D1273162

BATTLE FOR CHICAGO

By the same author

THE VANDERBILT LEGEND

(*Walter Scott Shinn from an original by Pirie MacDonald*)

MARSHALL FIELD

BATTLE
FOR
CHICAGO

by

WAYNE ANDREWS

NEW YORK
HARCOURT, BRACE AND COMPANY

first printing

PRINTED IN THE UNITED STATES OF AMERICA

FOR JOHN BAYLEY

Contents

Illustrations

Illustrations

BATTLE FOR CHICAGO

CHAPTER ONE: *Queen of the Lake*

MEET MARSHALL FIELD

"As A rule," said Marshall Field, "people do not know how to save." A quiet man in the loud city of Chicago, Field built his career on the principle of accumulating cash at all times for unseen emergencies and opportunities undreamed of. He had no use for daring. While other capitalists gambled on the future of the Middle West, he subjected the making of money to scientific analysis, and in the end very largely eliminated the element of risk in investing surplus profits.

There was nothing casual about Marshall Field's appearance. Though only five feet nine inches tall, he bore his slender frame with such dignity that his carriage was described as imperial. He dressed soberly, and yet there was an unobtrusive elegance about his waistcoats that was long remembered. A fellow clubman, recalling the spotlessness of his linen, the freshness of his complexion, the keenness of his blue eyes, and the premature grayness of his hair and mustache, thought that he "would pass at Voisin's for some foreign prince or diplomat rather than a successful businessman."

Unlike many a successful businessman, Field rarely alluded to his rise in the world. "When dining at his table on Prairie Avenue," remarked that most fastidious of Chicagoans, Hobart C. Chatfield-Taylor, "you were never forced to listen to long-winded tales of [his] early struggles and subsequent successes, nor were you overawed by any manifestation of his riches. Furthermore, your fellow guests were not bejeweled females in sheeny gowns, or bumptious males who in the smoking room inserted their thumbs in the armholes of satin waistcoats, whilst flicking with pudgy fingers the ashes from the ends of long cigars. On the contrary, your host was a silent man of quiet tastes who took delight in the intimacy of a few seemly friends to whom he extended his hospitality, but never his confidence; for if ever a man kept his counsel, it was this merchant prince." Everything considered, Chatfield-Taylor was satisfied that Field was "entirely free from the ostentation that impairs so frequently the man of newly made riches."

Field did not have to raise his voice to be heard. At work he had only to lift his eyes from his desk for chills to run down the spines of brave men. James J. Hill of the Great Northern, who was not easily frightened, broke into a cold sweat whenever he stopped by Field's office on his way through Chicago. "He has the damnedest eyes," Hill confided in the great merchant's nephew Stanley Field. "I go in there to ask him a question, and by the time I come out I've told him everything I know. He pumps me dry."

Stanley Field was not surprised. "My uncle," he told the author recently, "had the coldest eyes you ever saw and they read you through and through."

Too perceptive to be talkative, Field earned the nickname of "Silent Marsh" from businessmen who waited in vain for him to utter an indiscreet word. Sensing that his opinions carried the same weight as the commands of lesser men, he seldom discussed the trends of the times. Once, however, just as Chicago was braving a banking panic, another capitalist suggested that "if New York doesn't lend the West money, we are in for general ruin." The thought had already occurred to Field. "I am afraid," he predicted, "that many must be ruined."

Reporters, who did not know what to make of Field's detachment, labeled him "the merchant prince"—a title he abhorred. He loathed having his name noised about, although he had to insist on decent publicity for his store. No doubt he was grateful to the Chicago *Tribune* for pointing out that the formal opening of his firm on the corner of Washington and State was "the grandest affair of the kind which ever transpired, even in Chicago, the city of grand affairs." Of course nothing short of the stupendous was expected from the proprietor of "the largest and most fashionable dry goods store in the city." For months the first families had been "all agog with anticipation of the time when the wide portals of the retail department would be thrown open and an opportunity afforded for a gorgeous revel in the mazes of inextricable finery."

At last, on the evening of the 12th of October, 1868, the crowds edged their way to the counters. "The attendance of wealth, beauty, and fashion . . . was something unparalleled in Chicago's history," the *Tribune* announced. "One would have thought that the opening was an adjourned meeting of the Charity Ball, judging from the long line of carriages filled with the cream of the avenues. The attractions were unusual—a dry goods store in a marble palace. . . . It was the first of a series of grand affairs destined to transpire in the course of Chicago's progress, and as the inauguration of an era, deserves special notice."

On that portentous night Chicago was only thirty-five years old, and Field himself but thirty-four, having come into the world on the 18th of August, 1834, the third son and third child of John and Fidelia Nash Field, whose farmhouse stood on Field's Hill, a mile south of the Berkshire village of Conway, Massachusetts. As far as man could remember, the Fields had been Yankees. Though they had been tilling the land of Conway for less than a century, Zechariah, the first of the name to settle in America, had left Yorkshire for Massachusetts as long ago as 1629. At that detail Marshall Field would have yawned, for he despised the study of one's ancestors. "I have nothing to say, nothing to give you," he made plain to a gentleman who proposed to publish a volume on the Field pedigree. "Why do *we* need a genealogy?"

In his childhood Field had no time to think of family trees. "You mean you were poor?" asked a newspaperman.

"Yes," the great merchant acknowledged, "as all people were in those days, more or less. My father's farm was among the rocks and hills, and not very fertile." Field was not one to pretend that either of his parents was extraordinary. "My father was a man who, I consider, had good judgment. He made a success out of the farming business. My mother was more intellectually bent, if anything, and naturally, both parents were anxious that their boys should amount to something in life. Their interest and care helped me." According to a friend of the family, Field's mother "reared her sons to avoid the appearance of evil and to regard a fixed bad habit as one of the dangers always threatening success." Field filed the tribute in a memorandum book, and now and then read it out loud. "That had its influence," he used to say.

Field's schooling ended when he was seventeen. In later years he never regretted that he missed a college education, for he suspected that such advantages spoiled young men for business. "The truth is," he declared, "that for most young men a college education means that just at the time when they should be having business principles instilled into them, and be getting themselves energetically pulled together for their life's work, they are sent to college. Then intervenes what many a young man looks back on as the jolliest time of his life. . . . Often when he comes out of college the young man is unfitted by this good time to buckle down to hard work, and the result is a failure to grasp opportunities that would have opened the way for a successful career."

In Field's philosophy there was more to life than having a good time. Getting ahead, for instance. "The trouble with most young men," he said, "is that they do not learn anything thoroughly and are apt to do the work committed to them in a careless manner; forgetting that what is worth doing at all is worth doing well, they become mere drones and rely upon chance to bring them success. The business world is full of just such men, content in simply putting in their time somehow and drawing their salaries; making no effort whatever to increase their efficiency and thereby enhance their own as well as their employers' interest."

Field was earnest, even as a boy. One of nine children, only six of whom survived the Berkshire winters, he dutifully milked the cows, plowed the fields, and cut and husked the corn, all of which left him very little time to play games. When he played fox and hounds with the other fellows, it was not so much for fun as to prove his stamina. Once, in a fit of determination, he led the hounds in a 20-mile chase, returning untouched and unwinded in only two hours and a half.

There was a thrill to winning a race, as Field knew. But there was also a gray charm to saving money. All his life he pitied men who did not know the value of a dollar. "The average young man of today," he decided in his old age, "when he begins to earn is soon inclined to habits of extravagance and wastefulness; gets somehow imbued with the idea that irrespective of what he earns, he must indulge in habits corresponding to those of some other young man simply because he indulges, or imagines he cannot be manly without. The 5, 10, or 15 cents a day that is squandered, while a mere trifle apparently, if saved would in a few years amount to thousands of dollars and go far toward establishing the foundation of a future career." Was there any greater folly than scattering one's substance? "It matters not what a man's income is," said Field, "reckless extravagance and waste will sooner or later bring him to ruin."

When, at the age of seventeen, Field left Conway for Pittsfield to clerk in the dry goods store of Henry G. ("Deacon") Davis, nothing was further from his thoughts than unwise expenditures. He had his way to make in the world, it having already been decided that his oldest brother Chandler Augustus Field would inherit the family farm. In the same circumstances as Marshall were two other brothers, Joseph Nash Field, three years his senior, and Henry Field, seven years his junior. Bent on business both of them, they often visited him in Pittsfield, laying the groundwork for their common future.

Meantime Marshall Field studied storekeeping with the dry passion of a genius, noting the foibles of the lady customers. "He mingled with few of the young men of the town," a neighbor recollected. "He was not afraid of work, but he always appeared to be turning something over in his mind. As a clerk he was one of the best Pittsfield ever had, but his popularity was with the womenfolk. He seemed to know just what they wanted, and if that was not in stock, he was able without deceit to sell them something else." When his "day's work was done, he went to his lodging house instead of the town tavern."

Presbyterian that he was, it was only natural for Field to make decent use of his evenings. He liked to think that prosperity sought out sober men. "As a rule," he was confident, "the young man of high principles and fair ability, who saves his money and keeps his habits good, becomes valuable in any concern." Not that young men should yearn for money alone. "I would not have them believe," he said, "that success consists solely in the acquisition of wealth—far from it—as that idea is much too prevalent already. The haste to become rich at the expenses of character prevails to an alarming extent, and cannot be too severely denounced. What is needed today more than anything else is to instill in the minds of our young the desire above all to build up a character that will win the respect of all with whom they come in contact, and which is vastly more important than a great fortune."

Field, who thought all his life along those lines, was probably the most conscientious clerk in the history of New England. Yet the unlikely story has been told that "Deacon" Davis judged him too timorous to succeed; Davis has even been credited with grumbling in after years that "he was about the queerest looking boy I ever saw when he came to work for me. He was with me four years, and though he learned fast and seemed to have an uncanny knowledge of merchandise and a remarkable memory for stock and prices, I never thought he'd be a great merchant." At the suggestion that Field might make a name for himself in Chicago, Davis is said to have grunted: "You go West? You'll never make a success out there. You'd better take an older man's advice and stay nearer home. You go out there and you'll starve to death."

"I'm going," Field is supposed to have replied, "and some day

I'll have a store out there the doors of which will be worth more than your whole building here."

The truth was that Field and Davis got on very well. When John Pierpont Morgan, the son of the Hartford merchant banker Junius Spencer Morgan, accompanied his father to Pittsfield on business, Davis saw to it that young Field had the privilege of making young Morgan at home. Moreover, when Field announced his intention of starting anew in Chicago, Davis promised him a partnership in the store if only he would stick to Pittsfield. Finally, realizing that his gifted clerk had made up his mind to go West, Davis wrote out a letter of recommendation on the 19th of January, 1856. The tone of the letter was restrained, but then it was written in the heart of New England.

> The bearer, Mr. Field [Davis began], has been in my employ for nearly the past five years and now leaves me for the West. I can, without qualification, commend him as a young man of unusual business talent and worthy of the confidence of any who may employ him. His character and his principles, as well as his business qualifications, are such that I cannot doubt he will meet with that success in life which usually accompanies industry, perseverance, and integrity, when combined with strict integrity and energy of character.
>
> He has my warmest wishes for success in whatever situation he may fill or business he shall engage in.

THEY GOT THERE FIRST

Marshall Field, who was not one to squander his energies, ran very little risk in setting out for Chicago at the age of twenty-one. One hundred eighty-three years had gone by since Joliet and Marquette sighted the swamp from which the Chicago River drained into Lake Michigan, and 84,000 people were living close to the natural harbor at the river mouth, anxious all of them to capitalize on the westward expansion of the nation. Turnpikes, canals, and then railroads had struck farther and farther west, forcing the growth of Chicago, and now, in the last months of the presidency of Franklin Pierce, her future seemed certain.

At the close of the eighteenth century Chicago had been merely an Indian epithet for a river that oozed into a lake. If the word stood for "great" or "powerful" in the language of the Illini and the Miami, it meant nothing but "skunk" or "wild onion" in the Chippewa dialect of the Algonquin tongue. In 1800 a garrison was established at Fort Dearborn near the river mouth, only to be annihilated twelve years later by a band of Powattomies. In 1831, thirteen years after the State of Illinois was admitted to the Union, no more than a dozen families of traders and trappers were tempted to settle in the windswept, wooded marshlands near the second fort.

But in 1833, the year Andrew Jackson started upon his second term in the White House, the village of Chicago was incorporated, and three years afterward the Illinois-Michigan Canal was begun, linking Lake Michigan and the sullen Chicago River with the Illinois River and the riches of the Mississippi Valley. In 1837, when Jackson left Van Buren the problem of coping with an acute financial panic, Chicago was reincorporated as a city, and neither the panic nor the depression which followed hindered her expansion for long.

By 1845 the depression was over, Americans were streaming West, and New York and Boston bankers were thinking of the money to be made in railways beyond the Alleghenies. As bankers must, they thought twice before putting up any capital, and Chicago's first railroad, the Galena and Chicago Union—long since swallowed by the North Western—was launched by Middle Westerners with little encouragement from either Wall or State Street. December, 1848, saw the beginning of work on its right-of-way to the Mississippi.

Once started, there was no stopping. Little more than three years later—on the 20th of February, 1852, to be exact—the first train of the Michigan Southern and Northern Indiana Railroad, financed by the Litchfield brothers of New York, reached Chicago from Toledo, and for the first time the city was in direct rail communication with the Eastern seaboard. Three months after that, the Michigan Central, sponsored by the Canton trader John Murray Forbes of Boston, joined Chicago to Detroit.

Like a plant on water, Chicago fed on the very cinders of locomotives. In the two years following the arrival of the first Michigan Southern train the population leaped from 30,000 to 60,000, gladdening the heart of William Bross, an evangelistic schoolmaster who turned journalist to puff the wonders of the infant city. Bross was vexed by only one aspect of Chicago, the prudence of its storekeepers. "We have made repeated efforts," he wrote in *The Railroads, History, and Commerce of Chicago,* a broadside published in 1854, "to get at the exact figures in each department of trade, that we might make comparisons between the last and preceding years, but we are very sorry to say that many of our merchants are very reluctant to give us any figures, lest the extent of the commerce of Chicago should become known, and merchants from other cities should come here and divide their profits. A more narrow-minded, injurious policy, in our judgment, could not be adopted."

Bross was positive, even in 1854, that Chicago would one day be the railway center of the continent. Playing godfather to the city, he proposed the building of lines to tap the copper and iron mines of Lake Superior and the coal fields of Kentucky, prophesying that within five years Chicago and New Orleans would be knit by rail; within seventeen years, Chicago and San Francisco. Incidentally he noted that suburban real estate selling for $50 an acre in 1849 was already bringing $5,000.

With land values booming, what did it matter if dainty visitors found Chicago unattractive? The Swedish novelist Frederika Bremer, who visited the city in 1853, hurt no one's feelings by complaining that "Chicago is one of the most miserable and ugly cities which I have yet seen in America, and is very little deserving of its name, 'Queen of the Lake'; for, sitting there on the shore of the lake in wretched dishabille, she resembles rather a huckstress than a queen. Certainly the city seems for the most part to consist of shops. One sees scarcely any pretty country houses, with their gardens . . . and in the streets the houses are principally of wood, the streets formed with wood, or, if without, broad and sandy. And it seems as if, on all hands, people came here merely to trade, to make money, and not to live."

Chicagoans liked Chicago as it was. If a blanket of majestic gloom hung over the city, the happy lightning of vulgarity occasionally cleared the skies. There was a large force of Chicagoans, many of them New Englanders, many of them severely puritanical, who thought only of the solidity of the city's foundations, and if they had had their way Chicago would have been prim indeed. But there were other Chicagoans, many of them moneyed men, who knew that indiscretion was the one thing that made life worth living. They guffawed, saving Chicago from the contamination of good taste.

The new city, seemingly so sedate, and yet so easily roused to violence, had its share of smart real estate speculators. The coolest of these was William Butler Ogden, the first Mayor. "When you are dealing with Chicago property," he told worried investors, "the proper way to do is to go in for all you can get, and then go on with your business and forget all about it. It will take care of itself." It often did. "In 1844," Ogden recorded in his notebook, "I purchased for $8,000 what eight years later sold for $3,000,000." Though he did not have the foresight to hold on to that particular tract of land, he earned a national reputation for the niceness of his decisions on Chicago real estate. Samuel Russell of Middletown, Connecticut, who gathered a snug fortune in the Hong Kong trade, was only one of many Easterners to turn to Ogden for advice on how to get richer in Western lands. Ogden himself did so well that by the winter of 1853 he was worth more than a million dollars. "My God, Quigg, that's a lot of money!" he crowed to his secretary.

Though a native of uncultivated Delaware County, New York, Ogden needed no guidance in spending his income. Importing Chicago's first architect, the Baltimore-born John Mills Van Osdel, he had him surprise the corner of Rush and Ontario Streets in 1837 with a handsomely proportioned town house complete with cupola and porticoes. Here he entertained knowingly, dining Bryant, Emerson, Webster, and other celebrities who wandered West. A bachelor, he amused the ladies of Chicago by playing the piano on evenings when there were no lions to be had. His talk, however, was likely to be earnest and high-principled. "I was born close to a sawmill," he confessed to one of his dinner guests, "was left early an orphan, was cradled on a sugar trough, christened in a millpond, graduated at a log schoolhouse, and at fourteen found I could do anything I tried my hand to, and that nothing was impossible, and ever since, Madam, I have been trying to prove it, with some success." Certainly he had no trouble holding his own in a serious discussion. G. P. A. Healy, the conscientious portrait painter of the primeval Chicago millionaires, reported that "I found him in conversation a worthy rival of the three best I ever met, viz.: Louis-Philippe, John Quincy Adams, and Dr. O. A. Bronson."

Had Ogden remained in the East, his grave and calculating temperament could not have gone unrewarded for long. In Chicago luck was with him at the start. In June, 1835, when the mud of the town first spattered his boots, land values were hysterical, and he had only to gamble on the boom to realize a comfortable fortune. Subsequently he was embarrassed by the panic of 1837, but not critically, for he was elected the city's first Mayor in the midst of the crisis. At the time he was not yet thirty-two years old, but no novice in politics. At home in Walton, New York, he had been appointed Postmaster by Andrew Jackson, and in 1834 had been sent to the New York State Senate as the defender of the Erie Railroad.

Trained in the service of investors in railroad shares, Ogden was ever-sensitive on the subject of credit, and as Mayor argued shrewdly and successfully against the repudiation of Chicago's debt. "Above all things, do not tarnish the honor of your native city," he cautioned. Ten years later, when he traveled to Boston on behalf of the Galena and Chicago Union, he trusted that the capitalists of State Street would recall his devotion to municipal integrity. They did not. One of the Boston bankers not only scoffed at risking a penny in the railway, but even indulged in a malicious prophecy. "I do not remember," he declared, "any enterprise of this kind we Boston people have taken hold of upon statistics. You must go home, raise what money you can, expend it upon your road, and when it breaks down, as it surely or in all probability will, come and give it to us, and we will take hold of it and complete it, as we are now completing the Michigan Central."

Ogden, who was not easily discouraged by the cynicism of State Street, had the good sense to persevere with his plans for the Galena and Chicago Union. With the help of businessmen from near-by Rockford, he bought up a lot of rejected rails from the Rochester and Batavia Railroad and secured a second-hand locomotive for $2,400. Such was the start of Chicago's first railway, and such was Ogden's love of building new lines, that even when he had all he could do watching over his timberlands in Wisconsin and his iron works in Pennsylvania, he stayed with the railroad business. In 1853 he was appointed one of the original directors of the Chicago and Fort Wayne, today the right-of-way into Chicago of the Pennsylvania system. Eventually he was elected president of the Chicago and North Western, the consolidation of the Galena and Chicago Union and other roads whose credit he endorsed.

But the resourceful Ogden was not the only Chicagoan to fight the battles of the railways. Beside him on the original board of directors of the Galena and Chicago Union sat Walter Loomis Newberry, a Connecticut Yankee who entered upon prairie life with the blessing of the Astors and the wit to create a fortune of his own. Coached by his brother Oliver, the Buffalo agent of John Jacob Astor's American Fur Company, Newberry was not one to take the promises of the Middle West for granted. In Buffalo, where he did his brother's bidding, and later in Detroit, where he kept store for six years, he learned to discount the easy optimism of pioneers. In 1833, when he left Detroit for Chicago at the age of twenty-nine, he was on the trail of something far more substantial than an immigrant's hope. Having joined his brother Oliver, Lewis Cass, and William Backhouse Astor, John Jacob's son, in the purchase of thousands of acres in Wisconsin, Northern Michigan, and Chicago itself, he had the responsibility of looking after the syndicate's interests on the spot.

Though Newberry made few friends in Chicago, he had the reverence of the heartiest settlers. In the feverish boom of 1835 he thoughtfully unloaded his holdings of 1833, and then, at a cost of only $1,100, acquired 40 acres on either side of North Wells Street which came to be worth $2,500,000. Meantime he set himself up as a banker, candidly analyzing the credit of enthusiastic borrowers. And as if he were not making enough money already, he acted as the agent of many millionaires on the seaboard.

Newberry was unquestionably at ease in the homes of the New Yorkers whose funds he invested. His daughter Julia, when fifteen, was so far from embarrassed in the presence of the best blood of Manhattan that she set down in her diary that "Thursday evening I went to my first dinner party, & never in my life was so bored. I had the illustrious Mr. Stuyvesant Fish who in spite of his having a Grand-Father is little less than an idiot." At Richfield Springs, where so many Fifth Avenue heiresses endured the sulphur cure, she noted that one of the older families was "not very nice; too many diamonds."

Chicago, of course, was not the city for such distinctions. Whenever an important question was before the people, Walter Newberry played up to anyone, whatever his manners, who promised to bolster a conservative policy. Early in 1837, in the midst of the arguments over the city charter, he looked everywhere for supporters of a motion to limit the municipal debt. Spying at last at a town meeting a burly six-foot-seven-inch newcomer who had yet to utter a word either in approval or in protest, he snatched his coat collar with masterly impatience. "Stand up!" he commanded. When the silent giant complained that he was not a voter, Newberry groaned. "Don't you intend to live here, and don't you intend to get rich?" he asked. The stranger admitted that he did. "Well, then," Newberry cried, "stand up! Give these men the power and they will abuse it until they bankrupt us." The newcomer, one

John Wentworth from Sandwich, New Hampshire, not only raised his hulk to a right angle but forever after swore by Newberry's views on financial issues.

Wentworth, at whose bellow the biggest locomotive would blush for shame, was not the most delicate of Chicagoans. He had to have his whisky, and didn't mind weighing 300 pounds. With a broad-brimmed slouch hat on his head and a black swallowtail coat buttoned around his anxious abdomen, he rapped the pavements of Chicago with a monstrous black cane, a kind of heroic caricature of the pioneer. Withal, he was shrewd. "I have learned," he wrote, "that the secret of success is to be all things to all men; to be friendly with all and intimate with none."

He had been only twenty-one, and slender, that fall day in 1836 he got his first glimpse of Chicago. "Could you," he pictured his inglorious arrival, "have been on the sandhills between here and Michigan City on the southern shore of Lake Michigan, you would have seen me stretched out like a leather shoestring, tied up just after wading a prairie marsh, all length and no breadth, leaning over the country at an angle of 45 degrees, with my clothes under one arm and a jug of whisky under the other with which to bathe my blistered feet." With only $100 in his pocket, he had set out from his native Sandwich, traveling by coach to Concord, New Hampshire, thence again by coach to Troy and Schenectady, New York, thence in the railroad cars to Utica, thence over the Erie Canal to Tonawanda, thence by stage to Niagara Falls, thence by steamer to Buffalo and Detroit, thence again by stage to Michigan City, thence to Chicago on his own hind legs.

Chicago in 1836 was not exactly an oasis. Wentworth long afterward remembered that "the winters were long; no railroads, no telegraphs, no canal, and all we had to rely upon for news were our weekly newspapers. We had no libraries, no lectures, no theaters, and no other places of amusement. . . . You ask what society lived upon in those days? I answer, upon faith. But faith without works is dead. From the close to the opening of navigation, nearly six months in the year, we had nothing to do. Our faith consisted principally in the future of Chicago. Nearly everyone had laid out a town, and men exchanged lots with each other, very much as boys swap jackknives. The greatest storyteller was about as big a man as we had."

Never at a loss for an anecdote, Wentworth was never allowed to be lonely. Within two hours after his arrival he was baptized "Long John," and so fierce was his popularity that he was shortly elected to the House of Representatives for the first of six terms. He had a mind to keep himself constantly before the public, and was not above advertising his own tomb in Rosehill Cemetery. It stood 65 feet tall, but bore no inscription. "Long John" commented, "If there is no inscription on my monument, people will ask: 'Whose monument is that?' On being informed that it is John Wentworth's monument, they will ransack the libraries to find out who John Wentworth was. When they have found out, they will remember." The plot was sizable. "Long John" insisted, "I want a big place so that if I get tired lying on my back I will have room to turn over and kick."

Free and easy with all Chicagoans from beggars to bankers, Wentworth was not one to throw up to his neighbors that he was a relative of the last Royal Governor of New Hampshire, a grandson of a member of the Continental Congress, and a graduate of Dartmouth. For forty-nine years, unless he happened to be out of the city on business, he celebrated the anniversary of his coming to Chicago by dining with Mrs. Murphy, his first landlady. The gesture was typical of Wentworth; so was the message he left in his Bible. "This is John Wentworth's traveling guide," he wrote in the flyleaf. "If you think it will do you more good than it will him, take it with you. He knows where to get another. Perhaps you don't. This is the Lord's timetable. His trains are always ready, and they never wait."

Besides being a public character, Wentworth was very much of a businessman. Though his first job in Chicago was with the *Democrat,* a newspaper he later owned, he found out in no time that journalism was at best a precarious profession, and at the right moment switched his savings to the Galena and Chicago Union. Speculating in railroad stocks and Chicago land, he was soon several times a millionaire.

If Marshall Field in Pittsfield listened to stories of the real estate deals of Ogden, Newberry, and Wentworth, he almost certainly heard of the sharp Scotsman George Smith. Scrutinizing the Middle West for the first time in 1834, Smith was so delighted with its prospects that he began then and there to pick up parcels of land in and about Chicago. He was not, however, so infatuated that he forgot to sell out in 1835 and 1836. Returning to Scotland, he organized the Scottish Illinois Land Investment Company. Back in America in 1839, he collected prairie sites at demoralized prices for the portfolios of Caledonian investors. In that same year, dodging the Jacksonian Democrats who still controlled Middle Western legislatures, he obtained a charter for a certain Wisconsin Marine and Fire Insurance Company, under cover of which he carried on an illegal and highly successful banking business. He grew richer with every season until in 1856, when only fifty, he was ready to spend the rest of his life in the armchairs of the Reform Club in London, leaving his fellow Scotsman Alexander Mitchell of Milwaukee in charge of his American holdings. Mitchell did not do badly watching over Smith's stock in the Rock Island, North Western, and Saint Paul railroads, for he built himself a Moorish palace with the fees. But Smith was the wiser man. Legend had it he died worth $50,000,000.

FIELD FORGES AHEAD

Though 104 trains a day were rumbling in and out of the depots of Chicago in the winter of 1856, and every whiff of smoke was a symbol of hope to the businessmen who followed in the footsteps of Ogden, Newberry, Wentworth, and Smith, Marshall Field was not exactly excited by his first view of Chicago. "The town had plenty of ambition and pluck," he granted, "but the possibilities of greatness were hardly visible." Had it not been for his older brother Joseph, then passing through Chicago on his way to Omaha, he might even have tried his luck in another city.

But Joseph Nash Field, who was not easily put off, talked Francis B. Cooley, the senior partner of Chicago's largest dry goods house, Cooley, Wadsworth and Company of 205 South Water Street, into giving his hesitant young brother a job, and Marshall Field was fixed for life. "Joseph Field . . . called on us several times to recommend his brother for a position with us," wrote Cooley many years later recalling the event. "He was persistent in the face of some discouragement, and I finally consented to give the young man a trial. He came with many letters from the best people of Pittsfield, which his subsequent conduct amply justified. At first he appeared to lack confidence in himself to an extent that would be surprising to those who have known him in maturer years. It was not long, however, before the real substance of the man appeared, and he began to show the possession of those qualities which have made him successful in business and reliable in all matters pertaining to it."

How many dollars, if any, the trustworthy young man had in his pocket on the day he was hired is something that may never be known. In later life he never cared to hold forth on the subject. According to one tradition, he brought with him to Chicago as much as $1,000, according to another, as little as $100, and that borrowed from his father, and according to still another, he was down to his last dollar before he rolled up his sleeves for Cooley, Wadsworth and Company. Once employed, he set such an example of thrift that it is hard to believe he had less than $1,000 on hand when put to work. Sleeping in the store, and buying no new clothes except a pair of overalls, he saved $200 out of his first year's wages of $400.

Fate was kind to the frugal clerk in the nation-wide depression of 1857. In Field's own words: "The panic . . . swept almost everything away except the house I worked for, and I learned the reason they survived was because they understood the nature of the new country and did a cash business. That is, they bought for cash and sold on thirty and sixty days instead of giving the customers, whose financial condition you could hardly tell anything about, all the time they wanted. When the panic came, they had no debts and little owing them, so they weathered it all right. I learned what I consider my best lesson, and that was to do a cash business."

Only a few months before the boom in railroad securities collapsed, bringing on the crisis, the cautiously managed store had been renamed Cooley, Farwell and Company. Elisha Wadsworth, whose thinking was not half as conservative as Cooley's, was eliminated from the partnership, and John Villiers Farwell, a canny, thirty-one-year-old native of Steuben County in western New York who had put $10,000 in the old firm, was permitted to fasten his name on the new. A merchant of rigid principles, and a hardshell Presbyterian, Farwell not infrequently lectured his nieces on the frailty of their religious beliefs. "Anna," he reprimanded the daughter of his brother Charles, "you must believe in eternal damnation; the Bible teaches it. You will be punished if you refuse to believe."

"But, uncle, the Greek word is not 'eternal,'" interrupted Anna.

"I thank my heavenly father," Farwell groaned, "that I do not base my theology on a Greek word."

"And I, dear uncle," put in Anna, "am thankful that I need not base mine on a translation."

Farwell might find fault with his nieces, but not with Field. "He was an extraordinary salesman," he admitted admiringly later on. "He had the merchant instinct. He lived for it and for it alone. He never lost it."

Cooley, who had the very same opinion of Field, made a point of bringing customers up to the young clerk's counter. "Now Mr. Marshall Field," he would say, "is one of our finest salesmen. He'll take care of you." Eternally grateful for thus being put on his mettle, Field one day divulged that "Cooley taught me all I know about selling merchandise."

Cooley's standing in the community was so high that he was

(*Brown Brothers*)

(*Wayne Andrews*)

THE SPLENDOR OF THE REAPER KING:
Cyrus Hall McCormick, his Chicago home, his summer house and stables

(*Photos Wayne Andrews*)

(*Photo Kaufmann & Fabry Co.*
Courtesy the Chicago Tribune)

JOSEPH MEDILL

elected one of the original trustees of Chicago's first formidable bank, the Merchants' Savings, Loan, and Trust Company. Opening its doors on the 10th of June, 1857—the very eve of the depression—the Merchants' Loan and Trust Company (as it was later known) survived the break in the securities market and more than justified the hopes of its directors, one of whom was Newberry, another Ogden.

While Ogden was not unmanned by the panic, he was far from comforted by the depreciation in railroad stock and bonds, for he had been so indiscreet as to endorse $1,500,000 of the paper of the new Fond du Lac line. Fortunately he could count on his friends. Samuel Russell of Middletown was so affected by the news of his distress that he offered to turn over to him his entire fortune of half a million dollars. And a sympathetic Scottish peer was equally generous. "My dear Mr. Ogden," he wrote, "I hear you are in trouble. I have placed to your credit in New York 100,000 pounds. If you get through, I know you'll return it. If you don't, Jennie and I will never miss it."

Meantime "Long John" Wentworth, who had himself elected Mayor in the spring of 1857, installing the first steam fire engine and naming it after himself, was obligingly clearing the title to Ogden's holdings in "The Sands"—a strip of lake front where bums, hoodlums, and whores hid out in shacks. Fortified by a writ of ejectment, "Long John" marshalled out half the police force and a hook and ladder company; then, ax in hand at the head of his men, he marched down to slash the wretched shanties to bits. By the end of the day the site was rid of hovels, but Mayor Wentworth's clothes were sacrificed. Pounced upon by a mob of howling slatterns, he just missed being lynched.

"Long John" was not always so brave. In his campaign for Mayor he swore he was the truest friend of liberty and economy. He also promised a brawny Irishman a job on the police force if he would round up every longshoreman in Chicago on election day. The longshoremen voted as they were told, and the Irishman showed up at City Hall after the people's will was made known. "You promised me a job on the police force," he reminded the Mayor.

"Uh? Is that so? When did I do that?" "Long John" grunted.

"Before election day."

"I thought so," "Long John" replied. "It wasn't *after* election, though. We think you fellows are very nice before you vote, but when we get your ballot you can go to hell."

Suddenly the Irishman felt slighted. "Come outside," he muttered. "I can whip you, if you are big." He was added to the force.

Though not every complaint was adjusted as easily as this, "Long John" was re-elected Mayor in 1860, in time to greet the Prince of Wales on his way through Chicago. "Boys," he said, "this is the Prince of Wales. He has come to see the city and I am going to show him around. Prince, these are the boys."

The future Edward VII was enchanted with this reception. "Mr. Wentworth," he ventured as he bade farewell, "I have enjoyed my visit to Chicago immensely, and I should like to return the favor."

"Never mind!" said "Long John," cutting the Prince short. "We treat everybody that way out West."

In the end Edward showed the Chicagoan his gratitude by sending him his portrait and two Southdown sheep.

In the midst of these goings on, meticulous Marshall Field was memorizing the stock in hand of Cooley, Farwell and Company. Promoted to a partnership in January, 1860, when only twenty-five, he astonished his elders not only by knowing where everything was, but also by knowing what everything cost. "No matter what store he worked in," wrote his older brother Joseph, "he was not there a week before he knew more of the stock than the proprietor did. He carried purchasing and selling prices in his head or in a small black book kept carefully in an inner pocket." Thus equipped, he did miracles with the turnover. "He had a passion in those days which grew more marked after he became a businessman himself of getting rid of lines of stock as rapidly as possible and immediately adding a new and fresher line. . . . If Marshall had anything to sell, he would sell it if a customer came in; and if a customer did not come in, it was not beyond him to go out and find a buyer."

His mind on his work, Field had apparently little difficulty in coping with the financial crises of the Civil War. At the time of Meade's victory at Gettysburg the twenty-nine-year-old merchant was so prosperous that he thought of marriage. Happening to meet Nannie Douglas Scott, a delicate girl of twenty-three who was visiting friends in Chicago, he fell in love, and when she left town, followed her to the train, leaped on board, and proposed. Nannie Scott agreed to be his in a second. She had never seen such persistence in an admirer, either at home in Ironton, Ohio, where her father was a well-to-do ironfounder, or in Troy, New York, where she was graduated from Miss Willard's School for Young Ladies.

No sooner was the wedding over than Field shot ahead in business. In the beginning of 1864, when Francis Cooley retired to Hartford, Connecticut, he stepped into a junior partnership in Farwell, Field and Company, the successor to Cooley, Farwell and Company. But this was not all. Before the year was out he resigned to head his own store. Borrowing $100,000 apiece from friendly John Farwell, he and Levi Zeigler Leiter, the "Company" of Farwell, Field and Company, bought out the wholesale and retail dry goods store of Potter Palmer on Lake Street. Field, Palmer, and Leiter, as the new firm was entitled when it opened for business at the start of 1865, was capitalized at $890,000, $450,000 of which was provided by Potter Palmer, $50,000 by his brother Milton, $130,000 by Levi Leiter, and the remaining $260,000 by Marshall Field. He was then only thirty.

Dealing at Palmer's old address in Palmer's stock of dress goods, silks, cloaks, shawls, cloths, flannels, embroideries, Alexandre's kid gloves, and other items, Field inherited the good will created by fourteen years of pitiless attention to business. "I always hunted for customers," said Palmer, describing his life as a wholesaler. "If I learned of a man 200 miles away, buried in a clearing in a forest, who might buy, I got the name of my establishment to him and invited him in. After he once got acquainted with the store, we rarely lost him."

A slender, six-foot Quaker from Albany County, New York, Palmer was six years a clerk in northern New York State before he opened his fourteen-year siege of Chicago. Now, at the age of thirty-eight, he was taking his first rest from behind the counters. Sitting back and letting his brother Milton watch over his stake in the store, he fell to speculating as to when and where the city would expand, and what were the ideal sites in which to invest his earnings. Land for him spelled security and an old age of leisure. In two years' time he withdrew his capital from Field, Palmer, and Leiter, as did his brother Milton, and the firm was renamed Field, Leiter and Company.

Although Field, Leiter and Company dated from the first of 1867, the earliest partnership papers in the Field archives were signed on the first of January, 1869. According to this document, the store was capitalized at $1,200,000. These were the partners and their shares:

Marshall Field	$400,000
Levi Zeigler Leiter	$400,000
Joseph Nash Field	$100,000
Henry Field	$100,000
Henry J. Willing	$100,000
Lorenzo G. Woodhouse	$100,000

Joseph Nash Field, who had risen to be cashier of the Omaha National Bank before returning to Chicago, was never sorry he went to work for his brother. As early as 1870 he was doing so well at Field, Leiter and Company that he was given the responsibility of locating the firm's European headquarters. Deciding on Manchester, he settled down for the rest of his life within earshot of the Lancashire textile mills. From Manchester he supervised the buyers on the Continent, and kept tab on the representatives in Chemnitz, Belfast, Paris, and Calais.

Unlike Joseph Field, who paid in every penny of his share of the capital, Henry Field contributed only $70,000, borrowing the rest from Marshall with whom he had been clerking for eight years.

He seems to have had wit enough to marry Florence Lathrop, the granddaughter of a Governor of Virginia, and taste enough to collect Barbizon paintings, but not bluff enough to drive ahead in business. He is remembered, not as a merchant, but as a slim, rosy-cheeked youth with a craving for perfectly matched tandems and sleek dogcarts. One afternoon he rolled out on Michigan Avenue in the highest style and was not surprised to hear window after window rattle open in homage. But when crowds rushed after his carriage, he suspected that all was not well, and looked behind. To his horror he discovered that he was being followed by a turnout exactly like his, with horses of the very same shade, and with dogcart and harness of the identical hue, value, and chroma. At the reins lolled "Molly Mason," one of the ladies of the town. Aghast, Henry Field took the first turn into State Street.

Possibly Willing and Woodhouse were more slavish in their devotion to trade. Although neither was able to supply more than $70,000 in capital, both had made names for themselves at Cooley, Farwell and Company. Willing, who hailed from Chautauqua County, New York, was a mathematical genius with such a flair for calicoes, linens, and laces that Leiter was glad to lend him the $30,000 he required. Woodhouse, a native of New Hampshire who sweated long hours in the dry goods stores of Fitchburg, Massachusetts, and Hudson, New York, before coming to Chicago, had such a knack for driving bargains that he was made buyer and manager of the New York office, Field and Leiter each providing him with $15,000.

Surrounded by these men, Field had no reason to fear for the future. In 1867 he and his staff outsold every dry goods firm in Chicago, grossing over $9,000,000. Their nearest competitor, the wholesale house of J. V. Farwell and Company,* reported transactions of barely $7,000,000, and as for the Mandel brothers from Kerzenheim, Germany, they were the most modest of rivals in

* One of John Farwell's partners in this successor to Farwell, Field and Company was his brother, straightfaced Charles Benjamin Farwell—"Poker Charley" to his friends even after he entered the U. S. Senate.

these days. Beginning operations in 1865 on the corner of Clark and Monroe, they attracted practically no notice at all.

Those two knowing Scotsmen, Samuel Carson and John T. Pirie, were almost as quiet as the Mandels. Moving to Chicago in 1864 after ten years of storekeeping in Amboy, Illinois, they founded the wholesale end of what is today Carson, Pirie, Scott and Company without letting anyone discover the depth of their ambition. Three years afterward another Scotsman, Andrew MacLeish,* launched Carson, Pirie's retail division. MacLeish, who was at one time a Field employee, never spoke of Yankee thrift without respect. "Not even a Scotsman could live on that!" was his tribute to Field's wage scale. Whether Carson, Pirie paid much more is open to question. In 1867 it did a business of merely $700,000.

With his sales figures running thirteen times those of MacLeish's friends, Field kept the quiet joy of his success to himself. As calm as a banker, he was often taken for one. "I am a merchant," he continually reminded reporters, forgetting that his exquisite caution justified the confusion. He would have been remarkable anywhere for his prudence; on the optimistic prairie he was notorious.

He was far too circumspect to be an innovator. A. T. Stewart of New York and John Wanamaker of Philadelphia appear to have been much more daring, for the former is at least credited with introducing the one-price system, and the latter is supposed to have been the first merchant to allow customers to exchange goods. No such claims have been advanced for Field, whose mind rebelled at idle experimenting, and whose methods were assimilative rather than creative.

Unlike Stewart, he wasted not a single penny on ostentation after hours; unlike Wanamaker, not a single second on sentimentality. Saving every ounce of energy for the passion he spent on the store, he was at the same time too wise to become a drudge. He did not care to toil after the blinds were lowered, and thanks to his astonishing powers of concentration, he did not have to. When asked,

* Archibald MacLeish is his son.

toward the end of his career, if he had been a hard worker, he proudly answered no. "I have never believed in overworking, either as applied to myself or others," he explained. "It is paid for with a short life, and I do not believe in it." For businessmen who worked eighteen hours a day he had only pity. "My fortune has not been made in that manner, and as I have said, I believe in reasonable hours for everyone, but close attention during those hours."

Too attentive to his work to pass the time of day with anyone, Field was very likely exasperated by the cordiality of drummers. For years he clung to the superstition that it was undignified and unnecessary for the wholesale division to send roadmen out with samples, and it was only after squads of salesmen from Eastern wholesale houses had overrun the Middle West that he perceived the wisdom of allowing the carpet department the luxury of a traveling man. "I would rather have my business go under," he grumbled, "than have to peddle it out on the road." When Dixon Beam, the store's carpet expert, prophesied that within two years every department would have men on the road, Field groaned. "I would close up first," he predicted. Eventually, of course, he was compelled to sanction the use of traveling salesmen, just as he was bullied by circumstances into selling toys and contemporary furniture.

He had his doubts about opening a toy department, but once the venture turned out to be successful, he had the honesty to own he was wrong. "Your results are as good as anybody's, if not better," he told the firm's toy buyer Harry Grund. Selling the latest thing from Grand Rapids was much harder to square with his conscience. For a long time he held out against showing any furniture except antiques, murmuring "it is not good enough for our store" at each new sofa. When he did come around to approve of modern furnishings, he was wracked with misgivings. "If I were to put a banana stand on the first floor," he fretted, "I suppose I could sell more bananas than anyone else in Chicago. But I am not in the banana business."

In all things Field was dignified, and his employees knew it.

Once, coming upon four young clerks who were so indelicate as to sing at their work, he paused with the patience of an hourglass before risking a suggestion. "Sing it again, boys," he said, "but this time just a little softer." With a salesman who hid dirt and papers behind his counter he was equally cool. "What are you getting ready to do here, raise potatoes?" he inquired in a remote voice. The next day he restored the offender's self-confidence by stopping to say hello on his way through the store.

Field sometimes cheered the spirits of a repentant clerk, but almost never praised an employee to his face. When he did so, it was likely to be inexpectedly, as in the following interview. "What competition do you meet, Jimmy?" he one day asked of James O'Malley who handled carpets in Indiana.

"None, Mr. Field," O'Malley replied. "There may be others who sell as much as I do, but I do not know who they are."

"I am very proud of you, Jimmy," said Field, smiling faintly.

"You don't tell me that often, Mr. Field," O'Malley observed.

"No," Field agreed. "That might cost me too much money."

Meanwhile Field's partner Levi Zeigler Leiter was making it quite plain that he did not approve of spoiling the help. "You are an ass, you are an ass, you are an ass," he branded a salesman who happened to displease him. Another time he withered the self-esteem of one of the officers of the store by handing him a slip of paper with the command: "Write on this, sir, all you know."

A burly, bearded native of Leitersburg, Maryland, descended from eighteenth-century Dutch immigrants, Leiter never learned to be as tactful as Field. The same age as his partner, he reached Chicago a year ahead of him, finding his first job with the dry goods firm of Downs and Van Wyck. A little later he transferred to Cooley, Farwell and Company, developing from a bookkeeper into a credit specialist. There, as at Field, Leiter and Company, he plumed himself on the number of questionable accounts he scared away. "No, you cannot have these goods," he bellowed one morning at an individual who had ordered $700 worth.

"I am going to pay for them in cash," the buyer pleaded in self-defense.

"That makes no difference," said Leiter, sitting in judgment on his respectability. "Your record is bad."

At the sight of a patron who failed to keep his word, Leiter could hardly control himself. "You promised it, and you did not do it, so get out, or I will have the porter throw you out," he told one such customer. He was even harder on men who dyed their hair. "What do you want, sir?" he roared at a gentleman who dared to enter the store with a dyed mustache. When the stranger announced his intention of making a few purchases, Leiter was beside himself. "No, you don't!" he declared. "You are a thief—your mustache is dyed—so get out of here!"

Away in New York supervising the buying from 1864 to 1869, Field never knew what move Leiter might make in Chicago. When an Eastern house wrote in to ask about Field, Leiter's credit rating, Leiter was furious. "After such a letter, we'll never buy from them again," he said.

"You are mistaken," put in his partner. "We'll satisfy them as to our responsibility and then make closer future bargains."

If Leiter's temper was a worry to Field, his taste in hats was a constant offense. He wore a tall gray topper to work and kept it on all day. As if that were not enough, he annoyed his partner by insinuating there was no need to maintain a handsome cash balance twelve months of the year. For Field, who had to have his house in order at all times, the thought of doing business with insufficient cash on hand was a nightmare.

Taking care there was always plenty of money in the treasury, Field made a fetish of absolute honesty, and a Chicago artist with the imagination to realize there are those who live for solemn pleasures, called him "a cool gray man." Once upon a time he paid $300 for a horse which the seller, a customer from St. Joseph, Michigan, believed to be worth $350. Many years later he stopped the customer on the street. "That horse I bought from you," he said, "was a better horse than I thought." With that he forced $50 upon him.

If the law of the land had ruled that every business failure was proof in itself of a criminal conspiracy against society, Field could not have taken more seriously the responsibilities of his calling. Obviously, he suspected the worst of any storekeeper who went under. In his own inexorable words: "Merchants who keep their business well in hand, sell for cash, and pay for goods at short time, taking advantage of all cash discounts, keep good habits, and pay strict attention to business very rarely fail."

As for the successful merchant, in Field's eyes he was no happy-go-lucky operator but a man who conducted his business along certain definite lines. "He never gives a note; he never buys a share of stock on margin; he is against speculation; he has made it a point not to encumber his business with mortgages; he does business on a cash basis; he tries to sell on shorter time than his competitors; he tries to sell the same grade of goods for a smaller price; he holds his customers to a strict meeting of their obligations."

Following these principles to the letter, Field thought of a hundred and one ways to economize. Instead of advertising on Sunday, when rates were high, he bought space on Monday, when rates were low. Instead of dealing with middlemen, and letting parasites nibble at his profits, he made a practice of ordering in vast quantities direct from manufacturers. Soon he was controlling the entire output of strategic mills, compelling the owners to conform to his specifications. With things running so smoothly, it was no trouble for him to do the ladies a favor, and he allowed them to take home goods on approval. But when it came to chalking down figures on price tags, that was out of the question. There was no point in reducing operating costs, if all was not serene behind the counters. Like A. T. Stewart and Company, Field, Leiter and Company was a one-price store.

There was a reward for all this. In 1868, the year of the opening of the new store on the northeast corner of Washington and State Streets, Field, Leiter and Company grossed $12,000,000, which was more than any dry goods firm in the country with the exception of Stewart's in New York and Claflin's in Brooklyn. With profits piling higher and higher, Field felt obliged to stage a magnificent welcome to his customers the night of the 12th of October.

Rapturous newspaper reporters were reminded of the Alhambra by moonlight, and the first families of Chicago were themselves entranced, although, as they stepped from their barouches, phaetons, landaus, and clarences, they were half-blinded by the glare of hundreds of flickering gas jets within, maddeningly reflected in the plate glass windows of the façade. To calm the nerves of excitable women Field had five boys in blue uniforms with three rows of brass buttons down their jackets stand just inside the entrance to usher in the guests.

The building itself was the envy of the Middle West. Put up by Field's old partner Potter Palmer, it stood six stories high, adorned with Corinthian columns and crowned with a noble mansard roof. The second, third, fourth, and fifth stories were faced with white marble from Canaan, Connecticut, costing $105,000, and the Chicago *Times* was inspired to declare that the corner was "architecturally the most perfect and imposing in the country. Hardly so large as Stewart's in New York, it still bears the superiority of being more substantial as well as being better adapted to the dry goods business."

It was evident that the store had been designed to satisfy every need of Marshall Field. The first story was devoted to the retail division, the second to the private offices of the partners, the third to gloves, linens, woolens, and cashmeres, the fourth to soap, perfumes, hosiery, hoopskirts, and balmorals, while the fifth was saved for storage space and the sixth for boilers. The most electric spot in all six stories was the ladies' cloak department on the ground floor. It was railed off, richly carpeted, and fitted with a stand of sumptuous mirrors.

It is just possible that Potter Palmer put the architect in mind of these voluptuous details. Two years earlier he had sunk $2,000,000 in State Street land; in the interval the property had doubled in value, and he was now eager to stake his entire fortune on turning State Street into Chicago's shopping center. With Field, Leiter and

Company as his tenants he saw the fashion of Lake Street waning and his ambition secured. Small wonder he let it be known that he was contemplating the building of a glorious hotel on the corner of State and Monroe.

In this, the hour of Potter Palmer's joy and Marshall Field's triumph, Walter Loomis Newberry was deep in gloom. Ravaged by tuberculosis, he was informed he had at best only six months left on earth, and to live even that long must travel to the South of France with a nurse to watch over him. Newberry agreed to sail for Europe, but not to hire a nurse. "I cannot afford it," he said. A few weeks later, just as the Cunarder *Persia* was steaming into Le Havre, he sickened and died in his cabin, alone. Survived by his widow and two daughters, both of whom died young, he left an estate eventually valued at $4,298,403.*

For Field and the other leaders of the second generation in Chicago four million was not enough.

RISE OF THE HOUSE OF McCORMICK

Since the opening of Field, Leiter and Company's new store provoked comment in the home of every Chicago family that kept carriage company, it is reasonable to suppose that it was the topic of conversation at the breakfast table of the massive and intractable reaper king Cyrus Hall McCormick. More than likely, he greeted the news with a sigh. Offered a partnership in Field's future not so long before, he had turned the opportunity down. Cursed with passionate convictions, McCormick rarely attained the peculiar state of serenity necessary for the successful study of investments.

He was nervous, even in his own dining room. Less than six feet tall, the ruddy, bushy-bearded benefactor of the American farmer

* It remained for John Stoughton Newberry, the son of Walter's brother Elihu, to found the great Newberry fortune of Detroit. Based on railroad car building, it eventually financed the Packard Motor Car Company.

measured 54 inches around the waist when bundled up for winter, and weighed about 215 pounds, most of which was due to his ravenous appetite for roast beef, cherry pie, and mush. At breakfast, once grace was said, he applied himself to mush and milk with an energy that was wonderful to see. First he fastened a bounteous napkin with an elastic band around his neck; then he plunged spoonful after spoonful of steaming mush into a vast bowl of cool milk, always taking care that the very last grain of cereal was moistened by the very last drop of milk. One day—no doubt after a hearty meal—he cried out that "indomitable perseverance in a business properly *understood* almost insures ultimate success," and to tell the truth he attacked the problem of selling reaping machines with the very same eagerness he displayed at breakfast.

On the other hand he was so sentimental that the bare mention of Virginia, his native State, was enough to bring on a fit of tears. He is known to have wept at the sight of splendid mountains, saying that they reminded him of the landscape of the Old Dominion. He was also sweet upon the flowers of his childhood, and not ashamed to admit it. "I love best the old-fashioned pinks," he said, "because they grew in my mother's garden in Virginia."

The first, and the most emotional of the eight children of Robert and Mary Ann Hall McCormick, he was born on the 15th of February, 1809, at Walnut Grove, near Lexington, in Rockbridge County. His father, who was of Scotch-Irish stock, was a moderately well-to-do farmer with a markedly mechanical turn of mind. At one time or another he held title to 1800 acres, two grist mills, two sawmills, a smelting furnace, a distillery, and a blacksmith shop. In his odd moments he invented a hemp brake, a clover huller, and a bellows, besides experimenting with a primitive reaper. Cyrus's mother, who was also of Scotch-Irish descent, puzzled the neighbors with her haughty ways while her husband meddled with machinery. In the countryside she was famous for her flock of peacocks and her carriage, dignified with a set of folding steps.

To her son Cyrus, however, Mary Ann McCormick symbolized all the virtues of motherhood in the Shenandoah Valley. Years later, at a banquet of fellow Virginians in Chicago, he waxed wondrously grandiloquent on the subject. "Can any of us," he sermonized, "forget how the mother was enthroned in the Virginian homestead, and with what untiring, loving tact and sagacity she swayed her scepter? Her care for the comfort of the household and of her numerous dependents; her hospitality to strangers; her kindness in sickness; her hours of pious conversation with her children, and her daily assemblage of family and servants to worship; these united labors making her queen, mother, mistress, doctor, nurse, counselor, and friend. She was, in short, one strong element of Virginia's true greatness—her moral greatness." Appropriately, Cyrus ended on a Biblical note. "I may say of Virginia, as David said of the city of his love: 'If I forget thee, O Jerusalem, let my right hand forget her cunning.'"

Although McCormick could cite chapter and verse to prove his knowledge of the Bible, his education was meager indeed, apart from religious instruction. According to his definitive biographer William T. Hutchinson, he mastered little more than the three R's and a smattering of geography before he quit school at the age of fifteen. Later on, to catch up on his punctuation, he made a point of scrutinizing newspapers as faithfully as a proofreader. At all times he was earnest enough to pass for a scholar. When twenty-two, he wrote one of his brothers that "Mr. Hart has two fine daughters, rite pretty, very smart, and as rich probably as you could wish; but alas! I have other business to attend to, and can, as I told you, devote but a small proportion of my time to the enjoyment of their society or any other's."

When twenty-two, the serious-minded young man invented the reaper, trying it out during the harvest of 1831 on the fields of John Steele near Walnut Grove. It failed to cut Steele's wheat perfectly, but it was none the less the first feasible harvester in the history of the world. Subsequently modified again and again, the machine always embodied the seven essential principles incorporated in the first model, only one of which, a main wheel operating the gears, was original with McCormick. The other six features were a side draft, a vibrating horizontal knife, a divider, a reel, fingers, and a platform to receive the severed grain.

"The reaper is a success," Cyrus's father told a friend, "and I believe that I could not have made it so, but it makes me feel proud to have a son do what I could not." Then and there Robert McCormick discarded his own attempt at a harvester, but neither he nor his son was wide awake to the significance of the seven essential principles. Cyrus patented a plow in 1831, but didn't think of licensing the reaper until 1834, nor putting it on the market until 1840.

Meanwhile he and his father were drifting toward bankruptcy, having sunk the family fortune in a smelting furnace on the eve of the depression of 1837. Long after the ordeal was over, Cyrus mustered up the dignity to review the blunder without blushing. "Full of enterprise, and not satisfied to rest on my oars nor on my inventions," he recalled his youthful self, "an opportunity was presented to me to engage in the iron business. . . . The dignity and position of an ironmaster was somehow enviable." For all that, the McCormicks were in such straits by the fall of 1842 that they had to transfer the title to Walnut Grove before anyone would risk endorsing their drafts. They might have been ruined if Cyrus hadn't managed to unload 6 of his reapers.

To dispose of half a dozen of the McCormick machines in 1842 was something of a feat. In the years that Robert and Cyrus McCormick were busy with their ironworks, Obed Hussey, a one-eyed ex-whaler from Nantucket had stepped forward as the leading reaper manufacturer of the country. The supremacy of his harvester, which was patented prior to, but invented later than McCormick's, went virtually unchallenged until, on the 30th of June, 1843, it was pitted against the Virginian's at a public contest on the estate of Ambrose Hutchinson near Richmond. The duel was decided in McCormick's favor, who cut 17 acres to Hussey's 2, yet rested two hours at noon. Fired by this success, McCormick marketed 29 machines that season, and Hussey only 2.

Thenceforward McCormick more than made up for his previous neglect of the reaper, pushing its sale with a truculence which was both unremitting and exasperating. "Meet Hussey wherever you can and put him down!" he called out to his brothers, and the day was not far off when the old Nantucketer sank to his knees, a beaten man.

"I never experienced half of the fatigue in rowing after a whale in the Pacific Ocean . . . as I experienced year after year . . . in the harvest field," said Hussey when it was all over.

The McCormicks and their licensees having built 190 machines in 1846, Cyrus McCormick was ready to frustrate Hussey by setting up a factory near the westward-shifting grain belt. He tried to persuade his younger brother Leander James McCormick to settle in Brocton, New York, promising "regular and good Presbyterian teaching" as well as a look at Niagara Falls if only he would come on to supervise a harvester works. But Leander, who was never as enterprising as Cyrus, preferred to linger in the Valley of Virginia where he had just married Henrietta Hamilton of near-by Locust Hill. A little later, in February, 1847, in the midst of our war with Mexico, Cyrus proposed that Leander spend six weeks in the Middle West putting reapers into operation. "I presume," he wrote, "that this will be to you a desirable little enterprise, and possibly just as honorable, more profitable, and every way a more justifiable separation from Henrietta (if so bye the bye) than to go to Mexico to be shot *at,* if not shot down, not *faulting* that either, in those who have a taste for that particular sport." Impressed with the logic of this argument, Leander moved to Cincinnati, leaving his other brother William Sanderson McCormick in charge of the plant at Walnut Grove, and freeing Cyrus for the invasion of Illinois.

It was in the fall of 1847 that Cyrus opened his first factory in Chicago. Delighted with the bracing climate, and sure of an ever-expanding market on the edge of the prairie, he settled permanently in Chicago the next year. When a lawsuit brought an end to his first partnership, he drew up the papers for a new agreement, this time with William Butler Ogden for his backer. When neither that nor a later understanding worked out well, he struck out on his own. Beginning in 1850 he was the sole proprietor of the harvester business, fixing the salaries for which his brothers toiled.

Leander, who came on to Chicago with Henrietta in the fall of 1848, seems to have made a competent superintendent of the McCormick factory, and it has even been claimed that he suggested certain improvements on his brother's invention. Nevertheless he was painfully conservative. He did not approve of the theater, and at home did not tolerate cards, making matters worse for his family by getting up at dawn to torture plantation tunes out of an old violin. At work he was just as nostalgic, shaking his head when his brother talked of doing anything as foolish as promoting the reaper in England and on the Continent. At heart his wife was as unadventurous as he was. "The primitive life in this Western town is novel and extremely interesting," she wrote, "and the people as well, of whom many are New Englanders whose provincial ways and customs are quite amusing when contrasted with those of Virginia."

William, who did not desert Walnut Grove for Chicago until 1850, was probably more valuable than Leander to the McCormick firm. From the first he was in charge of sales, collections, and the purchase of supplies, and in a little while made himself Cyrus's financial adviser. Not for a second did he doubt the wisdom of locating the business in the Middle West. "Chicago," he said, "must be a success if any city in this country will be. The best men and capital are coming here." Yet he looked forward with pathetic eagerness to vacations in the Old Dominion, and Mary Ann Grigsby, his Virginia-born wife, was so little at home in Illinois that she was sorry "this wasn't a slave state because so easily cultivated."

Both Leander and William earned enough to set aside a substantial portion of their salaries, gratifying their appetite for Chicago real estate, but neither was willing to keep on working indefinitely without sharing in Cyrus's profits. "As I have said to you," Leander wrote Cyrus, "I have done not a little for the machine, and I am resolved not to be satisfied without a pretty strong interest if I am to remain in the business." Like his brother, William complained that he "calculated upon something considerable more than a salary."

There was money enough to go around, as Leander and William were well aware. If up until the time he settled in Chicago Cyrus had brought out only 1,278 machines, as early as 1850 he was turning out 1,600 a year, disposing of all except 50. Shutting down the plants at Brocton, Cincinnati, and Walnut Grove, and putting an end to other people's manufacture of the reaper under license spelled greater and greater profits for the Chicago works. In 1856 alone Cyrus cleared $300,000, and his earnings for the decade ending in 1858 amounted to a million. At last, in 1859, he capitulated, raising his brothers to the rank of partners. Under this agreement Leander and William received one fourth each of the net profits in addition to $5,000 a year in wages, while Cyrus supplied all of the capital at 8 per cent, furnished the factory with machinery at cost, and rented the plant to the company for $10,000 a year.

Even with his brothers helping, Cyrus McCormick never knew when to stop working, and the gusto with which he urged his invention on the world was stupefying to his competitors. In 1851 he entered the Virginia Reaper at the Crystal Palace Exposition, squelching Hussey at a public trial on Tiptree Heath and winning a Council Medal, an honor bestowed by a jury of fifteen judges from six different nations. This was glory indeed, thought William H. Seward. "No general or consul," he pointed out, "drawn in a chariot through the streets of Rome by order of the Senate ever conferred on mankind benefits as great as he who thus vindicated the genius of our country at the World's Exhibition of Art in the Metropolis of the British Empire."

It is only fair to add that Seward uttered this superb period in the Circuit Court, where he had been hired to represent McCormick in a suit over an infringement of the patent of 1834. The inventor had a touching faith in the law, which is another way of saying that he was the most litigious capitalist of the day. Perhaps the most famous of all the disputes he dragged into the courts was that with John H. Manny of Rockford, again over an infringement of the patent. With Abraham Lincoln and Edwin M. Stanton taking Manny's side, McCormick went down to defeat, embittered by

Stanton's reflection that "the model room of the Patent Office is not designed as an armory for patentees, but as a magazine for public defense against grasping monopolists, seeking to appropriate anything useful in the arts under pretence of being its first creator." According to the future Secretary of War, the Virginian was laboring under a delusion as to the patent law. "His claim," Stanton argued, "seems to rest on the notion that everything in the reaping machine belongs to McCormick that is not the subject of some other successful monopoly."

But the reaper king was to suffer an even crueler humiliation at the hands of the United States Government. Refused the right to renew his monopoly, he was also denied the privilege of extending the license on his improvements to the harvester. Sympathizing with Cyrus, William wrote that "your money has been made not out of patents, but by making and selling the machines," which was true, but no consolation for the unwelcome report of the Commissioner of Patents. Amused at the suggestion that the reaper had saved the American farmer up to $100,000,000, the Commissioner indulged in a flight of skepticism. "We are furnished," he declared, "with no statistics, either as to the amount of land in cultivation, or the quantity or value of the grain grown, nor . . . as to what part this particular invention played in producing this extraordinary result. The entire region from which this estimate is drawn . . . is one of absolute and wild conjecture, too dimly lighted to be pressed by the feet of public justice. . . . This item, vague, extravagant, and unsustained as it is, deserves not a moment's consideration."

Rebuffed at Washington, McCormick regained his self-respect by making things unpleasant for the heads of our railroads, many of whom lived in dread of his name on a summons. When a relative of his lost a trunk valued at $1,300 on the New York Central, the road's attorneys forwarded a check for the full amount the instant the complaint was filed. "We don't want a lawsuit with the McCormicks," ruled the wise, if trembling, counsel for the Vanderbilt system. If the president of the Pennsylvania Railroad had known what was good for him, he would have followed the Central's example, and settled on the spot when the inventor pressed a claim for luggage destroyed by lightning. As it was, he held out, and lived to rue the day. Year in, year out, the McCormicks kept after the Pennsylvania, peppering executives with memorandums demanding payment in full, and at last, after fighting the case in the courts for eighteen years, forced the weary railway to surrender, twenty-three years after the damage was done.

In the Presbyterian Church the irrepressible millionaire stuck up for his rights as grimly as in a court of law. He had no patience with abolitionist clergymen, as R. W. Henry, the rector of South Church, Chicago, could testify. Henry, who had fallen into the habit of borrowing money from McCormick, and of heating his home with free coal from the harvester factory, committed the indiscretion one Sunday morning of denouncing slavery from the pulpit. This was more than the reaper king could stand. Cutting off the culprit's fuel supply, he bore down on him at once for the payment of his debt. And ever afterward he worshiped at North Church, at the feet of a pastor who left controversial topics alone.

In spite of all this, McCormick was, in his way, a sincere churchman. "Business is not inconsistent with Christianity," he observed, "but the latter ought to be a help to the former, giving a confidence and resignation, after using all proper means, and yet I have sometimes felt that I came so far short of the right *feeling,* so worldly minded that I could wish myself out of the world." To put his conscience at rest, he gave $445,000 to the Presbyterian Church in his lifetime, $325,000 of which went to the Presbyterian Theological Seminary of the North West, now known as the McCormick Theological Seminary.

The pious manufacturer did not marry until he was almost forty-nine. Looking for a pretty girl with strict principles, he found her in the person of Miss Nancy Fowler, the 26-year-old daughter of a storekeeper in northern New York State. When he met her at the home of his brother Leander, there was no doubt in anyone's mind as to her religious affiliation, for she had taken it upon herself while visiting friends in Chicago to sing in the choir of North Church.

As dutiful all her life as she was in her girlhood, she made him a perfect wife, reading the Scriptures aloud each morning at seven. She also taught the children, five of whom grew to maturity, to write down how long it took them to brush their teeth and put on their clothes in the morning, reminding them in that way of their slowness in reaching the mush and milk on the breakfast table.

With his wife to comfort him, McCormick kept faith with the Democratic Party throughout the Civil War, a decision that earned him many an enemy in Chicago. Like August Belmont and many other influential bankers and businessmen, he prayed that the conflict might be staved off, or at least postponed, and in 1860 bought up the Chicago *Times,* consolidating with it the Chicago *Herald* in the vain hope of founding an effectual Democratic newspaper. A month after the guns blazed at Fort Sumter he resigned himself to failure as a publisher, disposing of the *Times* to Wilbur F. Storey of the Detroit *Free Press*. Under Storey's brilliant if erratic management the *Times* was notorious for its Copperhead editorial policy, finally being suppressed on the charge of sedition in the summer of 1863. By then McCormick was in England conferring with Junius Morgan, Charles Francis Adams, and the Rothschilds on the subject of his investments.

At home brother William worried over the best use of the firm's surplus capital, salting the profits away occasionally in gold, occasionally in Chicago real estate, but never in Government bonds, although by so doing he might have doubled the family fortune. The instant a crisis developed over the packet *Trent,* he had a cold fit at the thought that British warships might bombard New York. Wiring the McCormick bankers in the East, he directed that the company funds be transferred to bullion and shipped to Chicago for safekeeping. Meanwhile the American farmers were taking their own good time about paying off the million dollars they owed on reapers at the start of the conflict. Discouraged, William's wife complained that "the idea is with everybody to go ahead and see how much you can *swindle* out of everybody while this thing lasts."

For his part Cyrus McCormick was saddened by the cost in blood of Northern victories. In July, 1864, he boldly wrote the Chicago *Times* that there was no choice but to "stop the war, declare an armistice, and consider *terms* of peace. May the *Democratic Party* then not falter at this stupendous crisis. . . . Another Republican President elected and the country—*the Union is lost*. The Democratic Party only can—and *it can if it will*—save it. Will it not to the rescue? The ballot box is the only remedy." Thinking that Lincoln would understand that the time had come to cease firing, the inventor suggested to the President that he "be permitted to go to Richmond for the purpose of such conferences with the Confederates as might be obtained that might be useful. . . . My former residence in the South, and acquaintance with the people there might be rather favorable to the object than otherwise."

In September the troubled capitalist announced his candidacy for Congress on the Democratic ticket, bringing upon himself the scorn of the ever-Republican Chicago *Tribune*. "Mr. McCormick has not an instinct that is not in sympathy with the Rebellion," said the *Tribune*. "Like all the poor white trash of Virginia, he left that State a better friend of slavery than the slaveholders themselves, and the prejudices of his youth have built upon a defective education a perfect monomania in behalf of man-stealing. . . .

"He has been nominated avowedly for his money—that being the only qualification which he possesses—and we trust that he may be made to bleed as freely as his most greedy supporter can desire. But all the wealth which he has extorted from the loyal farmers of the West will not elect him. The voters of Chicago are not to be bought by all the reaping machines of the two hemispheres. Mr. McCormick will be beaten by a majority that will stifle his political ambitions for the rest of his natural life."

This was not the first time that McCormick and the editors of the *Tribune* failed to see eye to eye. "Stop [my subscription] to the dirty sheet instantly!" the reaper king had ordered his brother William not so long before. Now, in the midst of the Congressional campaign, the Republican organ outraged the Democratic candidate by insinuating that the basic idea of the harvester was stolen from Obed Hussey.

For this and other libelous accusations of the *Tribune* there was only one consolation, the eulogy of McCormick delivered by Secretary of War Stanton at the outset of the Rebellion. "The reaper is to the North what slavery is to the South," said Stanton, forgetful of his earlier indictment of the machine's creator. "By taking the place of regiments of young men in the Western harvest fields, it releases them to do battle for the Union at the front, and at the same time keeps up the supply of bread for the nation and the nation's armies. Thus without McCormick's invention I feel the North could not win, and the Union would be dismembered."

Not that anyone thought of Stanton's words at the polls. McCormick went down to defeat, the victorious Republican being none other than "Long John" Wentworth, who switched to Lincoln's party in time to help elect him President. Good-humored, like all born politicians, Wentworth bore the ambitious inventor no grudge. "Although Mr. McCormick and myself were at extremes in politics, we were always good friends," he revealed long after the election was forgotten. "I don't believe there was ever a party at his house that I was not present." Then he added: "Whenever the Democrats wanted money, they would always try to get Cyrus in to bleed him."

Crushed by the people's rejection of McClellan for President, crossed by his own unpopularity, McCormick was too weary by the end of 1864 to be a sound judge of investments. When the chance to put money in Field's business was thrown his way, he let the opportunity slip through his fingers. Fortunately the correspondence in question has been religiously preserved in the archives of the McCormick Historical Association, making it possible for us to examine every step in the negotiations between the inventor and the merchant.

It was in January, 1864, during the last days of the partnership of Cooley, Farwell and Company, that Marshall Field made his first call on William Sanderson McCormick in the hope of enlisting capital for a dry goods store of his own. "He would like a connection with us," wrote William to Cyrus, telling of the interview. "Is man of means I suppose and sharpe & capable." But no McCormick cash was forthcoming at the time, and Field went ahead with the plans for Farwell, Field and Company.

In the fall of 1864, when Field again urged the McCormicks to supply the money for a store, William McCormick was tempted to risk his own fortune in dry goods, but was hindered by the terms of the latest understanding with his brother. "Recently," he informed Field, "We have entered into a new agreement by which I have to find my share of capital, and hence I would not now enter into a new enterprise such as we talked of. I don't know what C. H. would think of it."

Perhaps Cyrus would advance the funds, thought William McCormick. "I consider Field a superior young man," he wrote his brother in New York. "Rare chance to find his equal probably. He has means, energy, intelligence, experience, application, etc. I will enquire further and in a day or two make some estimates—but I think he must know soon."

Weeks went by, and the McCormicks dallied with the idea of setting up their brother-in-law Hugh Adams with Field for a partner. "The *inducements,* if any, to start such a business *now,*" William told Cyrus, "would be a rare opportunity to make a connection with such a man as Field is supposed to be in that business & to work Adams and his boys into it. Adams could put up $25,000. . . . Suppose you have seen Cooly [sic] as to Field's reference & Field may not wait unless you telegraph.—Is talking of uniting with Parmer [sic] and has other offers. If you encourage & *desire* it, think he would go to see you or wait a few days—but not long, as spring trade to provide for."

Suddenly the discussions took an earnest turn. "I handed your telegram to Field today," William advised Cyrus the day after Christmas. *"He* seems confident that the present (or soon) is the better time to commence business—says will buy *light* as things now look. Says that *now* he can get some first class men whom he desires to secure. Says manufacturers of goods are doing little & that he considers risk of decline not great for this season—that inflation by National Banks will in the main tend to keep up prices, etc. Thinks in *any* event he can avoid positive loss first year by good management—buying light & selling according to the looks of things. Parmer offers to sell to him & retain an interest as special partner & think likely he will do this unless you join him. One opinion I have heard has been, that if war ended inflation would still make high prices. I think I should not at present want to get into it. My taste is to get a good *farm* somewhere to suit me & might not be able to get out of a store if I wanted. *You* can better afford to do it—while I confess to being more than ever at a loss as to the future."

Of course Marshall Field could not wait indefinitely upon the pleasure of the McCormicks. "I think Field is buying out Parmer," William warned Cyrus on New Year's Eve. "If you and I were in & we should be (as we *probably* will) able to realize large cash payments on this year's sales, we might have large means to invest & dry goods should be as good as gold—while one pays no income and the other should pay well. The store would be a convenient place to put means that would be of intrinsic value & convertible into gold. These are some advantages as it seemed to me—although I have bestowed little thought upon it. I suppose it's too late to deal with Field, but don't know." It was indeed too late.

A few weeks afterward, on an afternoon when customers were crowding into the salesrooms of Field, Palmer, and Leiter, William Sanderson McCormick collapsed, his nerves shattered by the ordeal of caring for the family portfolio. Plagued by his Calvinistic conscience, he took to brooding over his shortcomings, and his wife reported that he was the victim of "nervous headache, *low spirits,* and general debility—almost as he was some years ago." When neither ten days of Dr. Sealy's "water cure" in Cleveland nor two months of treatments at a hydropathic institute in New York brought any relief whatever, the fifty-year-old capitalist was removed to Jacksonville, Illinois, and put up at the home of Dr.

Andrew MacFarland, Superintendent of the State Hospital for the Insane.

For a while there was hope. Though dysentery was rife in Jacksonville, and Cyrus begged for the patient to be brought back to Chicago, William stayed on at Dr. MacFarland's under whose supervision he made great progress. Unfortunately he came down with typhoidal dysentery in mid-September, and on the 27th, having regained his peace of mind, he died. With almost his last gasp he warned Leander and Cyrus of the folly of worshiping Mammon; then, half suspecting that the two might quarrel, he implored them to "forbear one another in love."

This was not to be. Unmindful of William's last wishes, the two brothers were soon wrangling over the title to patents on the reaper. "I have not written him [Cyrus] a line since last winter or spring. I don't know *when I shall again,*" Leander told a friend in the fall of 1866.

Unyielding, Cyrus brooded over the points of contention, wondering when Leander would "be able to take a more proper view of my course and thus make the situation admit of a restoration of good feeling." Until then, nothing must be allowed to interfere with the orderly management of the harvester plant. William's widow's share in the business was purchased for $400,000, and the firm reorganized under the title of C. H. McCormick and Brother, Leander taking one third of the profits and Cyrus two thirds.

In these lonely days Cyrus made all sorts of visionary investments, even subsidizing a survey of the mineral resources of Santo Domingo on the chance that Grant would annex the island. He also dabbled in the stocks of Mexican railways and speculated in an elusive gold mine in western South Carolina, ennobling this last dream by building a town on the site. Luckily he never got over the habit of trusting most of his savings to Chicago real estate, and rents eventually totaled a quarter of his income.

Suspicious as he was of other reaper manufacturers, at heart he was guileless. A stockholder of the Crédit Mobilier and of the Union Pacific as well, he sat on both boards without quite comprehending what the Ames were up to. When it finally dawned upon him that his associates were not high-minded men, he sighed, sheepishly. "We all feel," he said, "that there has been large *stealing* in this business, while I have not an *equal chance* at that." In his own words he was "entirely *too slow* for this game."

He was not quick enough to guess the truth about Tammany Hall. When the New York *Times* opened its attack on the Tweed ring, he gallantly sided with his fellow Democrats, refusing to believe a word of the reformers' tirades. "They are honest men, and conscientious," he thoughtfully explained to Boss Tweed, "but they forgot the fable. Better prove all things, and hold fast to that which is good—not adopt the insane policy of burning down the barn to insure the extermination of unseen rats."

Bewildered by the turn of our politics after the Civil War, McCormick was glad to be appreciated abroad, and when the Emperor of France named him a Chevalier of the Legion of Honor, was overcome with gratitude. By way of showing his thanks he sent Napoléon III a mowing machine and an engraving of Schussele's worthwhile painting, *American Men of Progress*. If the Second Empire saw fit to honor his achievement, surely it did not matter so much what the *Tribune* said in Chicago.

MEDILL AND THE TRIBUNE

The *Tribune,* whose first issue was published on the 10th of June, 1847, only a few months before McCormick opened the doors of his Chicago factory, seems to have been an inoffensive newspaper in its early years, worrying no one until the summer of 1855 when it fell into the hands of two ambitious Republicans, Dr. Charles H. Ray, the former owner of the Galena *Jeffersonian,* and Joseph Medill, one-time editor of the Cleveland *Leader*. A disillusioned Democrat, Ray bought a one-fourth interest in the *Tribune* with one idea in mind, to help a Republican into the White House. His partner Medill, who took up a one-third interest in the *Tribune,* was equally anxious to see a Republican President. But above all he longed for a Republican Party alive to the danger of the aliens in our midst.

Filled with indignation at the sight of European immigrants overrunning our country, Medill made himself the champion of the Know-Nothing doctrine that America belonged to the Anglo-Saxon race, and whenever laboring men organized to better their living conditions, scented a conspiracy of the foreign-born against the American way of life. Holding these convictions, it is not surprising that he fought for the election of Abraham Lincoln without gaining any understanding of the great President's humanitarian ideals.

Very likely, Medill was racial-minded even in his boyhood. The son of an improvident Scotch-Irish shipwright, he was born in Canada, at St. John, New Brunswick, on the 6th of April, 1823. Nine years later the Medills migrated to Stark County, Ohio, and there he attended the district schools while his father tried his hand at farming. Somehow, despite the poverty of the family, he managed to memorize the fundamentals of the law, starting to practice at the age of twenty-three. But a lawyer's life was not for him. At twenty-six he bought out a small newspaper in Coshocton, changed its name from *The Whig* to *The Republican,* and installed himself as editor with his younger brothers as assistants. As a journalist, dealing in public opinion, he was supremely happy. "The law lingered a little while to reclaim the recusant," he afterward remarked, "but he had tasted the delights of Franklin's nectar, and he never returned."

In 1851 he moved on to Cleveland, founding a Whig morning newspaper, *The Daily Forest City,* which he later consolidated with a Free Soil journal and renamed *The Leader.* With the defeat of Winfield Scott an accomplished fact, and the repeal of the Missouri Compromise impending, he had the good sense to recognize that the Whig organization was crumbling. An astute opportunist, he was soon urging the union of Whigs and Free Soilers in a new party to which he gave the name of Republican. This christening of the G.O.P. was an achievement of which he was mortally proud. In spite of the fact that no reputable historian bothered to dispute his bid for fame, he prepared reams of evidence to substantiate his claim, and on losing Horace Greeley's letter of congratulation, wrote out a convincing version from memory.

It was in March, 1854, that the young editor first tried the word Republican on an audience. Calling a meeting of dissatisfied Whigs, Free Soilers, and Democrats in his office at *The Leader,* he talked them into agreeing that National Republican was the proper title for a party opposed to the spread of slavery. "It is not strictly true that we were the first to announce in public the new party and the new name," Medill observed at a later date, "but it is a fact that none of the other meetings in any State antedated our little gathering." From that day forward he never wavered in his Republicanism. "The honor of giving birth to the Republican Party ought to be divided between Stephen A. Douglas and myself," he said. "I began by preaching the death of the Whig Party in my little Whig paper; Douglas hastened it by pulling down the bars and letting the South into the Free Territory, and the North united under the name of National Republican to drive them out of it."

Analyzing political trends night and day, Medill valued his time too highly to waste a second chatting with a friend. The result was that he had no close friends at all. He was "rather cordially hated, which is true, probably, of nearly all editors," wrote Calvin Cobb, one of his contemporaries. To Cobb there was something unnatural in the idea of Medill's having a rollicking good time. "I ran across him in Denver once," he admitted, "and found him to be quite 'one of the boys' at the Denver Club, even joining them in a baseball match as chief rooter in a game against the Cheyenne Club Nine, composed of young cattle barons. He was extremely human that day, and it was difficult for me to believe that it was the sedate Joseph."

A tall, spare figure with red hair, Medill embalmed his dignity in clothes long since outlawed by fashion, decking himself out in congress gaiters, a stiff white shirt, a black tie, and a black frock coat. He chewed only one cigar a week and never touched wine or spirits of any kind until doctors prescribed a thimbleful of digitalis to speed his heart action. By then he was stone deaf and never without his ear trumpet.

In his deafness Medill had one consolation, a wife of the most patriotic American stock. She was the former Katharine Patrick, the daughter of a county judge in New Philadelphia, Ohio. The granddaughter of Abraham Westfall, a valiant soldier in the American Revolution, she was also the great-granddaughter of Peter Van Etten, one of the colonists' courageous marksmen in the French and Indian Wars.

With such a wife, Medill felt he must make his mark in the community, and if he grumbled from time to time, it was because he had so little opportunity to dictate the policy of the *Tribune* in the '50s and early '60s. Besides Ray, who shared the editorial authority up until the day he retired in 1863, William Bross and Horace White worked their will upon the newspaper. Thanks to Bross, who never lost interest in the story of the builders of the business world, the *Tribune* kept its readers well informed on all economic topics. Thanks to White, the *Tribune* occasionally glowed with humanitarian expectations.

A fearless abolitionist, White managed to earn a living as a journalist at the very time he was forwarding money, arms, ammunition, and supplies to John Brown and the Free State Pioneers. If he hadn't gone to work for the *Tribune* in 1857, he might have settled in Kansas himself. By the next year he was covering the Lincoln-Douglas debates, winning his way into the confidence of the future President, and making a lifelong friend of Henry Villard, the German-born reporter of the Cincinnati *Commercial* assigned to the Senatorial campaign.

With White on its staff, the *Tribune* emphasized what was most important in the news. Grateful for its support in the election of 1858, Lincoln wrote a letter of thanks the following spring. "Herewith," he said, "is a little draft to pay for your daily another year from today. I suppose I shall take [the *Tribune*] as long as it, and I both live, unless I become unable to pay for it. In its devotion to our cause always, and to me personally last year, I owe it a debt of gratitude which I fear I shall never be able to pay."

As soon as he was able to pay, the editors of the *Tribune* insisted on payment in full. Nothing less than the Postmastership of Chicago would do. "We want the office," Ray wrote Senator Lyman Trumbull in the winter of 1861, "not wholly for the money there is in it, but as a means of extending and insuring our business, and extending the influence of the *Tribune*. We claim to have done as much for Lincoln and the Republican cause as any other agency in Illinois and we do not see why our claim should be denied, nor why in the division of rewards our wishes should not be respected." Tired of the *Tribune's* importunities, Lincoln finally appointed one of Ray's assistants, John L. Scripps.

The *Tribune,* Postmastership and all, seems to have been a money-making organization throughout the Civil War. On the 18th of February, 1861, it was incorporated, with its capital fixed at $200,000. Among the original stockholders were William Rand, an unidentified investor, Alfred Cowles, the business manager, John L. Scripps, William Bross, Charles H. Ray, and Joseph Medill, the last four of whom had the power to veto editorials. Whether Horace White put any money into the venture at this time is not known, nor whether he had the right to prevent Medill from leaping into print.

Medill was frequently dissatisfied with Lincoln's leadership. "What a dismal retrospect is the past eighteen months!" he complained to Representative Colfax of Indiana toward the end of 1862. "That period consists of epaulettes and apathy, imbecility and treachery, idiocy and ignorance, sacrifice on the part of the people, supineness on the part of the government." A little later Medill was even gloomier. "By a common instinct everybody feels that the war is drawing toward a disastrous and disgraceful termination," he told Colfax. "Money cannot be supplied much longer to a beaten, demoralized, and homesick army. Sometimes I think nothing is left now but *to fight for a boundary*."

By the beginning of 1863 Medill saw no sense in continuing the struggle. "I can understand the awful reluctance with which you can be brought to contemplate a divided union," he wrote Representative Washburne of Illinois. "But there is no help for it. The war has assumed such proportions . . . the resistance is so desperate and stubborn, our finances are so destroyed and exhausted, the Democratic Party is so hostile and threatening, that complete success has become a moral impossibility."

Apparently the once eager editor did not recover his good spirits until the spring. "How do you like the news from Vicksburg?" he asked his brother William on the 24th of May. "The river opened, the rebel army destroyed, millions of property captured or burned, 24,000 prisoners taken, Louisiana conquered, Mississippi to be conquered and slaves all freed in a few weeks, the rebellion nearly played out in the whole Southwest, I tell you the Kingdom of Jeff Davis totters to its fall. A victory by the Potomac army would give it the finishing blow. It looks to me as if you will be able to join my family at Newport in August."

With his younger brothers Samuel and William at the front, Medill felt free to dream of the future of his adopted country. If other wars broke out when this was over, so much the better. "It is very possible," he told William, "that we shall have two wars when this one is ended—one to clear the British out of Canada and the other to clear the French out of Mexico. This continent belongs to the Free American Race and they are bound to have it, every inch of it, including the West Indian islands. We have got a taste of blood and learned the art of war and our tremendous strength and exhaustless resources. Our navy will domineer the seas and our army the continent. The insults received from England must be wiped out, and the only reparation she can give us is to vacate North America, peaceably if she will—forcibly if we must. And as to France, she has taken a mean and cowardly advantage of this nation to crush poor Mexico, which will not be allowed. We shall permit no nation to abuse Mexico but ourselves. We claim the right to turn her up on Uncle Sam's knee and spank her bottom for not behaving herself, as in 1846, but will permit no one else to touch her. . . . Louis Napoleon will get his eyes blackened within six months after our rebellion is put down and will find himself kicked out of that country.

"In future wars black and yellow men will be used freely to fight," the editor rambled on, his mystical mood deepening. "We will not be so careful about spilling the blood of niggers. England holds India with Sepoy troops who hate her. How easy for us to hold the South with black troops who love the North and are devotedly loyal. Old Abe says: 'Bring on your niggers. I want 200,000 of them to save my white boys. . . .' Our people are learning sense. The war has pounded new ideas into their heads and old prejudices out. It is a great teacher, and great progress is never made by a people except through war. The tree of liberty must be watered by the blood of patriots at least once in every three generations." *

For all his love of war, Medill had no understanding of the demands of an army. In 1864 he was surprised by the need for recruits. "When the call for extra troops came," he afterward told Ida M. Tarbell, "Chicago revolted. She had already sent 22,000 men up to that time, and was drained. When the new call came, there were no young men to go—no aliens except what were bought. The citizens held a mass meeting, and appointed three persons, of whom I was one, to go to Washington and ask Stanton to give Cook County a new enrollment. I begged off; but the committee insisted, so I went. On reaching Washington, we went to Stanton with our statement. He refused entirely to give us the desired aid. Then we went to Lincoln. 'I cannot do it,' he said, 'but I will go with you to Stanton and hear the arguments of both sides.' So we all went over to the War Department together. Stanton and General Frye were there, and they, of course, contended that the quota should not be

* One of those who watered the tree was William Medill himself, who fell mortally wounded at Williamsport, Maryland, a few weeks after he received this letter.

changed. The argument went on for some time, and finally was referred to Lincoln, who had been sitting silently listening. I shall never forget how he suddenly lifted his head and turned on us a black and frowning face."

The President was bitter indeed. "Gentlemen," he said, "after Boston, Chicago has been the chief instrument in bringing this war upon the country. The Northwest has opposed the South as New England has opposed the South. It is you who are largely responsible for making blood flow as it has. You called for war until we had it. You called for emancipation, and I have given it to you. Whatever you have asked for, you have had. Now you come here begging to be let off from the call for men which I have made to carry out the war you have demanded. You ought to be ashamed of yourselves. I have a right to expect better things of you. And you, Medill, you are acting like a coward. You and your *Tribune* have had more influence than any paper in the Northwest in making this war. You can influence great masses, and yet you cry to be spared at a moment when your cause is suffering. Go home and send us these men."

"I couldn't say anything," Medill confessed to Miss Tarbell. "It was the first time I was ever whipped, and I didn't have an answer. We all got up and went out, and when the door was closed, one of my colleagues said, 'Well, gentlemen, the old man is right. We ought to be ashamed of ourselves. Let us never say anything about this, but go home and raise the men.' And we did—6,000 men—making 28,000 men in a city of 156,000."

At the time of this rebuke from Lincoln, Medill was the master of the *Tribune,* having bought up Ray's stock and appointed himself editor-in-chief on the 20th of November, 1863. In his new job he mulled over many plans for the punishment of the rebel leaders, complaining in the summer following Appomattox that "General Lee is receiving rations . . . from the government whose citizens he has slain by tens of thousands. We are in favor of striking him off the list of recipients or of feeding him in some penitentiary where his work in hammering stone will be some small compensation for the bread he eats. But if he prefers liberty, we will hire him to tote paper for the *Tribune* pressrooms, provided no Union soldier applies for the job."

On the first of August, 1866, little more than a year after the publication of this interesting editorial, Medill was removed as editor-in-chief and replaced by Horace White who acquired the interests of John L. Scripps and William Rand. Under White's management the *Tribune* dared to disagree with the G.O.P. and went so far as to support Greeley for President. "Mr. Medill and I differed radically in our views on the tariff question and in party service," White wrote later on. "I was a free trader in principle and an independent all around, whereas he was a believer in protective tariffs and in close adherence to the Republican Party."

WHEN THE FLAMES STRUCK

Leaving Medill, White, and the other intellectuals to argue out the political future of the country, wide-awake businessmen were neglecting none of the opportunities thrust by the Civil War upon the city. With the Mississippi closed to traffic, river ports slumped while Chicago boomed. In the very first winter of the Rebellion Chicago took Cincinnati's place as the pork-packing center of the nation, curing over half a million swine, the next season over 900,000. And in the first three years of the conflict cattle shipments tripled in volume, guaranteeing splendid profits to Nelson Morris, Samuel Allerton, and other traders in livestock.

Morris was a stout-hearted Jew from the Black Forest, wishful whenever he thought of the education he missed. "A boy who took honors at Yale ought to be a successful man," he surmised. "One of the things I most deeply regret is that I didn't go to one of those great schools. When I came from Europe I was thirteen years old, and had to go to work for a man who was unsympathetic and unkind. Traveling through the New England States, I used to sit down by the road and watch the boys coming out of the schools and wonder if they were, like my notion of those across the water, all of them princes. I liked to think of the time when I could stop work and go to school."

Penniless the day he landed in Philadelphia in 1851, Morris came by a job as a huckster's helper, dropped it to wander into western Pennsylvania, where he labored in the coal mines as a charcoal burner. When sixteen, he reached Chicago, hiring himself out as a watchman in the old Myrick Stock Yards for $5 a month and board. At the end of a year he scrimped together $35 and began trading in disabled stock on his own account. In this he was not unsuccessful. In only eight years he bought back the family home in the Black Forest, built himself a comfortable house in Chicago, and married the daughter of Abram Vogel, a local packer.

"If Nels Morris ate a piece of beefsteak, he could tell you from what part of the country came the steer from which it was cut," said one of the old hands at the yards, amazed at his feeling for the hidden points of all livestock. In the war Morris put his insight to good use—on one occasion he delivered 20,000 head of cattle for the government in Baltimore, Philadelphia, and Louisville. While executing this and other glorious orders, he indulged his nervous temperament, forming the lifelong habit of whittling. When optimistic, he would pull the blade down the stick; when pessimistic, toward himself.

His sharpest competitor, Samuel Waters Allerton, had none of his nostalgia for higher learning. The phlegmatic descendant of one of the pilgrims on the *Mayflower,* Allerton grew up in Dutchess County, New York, in a world where nothing counted for much except a good day's work. At hard work, he had few equals. "When I was a boy and lived on a farm," he recalled, "I was considered the best boy to work in the country. I had a small interest in the farming, and this individuality gave me courage to work for something of my own. With self-denial, I saved $3,200 and established a character that enabled me to borrow $5,000 more. In this way my credit as a worker was worth more to me than what I had worked twelve years to earn. Nobody can succeed," he added, "unless he can build up character and credit."

Although Allerton was never without character and credit, his fortune was not so much based on self-denial as on the cornering of pork. In 1860, in his fifth year in Chicago, he bought up every hog in the city in a declining market, then held for the inevitable rise. A sagacious investor, he hugged his profits on this and other deals, biding his time for peculiar opportunities, one of which was the founding of the First National Bank of Chicago on the 7th of July, 1863. Growing richer as the war progressed, he suggested and brought about the unification of all the cattle pens in the Union Stock Yards, opened on Christmas Day, 1865. Nelson Morris, his fellow stockholder in the First National, was his partner in this venture as well.

The city in which Allerton and Morris made these happy investments had its splendor, even if mud ran in torrents in many streets, and buildings, slipping into the prairie slime, had to be jacked above the seepage of the swamp. Besides the marble palace occupied by Field, Leiter and Company, there was the Court House, conceived in a fit of Italian grandeur by Ogden's protégé John Mills Van Osdel, not to mention the ubiquitous masterworks of Van Osdel's rival W. W. Boyington. Twenty million dollars' worth of Boyington's architecture was put up in fifteen years, much of it gaudily French, like Crosby's Opera House, more of it romantically Gothic, like the rude gatehouse to Rosehill Cemetery, the triumphant water tower still standing on North Michigan Avenue, and the dark halls of the old University of Chicago, then located at Cottage Grove Avenue and 34th Street on the South Side.

In such a setting social life could no longer be forbidden. Meeting in January, 1869, in the parlors of a discreet hotel, The Sherman House, a few fastidious gentlemen organized the Chicago Club. The mansion of Henry Farnam, a banker who had gone back "to the more congenial surroundings of the East," was leased for a clubhouse, and a hundred citizens nominated for membership without a ballot. Unfortunately many whose names were suggested had doubts about the character of the proposed association. "It was like pulling teeth to get the first fifty," complained Philip Wadsworth of the committee on admissions.

All too many Chicagoans suspected that club life was a waste of time. "It is, perhaps, unnecessary to point out that the early settlers of Chicago did not come here for their health," the historian of the Chicago Club has written. "Few of them had enjoyed much previous experience of clubs, and if their opinion had been requested would probably have pronounced them an undesirable influence in the community." Yet there were those who did not hesitate. Robert Todd Lincoln, the President's son, Perry Smith, the railroad speculator, and Potter Palmer were among the charter members, and Marshall Field joined them before the club was a year old.

Before three years were over club life and all other pleasures were rudely interfered with. At nine o'clock on Sunday evening, the 8th of October, 1871, while the gentlemen of the Chicago Club were meditating, cigars in hand, on the profits to be realized during the amenable presidency of General Grant, a cow kicked over a lamp in the stable of Mrs. Patrick O'Leary at 137 De Koven Street on the West Side, kindling a fire which was not extinguished until rain fell early Tuesday morning. In the interval 2,000 acres were ravaged by the flames, bounded on the north by Fullerton Avenue, on the south by Taylor Street, on the east by the lake front, and on the west by Jefferson Street. Downtown Chicago was leveled, and so was the North Side with its neat villas. Seventeen thousand four hundred fifty buildings were reduced to ashes, 100,000 of the city's 340,000 were made homeless, and about 1,500 people were burned to death.

"Chickey, chickey, craney crow, I went to the well to wash my toe," moaned a crazed woman on State Street. Even as she sang, bullies fired piles of sofas and bedding, and ambitious criminals stole pianos from abandoned homes. Cinders fell like snowflakes, and wise bankers did not dare open their watches for fear the faces would ignite. A little girl ran through the desolate avenues, her golden hair ablaze. An idiot tossed a glass of whisky at her, and her scalp burned blue.

"The district where the fire got its first firm foothold was the Alsatia of Chicago," wrote Horace White, referring to Conley's Patch east of the O'Leary house. "Fleeing before it was a crowd of blear-eyed, drunken, and diseased wretches, male and female, half naked, ghastly, with painted cheeks, cursing and uttering ribald jests as they drifted along." Troubled, like other men of property, by the recent uprising in France, White trembled at the specter of communism. "And what if the *Commune* should go to work and start incendiary fires while all was yet in confusion? Those fiends were improving the daylight by plundering all along the street. Before dark the whole male population of the city was organized by spontaneous impulse into a night patrol, with pallid determination to put every incendiary to instant death."

Not everyone, of course, was as excited as Horace White. "The second day of the great fire," the historian of the Chicago Club has informed us, "a number of the members who had been burned out in the night . . . assembled for breakfast at the club, which was still standing. Some of these gentlemen had been up all night, and were indulging in what might be called a champagne supper for breakfast. In the midst of their meal, the house caught fire and the breakfasters, hastily filling their pockets with cigars, and taking a demijohn of whisky and one of the red satin sofas from the sitting room, finished their meal on the lake front."

Near by, pacing up and down the fiery sands, the Unitarian minister Robert Collyer was one of the thousands seeking some Biblical explanation for the catastrophe. "There was no reason why Chicago should have been made an example for the rest of the world," he fretted, forgetting that the city, with row upon row of wooden tenements, 56 miles of wooden block pavement, and 561 miles of wooden sidewalks, was protected in the rainless fall of 1871 by only fourteen fire engines and one wooden-roofed pumping house that went up in flames before dawn on Monday. Then he recalled that Chicago, like all large cities, was cursed with tricky politicians.

Satisfying his fury, he denounced them and "the only recognized aristocracy . . . a set of ignorant and recently enriched social swells and snobs."

The ashes were already cooling. On the morning of Wednesday, the 11th, when the troops summoned by General Sheridan marched in to restore order, J. V. Farwell and Company reopened for business, and so did Field, Leiter and Company. Surprising as it may seem, the fire was a blessing in disguise to Chicago's biggest businessmen. Having taken out all kinds of insurance with the best companies of the East, they made a fresh start untroubled by uninsured competitors.

Wilbur Storey, the volatile editor of the *Times,* was the only prominent Chicagoan prostrated by the disaster. "I shall not resume publication of the *Times,*" he murmured before the ruins were cleared away. "The city is destroyed. I am now an old man. I have about $80,000 with which I can live comfortably for the rest of my life. If I put that into a new paper, I would be a pauper in less than a year." Shortly afterward he forgot himself in the joy of watching the *Times* roll off the presses.

From all accounts, no other moneyed man faltered for a second. William Butler Ogden, who had moved to New York City five years before, marrying a maiden lady from Elmira whose funds were tenderly invested in real estate and railways, rushed back to Chicago on the morning of the 10th, undaunted. Though the fire gutted $1,000,000 worth of his buildings, and another blaze at Peshtigo, Wisconsin, razed lumber mills of his valued at $1,500,000, he quickly recovered his economic equilibrium and returned to live at "Boscobel," his mansion at High Bridge on the bank of the Hudson.

Like Ogden, Potter Palmer never doubted that the future of Chicago real estate was golden. In New York attending the last rites of his sister on the night State Street was obliterated, he hurried home to find that his new hotel the Palmer House, opened thirteen days before the fire, was a shambles. But he was too faithful a businessman to mope over ruins. As soon as he got rid of the débris of the Palmer House, he argued the Connecticut Mutual Life Insurance Company into lending him $1,800,000 for a much more splendid fireproof hotel. Owning as he did three quarters of a mile of State Street land from Randolph to 13th Street, he saw no reason to be discouraged. What if 35 of his buildings, bringing in $192,000 a year, went up in smoke? With his bride, the beautiful and imposing Bertha Honoré from Kentucky, he would wait for the revival of State Street.

Marshall Field, who carried insurance on $2,200,000 worth of merchandise, was calmer than Palmer both during and after the fire. Glancing at the violently tinted sky on the evening of the 8th, he quietly made his way to the corner of State and Washington Streets, where he consulted with Willing and Leiter on the decent measures with which to safeguard his property. In due time a squad of employees under Leiter's command began removing the most valuable laces, silks, shawls, and woolens from the endangered building, piling them on trucks, wagons, and street cars. Over $583,000 worth of goods was saved. Much of it was stored in Leiter's home at 23rd and Calumet; the rest was thrust under a tarpaulin in the neighborhood schoolyard.

Meantime the marble palace on State Street was being bravely defended. While a crew under Field's direction was soaking heavy blankets in water, hanging them in the windows on the chance they might ward off the worst of the heat, other more adventurous clerks, thinking of the pumps in the basement, raced to the roof with a hose which they played on buildings about to be attacked by the flames. Not that either blankets or hose could save the store. At three-thirty in the morning, with the waterworks on the North Side ablaze, all hope was abandoned. At eight the store was shattered by an explosion; the marble front was powdered to lime; the iron columns melted. In this desperate moment Marshall Field remembered to post a sign reminding wanderers of his liquidity. It read:

CASH BOYS AND GIRLS WILL BE PAID
WHAT IS DUE THEM MONDAY, 9.00
A.M., OCT. 16 AT 60 CALUMET AVENUE
FIELD, LEITER AND COMPANY

Within half an hour after the placard was stuck in the rubble, weary clerks were invading the parlor of Levi Leiter. Pretending not to notice that their host was in tears, they patiently waited for the coffee and sandwiches prepared by his wife, ambitious Mary Theresa Carver of Chicago. The calmer men couldn't help commenting on the devotion of Edward Nevers, who saved all the general books of account. Others congratulated Tony Mulligan, who labored all night long heaving packages from elevators into wagons, spurning the bids of strangers who offered higher pay. "No, sir," Mulligan kept saying to intruders, "I am working for Field, Leiter and Company."

Less than forty-eight hours later, Marshall Field was again open for business, having acquired for $9,785 the horse-car barns of the old South Side Railroad at State and 20th Streets. "This tells no story of a fire," remarked one of the journalists who visited the barns. "Here are hundreds of clerks and thousands of patrons a day." In what was once a manger "a richly robed body leans languidly across the counter and fingers point laces."

Naturally the firm was in no need of bank loans. "We have suffered some loss by the fire, as you are aware," Leiter informed the banker Henry Greenebaum on the 15th of November, "but our capital is ample to continue our business in the same magnitude as in the past. We had kept our affairs very snug—making our entire purchases for cash—never in a single instance having given a note for merchandise. We are therefore today in good shape. Before we received any money from insurance we met our obligations promptly. This was done exclusively from our daily receipts from collections."

All in all, the year 1871 was a profitable one. "You will see that we have left a very handsome capital to continue our business,"

Leiter wrote to Joseph Field in Manchester on the 28th of December. "Our sales since the fire . . . will yield us a net profit of at least $125,000—making a surplus of $2,750,000. This does not include the personal property of either of the partners outside the business. Marshall, you know, has considerable."

CHAPTER TWO: *The Cash Reward*

MEDILL AND HIS PEERS

THOUGH Marshall Field, like most American businessmen, found our government to his liking in the years that followed the Civil War, our intellectuals felt we had fallen upon evil times. Surprised there was no need for their talents in Washington, they bewailed our growing materialism. Henry Adams, who expressed intellectuals' class interest more clearly than anyone else, murmured he had no place "in a society of Jews and brokers, a world of maniacs wild for gold." Like Adams, Joseph Medill was ill at ease, not understanding there was no room for professional thinkers either radical or reactionary in a nation getting steadily richer despite depressions.

With his transparent dislike of immigrants, Medill was a lonely figure in politics. "I have had a dose or two of office-holding and I got about enough," he admitted. "I was once Mayor of Chicago and I had about as heavy a load as I could stagger along with and came out of office with some mud on my clothes, but most of it was knocked off all right, I guess. Politics and office-seeking are pretty good things to let alone for a man who has intellect and individuality. Generally he will get more happiness out of life, I am sure, tending to his business, respecting God, his conscience, and the grand jury, and doing only what those three powers will let him."

Elected Mayor in December, 1871, Medill was confronted not only with the problems of a city being built anew, but also with the emotional demands of a city half of whose population was foreign-born, one citizen in every six being a native of Germany. Thanks to these new Americans, Chicago passed St. Louis in the race for size, becoming our fourth biggest city by the time of the fire, outranked only by New York, Philadelphia, and Brooklyn.

Another Mayor, excited by the growth of Chicago, might have proposed startling reforms to capture the imagination of the people. Not so Medill. Beyond demanding an increase in the police force, reminding the Common Council of the wisdom of enrolling fire wardens, and urging the building of a bell tower to warn the citizens of fires to come, he did nothing to reassure the thousands whose homes were turned to ashes. Not knowing that the Treasurer of his administration would shortly be exposed as an embezzler, he boasted that "the public affairs of the city" were "conducted with as much care, fidelity, and economy as officers of well-managed private corporations bestow thereupon," which was "as high a standard of management as taxpayers can reasonably expect."

Medill might have spent a comfortable term, and passed into oblivion, another undistinguished Mayor, if he had not made the mistake of appointing Elmer Washburn of Joliet as Chief of Police. A tactless disciplinarian, Washburn revealed that Medill did not give workingmen and their pleasures a second's thought. Washburn's first move as Chief was to infuriate the patrolmen by ordering them on duty for twelve hours at a stretch. His second was to embitter all of the foreign-born—but especially the Germans—by enforcing at Medill's request an ordinance forbidding the sale of liquor on Sundays.

To A. C. Hesing, editor of the Chicago *Staats-Zeitung,* this decree of Medill's was intolerable. Why should the Germans of Chicago be forced to give up their beer on Sunday afternoons? They were, he felt, just as law-abiding as the native-born. "Are the Americans infallible?" he cried at a mass meeting of his fellow Germans. "Are the Americans models of morality? . . . Let us," he advised, "coalesce with all liberal-minded citizens, Irish, Americans, or others, and no matter whether they be Republicans, Liberals, or Democrats. Our personal and social freedoms have been infringed upon, and we must win them back at all hazards. Don't be afraid that we Germans will stand alone."

They didn't. Rallies were staged of angry Chicagoans of all races, and the People's Party organized to humiliate the Mayor in the next election. Long before Chicago went to the polls, however, Medill was out of the City Hall. Sick at the thought of compromise with immigrant voters, he resigned and went to Europe to recover from the fatigue of his few short months in office.

On his return to Chicago he was in a quandary. With his modest savings, he could not hope to found a newspaper of his own, or even to buy his way back into the control of the *Tribune*. It was then that he thought of Marshall Field. If the merchant would lend him the money, he could start life over again. Strange to say, this dream came true. Using no one knows what arguments, but probably pointing to the *Tribune's* earnings in the Civil War, he succeeded in borrowing a large sum. With this he drove White from the *Tribune,* buying up his shares and those of Alfred Cowles, and appointing himself editor-in-chief.

According to legend, Medill paid 10 per cent interest on the loan. In any event, there was no love lost between the editor and his creditor, and one of Medill's grandchildren long afterward hinted there were bitter arguments over editorial policies. "In 1874," he wrote, "he [Medill] came back to Chicago and borrowed from Marshall Field enough money to buy majority stock control of the Chicago *Tribune*. That was not all that Medill found he had bought. He had also bought a great deal of freely and frequently given advice from Marshall Field I on almost everything under the sun, especially on how to run a newspaper."

Perhaps Field insisted it was only good manners for Medill to pay a compliment or two to Horace White. On the 9th of October, 1874, the day after White left, Medill made curt mention of his predecessor. "The *Tribune,*" he said simply, "hereafter will be, as it formerly was under my direction, an independent Republican journal. It will be the organ of no man however high, no clique or ring however influential, or faction however fanatical or demonstrative. . . . Looking at the individual composition of the two parties . . . and at their respective records and underlying principles, I cannot hesitate to give decided preference to the Republican Party. Hence the *Tribune* will be conducted as a Republican journal."

As a Republican journal, the *Tribune* declared there was nothing more American than a good lynching. "If the Communists in this country," read an editorial in the fall of 1875, "are counting upon the looseness of our police system and the tendency to proceed against criminals by due process of law, and hope on that account to receive more leniency than in Europe, they have ignored some of the significant episodes in American history. . . . Judge Lynch is an American, by birth and character. . . . The Vigilance Committee is a peculiarly American institution. Every lamp post in Chicago will be decorated with a communistic carcass if necessary to prevent wholesale incendiarism . . . or any attempt at it."

Tramps were no better than communists, Medill reasoned. Annoyed to hear that the sentimental inhabitants of the suburbs were serving food to homeless wanderers, he had a recipe for the extermination of beggars inserted in the *Tribune*. "The simplest plan, probably," he explained, "where one is not a member of the Humane Society is to put a little strychnine or arsenic in the meat and other supplies furnished the tramp. This produces death within a comparatively short time, is a warning to other tramps to keep out of the neighborhood, puts the Coroner in a good humor, and saves one's chickens and other portable property from constant depredation."

At the height of his campaigns against communists and vagrants, Medill was likely to be absent-minded. Once, when the New York *Times* reprinted two columns from the *Tribune,* he quite forgot he had already published the piece. "I want this article to be reprinted in the *Tribune* tomorrow," he ordered. When a conscientious subordinate interfered, he flew into a rage. "What do you mean by neglecting my instructions?" he asked. "Print it anyway."

Reporters who hoped to earn a living on the *Tribune* knew better than to snicker at his eccentricities. When he hailed the wonders of simplified spelling, they cheerfully agreed to spell as he thought best. When he decided that Franklin was one of the greatest of Americans, they willingly took the apostle of common sense for a saint. When he discovered that sunspots were responsible for all the woes of the world, they congratulated him on his scientific mind. Later on, when he transferred his allegiance from sunspots to microbes, they admired his eagerness in keeping up with the times. It was only when he poured water in the mucilage cans on their desks that they dared to complain, and then only under their breath. "Mr. Medill's orders!" the janitor would tell them. "He says you fellows are using too much paste."

Many journalists, realizing that the *Tribune* under Medill emphasized the editorial page at the expense of the news, preferred to work on Wilbury Storey's *Times*. The *Times* was newsy, if nothing else. As one of the members of Storey's staff put it, "Scandals in private life, revolting details from the evidence taken in police court trials, imaginary liaisons of a filthy character, reeked, seethed like a hell's broth in the *Times'* cauldrons."

Like James Gordon Bennett the First, whose *Herald* outraged New York, Storey often ran the risk of being horsewhipped for his impudence. Once, out of pure malice, he printed a series of articles insinuating that the British Blondes, a troop performing at the Opera House, were not as chaste as they might be. When, one dark night, Miss Lydia Thompson, the star of the act, rushed after him and his wife, followed by her lover, her manager, and another girl in the cast, he grinned and more than held his ground. "That creature, there," he pointed out Miss Thompson the next day in court, "undertook to strike me with a whip. I caught her by the throat and would have choked out her life, when that little chap"—meaning her admirer—"jumped on my back, and that ruffian"—her manager—"attacked me from the front."

"Why did not you use your pistol, as Mrs. Storey asked you to?" he was questioned.

"Because," he answered, "I did not need it, sir."

There is no evidence he was ever intimidated. Before sending his men out on an assignment, he would chuckle at the reputations about to be ruined. "We must go for gut-fat," he would murmur. "We must go for gut-fat in so-and-so."

At the end Storey lost his gaiety. His mind unhinged by paralytic strokes, he dreamed he was in spiritual communication with "Little Squaw," the ghost of an Indian girl. " 'Little Squaw' tells me that I shall live as long as Commodore Vanderbilt," he bragged one afternoon. At her suggestion he jumped faithfully each morning into a cold bathtub. For the rest of the day he worried over his place in American history. "I don't wish to perpetuate my newspaper," he decided. "I am the paper. I wish it to die with me so that the world may know that I was the *Times*." At last, on the 27th of October, 1884, when only sixty-four, he died a blind imbecile in the white stone Gothic palace he built for himself on Grand Boulevard on the South Side. Defying his heart's desire, the *Times* went on without him.

Another daily, not half so brilliant, was the *Inter-Ocean,* founded in 1872 by Jonathan Young Scammon, a banker and real estate operator who happened to be "Long John" Wentworth's lifelong enemy. Not that "Long John" forgot how to enjoy himself. "Boy," he one day called the colored bellhop in his hotel, "here is a dime. Go and buy me a copy of the *Inter-Ocean*. I never read any other now. It is the best paper ever published in Chicago, except the *Democrat*. Don't you know it, boy?" When the bellhop returned with the latest issue, Wentworth beamed. "Damn smart paper!" he roared out in the lobby. "Some ability here. This man Scammon is pretty hard about some things; I had to fight him in the School Board, but he knows how to get out a paper. He missed his business. He was made for an editor. I am a judge of these things, for I know the trade. Political views all wrong, but they are stated devilish well. Smartest paper in Chicago." The very next morning there was a copy of the *Inter-Ocean* at Wentworth's door with a card attached: "Compliments of J. Y. Scammon." That afternoon the two shook hands in public. It was not until that evening that someone asked Wentworth if he actually read the *Inter-Ocean*.

"Read the damn thing?" he howled. "No! Never opened it!"

"We've been an enmity more or less for forty years," Scammon muttered on another occasion. "Or rather, he has; I have no quarrel with him, and haven't." Falling into disagreement over the proper way to dispose of the funds of a bank that failed, they never stopped arguing, even in public. "I once witnessed an open and loud oral battle between these two gentlemen on Lake Street, between Clark and LaSalle," said S. H. Kerfoot, a rival real estate dealer. "Of course it was simply disgraceful to both of them. Mr. Wentworth had largely the advantage of Mr. Scammon in lung power, and in his Saul-like overtowering height, while Mr. Scammon, of course, outdid Mr. Wentworth in the elegance of his diction and vocabulary. Mr. Wentworth seemed to be under special influence at the time, and some charitable persons have said that he is a spiritualist, and that he is often led to the indulgence of his merely physical and animal tastes from the fact of his bowing at this shrine and worshiping at that altar."

Far more influential than either Scammon's *Inter-Ocean,* Storey's *Times,* or Medill's *Tribune* was the Chicago *Daily News.* Though launched with only $5,000 capital, and published in the afternoon, the *News* grew to be Chicago's most popular newspaper, winning three times as many readers as the *Tribune* before the century was over. Staffed with distinguished journalists, and genuinely dignified, the *News* achieved a fame of its own as the paper that could be believed.

It was never humorless. On Christmas Eve, 1875, ten days before the first issue was put on sale, a trial number was run off in which the political inactivity of Joseph Medill was deplored. Blazoned on page two was the announcement:

FOR PRESIDENT
of the United States, Alaska, the Western
Islands, and perhaps Cuba
Subject to the Decision of the Republican National Convention of 1876
HON. JOSEPH MEDILL
of Illinois

"A great man in idleness is at once a dangerous and a pitiable object," the *News* remarked. "We have good reasons for believing that if the office of Chief Executive were tendered to Mr. Medill by the unanimous voice of the country, on a silver platter, as it were, he would accept. There is also good reason for believing that he is *in the hands of his friends.* Place in the Presidential chair this great man, and it would not only give employment to his exalted talents, but it would ornament the chair with a diadem as rare as it is beautiful."

One of those who smiled at this squib was Percy R. Meggy, an English remittance man who might be called the founder of the *News,* since he provided the initial $5,000 with which his good friends Melville Stone and William Dougherty went to work. Within a very few weeks, however, Meggy and Dougherty tired of the responsibility of the paper and sold out to Stone. He in turn, on the 27th of July, 1876—barely seven months after the first issue went to press—surrendered the control of the *News* to his landlord, young Victor Fremont Lawson, who forthwith hired him as editor and general manager for $25 a week and a third of the profits.

The son of a Norwegian immigrant who supposedly accumulated a million dollars in Chicago real estate, Lawson managed his inheritance and the money he made on his own with a God-fearing sobriety that was an inspiration even to New Englanders. He also kept the Sabbath strictly. When a Congressman invited him to lunch on Sunday, he sent his regrets. "I never attend a general social function, entertainment, or amusement on the Christian Sabbath as a matter of conviction," he explained. "I trust you will permit me to say so frankly without any thought that I am thereby criticizing any of my friends who think or do differently."

A concert on the Seventh Day was out of the question. When certain members of the *News* staff began sponsoring popular band concerts, he fixed his name to the list of guarantors—until he learned the concerts might be held on Sunday. He then withdrew his patronage. "I will never do anything knowingly," he said, "that would tend to draw boys and girls away from Sunday school and so deprive them of such instruction as I received."

Other Chicagoans felt for our Sunday schools, but very few lived as Lawson did on a diet of good works. Eager to help in the Americanization of our immigrants, he put up the money for free lectures in the public schools. Dreaming of the day when all workingmen would set aside a portion of their earnings, he called upon the government to establish postal savings banks. Aware of the importance of what we would now call socialized medicine, he founded the *Daily News* Fresh Air Fund and paid all the administrative expenses out of his own pocket.

At the same time he was too shrewd to ask newspapermen to be angels. A tolerant and considerate employer, he refused to be exasperated by the Bohemianism of anyone on his staff, and even allowed the perpetually insolvent Eugene Field to pester him for loans. Once, when a reporter at lunch defended himself furiously from the charge of drinking on the job, he listened absent-mindedly and then whispered to the waiter to bring up a bottle of the finest wine. "To your health, my friend," said Lawson, quashing the indictment with a toast.

Lawson was willing to forgive a reporter for getting drunk, but not a businessman for sporting cheap jewelry. "He is shallow. He wore a big showy ring. He is that kind of a man!" he mumbled after an overdressed visitor left the office. He himself dressed sensibly, with a faint suspicion of elegance, draping his majestic, thoughtfully massaged body in a frock coat of wool imported from the Tyrol. With his immaculate full beard and his extraordinary flat-crowned derby, made to order, he was a vision of serene opulence.

He rather enjoyed the few tense moments of his long and peaceful life. Comfortably educated at Andover, he was about to enter Harvard when his eyesight dimmed, making it impossible for him to go on studying, but giving him the chance to learn the fundamentals of the real estate business in his 'teens. He made the most of this, and when his father died in 1873, knew enough about titles, deeds, and rent rolls to take over the management of the family properties. Though only twenty-three, he saved the estate from embarrassment in the panic of that year. On Sundays he sang away his anxieties in the choir of the New England Congregational Church. There he met Miss Jessie Bradley, the Vassar graduate who became his wife.

Like many other Americans who sang in choirs and married two octaves above them, Lawson was a man of reasonable ideals. He didn't like to do favors for his advertisers, and he didn't have to. When Marshall Field urged him to invest in a certain face of display type and hold it for the exclusive use of the store, he let him know that was not the way he did business. "We shall be very glad to buy this face of type for use in setting up your advertisements," he said. "If, however, another advertiser later asks us to use this type for his advertisements, we must be at liberty to give him the same service that we give you in that regard. . . . You may say that certain other papers have done this for you. That is an old situation and does not in the least disturb our convictions. We have grown quite used to wrong methods on the part of our contemporaries."

Lawson thought it was wrong for publishers to accept liquor advertising. He himself took no money from distillers and brewers and never regretted it. Always open to new ideas for broadening the circulation of the *News,* he had the satisfaction of watching its earnings swell from year to year. In the beginning, when the *News* was Chicago's only penny paper, he showed the heads of the dry goods stores the wisdom of holding 99-cent sales, smiling the next morning at the piles of odd pennies shoppers spent on the *News*. Not long after this, in the summer of 1885, he and Stone had the joy of telling Chicago that the *News* had 100,000 readers. Borrowing a battery of artillery and a crew of gunners from the armory, they fired a salute on the lake front. Even without Stone, who threw over the editorship in 1888 to be free to travel and later to take charge of the Associated Press, Lawson did splendidly. Appreciating the need for trained correspondents abroad long before any of his competitors, he founded the famous world-wide news service of the *News* in 1898.

Perhaps because he was a businessman at heart and not an intellectual, Lawson suffered none of the delusions of grandeur so common to American newspaper publishers. When he died, childless, at seventy-five, there were no editorials he was sorry for. Nor did he have to apologize for his investments, for he left an estate of $20,300,000.

A TIME FOR HOTELS

While Medill, Storey, Scammon, and Lawson were chronicling the day-by-day recovery of the city from the fire, Potter Palmer was avidly watching over the future of State Street. In November, 1873, barely two years after the disaster, he threw open the doors of a new and fireproof Palmer House on the southeast corner of State and Monroe. Designed in the gaudiest French style by John Mills Van Osdel, it was a symbol of comfort in the Middle West for generations, and a godsend to travelers, very few of whom were as critical as Rudyard Kipling. "They told me to go over to the Palmer House, which is a gilded and mirrored rabbit-warren," he wrote, "and there I found a huge hall of tesselated marble, crammed with people talking about money and spitting about everywhere. Other barbarians charged in and out of this inferno with letters and telegrams in their hands, and yet others shouted at each other. A man who had drunk quite as much as was good for him told me this was 'the finest hotel in the finest city on God Almighty's earth.' "

The Palmer House was advertised as "the palace hotel of the world," and not without reason. Two hundred twenty-five silver dollars were embedded in the floor of the barber shop and reflected in 200 square feet of mirrors agleam with sizzling gas jets. It is hardly necessary to add that whenever General Grant dignified

Chicago with a visit he stopped at the Palmer House and had his beard trimmed in the shop, which was christened the Garden of Eden in honor of its proprietor W. S. Eden.

Potter Palmer, who was justly proud of the Garden of Eden, sometimes wondered whether the famous piles of the Old World could compare with the corner of State and Monroe. "The Palmer House," he pointed out, "is the final result of a perfect plan worked out to full completion. Most of the palaces and hotels of Europe are made up of disjointed buildings erected at various times and of mixed architecture. They are thus lacking in perfect form and well-defined taste. The Palmer House is a realization of an era of magnificence, and a luxury in architecture and appointments of which the older builders knew little."

It was true that nothing like the Palmer House had been seen before. In no other hotel was there a grand dining hall copied after the salon of the Crown Prince's palace in Potsdam, in no other hotel an Egyptian parlor "furnished entirely in the style of the ancient Egyptians." If other hotels, like the Palmer House, had staircases of Carrara marble, with voluptuous Venetian mirrors on the landings, where else was there a gigantic Egyptian chandelier dangling above the reception desk?

All this involved $3,500,000, which was not too much, provided the first families of Chicago dined handsomely and paid their bills. Fortunately there were not many millionaires as careful as Cyrus McCormick. Businesslike even in the grand dining hall, the reaper king insisted on a private price for dinner. Palmer hoped he would not brag about this. "The price that we agreed upon for dinners I wish confined to yourself only," he pleaded, "for the reason that 75 cents does not pay me the actual cost of dinners."

Palmer was in no mood to grant cut rates to anyone in the early days of the hotel. Hit by the depression that followed the failure of Jay Cooke and Company in September, 1873, he did not always know how he would meet his bank loans. Neither did he know how he could go on paying his help. One dark morning when the chambermaids struck for higher wages, he took up a broom and set about sweeping rooms himself. He had not brushed away many cobwebs before Lyman Gage, the benevolent but keen cashier of the First National Bank, caught up with him. "Mr. Palmer," Gage broke out, "your note for $500 in my bank is due today. I thought I would come over and tell you about it myself."

In his embarrassment Palmer let the broom fall from his hands. "That's the straw that breaks the camel's back," he murmured. "I can't pay it. I have paid every cent I can raise. I haven't a dollar in the world."

"I expected as much," Gage returned. "I will pay the note myself."

With Gage and the First National behind him, Palmer recovered his self-confidence. Furious at his rivals for pretending their hotels were fireproof when they weren't, he vented his rage in a series of strange advertisements in the daily papers. One of these ran in the *Tribune* for the 4th of September, 1878. It read as follows:

A CHALLENGE TO THE KEEPERS OF HUMAN FIRE TRAPS

To the proprietors of any hotel in Chicago, particularly of the Grand Pacific, who are falsely claiming that their houses are practically fireproof, and at the same time paying insurance for a hazardous risk:

Gentlemen: Having erected a fireproof hotel at an additional cost of $500,000 over what it could have been built for in the *practically* fireproof style, and being unwilling that any other hotel in Chicago should claim exception in this respect when the facts do not warrant it, I hereby invite such unscrupulous persons to build a fire in the center of any chamber or room of the Palmer House proper (the Wabash Avenue extension excepted), the furniture, carpets, mirrors, etc., to be undisturbed, and the doors and windows to remain closed for one hour. If, at the expiration of that time, the fire does not spread beyond the room, the person accepting this invitation is to pay for all damages done and for the use of the room. If the fire does extend beyond the room (I claim that it will not), there shall be no charge for damage done. The test can take place on January 1. If the invitation is not accepted by that time, I propose, with the consent of the Underwriters of Chicago, to make the test myself.

When not threatening to set fire himself to the corner of State and Monroe, Palmer was apt to be looking into the private lives of his employees. He liked to know whenever there was sickness in the family of anyone working for him, for he enjoyed walking up to a worried porter or waiter, slipping him a little money, and whispering, "Stop on your way home and get whatever will do the most good."

No wonder the service at the Palmer House was exceptional. It was not, however, the only noble hotel in Chicago. To mention only two competitors, there were the Tremont House and the Sherman House, the former designed by Van Osdel and the latter by Boyington, and both distinguished by opulent mansard roofs. A third rival, also in the Second Empire style, was the Grand Pacific. It cost a million dollars and passed for Boyington's masterpiece, fireproof or not. Bounded by Jackson, Clark, Quincy, and LaSalle Streets, it stood on the edge of the financial district, and was rarely without a railway king in the dining room. Jay Gould stopped there, and so did William Henry Vanderbilt, neither of whom disliked the hearty meals served by the Grand Pacific's proprietor, John B. Drake.

No one, not even Palmer, denied that Drake's game dinners were works of art. Once a year he paid homage to the biggest businessmen and their wives, inviting them to the Grand Pacific for a banquet of quails, pheasants, canvasback ducks, venison, antelopes, and carloads of other kinds of wild game. If the food was rich, the table decorations were richer. It was not unusual for the imaginative caterer Gaskell to spend days thinking up new ways to tease the appetites of weary bankers, tricking out the tables with ornamental and lifelike groups of stuffed birds, squirrels, and rabbits. Now and then he fancied himself a storytelling sculptor and gave his creations sentimental names such as "The White Pet," "The Coon at Home," or "The Lost Faun."

There was, of course, a limit to extravagance. C. V. Bemis, the genius of the Richelieu Hotel on Michigan Avenue, aimed at a more fastidious clientele than either Drake or Palmer, and failed.

Opened in 1885, the Richelieu soon shut down because very few Chicagoans cared to pay for the privilege of lunching off the plates "the French Napoleons ate from," strolling through a $100,000 art gallery, and gazing at Larkin G. Mead's realistic statue *Columbus Before Isabella.* Nor were there many Chicagoans who appreciated the depths of the Richelieu's cellars.

"For Chicago and the territory it served the Richelieu proved an anomaly," confessed one of the great gourmets of the Middle West. "In the early '80s, west of the Alleghanies, champagne meant Mumm's Extra Dry; there was no substitute. In such a world a kitchen and a cellar stocked for real epicures was bound to fail. What did Romanoff-Beluga caviar, terrapin à la Maryland, crêpes Suzette, pâté de foie gras, Dry Monopole or Veuve Cliquot, Steinberger Cabinet Spaet und Auslese of the greatest vintage years, Clos Vougeot or Château Yquem Lur Saluce signify to palates educated to prime roast beef washed down with Mumm's?"

H. M. Kinsley, who opened a splendid restaurant on Adams Street in the same year Bemis attempted Michigan Avenue, did not need to be told that such things were not for Chicago. The first restaurateur in the city to use solid silver tureens, and the first to import oysters from the Atlantic by express, Kinsley featured none of the foreign dishes on the menu at the Richelieu, and by keeping his cooking solidly American, won a large and loyal following. As a caterer he had no equal. No one dreamed of giving a dinner without consulting Kinsley, just as no one thought of giving a dance without asking Johnny Hand to lead his orchestra.

FIELD AT HOME AND AT WORK

Though Marshall Field, like all other rising businessmen, went to dinner parties where Kinsley's men did wonders with the chafing dish, he thought very little about fine cooking and the other luxuries of life, and no diversion distracted his attention from the store for an instant. His town house, which might have been the most beautiful in Chicago, was only a joyless monument to his sense of responsibility.

Cruelly dilapidated today and ruthlessly altered, Field's mansion at 1905 Prairie Avenue was erected in 1873 from designs by Richard Morris Hunt, the most fashionable American architect of the late nineteenth century, and the first to return from the Ecole des Beaux Arts; 1905 Prairie Avenue, however, showed neither learning nor good manners. Its mansard roof was prim, its pressed brick walls were as mean as its sash windows, and its only concession to elegance was a Louis XVI drawing room in white and gold damask. There was nothing anywhere to suggest the superb châteaux Hunt afterward created for the Vanderbilts. At any hint of such lavishness, Field would have held up his hands in horror. He tolerated a light claret at dinner, but only out of compassion for Alphonse Campion, his children's French tutor.

Fortunately for American architecture, the homes of Field's neighbors were pretentious. At 1729 Prairie Avenue, little more than a block to the north, stood the arrogant mansardic palace of the sleeping car baron George Mortimer Pullman. It was razed not so long ago to save taxes, but the tremendous château to the south conceived by S. S. Beman for the piano manufacturer W. W. Kimball has been left untouched. Facing Kimball's at 1800 Prairie Avenue is one of the masterpieces of the century, the somber Romanesque residence planned by H. H. Richardson for Cyrus McCormick's competitor J. J. Glessner.

Further south lived the packer S. W. Allerton, not far from his newest and bitterest rival P. D. Armour. With Allerton, Armour, and dozens of other millionaires dwelling side by side, Prairie Avenue became justly famous as the most expensive street in America west of Fifth Avenue. No one could walk down it without realizing that there was a cash reward simply for breathing intelligently the air of the Middle West.

If the air of Chicago was far from clean, what did it matter? Bordering for many blocks on the right-of-way of the Illinois

Central and Michigan Central railroads, Prairie Avenue was spattered with the soot and cinders of passing locomotives, a nuisance no Chicagoan could honestly complain of, least of all Marshall Field. There was a charm to golden grime.

At nine o'clock each morning, his business suit having been brushed free of the grit from which Chicago flowered, Field set out on foot for the store. His conscience told him it was ostentatious to ride to work in a carriage, and if his coachman drove at a convenient distance behind him, that was merely a precaution against thundershowers. Nearing 1729 Prairie Avenue, he would wait for his good friend George Pullman, with whom he would stroll as far as the Pullman Building on the corner of Michigan and Adams. Occasionally he would stop to chat a while in Pullman's office, but most often he would head for the retail store. He spent the morning there, saving the afternoon for the wholesale division. At exactly four o'clock he would shut his massive rolltop desk, serving notice on any caller, whatever his importance, that the business day was over.

There was, of course, a pause in the business day. Nearly every noon Field lunched at the Chicago Club, sitting at what was inevitably known as "The Millionaires' Table." Among those who pulled up their chairs beside his were George Pullman, T. B. Blackstone, the perennial president of the Chicago and Alton, John Crerar, the bachelor manufacturer of railroad supplies whose fortune finally endowed a distinguished library, Robert Todd Lincoln, the President's corporation-minded son, Lincoln's law partner Edward S. Isham, and Nathaniel Kellogg Fairbank, the impetuous creator of "Santa Claus" soap. Without Fairbank's financial sympathy, the $135,000 Venetian Gothic home of the club might never have been opened in the summer of 1876. Designed by the firm of Treat and Foltz, the clubhouse stood on Monroe Street facing the Palmer House. A provocative red carpet led immediately to the card room.

Fairbank, whose clever passion for processing lard allowed him to live finely, packed his family off each summer for Lake Geneva,

Wisconsin, where he put up a tasteful Swiss chalet planned by the very architects of the Chicago Club. Roundabout nestled the discreet cottages of Levi Leiter and other millionaires, not one of whom was capable of his spontaneous generosity. Once he even offered to give $100,000 toward a combined Chicago Public Library and Grand Opera House costing $1,000,000—provided nine other gentlemen came forward with $900,000.

Field was frankly critical of the project. "Would I subscribe $100,000?" he mused, somewhat taken aback, in the presence of a reporter. "Well, I am not prepared to say whether I would or would not today. Why should eight or ten gentlemen run the town as it might be with regard to a certain enterprise? Why should eight or ten gentlemen be called upon to subscribe $1,000,000? And will it take $1,000,000? Why is not the interest more divided? Answer me some of these things." In the end nothing came of all this, although Field was willing to think it over. "Give us anything," he said, "to elevate the tone of the people. Opera is elevating and instructing."

If Field was too cautious to enjoy playing the part of a philanthropist, he was not too wary for the good of the store, especially in times of panic and depression. In the fall of 1873, when bankers and brokers throughout the country were sick with worry, he kept his usual calm, sure there was plenty of cash on hand. "We are doing about as well this October as we did last," he announced, "but we are not doing as well as we expected. We like to sell cheap," he emphasized. "It pleases our customers. We turn our stock over rapidly. We are ready for a decline at any time."

Thanks to his cash reserves, Field studied the consequences of the failure of Jay Cooke and Company with a detachment matched by very few speculators. "We see no cause for general alarm," read a circular distributed by Field, Leiter and Company late in 1873, "and advise merchants and others to keep on in the even tenor of their way. The partial failure of crops in Europe, creating such a large demand for our breadstuffs and provisions, warrants us in assuring you that no action of bankers can long retard their movements, and as the business of the West is almost wholly dependent upon the money realized for its products, it cannot suffer to any great extent."

Unmoved by the panic of 1873, Field was not easily irritated by the threat of competition. When A. T. Stewart and Company opened a Chicago branch, he smiled at the folly of the New York merchant's executors in daring to attack him at home, and had nothing to say when the branch shortly afterward shut down. Nor did he waste any words on the founding of "The Fair" in 1875. Chicago's first department store—that is, the first store with booths leased to independent proprietors—"The Fair" thrived from the start on the "broken nickel" prices of its promoter E. J. Lehmann, but apparently without hurting the trade of Field, Leiter and Company.

There was room in Chicago for a man of Lehmann's resourcefulness. The son of a German basketmaker who settled in Wisconsin, he began his business life as a bellhop in a Chicago hotel, then tried running a jewelry store on Clark Street, and retired when only twenty-five to organize "The Fair." Though he had less than $1,000 in savings at the time, he knew how to make the most of crises that humiliated storekeepers with money to burn. Always on the lookout for the stocks of discouraged businessmen, he prospered by absorbing his rivals. When he broke down from overwork, Otto Young, a German with an intelligent eye for Chicago real estate, stepped in to manage "The Fair" for the Lehmann family.

Long before Young's time, long before Lehmann launched "The Fair," Field was examining the portentous question of his store's permanent site. As soon as Chicago cooled from the fire, he moved all of the wholesale division and part of the retail out of the car barns to the corner of Madison and Market, ten minutes' walk west of State Street. There, on the 25th of April, 1872, he staged a Grand Opening of the retail. Braving the ashes fluttering from the débris still to be cleared away, hundreds of women hurried to the counters. "Pater familias may expect to be ruined," was the *Times'* comment on the crowds.

But Field, if ready to house the wholesale division west of State

Street, couldn't conceive of the ladies' patronizing a store outside of the now traditional shopping center. Closing down the car barns on 20th Street, and abandoning Madison and Market to the wholesale, he brought the retail back to the corner of State and Washington. This time his landlord was the Singer Sewing Machine Company, who had purchased the site from Potter Palmer and thrown up five stories in the Italian style by E. S. Jennison.

At his old address Field schemed as dryly as ever for the trade of Chicago's most elegant women. In 1877, while assembling walking, carriage, dinner, and ball costumes for the spring opening, he had the presence of mind to import a few gowns fashioned in Paris by Pingat and by Worth himself, knowing quite well that no young girl whose father was reasonably rich or reasonable could resist a reception toilette by Worth costing, when all was said and done, only $400. If, by some miscalculation, the mother disapproved, she might be led to change her mind over a cup of coffee at the Viennese confectionery shop of John Kranz, located then as now at 128 North State Street, facing Field, Leiter and Company.

Who knows how many customers were planning to visit the store when, at four minutes past eight on the night of November 14th, 1877, an alarm sounded calling every fire engine in Chicago to the corner of State and Washington. Field, Leiter and Company was in flames. In a few hours the building was gutted and $750,000 worth of merchandise ruined. All this might have been mortifying if Field had not taken out $959,000 worth of insurance, divided among 152 companies.

The fire was a nuisance, however. Temporarily installing the retail in an exposition hall on the lake front, Field bided his time for the proper moment to return to State Street, and for once miscalculated. When the Singer Sewing Machine Company offered to sell him the corner lot and the shambles of the store, he hesitated and declined. He also turned down the chance to rent the new palace put up by Singer on the site, upon which Carson, Pirie and Company leased the premises. This was too much for Field. Rather than tolerate a competitor on the corner of State and Washington, he paid $750,000 for the building free of any encumbrance, groaning inwardly at the knowledge that $100,000 of the sales price was settled on Carson, Pirie in compensation for the cancellation of the lease.

The fact that Field was rich enough to lose $100,000 without feeling it was no consolation at all. If he were to leave a vaster estate than William Butler Ogden, who passed away in the summer of 1877 worth $5,000,000, he must have mountains of cash on hand for desirable investments. Downtown real estate was attractive, and so were bank stocks, particularly shares in the Merchants' Loan and Trust. Beginning with the first business day of 1877, Field was a director of this institution. Pleased with the Merchants' president, Solomon Albert Smith, he was very likely thinking of increasing his holdings.

Though Field asked of bankers that they live and die for their profession, he could find nothing to complain of in the past of Smith. In "Long John" Wentworth's judgment—and few cared to contradict "Long John"—Smith was "the safest and greatest financier of the Northwest." The son of a powder dealer at Southwick in western Massachusetts, he landed in Chicago in 1840 at the age of twenty-five and went to work for the Laflins, the manufacturers of the explosives that blasted the Illinois-Michigan Canal. For a young man he was unusually discriminating, selecting his friends as considerately as he did the real estate in which he invested his commissions from the powder business. In 1857, his talents having come to the notice of Ogden and Newberry, he was allowed to subscribe to the original offering of the Merchants' stock. Six years later, in the heat of the Civil War, he was elected president.

In the president's chair Smith grimly refused to compromise with the forces of evil. "I know of nothing in my life which should make me ashamed to meet my Creator," he told Wentworth, proud that neither the Civil War nor the fire nor the panic of 1873 had affected his capacity for indignation. When certain of the directors proposed to use the bank funds to contribute to the relief of a distressed city, Smith raged like a Biblical prophet. "What right have I to give away the property of which I am custodian?" he asked, dissecting the generosity of his associates. "I will not spend a cent that does not come legitimately under the head of banking expenses. These men want to get rid of paying their individual subscriptions by shouldering them on the bank." Much as he despised faithless bankers, he had an even greater contempt for politicians. He was willing to save the Fidelity Bank from closing—until he learned that ward heelers were close to the management. "If there were any hopes for the bank," he swore solemnly, "that class of men would obliterate them forever."

When, late in 1879, this high-principled capitalist surrendered his soul to the Almighty, he left something like a million dollars in cash and securities for Byron Laflin Smith, his twenty-six-year-old son by his second wife Marie Laflin. Recollecting that Byron Smith was already the cashier of the Hide and Leather Bank, "Long John" Wentworth uttered a prophecy: "That young man," he said, "will be another John Jacob Astor. Why, I tell you, he's the closest fellow financially I ever did know."

Unlike Wentworth, Field felt this was no time to be facetious. His thoughts fixed on the destiny of the bereaved bank, he was wondering whether it would survive Smith's loss. He very evidently decided that it would, for he added to his commitment until he became one of the Merchants' biggest stockholders.

RISE OF THE HOUSE OF ARMOUR

Meantime Marshall Field continued to leave home at nine o'clock each morning, closing his desk at four each afternoon. With such a schedule he was bound to outrage all of his neighbors who slaved for their millions. Philip Danforth Armour, the thick-set pork-packer of 2115 Prairie Avenue, bristled at the thought that any Chicagoan could indulge in such leisure. He himself got up at five, had breakfast at six, and reached the office at seven in his Goddard

(Brown Brothers)

P. D. ARMOUR

(*Photo Kaufmann & Fabry Co. Courtesy Swift and Company*)

GUSTAVUS F. SWIFT

buggy. He said he liked to get down to work "before the boys with the polished nails show up." He kept to his desk until six, staring blankly now and then at the bunch of fresh flowers his secretary stuck in the ox-horn vase beside his inkstand. At nine o'clock, having had a good wholesome meal in his own home, he went straight to bed, and so regular were his habits that policemen set their watches by his coming and going.

"Most men talk too much," Armour announced one morning after a good night's sleep. "Most of my success has been due to keeping my mouth shut." But it must not be forgotten that exasperation occasionally got the better of the bull-necked, sandy-haired packer. Once, when inspecting the Saint Paul railroad in company with Pullman and Field, he let the merchant know exactly what he thought of his easygoing ways. Nine o'clock struck, and Field, forgetting that Armour's bedtime had come, proposed a game of cards. "I have not broken my retiring hour for Mrs. Armour," the packer replied when asked to take a hand, "and I see no reason to do it for you." Later he turned on Field, muttering that "it must be wonderful to have a business like yours . . . and keep banker's hours."

Toiling from seven to six, Armour was a puzzle to reporters. "You have made your pile; why not clear out?" one of them asked him.

"I have no other interest in life but my business," the packer proudly explained. "I do not want any more money; as you say, I have more than I want. I do not love the money. What I do love is the getting of it. All these years of my life I have put into this work, and now it is my life and I cannot give it up. What other interest can you suggest to me? I do not read. I do not take any part in politics. What can I do? Besides," he added, "I think it is well for me to remain in business in order to set an example to the younger men who are coming up around me."

As long as Armour was on the job, the younger men would have to keep their feet on the ground. "When I am done with work, George," the packer told a favorite employee, "remember this—that I always had a great respect for facts. If there were fewer theorists in the world, there would be more successes. Facts can be discounted in any bank, but a theory is rarely worth par. Stick to facts!"

Fond as he was of facts and figures, Armour dearly loved to moralize on the spiritual significance of a business career. "I believe life is all right," he said. "I think the difference in men's natures is all right. Everything is good and is coming out satisfactorily, and we ought to make the most of conditions and try to use and improve everything. The work is here for us to do, and everybody is equipped by nature to do some part of it. I can't do everything." What he could do, he emphasized, was to feed the world. "Have you any ministers out in the part of town where you live?" he quizzed a visitor to his office. "They would preach better sermons if they included more of Armour's sausages in their diet."

For Armour there was no such word as shyness. "I can stand a lot, for my hide is thick," he bragged before a crowd of newspapermen. "That is the result of my early habits. I was raised like a farmer, and I still have a pitcher of water in the center of the table as we used to at home." The fourth of the eight children of Danforth and Julianna Brooks Armour, Connecticut Yankees who settled on a farm at Stockbridge, Madison County, New York, he was born on the 16th of May, 1832. He grew up not far from the socialist community of Oneida, but it did no damage to his ideals. "Oneida is for those whose dream did not come true," he grinned. "Mine has."

Like his five brothers and two sisters, Armour as a youngster was more sensitive to soap than to things of the mind. "On Saturday night," he recalled, "my mother would take us boys down to Oneida Creek for our weekly bath. Homemade soap would be poured upon our heads and then rubbed in. Often when the soapsuds were running into my eyes, making them smart like fire, I felt as though I would like to bite mother's hand, but I knew better than to do it. I felt that her power was supreme, and that I must submit to it."

Education was something to which Armour did not submit tamely. "My culture is mostly in my wife's name," he told Elbert

Hubbard, skipping over the subject of his schooling. At the academy at near-by Cazenovia he went buggy-riding with a young girl in the moonlight, and was expelled. Many years afterward one of the teachers called at his office in Chicago. "Mr. Armour," he began, "perhaps you remember me? I was the only member of the faculty to vote against your expulsion."

"It took you a damn long time to tell me that," said the packer, confounding his visitor by taking a glowering sniff at the flowers in the ox-horn vase. He was suspected of reading only one book in his life, and that was *David Harum*.

"God did not overlook me," Armour reminded an interviewer who wondered at his cultural shortcomings. Though his talent for trading and speculating was always alarming, he meddled in many lines before discovering it fitted him for the packing business. At twenty he set out for California with $100, which was all he had saved from his earnings as a farm hand and grocer's clerk. Four years later he was back with $3,000 collected from panning gold. Moving to Milwaukee, he built a soap factory which promptly burned to the ground. For the next two years he sold hides in Saint Paul. He then went back to Milwaukee for a fling at the provisions business, dickering so sharply that the thriving packer John Plankinton was left speechless. "I would like to have you go into business with me," said Plankinton, sidling up to Armour one day in 1862.

"But I haven't got enough money," Armour protested.

"Oh," Plankinton replied, "I don't care about the money. I don't care if you haven't got a cent. I would rather have your experience and business ability than all the money you could put in." With that the packing firm of Plankinton and Armour was founded.

In the very same year he went into partnership with Plankinton, Armour married Malvina Belle Ogden, a young lady from Cincinnati. Once, while chatting with an employee who had just become engaged, the packer carelessly revealed the method he used to select his bride. "You've got a good girl, and I know it, although I never saw her," he said, jollying up his subordinate. "I know her parents, and they're fine. She's sure to be all right, for she has a good mother. That's the way I picked out my wife. I looked around for a long time for a good mother with daughters, and I found her in Cincinnati. I went down there and picked out the youngest and prettiest of the girls. Then I went to the mother and told her that I meant to marry her daughter. My frankness to her mother rather scared the girl at first, and she seemed quite afraid of me. But when she found out that I wasn't such a bad fellow, she said yes, and we were married. And you may be sure we have been happy. She couldn't help but be a good wife and mother, for her own mother was both."

With his wife and family as well as a business to look after, Armour never lifted a musket in the Civil War, but one of his younger brothers did, and was killed in action. The longer the conflict lasted, the more the packer meditated on the coming downfall of the Confederacy, keeping close tab all the while on pork prices in the Middle West. Finally, with pork bringing $40 a barrel, and with Union troops ready to rush over the South, he came to the conclusion the time had come to sell pork short—that is, to sell barrels he did not yet own for delivery at a date when he had good reason to suppose prices would have fallen. Boarding a train for New York, he went to call on the bullish trading firm of Wallace and Wicks. "I'll sell you a thousand barrels, if you want it," he said, promising to deliver the meat at $40 a barrel a month or two hence.

"When pork is $60 a barrel," Wallace and Wicks countered, "you will want to get a thousand back."

Armour smiled, scorning the brokers' opinion. "I will deliver you that pork," he said, "when I can get it for $18 a barrel." He kept on selling until pork tumbled to $35, and then went back home to wait for the great Union victories and the collapse of pork prices. When the time came to settle, he and Plankinton made a profit of $1,800,000.

But Armour didn't like to think of himself as a gambler. "I have never speculated as men ordinarily use the word," he objected. "I have invested because I believed it was the best thing for me to do.

I think that this is one of the reasons why my business grew." Quite often the packer disagreed with popular interpretations of his actions. "Good heavens, Mr. Armour!" cried a visitor in the middle of one of his success stories, "do you run your business on sentiment?"

"My friend," Armour shot back, saddened by his guest's suspicions, "I never could run it on anything else."

Yet Armour was not sentimental about Milwaukee. In 1875, at forty-three, he moved to Chicago, ending his partnership with Plankinton two years later. Exactly what made the packer change cities is not known. Possibly he decided that he could not afford to be far away from Nelson Morris and Samuel Allerton, whose operations were certainly worthy of the closest study. In 1873 certain individuals in Chicago—later revealed to have been Morris and Allerton—persuaded the New York Central, Pennsylvania, and Erie railroads to charge $115 for each carload of cattle shipped to New York, with the understanding that $15 a carload would be refunded. The result of this deal, which is usually referred to as the Eveners' Combination, was to throttle the previously prosperous St. Louis cattle market, and to fix the trade once and for all in Chicago.

Armour never cared to believe that St. Louis had been cheated of her rights. "St. Louis," he conceded, "has many features which make it quite well adapted to certain kinds of business, but her great trouble lies in the fact that she hasn't quite enough vitality and Chicago *zip* to make her amount to anything. A place may have every natural advantage for a great city, but if the businessmen are not of pushing, energetic character, it will never amount to anything."

Morris was pushing, but so was Armour. When he discovered that the German was getting down to the yards at four to bid for hogs ahead of him, he started bidding at midnight, eager to roast his competitor at dawn. "To think you came all the way from Bavaria to get the start of me," Armour threw off at four, looking his most amused. His rival gave him a wry smile in return. Within a few hours trainloads of hogs were moving into Chicago consigned directly to Morris, who had taken the precaution of sending his agents out in the country to buy from the farmers' pens. A day or two later the two capitalists met for lunch. Armour enjoyed a huge meal, but Morris ate sparingly, saving his appetite for three cups of tea. "Boys," Armour greeted his staff that afternoon. "I've just lunched with Nelson Morris. I think we had better come to a definite understanding with him as to a few things we shall do, and a few things we shall not do. He's all right. He drinks only tea." For the newcomer from Milwaukee a tea drinker was a man who kept his mind on his work.

His own mind always on the packing business, Armour lived meanly on Prairie Avenue, in a drab house probably put up by a contractor. "I don't go to theaters and clubs, and the mild enjoyment of home does not wear me out," he said, prompting his employees to go to bed at nine. The only luxury he ever allowed himself was an English coachman, a blunder about which he guffawed in public. The packer thoughtlessly offered to outfit the servant, never dreaming he would have to pay for an entire wardrobe. But the Englishman had the effrontery to order a $90 boxcoat, an $110 topcoat, an $85 livery suit, besides gloves, breeches, and waistcoats that brought the bill to $500. At this, Armour fairly split with laughter. "Come here, Thomas! Come here, Webster!" he roared, ringing for men who respectfully whistled at the expense. "That's the kind of coachman to have," he chortled. "He knows his business." How much longer the culprit remained in the packer's service is not known.

"I make mistakes," Armour confided in Elbert Hubbard, "but I do not respond to encores."

Disappointed in this remark, the pamphleteer from East Aurora devoted a critical paragraph to the packer's career. "Philip Armour was a diamond in the rough," he wrote. "He was a diamond all right and at times he was rough. There were several very noticeable flaws in the Armour crystallized carbon. His exuberance was magnificent, but his habit of giving advice would have been a weariness to the flesh if anyone else had tried it. . . . His vocabulary . . . surely needed to be put on a buffing-wheel. His stories often required formaldehyde."

The millionaire whose conversational gift was so lightly dismissed was frequently the topic of talk in the very best parlors of Chicago, for his feeling for investments was admired from one end of Prairie Avenue to the other. He spent many months calculating the future earnings of Middle Western railroads, eventually deciding that Saint Paul at $65 was a bargain. Buying up $4,000,000 worth of the stock, he had the satisfaction of watching it rise to $95 a share.

Whether Saint Paul went up or down, the packer was never too busy to look into the affairs of his brothers. "You must all stand together," his mother had cautioned him, and he did not need to be told that family loyalty could be converted into cash for emergencies. Whenever a banker pressed an Armour for the payment of a loan, the brothers, all five of whom were involved in the packing business, met and relieved the tension. Brothers Simeon and Watson built up a prosperous branch in Kansas City. Brother Herman settled down in New York as the family broker. Brother Joseph, who died of Bright's disease when middle-aged, moved to Chicago in the late '60s, smoothing the way for Philip. "We brothers do stand together," P. D. Armour hummed. "I would give my last dollar before I would see any of them fail."

With his employees, the packer could not afford to be so considerate. When a clerk with a good voice took the liberty of singing at a banquet of packing-house managers, he groaned. "I wonder if he knows as much about hogs as he does about singing," he commented. Singing was bad enough, but insubordination was worse. One morning he rang for Calvin Favorite, his confidential broker on the Chicago Board of Trade. "What's this I hear, Calvin, about your son forming a new company?" Armour asked.

"I guess that's true," Favorite answered.

"I hear that he is taking some Armour men along with him," Armour went on.

"I guess that may be true," Favorite allowed, "but I don't see how I can stop that."

"I don't see how you can either, Calvin," said Armour, "but I do know that if you don't, you and I part company."

At heart, however, the packer loved to patronize the help. "Get yourself a suit of clothes!" he would shout at any clerk who happened to please him. If the lucky man was not wearing a new outfit at the end of ten days, the boss would lose patience. "I thought I told you to take orders and not to talk back," he would rail at anyone who didn't take advantage of the offer. Then one day an Englishman in the plant denied he needed new clothes. "Mr. Armour," he pleaded, "I have plenty of suits. Won't it be all right for me to get a bicycle?"

"By all means!" the packer replied, delighted with his spunk. "But let me see it after you get it." And for the next few years bicycles instead of suits of clothes betrayed his favorites.

Deep in his homely soul Armour yearned to be truly generous. Once upon a time he handed out $5 to a minister who begged it for a woman in distress. "I have discovered," the preacher afterward notified him, "that this woman is not deserving of charity, and I have therefore brought back the money you gave for her."

"Isn't she needy?" the packer fired at him.

"Ah, needy, no doubt, but not deserving," the clergyman reported.

"Is she not sick and without means?"

"Yes, but . . ."

"Oh," Armour concluded, "I suppose you have done your duty as you have the charity to see it. Good day." He then sent the pauper a check for $15.

Yet an employee had only to mention the name of Gustavus Franklin Swift to feel the hot breath of his indignation. "I have ordered a rule posted in our House," he decreed, furious at the attention paid his competitor, "that anyone who refers to business in the future, and says we ought to do so and so because Swift is doing so and so, will be shot. Only a few days ago Favorite was in my private office and said that if we did not take the Fort Worth packing house, Swift would. I told him that if I ever heard of another man within 100 miles of me that used that argument again, he could consider himself shot, without even a court-martial trial. It is such damnable nonsense to do something because somebody else does it, that I have no patience with it whatever. I don't know about the other fellow, but I ought to know about Armour and Company, but I guess I don't."

For Swift, Armour was above all a happy gambler on the Chicago Board of Trade. "He was . . . a born speculator," he let fall, sizing up his adversary, "and coupled with the power to speculate safely, he had the great faculty of being able to keep a great number of irons in the fire all the time. Mr. Armour's attention to the details of his vast business was marvelous to me when examples of it would come to my notice, and to that can be attributed much of his success."

In his brilliant moments on the Board of Trade Armour would even use an old friend to hide his hand. Once, having made up his mind to drive the price of wheat to a new low, he sent for George Seaverns, a crony of his for years. Asking him into his private office, he shut and locked the door, and after swearing him to secrecy, tipped him off that "a certain commodity was bound to rise." With that the trustful Seaverns went out and mortgaged "everything but the children's toys," put his last penny into wheat, and incidentally let a few of his friends in on the good thing. When the market collapsed, precisely as intended, Armour rang for his friend, braving his despair with a smirk. "George," he said, "I knew you'd tell." And he made out a check to cover his losses.

RISE OF THE HOUSE OF SWIFT

Swift, who had no idea of risking his cash in romantic frays on the Board of Trade, minded his packing business so sharply that he rarely bandied words with reporters. One afternoon, however, riled by the tales that reached him of businessmen clearing out for the East after making a killing in the Middle West, he felt he had something to say to the newspapers. Sending for a man from the *Inter-Ocean,* he denied that he, Gustavus Franklin Swift, would ever desert his adopted city. Like Armour, he had located in Chicago in 1875. Like Armour, he had gotten richer every year. Of what could he complain?

"Chicago," he said, "is the finest city in the world for the moderate, natural, average man of affairs in which to live. The New Yorker who says Chicago is a city of no luxuries is probably one of that constantly growing number who are insatiable in their greed for the softer things of life. To those men who have families and who find in their homes the greatest of their pleasures, Chicago offers all that New York offers, and, in my opinion, more. A man can get wholesome food in Chicago more cheaply than he can in the East, and he can live as well on a smaller amount of money. I do not go in for luxuries myself," he made plain.

"I do not know," he continued, "whether or not eloquent preachers are looked upon as luxuries in New York, but they certainly offer enough money to get them there. Their best and most famous ones come from Chicago, but Chicagoans seem to have succeeded in finding others equally good to fill their places. No," he said thoughtfully, "Chicago is good enough for me. I can spend my money fast enough here."

Satisfied with anything in the way of architecture, he kept his family for many years in a nondescript dwelling on the corner of Emerald and 45th, down near the yards. When, toward the end of his career, he moved to a comfortable home at 4848 Ellis Avenue, he ran into an unforeseen complication with his wife. "Gustavus," Mrs. Swift informed her husband one evening, "everything is ordered except the draperies and laces."

"Draperies and laces?" he gasped.

"Yes," she said, "draperies for the doors and lace curtains for the windows."

"We're not going to have any of those fool things for the windows!" he told her.

"I think we are," she advised him.

"But—why, Ann, I hate curtains!" he pleaded.

"Yes," she answered, "I know you do."

"Well," he decided, "I won't have them in my house, and that's that."

There was a pause. "Well," she hinted, "I think you will have to find someone else to live with you in *your* new home, and that's that."

"What do you mean?"

"Just what I say. I've lived thirty odd years in houses that were as you liked them, Gustavus, or at least, not as I liked them."

"Oh, very well," he sighed. "I don't have to have them in my bedroom, do I?"

"No," she conceded.

Though he left his muddy boots in the front parlor for all to see, he never intended to plague his wife. Neither did he mean to frighten his children, but he sometimes scared them teaching arithmetic after dinner. "How many are 12 and 13?" he shot one night at little George Swift, aged five.

"I don't know."

"Of course, you know," he fired back, frowning.

"I don't know," said George again, imploring his parent's mercy. "That's too hard for a little boy."

"Now, George, listen! If you had 12 cents and I gave you 13 cents, how many would you have?"

At that the youngster's face lit up. "Oh, a quarter, of course! Why didn't you say you meant *money?*"

Upon which the huge packer grinned from ear to ear. He weighed 190 pounds and stretched six solid feet tall.

To the last ounce and to the last inch Gustavus Swift was a Yankee. The eighth of the twelve children of William and Sally Sears Swift, he came into this world on the 24th of June, 1839, at Sandwich, Massachusetts, on Cape Cod. He grew up on his father's farm, close to the site where William Swyft, the first of the name to land in America, had settled in 1631. As a boy he yearned to be a butcher, an ambition his father was ready to encourage if he promised not to move to New York. "Don't go, Gustavus!" the senior Swift begged him. "Stay at home, and I'll buy you an animal to kill, and you can start in the meat-market business yourself."

Of course a mettlesome young man could not keep to Cape Cod forever. With his father's blessing, and with $400 borrowed from an uncle, Gustavus began buying pigs in the Brighton stockyards, selling them in markets he opened at Eastham and Barnstable. Later he was unloading Cape Cod cattle in Brighton. Still later he was slaughtering livestock on a wholesale scale and supplying retail markets all around the Cape. Anxious to be near bigger stockyards, he made his home first in Brighton and then in Albany. Finally, at thirty-six, he set out for Chicago to face his peers.

Nelson Morris, whose son Edward was afterward married to Swift's daughter Helen, thought he could explain the young man's urge to go West. "I was responsible for his coming to Chicago," he told Helen. "Well, 'twas while he was in Albany. I shipped a load of cattle from Chicago to be sold there. Got a wire from my agent that he'd sold them for 4¼ cents a pound. I was mad. They were good cattle—ought to have brought more. I wired the agent: 'Cattle sold too cheap. Buy them back at a quarter of a cent profit.'" Here Nelson Morris snickered. "What do you think that man wired?"

"Can't imagine," said Helen Swift.

"Well, he wired: 'Can't be done. Cattle sold to Swift. He knows a bargain as well as you do.'"

"But how does that make you responsible for father's being here?"

"Why, don't you see? Uncle Swift figured that if cattle could be shipped from Chicago and sold in Albany for 4¼ cents, that was the place money could be made, right on the ground floor. I always held it against him, a little. But now I'm even with him. I've got his daughter."

Long before Albany, long before leaving home for Brighton, Swift was married to Annie Maria Higgins, a conscientious Cape Codder who never went willingly to the theater. She bore him eleven children, nine of whom survived him, and only pretended to object when he set her on top of the icebox the better to admire her. "Gustavus!" she would screech, "don't be silly! Take me down!"

"You know, Ann," he would murmur, "I like the looks of you up there."

In his way, Gustavus Swift was as loyal to his family as P. D. Armour to his. He made his brother William his Fitchburg representative, and he put his brother Edwin in charge of all Eastern sales. But he never could count on his brothers' bank deposits in an evil hour. Nor could he persuade his brother Noble that packing was a worthwhile business. When asked if he wished to increase his commitment in the firm, Noble Swift indulged his sense of humor. "Brother Gustavus," he wrote, "I do not care for any more Swift and Company stock. Do you remember when we were boys, that everybody on the coast fished? What has become of the fish now? Fished out! Where will Swift and Company be when the cattle are killed off? I don't want any more stock. Perhaps I have too much already."

Though his own brother hung back from investing in the family business, Gustavus Swift contributed far more than anyone, including Armour, to the evolution of the packing industry. To use a tired word, he was a pioneer. Drawing on his savings, which amounted to $30,000 the day he arrived in Chicago, he made up his mind to experiment, and if possible to undermine the prosperity of the old-time packers. Taking note of the fact that Nelson Morris shipped frozen meats to the East in the winter of 1874, he kept his eyes open for the proper refrigerator car for summer and winter use. Finding the solution in the Tiffany patent, he broke precedent by sending a lot of dressed beef in a Tiffany car to Boston in the summer of 1879. It reached the Hub on the 3d of September in good condition, and if Armour, Allerton, and Morris lost no sleep over this, they very well should have. Swift was irrepressible. When the railroads, fearful of losing the profitable live steer traffic, refused to build him refrigerator cars, he had his own manufactured. When the great roads to the seaboard banned dressed beef shipments, he recalled that the Grand Trunk, no party to the boycott, was starving for freight. Calling on the Grand Trunk officials, he talked them into an attractive agreement. In time, of course, the railroads capitulated, and in time his rivals flung their refrigerator cars across the continent. But it was Swift who laid the foundations of the business.

"The best a man ever did," he thought, "shouldn't be a yardstick for the rest of his life." Dissatisfied with himself, the packer was not easy to please. To quote one of his children, "Sarcasm was my father's working tool in handling employees." If a clerk took a glass of whisky once too often, he could expect no mercy from Gustavus Swift. "You like your job, don't you?" he grilled a hand whose breath betrayed him.

"Oh, yes, I'm very well satisfied," the guilty one stammered. "I'm trying to do my very best."

"Well," said Swift, "you've been doing a lot of things you hadn't ought to, a lot of things we don't stand for. I'm glad you liked your job, for you ain't got it now."

On another occasion he hired a man for twelve months and sacked him at the end of eight weeks. "You're not getting the results you said you'd get, are you?" Swift asked.

"Not yet," the trembling man nodded. "But I was hired for a year, Mr. Swift."

"All right," the packer agreed. "You go over to Mr. So and So in the packing house. He'll have a job for you."

That afternoon the unfortunate employee was handed a squeegee and told to keep the blood running into the blood gutters. He resigned.

"I don't have to go out and hire many managers," Swift boasted. "I can raise better than I can hire." Higher-ups broke into a cold sweat whenever he inspected operations. "You never felt at ease with G. F. unless you knew him extremely well," the manager of one plant confessed. "He would ask you questions he knew the answer to, to see if you knew." Before walking into a manager's office, he never failed to glance at the thermometer outside the door. One morning in Kansas City it read 80 degrees. "It's a wonder your brains ain't cooked," he told the unlucky man behind the desk.

Swift couldn't stop to consider the feelings of thin-skinned underlings. As one of his sons expressed it, "The employee who required a lot of attention and waiting on did not interest him much." Besides, there were more important things than personalities. "Swift and Company can get along without any man, myself included," the packer felt. "This business will be bigger after I'm gone. That's what I'm building for." Naturally he was furious when all of his executives voted yes on an important question. "I vote no," he said, "and the noes have it. You men voted yes because you thought I would. I pay you for your real opinions, not to say what you think I think."

But only the bravest of men dared to suggest that alterations or additions to existing buildings were necessary. At the sight of a workman with a hammer or saw, Swift could not always control himself. "Whenever you see a lot of mechanics at work anywhere you are in charge, fire 'em," he ordered a department head.

"But sometimes they are needed, Mr. Swift," the department head pleaded.

"They'll find their way back, then," said the packer. "They're a luxury. We can't afford luxuries. It isn't only the high wages you pay 'em—it's the lumber and nails and brick and hardware they use, too. No, sir, when you see a gang of 'em around and you don't know that you have to have 'em, be on the safe side and fire 'em. That's the way I always work it."

Swift was so close to the business that he got up an hour earlier than Armour, riding off to the yards at five on a tall gray mare. "Any hogs die during the night?" he would cry as he dropped from the saddle. He knew that swine never smother if allowed plenty of room. Having checked the health of his cattle, he would often as not dart over to the Bubbly Creek, where the sewage of his own and other plants gurgled into the open air. At the faintest trace of waste fat, he would call for the superintendent and dress the man down.

For Swift a penny saved was a penny made. When a boy handed

him a slice of cheesecloth to wipe his oily hands with, he prudently and fiercely inquired: "What did it cost? How much is in it?"

"A cent and a quarter a yard," volunteered a foreman standing near. "There are about four yards in that piece."

"Thank you," said the packer. "I will use my own handkerchief. I think you should see that the company's supplies are not wasted."

In his personal expenses Swift was a model for everyone in the firm. At the end of the business day he usually tossed the urchin who held his horse a nickel for carfare home. But if he kept the lad after hours, he cross-examined him as to his destination. If he was heading for the yards, he got the customary nickel. If he was heading for home, which might after all be close at hand, he got nothing.

Thrifty in all things, Swift was not one to overlook the money to be made from the by-products of the industry. Eventually a pleasant proportion of his income came from offal, a circumstance in which he took an honest pride. What did dignity matter, when profits were at stake? He liked to get down and run his hand over the rumps of cattle, that being the very best way to test their fat. Daintier dealers tittered, but Swift wouldn't give up the habit. "Back where I ship these cattle to, they're bought that way," he spoke up. "That's how I sell 'em, and that's how I buy 'em." One day, coming upon a lot of hogs that had been scalded with their hair on, contrary to the correct procedure, he picked up a knife and started scraping the hirsute flesh himself. His employees helped, and in a few minutes the porkers were bald. "You know, when you're dressing hogs, you ought to take the hair off, you ought, ought to take the hair off," he grumbled, groping in his pocket for a handkerchief to dry his greasy fingers. "Never ought to leave a hog like that." To Swift anything to do with packing was fascinating, even the marketing of meat to housewives. "Cut it up and scatter the pieces!" he scolded a retailer for setting out grotesque chunks of beef. "The more you cut the more you sell." In his own butcher shop the packer learned as a boy that it was wiser to display cuts than carcasses.

When away from work, Swift always thought in terms of the yards. Though a staunch Methodist, he seldom heard out a sermon without getting up six or seven times to open or shut a window. "He wanted the ventilation of the church just right," one of his sons explained, "just as he wanted every one of his refrigerator cars scrubbed out and cleaned with live steam between trips." As time went on the tolerant members of the congregation abandoned all hope of talking him out of his idiosyncrasy and respectfully referred to him as "the ventilation committee."

One reason the packer was restless in church was that he was often deep in debt and harried by his creditors. One afternoon, galled by a rumor that his firm had failed, he rushed to the floor of the Board of Trade, "a place he had probably not been half a dozen times in his life." Marching over to a table, he pounded for order with his fists. "Attention!" he cried. "Attention! It is reported that Swift and Company has failed. Swift and Company has not failed. Swift and Company cannot fail." For thirty minutes after he left the room there was absolute quiet on the floor.

On another dark day he learned that certain financiers were meeting in secret to agree on terms that would mean his ruin. Lashing his carriage horse with a fury that would have been despicable on the part of anyone but a desperate man, he reached LaSalle Street in twenty minutes. Papers had just been drawn demanding his resignation. "You, gentlemen," Swift began, taunting the architects of his destruction, "think you might be better off by bringing pressure to bear upon us. I'm sorry, gentlemen, but we have to have more money, not less. It is up to you to lend it to us. If we don't get it, we go down—and a great many of you go down with us." And he browbeat the conspirators into increasing his line of credit.

With practice Swift became a past master at the fine art of saving his property from foreclosure. When a fidgety creditor sent a messenger to the yards after hours, ghoulishly inquiring into his assets and liabilities, he called in person the next morning on the offensive money-lender, bringing with him a sworn statement proving that he was solvent, if heavily in debt. He then made free to leave the balance sheet with four other financiers, and from each obtained additional funds. "There's no use in trying to deal with a banker and not letting him know where you stand," he cheerfully remarked. Another lender summoned him to pay a note not yet due, and on his refusal threatened to hawk the paper in question from the Court House steps. "Well, that's right neighborly," the packer decided. "If you get anybody to bid on it, let me know, and I'll go and sell him some more."

Although Swift was no speculator in Armour's sense of the word, he strained his credit whenever there was a chance of his embarrassing a competitor. One afternoon, having been informed that the New York cattle market was due to rise within a very few days, he began buying all the steers he could lay his hands on for shipment to the East. At the end of an hour or two his weight tickets—sight drafts on the National Live Stock Bank—totaled an appalling sum, and Levi B. Doud, the bank's president, ordered a boy sent to the yards to call Swift in for consultation. When one, two, and then three messengers came back without the packer, Doud mounted a horse and went himself in search of him. "You're buying a lot of cattle, Mr. Swift," said Doud, on catching up with his client.

"I know it," Swift agreed. And he turned to a commission man near by. "Weigh 'em," he said, indicating that he was acquiring another lot.

"To tell you the truth," Doud broke in, "your tickets have overdrawn your credit. I'm worrying about you, Mr. Swift."

"Glad to hear it," the packer returned. "I was worrying a little myself until now, but there's no use of the two of us worrying. I'm not worrying any more. Good-bye, Mr. Doud."

THE PANIC AND THE PROFITS

Clear-headed and two-fisted, Gustavus Swift looked out for himself in good and bad times, even in the dreary years following the panic of 1873. To thousands of other Americans, however, the '70s spelled misery and unemployment from which there was no apparent escape. Embarrassed by the decline in property values, respectable citizens blew out their brains. One of these unfortunates was William F. Coolbaugh, for fifteen years the president of the Union National Bank of Chicago. Arising at dawn on the 14th of November, 1877, he oiled his silver-plated revolver, fingered its pretty pearl handle, and then, at the foot of a statue to his good friend Stephen A. Douglas, pulled the trigger. His blood stained the base of the monument, pricking the curiosity of a passing locomotive engineer who notified the police.

The masses, whose discontent was quite as real as that of the banker Coolbaugh, spent their despair in strikes. When, on the 17th of July, 1877, workmen on the Baltimore and Ohio quit in protest against wage cuts, the agitation spread from railway to railway and from city to city, distressing our business leaders and petrifying our intellectuals. Violence was answered with violence, and in Baltimore, Buffalo, Pittsburgh, and Chicago, guns were turned on sulking crowds. Watching the uprisings from the comparative safety of Cleveland, the ambitious journalist John Hay was mortified by the marksmanship of the Federals. "The army has been destroyed by the dirty politicians," he complained, "and the State militia is utterly inefficient. Any hour the mob chooses, it can destroy any city in the country—that is the simple truth."

Rioting was anticipated in Chicago on the evening of the 23rd. Switchmen in the Michigan Central yards walked out on their jobs, and Levi Leiter, prepared for the worst, armed the employees of the wholesale store. On that very day a certain Albert Parsons, a typesetter at the *Times,* was working on the resentment of a gathering of laboring men, twitting them for doing the bidding of Jay Gould and other capitalists equally insolent.

The businessmen of Chicago were far from pleased with Parsons' remarks, as he discovered when he was arrested, brought before Mayor Monroe Heath, and badgered with questions from Board of Trade men about his membership in the Workingmen's Party.

Finally he was set free, but not before being told what was good for him. "Parsons," said Mayor Heath, "your life is in danger. I advise you to leave the city at once. . . . Do you know you are liable to be assassinated at any moment on the street? Why, those Board of Trade men would as soon hang you to a lamp post as not."

Cashiered from the *Times* for advertising his dislike of millionaires, Parsons found himself blacklisted at every printing plant. On the faint chance of getting work through friends on the *Tribune,* he wandered into its composing room where he met with two toughs who pressed a pistol to his ribs and rushed him down five flights of stairs. "If you ever put your face in this building again, you'll be arrested and locked up," one of the bouncers drawled. There was tension everywhere following the declaration of a general strike by all railroad workers in Chicago on Tuesday, the 24th.

Wednesday morning Field, Leiter delivery wagons were whisking policemen from one disaffected area to another. There were skirmishes, and the *Tribune* claimed that "red war" had broken out. Three hundred men and women collected in front of the Field wholesale store, scattering at the first blank cartridge fired into the air. Eight thousand stormed the Burlington roundhouse, retreating only after three men were shot dead and eight wounded. Another mob of two or three thousand overran the railroad yards from Canal to Halsted Streets. According to the *Tribune* the leaders were Bohemians and Polish Jews.

Overwrought by newspaper stories of this uprising, the Unitarian minister Robert Collyer called his congregation to arms. "I cannot expect to live long, in the course of nature," he babbled to reporters. "I thought I might live twenty years—I would like to. Do you know, fellow citizens, as God lives, and as my soul lives, I would rather die in twenty minutes in defense of order and of our homes against these men, than live 20 years of as happy a life as I have lived in all these fifty years?" Fortunately for Chicago, there were cooler heads than Collyer's in this crisis. Marshall Field was already meeting in conference with Mayor Heath.

At eight o'clock the next morning 10,000 sympathizers of the strikers swarmed about the Halsted Street viaduct, beating back the police at a cost of only ten lives. Yet the victory, if such it can be called, was meaningless. In the afternoon Federal troops marched into Chicago, and the passions of the people subsided. "The fight with the communists is at an end," cheered the *Tribune*. "The potent argument of bullets and billies did the work." At least 30 lay dead; at least 100 lay wounded.

Dumbfounded by the outcome, and knowing next to nothing of political or economic theory, young Albert Parsons was in a mood to be easily influenced. Turning for inspiration to the German anarchists who, having been disowned by Marx and Engels, were then trying to wrest control of the American labor movement, he glibly adopted all of their catchwords, ranting of civil war at the slightest provocation. "If the armed assassins and paid murderers employed by the capitalistic class undertake to disperse and break up our meetings, they will meet foes worthy of their steel," he bragged to a *Tribune* reporter in the spring following the railroad strike.

Parsons was always courageous and almost never intelligent. As a boy of thirteen he joined the Confederate Army, fighting the next four years for ideals he inwardly abhorred. Later he became a gallant if headstrong champion of the Negro race in Texas. Siding with the radical Republicans and their reconstruction measures, he edited a weekly newspaper pledged to equal rights for black men. Of course he had to leave the State. In Chicago he aired his opinions in the columns of the *Tribune,* never suspecting that if newspapermen were forever asking him for interviews, it might be because his bombast discredited the reforms advocated by the level-headed leaders of the working class.

But Parsons, although much more of an anarchist than a communist, and much more of a crank than a labor organizer, succeeded in frightening Chicago's millionaires as effectively as any graduate of the Paris Commune. At the best breakfast tables the talk was of barricades and gatling guns. Mrs. Cyrus Hall McCormick, who was one to keep herself informed of any threat to her husband's interests, forwarded a newspaper clipping on the communist menace to her son Cyrus at Princeton. "I wish," she wrote, "that you would pass it on to some of the young men who, from their position, will probably be called upon to meet these questions in the future. *All* young men will have to deal with them—but some will have a *controlling* position."

Big businessmen did not intend to be caught napping. In the spring of 1878 J. W. Oakley, an agent of the McCormicks, furnished the reaper company with a detailed report on the measures taken to ward off the revolution. "Thirty or forty citizens," he disclosed, "have had during the last two weeks several private meetings to ascertain by means best at hand what danger if any was to be anticipated during the coming summer from the communistic element in the city. A committee . . . recommended the purchase of arms and guns, etc. I think it most important," he reminded his superiors, "that our subscriptions are kept strictly private." In this quiet way the funds were raised for Napoleon guns, gatling guns, and uniforms for the Illinois National Guard.

While Cyrus McCormick, Levi Leiter, Marshall Field, and other moneyed men were taking the lead in arming and equipping the Guard, P. D. Armour was busy breaking a butchers' strike. "The ultimatum has been given us, you know," he told a reporter one December day in 1879, "that only *union men* shall work after tomorrow. But it is we who are going to run that house or quit the business here. We have two large houses in Kansas City and another in Milwaukee, where we can do this work cheap—for half the price we can here. Chicago can see this business killed if she likes." The packer was not threatening in vain, the butchers decided. At the end of a few weeks they resigned in hundreds from the union, promising never again "to join any society or association inimical to the interests" of their employer. Those whose jobs were not already filled by strikebreakers had some hope of being reinstated, but only if they had not been active in the union. "There will be plenty of men to work for us," Armour prophesied. "All we want is hogs enough to run with."

The packer often had other things on his mind than the troubles of his employees. Just then he was demoralizing the price of pork with the help of the most cunning brokers in Chicago. Making their first purchases in July, 1879, at $8 a barrel, he and his confederates unloaded their holdings at the end of the year when pork was selling at $14, netting $2,000,000 in one operation. Dissatisfied with these pickings, they kept on bidding until pork slipped to the disheartening quotation of $9.25. This time they lost $3,000,000. In April they plunged again, picking up 350,000 barrels at $10. Disposing of these at from $16 to $18, they cleared $7,000,000. This meant that in little more than a year's trading, they were $6,000,000 to the good.

There were Chicagoans who objected to this sort of thing. Orrin W. Potter, the president of the North Chicago Rolling Mills, held Armour and other gamblers in foodstuffs directly responsible for the unrest gripping the working class. "The laborers oppose the reduction of wages for the very good reason that they cannot live on any lower wages," said Potter, referring to a recent strike of iron workers. "They cannot stand the reduction with the high price of living. There are some things that are not to be talked about in public that bring this about, and one of them is the cornering of foods on the Board of Trade."

Henry Demarest Lloyd, a young journalist writing in the *North American Review* for August, 1883, had even less admiration for Armour's daring. "This is the communism of the syndicate," he declared, blasting the speculators' loyalty to each other, "and it is the only communism that the United States have yet produced." Lloyd also had no patience with the timid operators who connived at these raids. "It is the code of honor among wolves that no high-minded lamb will squeal," he fleered.

ON THE NORTH SIDE

Marshall Field, whose money was coolly made, seems to have had nothing to do with the high adventure of the Board of Trade, or indeed with any gambling in the usual sense of the word. Late in the '70s he and Levi Leiter placed an insignificant amount—some say $20,000 apiece—in the silver mines of Leadville, Colorado, but only after the investment had been urged by John Borden, Chicago's outstanding real estate attorney. Eager even when away from the office, Borden struck up an acquaintance with "Silver Dollar" Tabor while spending his vacation out West, and with him organized the firm of Borden, Tabor and Company to exploit the properties in which Field and Leiter took an interest. The actual development and operation of the mines was in the hands of John Borden's son William, a young man trained in geology at the Universities of Heidelberg and Freiburg. Neither Field nor Leiter had any right to find fault with William Borden's schooling, for each made a million dollars from the lodes he worked. As for the Bordens, they unearthed something like $2,300,000 all told.

Most of the Borden winnings were shrewdly and immediately reinvested in downtown Chicago real estate, but a fascinating sum was set aside for architectural splendor. In 1880 John Borden had the then unrecognized firm of Adler and Sullivan design him a robust red brick mansion capped with a mansard roof. It is still standing at 3949 Lake Park Avenue, though drearily in want of repairs. Four years after John Borden's house went up on the South Side, William Borden had Richard Morris Hunt plan him a limestone château in the heart of the Near North Side, on the north corner of Bellevue Place and Lake Shore Drive. This, the most exquisite residence in the history of the Middle West, has been happily preserved, a reminder of Hunt at his eclectic best.

The neighborhood was worthy of the monument. Although Lake Shore Drive was the home of fewer millionaires than Prairie Avenue, it was the richest street on the North Side and nobly situated. Looking out on Lake Michigan instead of the railroad tracks, it shook on stormy nights to the roar of the surf instead of the rumble of express trains. One of those who appreciated this was the corporation lawyer Robert Todd Lincoln. Another was the wholesale groceries dealer Franklin MacVeagh, whose Romanesque town house, one of the last works executed by the office of H. H. Richardson, was pulled down many years ago. Another was Potter Palmer, whose angry Gothic castle still threatens the corner of Lake Shore Drive and Banks Street.

"The age of Pericles seems to be dawning in Chicago," the *Inter-Ocean* decided, chronicling the building of the Palmer castle in the spring of 1882. "The plans call for a larger structure than any of the Vanderbilt row, and it will have no equal in size in the country among private residences except some two or three Pacific slope homes of the bonanza kings." The architect, young Henry Ives Cobb of Boston, concluded that nothing but "the English battlemented style" would soothe the troubled imagination of his client. In this he was sound, for the cost of the castle leaped from $200,000 to $250,000. "A high day, and already being prepared for, no doubt, by the queens of fashion, will be the housewarming of this most palatial of Chicago palaces," mused an enthusiastic reporter.

The turreted Wisconsin granite fortress that finally loomed above the lake front was such a frank revelation of the night side of man's nature that Potter Palmer himself took fright, setting his heart in the spring of 1883 on selling the castle to some braver millionaire. Failing in this, he made the best of his dilemma by driving clever deals in North Side real estate. He had one other consolation—the number of compliments his wife received on her Louis XIV drawing room. "I have been in palaces of crowned heads in both the Old World and the New," charmingly cried one of her guests, "but not in Brazil, not in Russia, shall you see such taste, such elegance! It is a throne room fit for Liberty herself!" The French dandy Boni de Castellane was not so easily pleased. Chilled by the gloom of the porte-cochere, he pronounced the castle "sumptuous and abominable."

The North Side was unmistakably moneyed, wherever one turned after leaving Mrs. Palmer's drawing room. On Astor Street, a block west of the Drive, the cleverest attorneys in the city fondled their after-dinner cigars in the parlors of patient Romanesque mansions. On Pearson Street, south of William Borden's château, the brothers

John and Charles Benjamin Farwell dwelled side by side in imposing, if not exactly graceful memorials to their merchandising millions. Near by, on what is now the corner of Michigan and Huron, Perry Smith of the Chicago and North Western Railway made his home in one of the gaudiest town houses created by Cudell and Blumenthal. Its three stories of Joliet marble, its stairway of ebony enriched with gold, and its dining room with carved panels portraying rabbits, ducks, squirrels, and prairie chickens were famous throughout the Middle West. "The style is Greek Renaissance, with proportions of Italian palace architecture," the *Tribune* insisted.

Today not a stone remains of Smith's magnificence, but at 675 Rush Street, only a block away, Chicagoans may still admire the greatest of all the designs of Cudell and Blumenthal, the Lake Superior sandstone residence of Cyrus Hall McCormick. Completed in 1879, just eight years after the burning of the Tuileries Palace, this was a masterpiece in the Second Empire style, surpassed only by the great hotels of Saratoga. As for the interior decoration, superintended by Marcotte, it was worthy of Saratoga itself. The master's library was of walnut and ebony, curtained with raw silk lambrequins. The grand library was of ebony set off with silver. The music room was of satinwood inlaid with rosewood. The dining room, distinguished by a Gobelin tapestry, was finished in delicately carved mahogany. On the ceiling was a fresco picturing the emblem of the Legion of Honor, a few sheaves of grain, and the McCormick reaper.

Upstairs was the private theater which seated 200 with ease. There, on the 24th of May, 1880, the first families of both North and South Sides gathered for a *soirée musicale* in honor of the coming of age of Cyrus's first-born Cyrus Hall McCormick II. An orchestra led by Julius Fuchs performed Goldmark's *Rustic Wedding* for the first time in Chicago, and then, at the close of the evening, broke into music for dancing, but not before everyone had lingered over the banquet prepared by Kinsley.

McCormick was seventy-one on the night of this party. Next year he asked McKim, Mead, and White, then the most inventive firm of architects in the country, to draw the plans for a summer home at Richfield Springs, New York. This new house, christened "Clayton Lodge" in memory of Mrs. McCormick's birthplace in near-by Jefferson County, remains today the most beautiful summer home ever built by a Chicagoan. A rambling, shingled mansion in the picturesque style originated by Norman Shaw in England, it was set down on top of a gentle hill, to one side of a line of fir trees planted by Frederick Olmsted. To the rear were the stables where Stanford White, using bits of broken glass glued in sand to imitate precious stones, filled the space between the first floor windows with preternatural flower-like patterns.

All this, sad to say, has been neglected for so many years that the stone and plaster piazza of the mansion has been half eaten away by storms and winters, and the shingles scorched dry of paint. When the author last visited the site, only the lawn, faithfully tended by an old retainer, revealed that Clayton Lodge was once the estate of an exacting millionaire.

Crippled with rheumatism and tortured by carbuncles, McCormick was not unnaturally demanding in his old age. At Richfield Springs, unmoved by the wailing of his children, he ordered the whole family to submit to the sulphur cure. At home on Rush Street he was short with the servants, and if they talked back, he fired them then and there. Meanwhile, perhaps because he never intended to spend so much on his town and country homes, he was ever ready to argue over the items in his personal expenses. On his way to the waters at Eureka Springs, Arkansas, he traveled in a private car of the Illinois Central from Chicago to Seligman, Missouri, but made up for this on the next and last lap of the trip by bringing the stage driver to terms. In spite of the fact that the standard fare from Seligman to the Springs was $21, he beat the coachman down to $15. In France he was not so successful. When, after having a carbuncle removed in Paris, he complained of the doctor's fees as a matter of course, he was told he owed his life to the operation.

Keen to the very end, at seventy-four the reaper king shot a memorandum at the head waiter of a country hotel. "Ordered oatmeal with sweet milk—sent to me cornmeal mush," he protested. "Waited then & received cracked wheat—had ordered balance of breakfast in 20 mins. from first order & finally this breakfast was brought to me in about ½ hr. after the time it was to be here, thus losing ½ hr. of my time in waiting."

To be idle for even half an hour was a punishment to McCormick, who once said he knew "of no better place for a man to die than in harness." True to himself, he ran through his last days on earth talking business with the department heads of the reaper works. "I want to tell you what a touching and profound impression I brought away . . . ," one of his last visitors wrote the family. "Though struggling with the infirmities of age, he took on a kind of majesty, which belonged alone to the combination of great mental and great moral strength, and surprised me by the power with which he grappled the matters under discussion, and the strong personality before which obstacles went down as swiftly and inevitably as grain before the knife of his machines."

The end came on the 13th of May, 1884, eighty-eight days after his seventy-fifth birthday. "Dearest of all—dearest to all!" he wept as he pressed his wife's hand in his.

"Do you wish anything?" a nurse whispered presently.

"I want nothing now but Heaven," he replied. "All right," he murmured a little later. "All right. All peace." Then, gathering all his strength, he led his family in prayers, repeating "Christ, Our Spiritual Head" at the close of the ritual.

"Now you have done your work," a kindly physician suggested.

"Yes," he answered, ever so faintly. "Work . . . work." With that he gave up the ghost.

He left a fortune of $10,000,000, one fourth of which was in real estate. Properly awed by this, young Cyrus Hall McCormick II, just turned twenty-five, made a modest president of the reaper works. "I was elected president," he recollected long afterward, "but you may believe me when I say that, in fact, I was not the president at all. My mother was the real president of the company, and she gave me my instructions on all points and all problems."

To Mrs. McCormick, whose religion was rock-ribbed, the harvester plant was a God-given trust, her five children the instruments of the Divine Will. She herself was capable of more than devotion to the business. "I remember," said Cyrus the Second, "that on one Fourth of July, an unusually hot day, she called for her carriage, an old-fashioned rockaway where the driver sat on the same level as the passengers, and drove down alone to the McCormick works, which were located at 26th Street and Western Avenue on both sides of the Chicago River. It being a holiday, the gates of the works were closed, but after knocking on the door, it was opened by the watchman, who was greatly surprised at her visit. She said to the watchman: 'I would like to go with you to see Captain Crowley,' the head of the fire and watch department. When she promptly found him in his small office in the courtyard of the works, she said to him, 'Captain Crowley, this is a hot and blistering day, and since early morning I have been thinking of you and the great responsibility you have in your hands for the care of the buildings of this great plant on such a day of extreme heat.' She went all over the works with Captain Crowley, shook hands with the leading men of his department, expressed her intense satisfaction and departed for home."

Back on Rush Street Mrs. McCormick most likely spent the rest of the afternoon studying the needs of the Presbyterian Church, to which she turned over $475,000 from her husband's estate. One of the many monuments to the piety of the family was McCormick Hall at the Theological Seminary, dedicated by Cyrus the Second in the fall of 1884 "with the prayer that it may help on the great work of preparing young men for the ministry, and thus advance the cause of Christ's kingdom on earth."

The cause of Christ's kingdom on earth was not exactly advanced by the publication in 1885 of a little booklet entitled *Memorial of Robert McCormick*. The work of Leander James McCormick, the brother of Cyrus the First, it developed the astonishing thesis that not he, but his father Robert McCormick, was the inventor of the reaper. More than half a century after the first machine cut John Steele's grain, Leander McCormick rounded up a number of aging Virginians who all recalled, obligingly and distinctly, the technical points at stake. Leander's wife Henrietta was most emphatic. "I learned for the first time, shortly before the death of Mr. Robert McCormick, that he had given the invention to Cyrus," she testified. "This I was surprised and chagrined at, as I had expected my husband to share with the family in the benefits growing out of it. I had frequent talks with Mrs. McCormick and the family, and she tried to reconcile me by saying that Cyrus had promised to 'make all the family rich if he ever made anything out of it.'"

Since Dr. William T. Hutchinson, the definitive biographer of Cyrus Hall McCormick, has so carefully examined and ably disposed of the legend that Robert McCormick was in any way responsible for the reaper, there is no need to look into the controversy here. For all that, the *Memorial* was a literary achievement. Splitting the House of McCormick, it started the bitterest feud in the history of American capitalism. The heirs of William Sanderson McCormick, sorry they received only $400,000 for their interest in the business, at once took up Leander's side of the argument, crying out in their humble drawing rooms that Cyrus the First did not deserve to be extolled as the benefactor of the farmer. There were words even in the harvester plant. Irritated at the attention paid Cyrus the Second, Leander's oldest son Robert Hall McCormick did battle for his rights. Finally, in 1890, there was a settlement. Selling out for $3,250,000, Leander and his offspring left the absolute control of the company in the hands of the widow of Cyrus the First and her five children. Though this put an end to arguing at the works, it did not decide the question of who invented the reaper. Even today the McCormicks are divided on that.

Marshall Field, who stood apart from all this, focused his serene mind toward the end of 1885 on a party for his two children, Marshall, aged seventeen, and Ethel, aged twelve. He had no intention of indulging in any unwholesome extravagance, but he realized that if a man in his position entertained at all, elegance was understood. After considering every type of amusement, he and his wife agreed on a Mikado Ball for the young people. On New Year's Night stage sets from the original *Mikado* at the Fifth Avenue Theater turned the first and second stories of 1905 Prairie Avenue into a Japanese wonderland. Four hundred boys and girls, many of whom came from Baltimore, Boston, and New York, danced to the music of Johnny Hand, whose orchestra was hidden away in a tiny pagoda. Kinsley's men served a superb collation, but neither his dishes nor Hand's waltzes could compare with the favors presented to the young ladies. These were designed in London by James McNeill Whistler.

Sure of his rank in the social as well as the industrial world of the Middle West, Marshall Field could afford to be disillusioned. "How do you like newspaper work?" he asked a reporter sent to interview him at home. "It must be interesting to one who wants to study life." Then he added: "Do you find life interesting?"

(*Photos Chicago Historical Society*)

MR. AND MRS. POTTER PALMER AND CASTLE

(*Chicago Architectural Photographing Co.*)

(Wayne Andrews)

(Brown Brothers)

THE MASTER OF THE MODEL TOWN:
George M. Pullman, the factory,
and Hotel Florence, Pullman, Illinois

(Wayne Andrews)

CHAPTER THREE: *The Cost of Grandeur*

FIELD WITHOUT LEITER

J. Pierpont Morgan, whose interest in the career of Marshall Field dated from the days when the merchant prince was clerking for "Deacon" Davis in Pittsfield, seems to have had the proper respect for his insight into business. Whenever the great banker descended on Chicago, he made a point of getting in touch with his old acquaintance, who invariably prevailed upon him to spend the night at 1905 Prairie Avenue. One morning, tingling with the stimulation of Field's talk, Morgan happened to come across one of the bright young men in the store. "Mr. Field has the keenest financial mind of any man in the country, don't you think?" the New Yorker suggested.

"He has an exceptional mind, Mr. Morgan," replied Field's alert subordinate, "but it would be hard for me to say *the* keenest in your presence."

Blessed with a sixth sense when it came to investing money, Field plotted the operations of the store so that nothing could rob him of the joy of putting stupendous sums at work in other enterprises. The resignation of a partner might be regrettable, but it must not be allowed to interfere with the orderly profit-taking of the day. "What would you say," a reporter inquired one afternoon, "if one of your partners were to leave?"

"Hire another office boy!" the great merchant rejoined.

When Levi Leiter withdrew from the business on the 26th of January, 1881, Marshall Field absorbed the shock.

"Is it true that there has been a dissolution of the firm?" asked a journalist who broke into Field's office.

"Yes," said Morgan's good friend, "you'll find it in the evening papers and an advertisement in the *Tribune* tomorrow will notify its readers."

"And the new firm will consist of—?"

"Oh," Field laughed, "you'll find that in the advertisement."

"This is a genuine surprise to the trade?" ventured another newspaperman.

"Yes, we kept it very private."

"And the terms—?"

"Are strictly private. Mr. Leiter retires from the business. He has been anxious to do so for some time."

"And the name of the new firm is—?"

"Marshall Field and Company."

Sooner or later Field and Leiter were bound to take leave of each other. Field was suave with customers; Leiter, sharp. Field gloried in the retail division; Leiter, in the wholesale. "There is nothing too good for the retail," Field observed, sure that his point of view was sound. Outside of the business hours the two capitalists had even less in common. To Field social ambition was a mild form of insanity. To Leiter social recognition was a necessity.

With three daughters to marry off, Mr. and Mrs. Leiter had to live in a high style. Falling in with the fashion of other wealthy Chicagoans, they traveled to the Continent and to Russia, bringing back to Calumet Avenue the novelty of tea served from a samovar with slices of lemon. Then, after a fling at Presbyterianism, they pinned their hopes of Heaven on the Episcopal Church. Marshall Field looked on all these things and was not pleased. He took his partner to task on the details of the lease of the retail store, and for a time neither spoke to the other.

At length Field broke the silence. "I will buy or sell according to the books," he casually announced, offering to buy out or sell out on the basis of the book value, that is, on the basis of the capital each contributed in addition to the accrued and undistributed profits and gains. Catching at what seemed to be a handsome proposal, Leiter agreed to think the matter over. But it was only after he talked to the key men in the store that he began to realize how astute his partner was. All of the worthwhile employees had given their word to stand by Field in the crisis; not one was willing to work for Leiter alone.

So Leiter resigned, as trapped men have done before and since. Screwing up his courage to face the reporters, he let on that a life of ease was his heart's desire. "I have made enough to live on," he declared, "and the time has come when I should take a rest. I have a good many outside investments that will occupy as much time as I care to devote to work. Some of my leisure I shall devote to trout fishing."

The store may not have missed Leiter, but Leiter most certainly missed the store. In 1880, with sales of $24,500,000 netting $2,450,000, he and Field earned $800,000 apiece. Gossip had it he received only $2,700,000 for his share in the partnership, and that his savings amounted to no more than $3,300,000. Of course a man may live bravely on $6,000,000. Moving to Washington, he and his wife opened one of the great social campaigns in American history.

Meantime Field roamed at ease about the store. Coming upon a clerk arguing with a lady customer, he tugged his sleeve gently. "Do as the lady wishes!" he whispered. The offender trembled, and sinned no more. Another clerk made the mistake of keeping his tall gray silk hat on while at work. "Don't you think you could sell as many goods with your hat off?" Field asked, eying his natty patent leather shoes. The culprit apologized, and not only removed his hat but forever after dressed as meekly as a bank teller.

If Field was critical, he was also considerate. "How many boys came down without overcoats and mittens?" he asked one horrid winter morning. "Outfit them all and say nothing about it." Too sober a businessman to forget his own humble beginning at Cooley,

Wadsworth and Company, he did not like to make fun of ambitious underlings. When told that a clerk was calling on his daughter Ethel, he remarked "Why not?" adding, "Thank God, there is no disgrace in being a clerk."

Positive of the loyalty of his staff, Field carried on cheerfully, watching the profits rise from year to year. In 1881, with sales totaling $25,000,000, the store netted $2,500,000, out of which he probably kept $1,600,000 for himself. He was willing to do so much for his partners, but no more. If they idled away their time, he filled their places with younger, abler men, and the dinner he gave every New Year's Night to those close to him in the business was not altogether delightful. Late in the evening, long after the cigars were lit, he was apt to report the resignation of any partner whose work was not up to standard. This was often the first the man heard of his fall from favor.

None of Field's partners, even those in his good graces to the end, grew enormously rich. Neither Thomas Templeton, his ace at mathematics, nor Robert M. Fair, for many years the general manager of the store, succeeded in piling up more than $2,000,000. And if John McWilliams, the superintendent of wholesale notions, accumulated $5,000,000, his brother Lafayette, who looked after general sales, amassed merely $1,000,000. As for Harlow N. Higinbotham, the eagle of the credit department, he had to be satisfied with $3,300,000, which was over three times the sum on which Henry Field retired to collect Barbizon paintings.

THESE WERE THE ARCHITECTS

Marshall Field, who asked so much of his partners, asked even more of an architect. H. H. Richardson, commissioned in the spring of 1885 to design him a new wholesale store, died with the merchant's name on his lips, whispering to the doctor that he longed "to live two years to see the Pittsburgh Court House and the

Chicago store complete." On those two works he felt his reputation would stand or fall, and rightly. A gigantic seven-story granite block, bounded by Wells, Franklin, Quincy, and Adams Streets, the Field wholesale store was a noble answer to the demands of a commercial building; its destruction in 1930, a tragedy.

The younger architect Louis Sullivan went into rhapsodies over its simplicity, calling it "in a world of barren pettiness, a male; for it sings the song of procreant power, as the others have squealed of miscegenation." Marshall Field could scarcely sympathize with so lyrical an approach to architecture. Depressed on the opening day by 530,343 square feet of floor space, he calculated two or three problems in mathematics and winced. "Nevers," he said, confiding in a faithful employee, "we will never fill it."

For once Field was unduly pessimistic, the future richer than he dared conceive. Before the decade was over, the population of Chicago doubled, broadening the market for dry goods and incidentally boosting the value of his favorite form of investment, downtown real estate. Land selling at $130,000 the quarter acre in 1880 brought $900,000, or nearly seven times as much, ten years later. With 1,100,000 inhabitants, or 50,000 more than Philadelphia, Chicago was then, as now, America's second city.

Goaded by the prices paid for choice lots in the metropolis, architects dreamed of taller and taller buildings, and William LeBaron Jenney, an engineer lately on Sherman's staff, daringly broke with the tradition of masonry bearing walls. If neither the Home Insurance Building, planned in 1884 and leveled in 1930, nor the Second Leiter Building, conceived in 1889 for Field's old partner and still standing, was a work of art, both were technical achievements of historic importance. In the first he heralded the age of skyscrapers by creating a business block chiefly, if not entirely supported by a metal skeleton. In the second he forced the skeleton to do all the work of the walls. Experimenting along these same lines, the firm of Holabird and Roche presented Chicago with the Tacoma Building, now demolished, in 1887. Even though the iron skeleton here carried less than half the weight, the cage-like façade betrayed the triumphs to come in engineering.

Meanwhile Henry Ives Cobb, the architect of the Potter Palmer castle, was designing massive monuments in the Romanesque manner of H. H. Richardson. For the estate of Walter Newberry he planned the superb, if symmetrical Newberry Library on Walton Place. About the same time he completed the august home of the Chicago Historical Society on the northwest corner of Dearborn and Ontario Streets, now abandoned for a Georgian pile in Lincoln Park.

Fascinated, like Cobb, by Richardson's dramatic reinterpretation of the Romanesque, the firm of Burnham and Root dealt in medieval shadows, turning out delightfully ornamented skyscrapers and snug homes built of boulders. The Women's Temple and the Masonic Temple, office buildings torn down in our irreverent century, were darkly Romantic memorials to Richardson's influence. The Rookery, pondering the convulsions of LaSalle Street since 1885, was an airier business block; its rich marble lobby, recently and lamentably altered, a masterpiece. But Burnham and Root's surest work was the 16-story Monadnock, the last tall building erected with masonry bearing walls. Bare of all ornament, it has been ennobling Jackson Boulevard since 1891.

Both Burnham and Root were sociable men. The former, whose father grew wealthy in the wholesale drug trade after moving to Chicago from northern New York State, was glad to hobnob with the biggest businessmen, impressing them with his organizing ability. The latter, whose father was a disappointed Georgia storekeeper, made up for his inconspicuous youth by shining in the society of the North Side, playing the piano dreamily and charming young women with his after-dinner wit. A man of flexible artistic ideals, Root lacked the grit of his salesman-partner. Sometimes he mistrusted his own undeniable genius.

Chicago's greatest architect was Louis Henri Sullivan, the son of an Irish dancing teacher who settled in Massachusetts after marrying a Swiss pianist. Lonely, like too many of the intellectual leaders of the Middle West, Sullivan bewildered many of his true friends. "He liked to be alone, to think and write," one of them recollected. "He lived alone most of his life, and when he drank, he drank alone." In his solitude he worried over the meaning of the word "democracy" and cursed the criteria of his profession. "Architecture has been a plaything long enough," he spoke out. "I am tired of the farce."

On the subject of Chicago, he was bitter. "It is, *facile princeps,* the 'City of Indifference,' " he complained. "Nobody cares about anything: Its nominal motto is 'I will.' Its actual shibboleth: 'I won't,' with the subscription, 'Not how good but how cheap!' Cheap is the word, cheap is the thought, and cheap is the deed. Poverty of heart, mind, and sympathy are here conjoined, and they glory in the conjunction." Taking heart, he added: "Chicago at least has youth, and where youth is, there is hope, and where there is hope, let us cling to it."

In his own youth Sullivan never knew his own mind. Dissatisfied with the teaching at the Massachusetts Institute of Technology, he quit at the end of a year and went to work for the Philadelphia firm of Furness and Hewitt. When he lost his berth in the depression of 1873, he tried his luck in Chicago and found a drafting job in Jenney's office. Still questing for an architectural ideal, he left to study two years at the Ecole des Beaux Arts. The academic point of view of most of his teachers discouraged his curiosity, but a phrase of his tutor in geometry, Monsieur Clopet, quickened his mystical imagination. "Our demonstrations," said Clopet to his pupil, "shall be so broad as to admit of no exception."

"If this can be done in mathematics, why not in architecture?" Sullivan wondered.

Back in Chicago, Sullivan entered the office of Dankmar Adler in the spring of 1880. One of the countless architects who descended on the city following the great fire, Adler was a conscientious, deservedly busy draftsman with the presence of mind to humor the newcomer's lyrical yearnings. In a little while the two went into partnership, beginning by laying out ponderous town houses frantic with ornament. Neglecting the achievements of McKim, Mead, and White in the new picturesque style, Adler and Sullivan attracted little attention until the Auditorium opened on the 9th of December, 1889. A majestic granite pile in the tradition of the Field wholesale store, it was one of the artistic justifications of the nineteenth century.

The project, involving a hotel and a theater seating 4,000 in addition to business offices, was the brainchild of Ferdinand W. Peck, a real estate promoter with an eye for Michigan Avenue values. Situated on the lake front, on the southern half of the block bounded by Congress, Wabash, Van Buren, and Michigan, the Auditorium was intended to be the elegant center of an already prepossessing neighborhood. When jewelers and picture dealers rented shops near by, and other speculators threw up other hotels, Peck congratulated himself.

As early as the opening night, however, Peck knew he could not fail. The house was packed, the boxes filled with the N. K. Fairbanks, the George M. Pullmans, the Potter Palmers, the Marshall Fields, and the other seigneurs of Chicago, all of them struck with the sumptuousness of Sullivan's imagination. So were the guests of honor, the President and Vice-President of the United States. Glancing now at the distant galleries, now at the great golden arches spreading above the stage, President Harrison only half listened to Adelina Patti's trilling of "Home, Sweet Home." At last he leaned over and nudged Vice-President Morton by the elbow. "New York surrenders, eh?" he grunted.

Next night the operatic season began in earnest, with the first families back in their boxes, and Patti starring in *Romeo and Juliet*. Now and then, in the middle of an aria, a nervous capitalist would forget himself and mumble commodity quotations to a neighbor. Out of such scenes Frank Norris composed the masterly first chapter of *The Pit,* the only great novel inspired by American capitalism.

Blissfully unaware of the desperate world pictured by Norris, Adler and Sullivan reveled in their new-found freedom. Having suddenly and splendidly acquired a national reputation, they no longer needed to vie with contractors in lining the streets with town houses. In 1890, waking from a mathematical daydream, Sullivan honored the memory of Carrie Eliza Getty by designing her an exotic tomb encrusted with a new ornament, half-orchidaceous, half-geometrical. But at bottom he was seeking the solution to something more difficult than the proper decoration for artistocratic graves. Eager as he was to invent a new system of ornament, he was even more anxious to realize the esthetic possibilities inherent in the skyscraper. In 1891 he and Adler planned the serene, sensitively decorated Schiller Building, the theater combined with business block now known as the Garrick. Two years later the firm drew in the last details of the Stock Exchange, then as now the most straightforward building on LaSalle Street. Both skyscrapers were landmarks in the history of American architecture, and yet Sullivan was not satisfied he had expressed the dignity of steel frame construction. He went on experimenting.

TRAGEDY AT HAYMARKET SQUARE

While the architects of the '80s were blessing Chicago with the greatest commercial buildings in the world, capitalists and workingmen were wrangling over the eight-hour day and the other disturbing demands of labor leaders. Though many a businessman was willing to compromise, right-wing intellectuals in Chicago as in other cities were calling for a showdown, and Joseph Medill, always awake to the danger of aliens, insisted labor unions were implicated in a communistic conspiracy of the foreign-born. If he made much of this discovery, it was to prove he was independent, having paid off the last of his debt to Marshall Field on the 2d of January, 1883. "Now again, Mr. Field, we meet as equals," he reminded the merchant on what he told his family was the happiest day in his life.

In 1885, when a Senate committee delved into the reasons for labor's unrest, Medill gladly testified that if workingmen were wretched, bad habits were to blame. "The chief cause of the impecunious condition of millions of the wage classes is due to their own improvidence and misdirected efforts," he explained. "Too many are trying to live without labor—that is, industrial or productive labor, and too many squander their earnings on intoxicating drinks, cigars, and amusements. . . . While they continue to spend their surplus earnings on these things, they will not get on in the world, and will fail to accumulate property."

Medill could not forget that the German-born citizens of Chicago had cheated him out of a tranquil term as Mayor. "Our trade unions, composed chiefly of foreigners, are almost universally hostile to American boys learning trades," he made clear. "Of the present American mechanics, the enormous majority of them are of foreign birth, and they prefer, when there is a vacancy, to send for a brother, or cousin, or chum of their own in the old country, if a mechanic; and so they secure places for them and limit the places which might be had by Americans, and in that way they keep the Americans out." But that was not all. "The trade unions of this country," he added, "are feeling more and more dissatisfied with their position, and they are developing more of what might be called a communistic feeling—a tendency or desire to resort to what may be called revolutionary and chaotic methods of rectifying things."

Once the eight-hour day was adopted, alien hordes would overrun our boundaries, of that there was no doubt. "Increased wages for short work would instantly attract to this country multitudes of foreign workmen," Medill warned. "They would rush hither as fast as fleets of steamers could bring them, and quickly swamp the demand for extra labor caused by short work. In a little while they would be soliciting employment at reduced wages, and offering to work for ten hours a day for probably half the pay that had at first been demanded for six hours' work."

Even more absurd than the demand for the eight-hour day was the cry for higher wages. "There is a universal impression prevailing," Medill pointed out, "that the employers in the United States could afford to pay much larger wages than they do if they wanted to without increasing the price of their goods, and that they do not do so out of pure selfishness. I think the dissipation, if it were possible, of that fallacy would be the most useful thing that could be done. I think that if the laboring classes of the United States—the mechanics especially—could be brought to see that under the fixed laws of trade, of supply and demand, the employer has really little more control over prices where not protected by patents than over the winds and the weather, the largest possible good would be done; for if the mechanics saw that they are really, as a whole, paid about as much as it is possible to pay them they would then yield to the inevitable and seek other ways of improving their condition, and the feeling that they were being systematically cheated all the time would die out."

Paying no attention to the editor of the *Tribune,* laboring men kept right on smoking, drinking, and striking for better pay. In the spring of 1885 the workmen at the McCormick plant walked out on their jobs, puzzling the reasonable widow of the reaper king. On the second day of the strike Pinkerton guards fired on a crowd of restless workers, and one fell wounded. When the police nabbed the Pinkerton men involved, young Cyrus the Second went bail on their behalf, perhaps against his mother's better judgment. Twenty-four hours later Mrs. McCormick capitulated to the strikers, promising day-workers a 10 per cent raise, piece-workers, 15 per cent.

"The strike is a sad experience to us all, a *new* experience to us all," Mrs. McCormick wrote. "Our men have always felt a kind of loyalty to our interests, and attachment to us as employers, but the strike shows a change in their attitude, whether with reason or not. . . . I would like to get at the bottom of this matter. I would like to know exactly the facts."

She could not afford to be cocksure. "Humanitarian reasons alone would lead us to wish to do fairly with out workingmen and to pay the price their work is worth, not getting a dollar's worth of work for 50 cents. To do *justly,*" she reflected, "does not mean to make hasty concessions under compulsion. It would be a very grave mistake to yield to the dictation of our workmen. This would never do, because we should soon have the fresh trouble on our hands of a new demand for another increase of wages.

"Concessions on both sides, I think, is the right way," she decided. "Capital and labor must both make concessions. It is very evident that as a class, *those who win strikes are not much better satisfied than those who lose.*"

A week after the strike was settled in the workers' favor, Albert Parsons was busy cultivating the McCormick employees, nursing their grudges and spreading the gospel of the Working People's International Association. "We are called by some communists, or socialists, or anarchists," he told a crowd on the corner of Blue Island and 22d Street, not far from the McCormick plant. "We accept all three of the terms. We even accept the name of dynamiters. What is dynamite? It is the latest discovery of science by which power is placed in the hands of the weak and defenseless to protect them against the domination of others. Science says to the poor through the voice of dynamite: 'Be of good cheer, I will make you the equal of all other men.'"

The *Alarm,* the anarchist newspaper of Parsons and his friends, was constantly discovering new uses for explosives. "One dynamite bomb, properly placed, will destroy a regiment," it revealed, taunting Field and other rich men for equipping the National Guard. "The revolutionist should experiment for himself," Parsons urged. "Especially should he practice throwing bombs."

Though he did not run amuck at the dedication of the new Board of Trade in the spring of the McCormick strike, Parsons had to show his feelings.* Anxious to spoil the ceremony for the brokers and their ladies, he ordered a grand march of his followers to the "temple of usury, gambling, and cut-throatism, where they will serenade the high priests and officers of King Mammon." When Company C of the National Guard blocked off the surrounding streets, stopping the parade short, he told off the militia in a speech to his fellow anarchists. "They're Marshall Field's boys," he sneered.

* Recently replaced by an innocuous skyscraper, the Board of Trade was a sepulchral tower designed by W. W. Boyington. It cost $1,500,000.

"If," he went on to say, "we would achieve our liberation from economic bondage and acquire our natural right to life and liberty, every man must lay by a part of his wages, and buy a Colt's Navy revolver, a Winchester rifle, and ten pounds of dynamite."

Parsons' rash words preyed upon the minds of capitalists, stiffening their resistance to the demands of sober labor leaders. Next winter, when the Metalworker's Union of the Knights of Labor asked young McCormick to discharge five non-union molders, he refused. His mind made up on the question of the closed shop, he forestalled a threatened strike by shutting down the works on the 16th of February, 1866. Two weeks later he reopened the plant to those willing to work side by side with strikebreakers, positive he had broken the stranglehold of the union.

Meanwhile laboring men all over Chicago were agitating for the eight-hour day. On the 25th of April 5,000 champions of shorter hours staged a demonstration on West Randolph Street, trying the patience of Joseph Medill. Next morning's *Tribune* reported that the "so-called" eight-hour-day meeting was "mainly communistic."

Young McCormick, who could not bring himself to believe that this was all a communist plot, surprised his employees on the 3d of May by granting ten hours' pay for eight hours to all at work in the factory—leaving out of his consideration the union members still on strike. That afternoon the socialist orator Fritz Schmidt drew a larger crowd than usual near the gates. "On to McCormick's!" he howled. "On to McCormick's, and let us run every one of the damned scabs out of the city. Strike for your freedom, and if the armed murderers of the law interfere, shoot them down as you would the scabs." Cool-headed union leaders tried to reason with the strikers, but Schmidt's tirade was too heady for logic. Hoodlums threw rocks at the outgoing shift, and the McCormick guards fired, at first into the air, and then into the mob.

Late in the evening Albert Parsons' good friend August Spies, the editor of the *Arbeiter-Zeitung,* flooded the West Side with the following circular, in English and in German:

Revenge! Workingmen, to arms! Your masters sent out their bloodhounds—the police; they killed six of your brothers at McCormick's this afternoon. They killed the poor wretches because they, like you, had the courage to disobey the supreme will of your bosses. They killed them because they dared ask for the shortening of the hours of toil. They killed them to show you, free American citizens, that you must be satisfied and contented with whatever your bosses condescend to allow you, or you will be killed. You have for years endured the most abject humiliations; you have for years suffered unmeasurable iniquities; you have worked yourself [sic] to death; you have endured the pangs of want and hunger; your children you have sacrificed to the factory lords—in short, you have been miserable and obedient slaves all these years. Why? To satisfy the insatiable greed, to fill the coffers of your lazy, thieving master. When you ask them [sic] to lessen your burden, he sends bloodhounds out to shoot you, kill you.

If you are men, if you are the sons of your grandsires, who have shed their blood to free you, then you will rise in your might, Hercules, and destroy the hideous monster that seeks to destroy you. To arms we call you, to arms!

Your brothers.

Capitalizing on the indignation spreading through the city, Parsons and the other anarchists called a mass meeting of protest at seven-thirty the following evening at Haymarket Square, a vacant lot on West Randolph Street between Desplaines and Halsted.

Chief of Police Ebersole, who read the manifesto many times over, laid plans to have his men break up the gathering. "This is going to have a bad effect on the police," brooded young McCormick, consulting his conscience. "If they are ordered to disperse a crowd, I am afraid they will begin to use their revolvers too early, in place of waiting for bombs. I am opposed to indiscriminate shooting and killing of everybody, and in a crowd that worst cannot be picked out from the good. The police are exasperated, and they will be dangerous for the mob to meet, and so you see in this way they will be demoralized."

"It was said that I inspired the attack on McCormick's. That is a lie," August Spies swore to the 1,500 workers who thronged to Haymarket. "McCormick is the man who created the row, and he must be held responsible for the murder of our brothers."

"Hang him!" someone cried out, worrying the earnest speaker.

"Don't make any threats," Spies pleaded. "They are of no avail. Whenever you get ready to do something, do it and don't make any threats beforehand."

Albert Parsons, the next man to play on the anger of the crowd, was almost as calm as Spies. "I am not here for the purpose of inciting anyone," he protested, "but to speak out and tell the facts as they exist, even though it shall cost me my life before morning. Do you know," he asked, "that the military are under arms and that a gatling gun is ready to mow you down? Is this Germany, or Russia, or Spain?"

"It looks like it," one of his sympathizers yelled.

"Whenever you make a demand for an increase in pay," Parsons rambled on, "the militia, and the deputy sheriff, and the Pinkerton men are called out, and you are shot and clubbed and murdered in the streets."

"He is making a good political speech," murmured Mayor Carter H. Harrison, who had ridden up to the meeting on his superb Kentucky mare, and was now moving on, his famous black slouch hat aslant his head. A descendant of Princess Pocahontas and of Robert "King" Carter, the great Virginia landowner, Harrison was as generous as he was well-born, which was one reason why the people of Chicago took him to their hearts, sending him to the City Hall for his fourth consecutive term in 1885. Too good-natured a friend of the laboring man to take the babblings of the anarchists seriously, he made a practice of asking socialists into the city government. Little did he care if this policy infuriated Joseph Medill.

Harrison always had an easier time of it than the editor of the *Tribune*. A graduate of Yale, he traveled leisurely through France and Germany before abandoning his native Kentucky for Chicago in 1855. He was then thirty. Borrowing what funds he needed from William Butler Ogden, he launched into a series of happy real estate speculations, in many of which Mrs. Potter Palmer's father was his partner. As Mayor he lived comfortably, if not finely, near a number of other Southern-born businessmen on Ashland Avenue on the West Side, and dined so frequently on clabber and watermelon that he eventually weighed 225 pounds.

Not long after Harrison ambled on his way, Samuel Fielden, a Lancashire teamster with fierce political opinions, followed Parsons on the platform. "Men, women, and children have not been spared by the ruthless minions of private capital," he reminded his audience, most of whom were now scurrying to cover from a drizzle. "You have been robbed. You will be starved into a worse condition," he prophesied to the 600 still hearkening to his words.

At that very moment Captains Bonfield and Ward, at the head of a police column of 180 men, were drawing near the square. "In the name of the people of the State of Illinois," Ward proclaimed, "I command this meeting immediately and peaceably to disperse, and I call upon you," motioning to the bystanders, "to assist. . . ." "We are peaceable," Fielden muttered, and then, rather than argue with law and order, climbed down off the stand. The excitement was apparently over when someone—no one knows who—hurled a bomb at the police squad, blowing one officer to bits and injuring 70 others. A second later Captain Ward's men lunged at the crowd, wreaking a ghastly vengeance. Some said the police killed 6 and wounded 72.

Fearing that Carter Harrison might not do his duty strictly, Marshall Field paid a call at the City Hall. "Mr. Harrison," he said, recollecting that he spoke for Chicago's biggest businessmen, "we represent great interests in Chicago."

"Mr. Field," Harrison returned patiently but imposingly, "any poor man owning a single small cottage as his sole possession has the same interest in Chicago as its richest citizen." He had already issued orders to the police.

Set on the heels of every agitator in town, the force rounded up 31 anarchists, 8 of whom were indicted. Besides Parsons, Spies, and Fielden, the courts arraigned Michael Schwab, Adolph Fischer, Louis Lingg, and George Engel, all four German-born, and Oscar Neebe, born in New York City of German parents. Of these last five, only the first two were present at Haymarket Square on the evening of the 4th of May.

Marshall Field was satisfied that justice would be done. "I think," he said, "that the prompt measures which the police have taken will tend to prevent any recurrence of the fearful riot. The police have acted nobly and deserve the highest commendation of all good citizens."

P. D. Armour was not so sure the reign of terror was over. "I don't think that the backbone of this trouble is broken yet," he argued. "Those fellows have gotten a taste of blood, and will not lie down so quietly as many think."

Although the State was unable to fix the identity of the man who tossed the bomb, or even to prove that the incident was inspired by the anarchists' preachings, the eight agitators were presently tried before Judge Joseph E. Gary and sentenced by the jury to be hanged, with the exception of Oscar Neebe, who was condemned to fifteen years of prison. "Whoever advises murder is himself guilty of the murder that is committed pursuant to his advice," Judge Gary decreed, and the Illinois Supreme Court sustained him.

There were those, however, who maintained that Gary was a deplorably eager magistrate, and that the trial was a travesty of justice. Marvin Hughitt, president of the by then Vanderbilt-owned Chicago and North Western, put his signature beside Potter Palmer's at the foot of a petition requesting clemency for the defendants. In London George Bernard Shaw and William Morris spoke before vast meetings in favor of the accused. In Boston William Dean Howells went to work on the conscience of American authors, hoping—in vain—that Whittier could be induced to write a letter of protest to Richard James Oglesby, Governor of Illinois.

Henry Demarest Lloyd, who had no sympathy with the rabid philosophy of the doomed men, gallantly insisted the courts had been unfair, and when old friends cut him dead, smiled and took no offense. "Do not let us notice or appear to notice any change in them," he gently cautioned his wife. "They are and must be too good and dear friends to be lost in such a way." Though Lloyd was perpetually crusading, pricking Armour's reputation with a magazine article, and wittily exposing Standard Oil in his unique book *Wealth Versus Commonwealth,* he was too affectionate for the role of a messiah. A prideless intellectual, he never gave way, even when disheartened, to the peculiar contempt for humanity that characterized Henry Adams.

Lloyd was a native of New York City, the son of a pulpitless clergyman of the Dutch Reformed Church who turned bookseller to support his family. After graduating from Columbia and taking a hand in reforming local politics, he went to Chicago in 1872 to write for Horace White's *Tribune.* Next year he married Jessie, the only child of William Bross. When White left for the East, he stayed on at the *Tribune,* following in Bross's footsteps by becoming an authority on financial topics, and finally earning from his delighted father-in-law a bonus of ten shares of *Tribune* stock. In 1885 he resigned, free to devote the rest of his life to whatever books and articles he pleased.

Joseph Medill, who couldn't see why a native American should go out of his way to befriend an alien convicted of murder, was perplexed by his ex-employee's interest in the fate of the anarchists. "Do you realize what you are doing?" he asked Lloyd's wife on the street. "Have you and Mr. Lloyd considered how this will influence your future?" He talked of the cash at stake, of William Bross's stock in the *Tribune.* Were Henry and Jessie Lloyd willing to be disinherited?

"Do you suppose," Mrs. Lloyd replied, "that any such consideration will stop Henry Lloyd from doing what he believes is right?" *

Potter Palmer's good friend Lyman Gage, by now the vice-president of the First National Bank, looked forward with something of Lloyd's dread to the date set for the execution. When Governor Oglesby agreed to commute the sentences of Parsons, Spies, Fielden,

* Bross behaved exactly as Medill prophesied. On his death in 1890 he left his fortune to the Lloyds' children, cutting Henry and Jessie off from the guardianship and the care of the property.

and Schwab, provided the leading citizens of Chicago approved, Gage called a meeting of 50 magnates and pleaded for the anarchists' lives, reasoning that the majesty of the law had been vindicated, that the community would be safer with the troublemakers in prison than made martyrs, and that capital punishment would only embitter the working class, damaging labor relations for years to come.

As soon as Gage was through, Field arose and introduced his spokesman, State's Attorney Grinnell, who hammered home the conviction that the rabble-rousers should pay for their ravings with their lives. One by one the businessmen cast their votes as the great merchant intended, and the conference ended in utter humiliation for Gage. "It was terribly mortifying for me," the humane financier confessed. "Afterwards many of the men present came around to me singly, and said they had agreed with me in my views, and would have been glad to join me in such an appeal, but that in face of the opposition of powerful men like Marshall Field, they did not like to do so, as it might injure them in business, or socially."

Yet there was room for hope. A few days after the 50 magnates met with Gage, Lloyd left for Springfield, bearing with him a petition signed by Ex-Senator Lyman Trumbull and 41,000 other men of good will. Struck with the length of the list, and its authenticity, Governor Oglesby commuted the sentences of Fielden and Schwab to life imprisonment. This meant that on the 11th of November, 1887, only Parsons, Spies, Fischer, and Engel walked to the gallows, Lingg having blown himself to bits in his cell. Though Fielden, Schwab, and Neebe were still within prison walls, they had an advocate in John Peter Altgeld, a homely, harelipped German with gleaming eyes whom the people of Chicago had just elected Judge of the Superior Court of Cook County. "Hell," Altgeld admitted, "if I had to depend upon my looks, I'd have been hung long ago."

Brought to America in 1848 when one year old, Altgeld faced a cheerless childhood in Ohio that worked upon his sympathy for the underprivileged and for all other hard-pressed immigrants. "In school the boys all picked on me," he broke down long afterward and acknowledged. "No one of them ever thought of protecting me from abuse. It was the crowd on one side and John Peter Altgeld on the other." At twelve he was taken out of his classes and put to work on his discouraged father's farm. In the field he stumbled into the melancholy moods that marked him as a man. "I have thought there must be something about me that repels others," he confided to a close friend at the zenith of his political career.

After volunteering in the Civil War and coming down with the Chicahominy fever, Altgeld astonished his dull-witted father by enrolling and graduating from the Mansfield high school. At nineteen he began teaching in a nearby country town where he made the mistake of falling in love with a girl whose father had no compassion for needy aliens. Unhinged by the anger and suspicion of his prospective father-in-law, he drifted to St. Louis and did odd jobs in a chemical plant, earned his hire as a day laborer on the Missouri-Kansas-Texas Railroad, and then succumbed to an almost fatal attack of the same ague that invalided him out of the army. While recuperating from his illness he again took up teaching and this time cultivated a few influential friends. At twenty-six, after mastering enough law to pass the bar examination, he was elected Prosecuting Attorney for Andrew County, Missouri. Two years later, for no one knows what reason, he resigned and moved to Chicago.

In two years' practice in Chicago he saved enough money to marry the girl he left behind in Ohio, her obdurate father having died a natural death in the meanwhile. Though never an authoritative lawyer, Altgeld managed his affairs with some shrewdness. He speculated in downtown real estate and at one time was said to be worth a million dollars, most of which was invested in the Unity Block, a skyscraper of his own on North Dearborn Street. He mixed with the comfortable Teutons at the Germania Club, but what he most unmistakably longed for was not good company but the strife of politics. In 1884, with the backing of three warm friends, William C. Goudy, an attorney for the Vanderbilt interests, George A. Schilling, a labor leader, and Joseph E. Martin, a gambler who stopped betting to please him, he secured the Democratic and Socialist nominations for Congress. He lost the election but two years afterward ran for Judge on the Democratic ticket and won. "Lawyer Altgeld is a foreigner by birth," the *Tribune* commented, stunned by his success.

At the start Altgeld was unwilling to air his real opinions. "You know," he told Schilling, "I have some of the same ideas you have. But if I talked as radical as I feel, I could not be where I am. I want to do something, not just make a speech. I want power, to get hold of the handle that controls things. When I do, I will give it a twist." He could not hold his tongue forever. Late in 1889, piqued by an article in the *Forum* that pointed up the criminal traits of our foreign-born, he came to their defense in a calmly reasoned essay. "But for the assistance of the immigrant," he submitted, "the election of Abraham Lincoln . . . would have been an impossibility."

Joseph Medill, who did not like to think that a pack of refugees had put Lincoln in the White House, was mortally offended. "Judge Altgeld is a follower of Jefferson and Karl Marx," the *Tribune* observed. In the spring of 1892, when Altgeld was nominated for Governor, the *Tribune* went further, predicting that "the criminal classes will take kindly to a man who thinks they are the victims of society, rather than its enemies." But no matter what arguments the *Tribune* used, it failed to sway the voters. In the fall America went Democratic, returning Cleveland to Washington and sending Altgeld to Springfield.

As Governor, Altgeld could not help noticing that the *Tribune* was paying taxes on an assessment of only $18,000 while its annual earnings amounted to more than $250,000. "The publishers of this great paper assume the right, almost to dictate to the community upon every public question," he emphasized. "They assume the right to denounce whomever they please. They are in a sense above and beyond the law, for a poor private individual has no practical remedy against an unjust attack upon its part, and yet they manage to throw the burden of supporting our government upon the shoulders of others."

The *Tribune,* he went on to explain, had been leasing a piece of real estate from the Chicago School Board, subject to revaluation every five years, and now proposed to execute a new lease, during the life of which the land would not be reappraised. "In comparison with what other property in the same locality is paying," he reported, "it is clear that the *Tribune* lot is worth nearly three times the rent it now pays, and that the owners of the *Tribune* have for a number of years been pocketing in the neighborhood of $25,000 a year that should have gone to the school fund."

The *Tribune's* claim to rent school lands without being embarrassed by periodic revaluations was eventually settled in its favor by the highest courts, but only after Medill and Altgeld were both dead. The Governor was so certain the *Tribune's* position was unethical that he questioned the editor's Americanism. "Waving the flag with one hand and plundering the public with the other is a form of patriotism that is getting to be entirely too common and is doing infinite harm to our own country," he remarked.

Learning that the cashier of the *Tribune* was in prison for misappropriating funds, Altgeld pardoned him. "This young man had charge of the financial department," he noted in a State paper. "He saw that the Tribune Company annually pocketed upwards of $60,000 which, in equity and good conscience, should have belonged to the public treasury; and he saw that, notwithstanding this fact, the owners of the *Tribune* were eminent and highly respected citizens. The natural effect of all this was to weaken the moral force of the young man, as well as his sense of integrity. There is no question but that similar conditions exist in other large offices, and while this cannot be any excuse for the commission of crime by employees, it is a fact that is to be deplored, and some remedy should be found."

Though Altgeld was perfectly aware that any move he made on behalf of the anarchists would be interpreted as treason by the *Tribune,* he found that Fielden, Schwab, and Neebe had to be freed in the interest of justice. Aside from the fact that nothing whatever had been found to implicate Neebe beyond his stock ownership in the *Arbeiter-Zeitung,* none of the accused were shown to be guilty, the jury was packed, and Judge Gary was prejudiced.

Sure of his facts, and surer of his logic, Altgeld also sensed that the liberation of the three prisoners would mean the end of his political career. "Don't deceive yourself," he leaned over and told Clarence Darrow. "If I conclude to pardon those men, it will not meet with the approval you expect. Let me tell you—from that day, I will be a dead man."

On one of the last days of June, 1893, Altgeld was ready. "I am going to pardon Fielden, Schwab, and Neebe this morning," he informed the Secretary of State, a certain Mr. Hinrichsen. "I thought you might like to sign the papers in person rather than have your signature affixed by your chief clerk."

"Do you think it is good policy to pardon them?" Hinrichsen asked, looking up.

"It is right," Altgeld answered.

"It was generally understood that they [the anarchists] were to be let go in the event of Altgeld's election," said the *Tribune.* "The anarchists believed that he was not merely an alien by birth, but an alien by temperament and sympathies, and they were right. He has apparently not a drop of true American blood in his veins. He does not reason like an American, nor feel like one, and consequently he does not behave like one."

Young Brand Whitlock, then a clerk in the Secretary of State's office, came upon the Governor the next morning. "Well, the storm will break now," he threw off sympathetically.

"Oh, yes," Altgeld replied, wanly smiling astride his horse. "I was prepared for that. It was merely doing right."

"He rode away with that wan, persistent smile," Whitlock set down in his autobiography. "And the storm did break, and the abuse it rained upon him broke his heart, but I never again heard him mention the anarchist case."

FIELD AND THE FUTURE

As early as the spring of 1885, a good eight months before the pardoning of the anarchists, Marshall Field pointed out that the United States Army was useful in enforcing the law in labor disputes. Coming before the Commercial Club of Chicago, he proposed that the members put up the money for a military training station not too far from their homes, offices, and factories. This was such a welcome suggestion that the club presented the government with 632 acres on the lake front 30 miles north of the city—the site of Fort Sheridan. When a rival group in the Merchants' Club gave the land for a naval training station at Great Lakes, Field and the Commercial Club had good reason to believe that Chicago was ready for any emergency.*

Then as now, the Commercial Club was a confraternity of Chicago's best business minds. Organized as a monthly discussion group in the winter following the railroad strikes of 1877, its membership was limited to 60 men of "clean thinking and high ideals," with no more than two representatives from any line of trade. Field was one of the founders. Though asked often enough to accept the presidency, he declined, knowing that he did not need to take office to have his views respected. By 1888, when "Long John" Wentworth passed away leaving an estate of $5,000,000, he was drawing something like $2,000,000 a year from the store alone, and he had only to whisper for his peers to hearken to his words.

In the summer of 1889 Field lent his prestige to the founding of a bank, taking up a fat block of stock in Byron Laflin Smith's Northern Trust Company. The son of the late Solomon Albert Smith of the Merchants' Loan and Trust, Byron Smith challenged the careless bankers of his generation by managing trust funds with the admirable care of a physician at the operating table. Golf was

* The Merchants' Club has since been absorbed by the Commercial Club.

his only distraction. Joining every country club for miles around Chicago, he swung a mashie with the fervor of a hardened sportsman but never dreamed of going out on the links on Sunday. Each and every Sabbath found him in his pew at the Presbyterian Church.

Ever eager to keep his personal expenses at a thoughtful level, Smith usually removed tempting bills from his wallet before beginning the business day. One noon, while lunching with a good friend, he pulled half a dollar out of his pants pocket and laid it ringingly down on the table. "That's all I have," he said, "and that's all I am going to spend." This was too much for his friend, who excused himself after pocketing the 50 cents on the sly. He then went over and hinted to the cashier that that man over there, meaning Smith, would try to get out of paying for his lunch, but not to let him off easily, for he always carried plenty of money. Before a messenger arrived from the Northern Trust with another half dollar, the cashier threatened to call the police. With time Smith appreciated the humor of his predicament, and told the story around town.

Not everyone Field sponsored was as modest as the president of the Northern Trust. In July, 1892, when an Englishman by the name of Samuel Insull took charge of the ailing Chicago Edison Company, the great merchant loaned the newcomer $250,000 with which he bought enough Edison stock to start a career.

"There is nothing like being fired to take the conceit out of a man!" Insull hummed one evening to a group of accounting students, driving home the fact that he had come up the hard way and knew what it was to be out of a job. But he was not one to sing small no matter how dark things seemed. A portly man with a reproachful mustache, he strode through the streets looking neither to left nor right, the curve of his lips betraying his estimate of other people's intelligence.

He was bright to have traveled so far. The son of an itinerant Presbyterian preacher whose wife ran a temperance hotel, he was born on Westminster Bridge Road, London, on the 11th of November, 1859. At fourteen he was yanked out of school and told to make his way in the world, which he did by finding work as an office boy at 5 shillings a week. By night he read through all of Samuel Smiles, the British Horatio Alger. By day he was always ready to pick a fight. Once he went down into an old wine cellar and beat the stuffings out of the office bully. "His claret was easily tapped, as testified to on his gray suit of clothes," Insull recalled the incident. "I almost lost my job, but I pleased the office force."

"Look out for opportunity! Train yourself for sacrifices!" Insull prescribed to beginners in business. As a boy he studied shorthand and accounting after hours and at last landed a bookkeeper's job. In the evening, instead of going straight home, he took dictation from a journalist. "Things were not always smooth," he remembered, thinking of the day he was no longer needed to keep accounts.

"The man I worked for," Insull reflected fifty years afterward, "did not have sufficient appreciation of my marvelous talents. When I was nineteen the senior partner said to me one Saturday morning that an articled clerk was coming on Monday who was paying 100 pounds a year for the privilege of doing my work, and would I please look for another place as soon as possible. I told him I was ready to leave at that moment. It was a severe blow, but I put on a bold front. The other day in London I looked at that basement. I always like to look at that room where I got fired. I think it helps me to the preservation of a sense of proportion."

As a businessman Insull was not inclined to emphasize the problems of the unemployed. "My experience is," he said, "that the greatest aid to efficiency of labor is a long line of men waiting at the gate." Not long after the articled clerk pushed him off the bookkeeper's stool, he answered an advertisement in the *Times* and found himself the secretary of Thomas A. Edison's English agent. A few years later, when not yet twenty-two, he walked down the gangplank of the *City of Chester* in New York harbor, Edison's personal secretary.

The young Englishman threw himself gloriously at the task of learning all about the electric light. "I finished my first night's business with Edison somewhere between four and five in the morning," Insull related, "feeling thoroughly imbued with the idea that I had met one of the master minds of the world. You must allow for my youthful enthusiasm, but you must also bear in mind Edison's peculiar gift of magnetism. I fell a victim to the spell at the first interview. I did whatever he told me, and looked after all kinds of affairs, from buying his clothes to financing his business. I used to open the correspondence and answer it all, sometimes signing Edison's name with my initial, and sometimes signing my own name. I held his power of attorney, and signed his checks."

Perhaps because he was too forward, Insull occasionally irritated Edison. "You are always thinking of the dollar angle," the inventor concluded one afternoon, forgetting for an instant all the hard work his helper was putting in. When the first underground wires were laid in New York City, he was kept on the job four nights out of seven. Afterward, when the Edison Construction Company was formed to build, sell, and finance generating plants, he was deservedly given full responsibility for its operations. Still later, when a number of the Edison companies were consolidated by Henry Villard, he was named vice-president of the new Edison General Electric Company at a salary of $33,000.

But in 1892, the year Edison General Electric was merged with Thomson-Houston to create General Electric, Insull was rewarded with nothing higher than a second vice-presidency in the new firm. "I was demoted from top to bottom," he objected. When Byron Smith offered him the presidency of the Chicago Edison Company, the thirty-two-year-old executive leaped at the chance. There were then forty electric light companies in the Chicago area, and if one could be combined with another, and yet another, first the savings, and finally the profits would rise higher and higher. Besides, Field was interested. . . .

Temperamentally Field was the exact opposite of the self-confident Englishman. Though he charted the future of the utilities business by helping Insull on his way, and fortified conservative banking by investing in the Northern Trust, he never overcame an inner timidity. One morning, just as he was taking off his coat in the office in the retail store, a messenger from the Chicago Title and Trust Company walked in to serve a trifling legal document. Startled by the errand boy's mention of the courts, he dropped his coat to the floor and trembled from limb to limb like a culprit caught in the act. A second later he recovered.

Old Peter Funk, a kind-hearted salesman devoted to the store, understood that there was another side to Field than the successful businessman. One day, having heard that Mrs. Field had gone to live in the South of France, an invalid for life, he stole a glimpse of her husband through the half-open door of his office. "Marshall," he said, taking the extraordinary liberty of calling him by his first name, "you have no home, no family, no happiness—nothing but money."

There was no answer.

CHAPTER FOUR: *The Men and the Monuments*

THE WHITE CITY

IF MANY New Yorkers in the spring of 1893 were surprised to learn that Chicago was actually launching a World's Fair, no one was more excited by the news than Mrs. Astor's great and good friend Ward McAllister. "The contact of New York and Chicago society during the World's Fair cannot help but open the eyes of our Western natives to our superiority," he explained to the gentlemen of the press. "I do not wish to belittle Chicago in using the word 'superiority.' The society of Chicago is behind that of New York, but there is no reason why it should not eventually catch up. Chicago is moving in the right direction and should be encouraged in every way."

As far as he was concerned, McAllister had nothing against Chicagoans. "The fact that a man has been brought up in the West does not mean that he is incapable of becoming a society man," he pointed out. "I could name over many men and women who have been forced to spend a large part of their early life in the West, but who have nevertheless established themselves in a good position in Eastern society."

There was, of course, a danger in indiscriminate dinner parties. "I see that the newly elected Mayor of Chicago has announced that visitors to the Fair need not fear a lack of hospitality. 'It may be a little rough,' he said, 'but it will be genuine.' In reply to this I may say that it is not quantity but quality that society people here want. Hospitality which includes the whole human race is not desirable."

Later, after reading the comments of Chicago newspapers on his helpful hints, McAllister wondered whether it was worth while to try to improve the tone of the Middle West. "We in New York are familiar with the sharp character of the Chicago magnates," he said. "These Chicagoans should not pretend to rival the East or the Old World in matters of refinement." Moreover, it was rather odd to hold an exposition in honor of Columbus. "In a social way Columbus was an ordinary man."

Untroubled by McAllister's suspicion that all was not well on the lake front, Grover Cleveland dedicated the World's Columbian Exposition on the 1st of May. Four hundred thousand people poured through the gates before the day was done, gladdening the heart of Carter Harrison, then serving his fifth term in the City Hall, and reassuring Marshall Field, who sank $250,000 of the store's funds in the Fair besides lending his partner Harlow Higinbotham for president.

For Mrs. Potter Palmer, the president of the board of Lady Managers, the Fair was the most delightful chapter in the social history of Chicago. When a personality problem arose at the reception for the Duke and Duchess of Veragua, the representatives of Spain, she faced the disturbance with a confidence that marked her as the Mrs. Astor of the Middle West. The fact that a certain lady manager complained in public of not having been asked to ride in the Duchess's carriage was not allowed to damage the splendor of the hour.

"We have thought that we were working together for something high," Mrs. Palmer declared at a meeting of her Board. "If I am mistaken in that estimate, if it is only a struggle for a few passing honors, and we are all torn up and pulling hair over an introduction to a duchess, my time is too valuable, your time is too valuable, the Government's money is too valuable to be wasted in this way."

"I beg that there be some expression offered here to our president in token of our love and esteem for her," interrupted a loyal lady manager from the South, her cheeks moist with tears. "I boldly say for the State of Louisiana that she is the only woman that can lead me, and I bow to her character and amiability as it goes out to the world as our American queen."

"I beg to state," Mrs. Palmer began again, "that I am not calling for any personal endorsement. It would make me feel uncomfortable."

"I am as much hurt as Mrs. Palmer," broke in another lady manager. "I believe so in the power of womanhood that no queen is above me. I cannot understand why any of you should want to ride with a duchess."

"I am moved to tears," said another worthy woman.

In June, when the Infanta Eulalia of Spain alighted from George M. Pullman's private car, Mrs. Palmer had one more opportunity to prove her social powers. The Infanta, though perfectly willing to be breakfasted by the Carter Harrisons and dined by the Harlow Higinbothams, hesitated to be the guest of honor at a reception at the Potter Palmer castle. "I prefer not to meet this innkeeper's wife," she dropped. At length she appeared at the reception, but not without exchanging a few words with her hostess. She came off second best, of that Chicagoans were certain. A few years later, when asked to grace a fête in Paris for the Infanta, Mrs. Palmer sent her regrets. "I cannot meet this bibulous representative of a degenerate monarchy," she said.

While Mrs. Palmer was fixing the social standards of the Middle West, 28,000,000 visitors strolled through the Fair grounds. At first glance "The White City," as the 600-acre site was named, was a glorious spectacle, with palace after palace reflected on the surface of a series of lagoons laid out by Frederick Law Olmsted, the creator of New York's Central Park. This was, however, an academic paradise. . . .

Everywhere were white classic piles, the most pretentious of which was Richard Morris Hunt's high-domed Administration Building. Near by stood the Agricultural Building, whose façade betrayed the sterility of the once-original firm of McKim, Mead, and White. Except for the Fisheries Building by Henry Ives Cobb and the gaily colored Transportation Building by Louis Sullivan, none of the exposition halls broke with the pattern.

As chief of construction, in charge of selecting the architects, John Root's partner Daniel Burnham bore most of the responsibility for this. Weary of the ordeal of designing creatively, he envied the prestige of Hunt, McKim, and the other academicians of the East, and even apologized in their presence for the cultural inferiority of the Middle West. This was not the play to please everyone. "Hell!" interrupted Hunt, "we haven't come out here on a missionary expedition. Let's get down to work." Shortly afterward Burnham gave in to the Easterners' suggestion that the Fair follow a classic motive. And when John Root died during the discussions, he replaced him with Charles B. Atwood, the author of the prudent Fine Arts Building.

Enchanted by the "pure ideal of the ancients," Burnham went down on his knees to beg forgiveness for the romantic skyscrapers of his youth. "We have been in an inventive period, and have had rather a contempt for the classics," he dogmatized. "Men evolved new ideas and imagined they could start a new school without much reference to the past." That he now knew to be an error.

Saint-Gaudens liked him for his candor. "Look here, old fellow," the sculptor called out at the end of a conference at which Hunt, McKim, and the rest had had their say, "do you realize that this is the greatest meeting of artists since the fifteenth century?" In Saint-Gaudens' judgment the Fine Arts Building was "the best thing since the Parthenon."

Carried away by the obvious grandeur of the general scheme of the Fair, the American public was largely taken in. But visitors from France were not so easily impressed. "The only things they had a good word for were the Transportation Building and parts of the Fisheries Building," noted the architectural critic Russell Sturgis. "As for the Roman colonnades, they sneered at them as being the school work of their authors, revived for the purpose;

and they intimated very plainly that this returning to their schoolboy work signified merely the adoption of what was easiest and quickest done."

Sturgis's fellow critic Montgomery Schuyler was fascinated by the theatricality of it all, but also horrified. Supposing an epidemic broke out of Roman banks, post offices, and railroad stations? "Arcadian architecture is one thing and American architecture another," he cautioned. "Men bring not back the mastodons nor we those times."

Schuyler's cry of alarm went unheeded. From coast to coast architects took to borrowing from past styles, neither for poetic reasons, like the Greek and Gothic revivalists of the early nineteenth century, nor for experimental purposes, like the Romanesque revivalists, but simply because they had lost faith in their own creative powers. "The damage wrought by the World's Fair will last for half a century . . . if not longer," Louis Sullivan calculated. "It has penetrated deep into the constitution of the American mind, effecting there lesions significant of dementia."

Harried by the triumphs of Burnham and McKim, Sullivan watched his practice dwindle. Eventually he withdrew from the world to brood over the decline of the architectural profession, but only after he reached a solution for the problem of the skyscraper. From 1899 to 1904 he worked out the startling horizontal design of Schlesinger and Mayer's dry goods store on State Street, the building occupied today by Carson, Pirie, Scott and Company. Though this was the greatest achievement of his career, little or no attention was paid to it at the time. For most of his contemporaries there was no point in stretching windows ribbon-like around a store when one could mimic the fenestration of the Renaissance.

Sullivan's battling pupil Frank Lloyd Wright was the only architect who held out against the new academic age and yet managed to earn a good living. With the self-confidence of a genius, he frightened the moderately well-to-do citizens of Oak Park and other West Side suburbs into putting up homes in the horizontal "Prairie Style." Many of these were surprisingly lovely and even elegant, no matter if the eaves sometimes seemed too heavy and the interiors too dark.

Bleak as was the old age of Sullivan, it would be a mistake to blame the moneyed men of Chicago for the architectural consequences of the Fair. For many a capitalist the pomp and circumstance of the lagoons and colonnades was a questionable investment, and Marshall Field, when asked for the loan of Higinbotham, held off until near the opening. Perhaps he half suspected that before the Fair was over America would be deep in depression.

Following the failure of the National Cordage Trust in May, factories began shutting down all over the country, turning thousands of workingmen into the streets. There were runs on the best of banks, even on Chicago's imposing Illinois Trust and Savings. If Armour and Field, both of whom were stockholders, had not taken the trouble to show up at the tellers' windows one June morning, the Illinois Trust might have been embarrassed. As it was, the crowd melted away as soon as Field began to speak. "If you will take your bankbook to my store, your deposits will be honored," he said. "My name is Marshall Field."

In Joseph Medill's opinion this was no time for trifling. In August, when a few hundred unemployed paraded through the streets, he complained that Carter Harrison was not the Mayor the situation called for. "It is astonishing," read an editorial in the *Tribune*, "in view of what happened in 1886, that he, in his insane craze for the praise and cheers of loafers, tramps, black-flag anarchists, and red-flag socialists, should have allowed the busy thoroughfares of the business center of the city to be blockaded and occupied by processions of anarchists, agitators, and ruffians pretending that they wanted work."

A few weeks after this editorial was published, Harrison was assassinated by a disappointed office-seeker.

THE DISCIPLINE OF DOING GOOD

Although there is no truth to the legend that the biggest businessmen of Chicago were a band of open-hearted pioneers, there is no use in denying the fact that they contributed to a number of good causes. Moreover, they honored their charitable obligations, such as they were, in the hectic year of 1893. Hull House, the Chicago Symphony Orchestra, the Art Institute, the University of Chicago, and the Field Museum all weathered the financial crisis.

Patterned after the famous London settlement house of Toynbee Hall, Hull House was opened in the fall of 1889 on Halsted Street on the West Side in what had once been the country home of Charles J. Hull, an early real estate operator. Its founder was Jane Addams, the daughter of the largest landowner in Stephenson County in western Illinois. Told she could never bear children because of a spinal curvature, Miss Addams felt for the problems of the immigrants who packed the tenements of the neighborhood, the Bohemians, the Italians, the Germans and the German Jews, the Poles and the Polish Jews, the Russians and the Russian Jews. In their daily rounds she and her staff washed new-born babies, minded children, nursed the sick, and even prepared the dead for burial.

Though she refused to believe in radical cures for the ills of this world, Miss Addams was not above protesting against the glaring abuses which bore down on the poor of the West Side. She never tired of attacking sweatshops. In 1893, after an investigation of the sweating system by one of her co-workers, the Illinois Legislature was prodded by Governor Altgeld into passing what Henry Lloyd called "the best anti-sweatshop law of any civilized community."

Once, in the midst of explaining her aims to a crowd of laboring men on the corner of Halsted and Madison Streets, Miss Addams was interrupted by an unsympathetic listener. "You won't talk like this when the millionaires begin to subsidize you," he sneered.

"I don't intend to be subsidized by millionaires, or bullied by labor unionists," she replied. She was frequently misunderstood.

Troubled by the "fast growing number of cultivated young people who have no outlet for their active faculties" and whose "uselessness hangs about them heavily," Miss Addams trusted that social service would bridge the gap between rich and poor. She always kept an eye on the dissatisfied sons and daughters of good families. "This young life," she declared, "so sincere in its emotion, and yet so undirected, seems to me as pitiful as that of the other great mass of destitute lives; one is supplementary to the other, and some method of communication can surely be devised."

Probably no one was nearer Jane Addams than Mrs. Louise De Koven Bowen. The granddaughter of one of the original settlers at Fort Dearborn, and the daughter of a banker, she did not hesitate to put her social prestige at the service of Hull House. She also started a country club to provide outings for the poor, saved Jane Addams the trouble of thinking about the budget by serving as her treasurer, and kept in touch with the new Americans on Halsted Street by becoming the president of the Hull House Women's Club. When she found out that the club members liked her for her fashionable self, she dressed smartly to please them and went to balls, operas, and concerts out of a new sense of duty. Ever so often she told businessmen what she thought of them. Horrified by the tuberculosis rate of the painters at the Pullman plant, she shamed the executives into taking humane precautions.

Charles Norman Fay, the utilities expert who founded the Chicago Symphony Orchestra, moved in a far less fashionable world than Mrs. Bowen, which was not surprising, for in the United States men of relatively moderate means have always had a greater influence on the fine arts than the very rich. Running across Theodore Thomas one day in New York, Fay asked the conductor if he would consider moving to Chicago. "I would go to hell if they gave me a permanent orchestra," Thomas returned. The sketchily financed Theodore Thomas Orchestra had just been disbanded, forcing him to plan searchingly for the future. Though a great musician, and an even greater popularizer of the best in music, Thomas had never known anything like economic security. His trials were over, however, when he lifted his baton at the first concert of the Chicago Symphony in the fall of 1891. At Fay's insistence 50 prominent Chicagoans led by Marshall Field subscribed $1,000 apiece to a guarantee fund. With this to rely on, Thomas outdid himself.

The Art Institute, organized a dozen years before the first Chicago Symphony concert, owed little to the benevolence of arch-millionaires. Its greatest patrons were Martin A. Ryerson and Charles L. Hutchinson, neither one of whom was enormously rich, but both of whom were public-spirited in the grave Middle Western meaning of the word.

No relation of the ironmonger Joseph T. Ryerson whose descendants manage the Inland Steel Company, Martin A. Ryerson was the only son of a certain Martin Ryerson from Paterson, New Jersey, and his third wife, Mary Campau from Grand Rapids. The older Ryerson, who slipped into the forests of Michigan in 1834 when only sixteen, laid the foundation of his fortune trading with the Indians. Afterward he broke into the lumber business, settling first in Muskegon and finally in Chicago in 1851. At his death in 1887 he left an estate of $3,200,000, a fraction of which was spent on a majestic tomb in Graceland Cemetery designed by Louis Sullivan.

The younger Ryerson, who has been described as "Quaker-like, gentle of voice and act," seems to have had a Calvinistic conscience, a rare sensitivity to the fine arts, and a passion for learning. Educated abroad and at Harvard, he might have lived out his life in France, sipping a civilization of which he was evidently quite fond. Instead he returned to Chicago, practiced law for a while, sat on the board of the Northern Trust, and directed the current of taste by playing godfather to the Art Institute. By the time he passed away in 1932 the once provincial museum had become one of the first art galleries of the world, with a good many fine examples of the early

Italian, Flemish, Dutch, and German schools, and a wise emphasis on nineteenth- and twentieth-century French painting.

If Ryerson had not been born a millionaire, he might have been a courtly professor. He was always studying the history of art, comparing what the Art Institute was buying with what was known to be "the best." "There is hardly a cathedral in Europe that Mr. Ryerson did not know, and hardly a collection he did not visit," said a friend after his death. But he was also a keen trader in works of art, dickering for them with something of the shrewdness of his father in the Michigan woods. Rushing from breakfast one morning in Paris, he and Hutchinson snatched up four panels by Hubert Robert from under the nose of an agent for the Louvre. Another time, after cabling Field and Armour for a loan, the two friends dashed to Florence and closed a deal for the dozen best paintings of the Demidoff Collection just before it was put up for auction.

Though Mrs. Palmer was the first Chicagoan to collect Impressionist paintings, placing her orders through an agent in Paris, Ryerson was much more enthusiastic, buying canvas after canvas at a time when the investment seemed unsound. He and his wife, who had no children, hung so many Renoirs in the dusky rooms of their Romanesque mansion on Drexel Boulevard that the air literally glistened with the warm golden hair of the Frenchman's young girls. All of these treasures may be seen today at the Art Institute, to which the connoisseur left two ninths of his $6,000,000 estate.

Charles L. Hutchinson, the president of the Art Institute for thirty-two years, was a bolder man than Ryerson. When told that the trustees were considering the appointment of a conservative director, he growled. "I am afraid," he said, "that they may get someone who will make a mausoleum out of the Institute instead of a three-ring circus." Letting Ryerson give the staff the benefit of his mellow scholarship, he went the rounds scolding businessmen out of thousands of dollars. The only unfortunate result of his pleading for funds was that the Art Institute had to move out of its original home, an interesting Romanesque design by Burnham and

Root, into the larger, less imaginative building it occupies today. The old quarters were then altered to suit the Chicago Club.

The persuasive Hutchinson did not come of sluggish blood. His father, Benjamin Peters Hutchinson, terrified the Board of Trade for over a decade, driving wheat from 89 cents to $2 in the most successful of his raids. Half whimsically, half respectfully, brokers used to sing this song when he left the floor for lunch:

I see Old Hutch start for this club,
Good-bye, my money, good-bye.
He's given us all a terrible rub,
Good-bye, my money, good-bye.

But Charles L. Hutchinson, who always gave away half his income, was meant for other things than the cornering of commodities. As president of the Corn Exchange Bank he incarnated the solid, dutiful tradition which has always flourished in Chicago side by side with the rowdyism of which "Old Hutch" was a picturesque example. In addition to being a director of the Northern Trust, he was superintendent of Saint Paul's Universalist Sunday School for over a quarter of a century, and met his wife, the daughter of the caterer Kinsley, while fixing religious principles in the hearts of the young. When he died at seventy in 1924, survived only by his widow, he was in the thirty-first year of his usefulness as chairman of the Committee on Finance and Investments of the University of Chicago.

There were not many Chicagoans with Hutchinson's reverence for higher education, as the history of the University of Chicago shows. The old University, of which William Butler Ogden had been president of the Board of Trustees, went bankrupt and closed its doors in 1886. The new University was founded and magnificently endowed by the Clevelander John D. Rockefeller.

Rockefeller had long been thinking of financing a seat of learning, but might never have supplied Chicago with a full-fledged university if he had not been encouraged by three canny Baptists, one of whom, Dr. Frederick T. Gates, the corresponding secretary of the American Baptist Education Society, was shortly made his confidential adviser, and ordered to feed him suggestions on both philanthropies and investments. At Gates's elbow were Dr. Thomas W. Goodspeed, the financial secretary of the Rockefeller-supported Baptist Theological Seminary at Morgan Park, Illinois, and Dr. William R. Harper, Yale's most brilliant professor of Greek.

It was in the fall of 1888, in a speech to the Baptist ministers of Chicago, that Gates first deplored the lack of facilities for higher education in America's second city. Catching at this opportunity, Goodspeed and Harper forwarded the text of the jeremiad to Rockefeller in New York. Harper was no shy pedant, even though he had written his doctor's thesis on the "comparative study of the prepositions in Latin, Greek, Sanskrit, and Gothic," and even if a friend swore that "he could read a German grammar about twice, and take the whole thing in just like a sponge." When the ruler of Standard Oil asked his advice on a college, the Greek scholar insisted that nothing less than a university would do.

In November Goodspeed made the same point, suggesting that Rockefeller give $1,500,000, and promising to raise $500,000 more if the first sum was forthcoming. The multi-millionaire murmured that the proportion assigned to him was "large," and then, on the following 15th of May announced he was willing to provide $600,000 if $400,000 could be gathered from other sources before the 1st of June, 1890.

With Gates and Goodspeed heading the campaign, $200,000 was pledged by Chicago Baptists in two months and a total of $419,000 subscribed in the time allotted. Of this $233,000 came from Baptists in Chicago and the Middle West, $70,000 from local businessmen, and $116,000 from philanthropists outside Chicago. Not counted in these figures was $125,000 worth of land, the gift of Field. Ten acres on the Midway Plaisance on the South Side, it was an ideal site for the university-to-be.

Field was in no rush to surrender the title, however. When Goodspeed paid his first call to discuss the 10 acres, he begged him to return in six weeks, after the inventory of the store was taken. At the end of the six weeks he was still thinking it over. "I have not yet made up my mind about giving you that 10 acres," he said. "But I have decided one thing. If I give it to you, I shall wish you to make up the $400,000 independently of this donation."

Goodspeed agreed, and then asked if Gates could telegraph Rockefeller that the gift was as good as guaranteed. "Mr. Field," he pleaded, "our work is really waiting for your decision. We are anxious to push it rapidly; indeed, we must do so; and if we can say that you have given us the site, it will help us immensely with every man we approach."

"Well," Field reflected after a pause, "I suppose I might as well decide it now as at any time. If the conditions are satisfactory, you may say that I will give this 10 acres as the site."

Goodspeed was shocked by Field's deliberation. "When he came to have more money than anyone else, he held back both money and service," the Baptist complained. "He listened coldly to appeals for approved causes of charity, education, and the public welfare when regard for the general good dictated the largest liberality."

In all of his transactions with the University Field was faithful to the ideal of caution on which he built his business. As if to prove that he was aware of his civic duty, he made Gates and Goodspeed a present of one and a half blocks of land, and then sold them the adjacent block and a half for $132,500. A little later he unloaded another block for $150,000. This time he canceled $5,000 of the purchase price, and after the first $40,000 was paid in, gave the University ten years to meet the rest of the obligation. It was the ever-thoughtful Ryerson who provided $25,000 of the necessary $40,000. Afterward, when Field promised $100,000 on condition that $900,000 more was raised in ninety days, Ryerson advanced $150,000 on an instant's notice. Any such lavish impulse was foreign to Field. Yet he once bestowed $135,000 with no strings whatever. He also deeded the land for "Marshall Field," the first athletic grounds, and co-operated with Rockefeller in presenting "Stagg Field," an additional plot for physical education. Finally, when the time came to consider the question of trustees, Field and Rockefeller together passed on the list before it was voted upon. All told, the great merchant donated $361,000, approximately one thirtieth of the $10,600,000 the head of Standard Oil settled on the University between 1889 and 1902.

"I am," said Rockefeller, "profoundly thankful that I had anything to do with this affair. The good Lord gave me my money, and how could I withhold it from Chicago?" Back of Rockefeller, back of masterful President Harper, stood Ryerson, who served thirty years as president of the Board of Trustees. In his lifetime he contributed over $600,000, $200,000 of which was used to build the Ryerson Physical Laboratory in memory of his father. In his will he left the University, like the Art Institute, two ninths of his estate. Another two ninths of the Ryerson fortune went to the Field Museum, recently rechristened the Chicago Natural History Museum.

Edward E. Ayer, a Chicago lumberman with a passion for American Indian relics, played a large part in the founding of the Field Museum. When, in the last days of the Fair, Field refused him money for natural history exhibits, he took it as a challenge and paid a second visit. "Mr. Field," he asked, "how many young men of today know even the name of that great merchant of only a few years ago, A. T. Stewart? Yours, likewise, may be lost unless you do something outside of a business way to perpetuate it. In the second place, how will the teachers, students, and others who want to know and ought to know about natural history have an opportunity to study representative collections unless you or somebody else provide them, and what other opportunity will ever be presented as favorable as the present one?"

"Let me think of it a few days, and then come to see me," Field replied, already calculating what was proper for him to give. Pleased with the vista Ayer opened, he promised $1,000,000, provided $500,000 was pledged by other businessmen, and $2,000,000 in World's Fair stock assigned to the trustees. These conditions were speedily fulfilled, and the name of the projected institution changed to the Field Museum of Natural History.

In his will Field remembered the Museum with $8,000,000,

bringing the total of his benefactions to $9,430,000. If he was never a civic leader of the stamp of Hutchinson or Ryerson, at least he grew to recognize his charitable duty, Goodspeed to the contrary. Since Field's death his family has contributed nearly $10,000,000, a glorious endowment for the tremendous classic building D. H. Burnham designed on the lake front.

The lake front, with its parkways spreading from the Far South Side to the Far North Side, shows to superb advantage the "Chicago Plan," that remedy for the evils of industrialism first put forward by Burnham in 1897, four years before he and McKim devised their grandiose pattern for Washington, D. C.

"Beauty has always paid better than any other commodity, and always will," Burnham argued when asked to explain the Chicago Plan to the Merchants' Club. "You all know," he went on, "that there is a tendency among our well-to-do people to spend much time and money elsewhere, and that this tendency has been rapidly growing in late years. We have been running away to Cairo, Athens, the Riviera, Paris, and Vienna because life at home is not so pleasant as in these fashionable centers. Thus a constant drain upon the resources of the town has been going on. No one has estimated the number of millions of money made here in Chicago and expended elsewhere, but the sum must be a large one. What would be the effect upon our retail business at home if this money were circulated here?"

In his opinion Chicago was unattractive. "Does anyone grown rich in the mines, the forests, or the plains of our country come here to live, or even linger for the sake of pleasure? Does he not pass through the city, remaining only so long as he is compelled to, so that we get the benefit neither of his money nor of his presence among us?"

Enraptured, Burnham dreamed of civic centers, post offices, and railway terminals, all of them strikingly located, of magnificent highways clearing all congestion, and of a boulevard along the lake from Jackson Park to Milwaukee with palatial homes on the banks of lagoons. "What," he asked, "would be the effect upon our prosperity if the town were so delightful that most of the men who grow independent financially in the Mississippi Valley, or west of it, were to come to Chicago to live? Should we not, without delay, do something competent to beautify and make our city attractive for ourselves, and especially for these desirable visitors?"

Burnham did not go unanswered. Richard T. Crane, a valve and fittings manufacturer with an independent turn of mind, wondered why the underprivileged had been forgotten. "Do not misunderstand me," said Crane. "I have no quarrel with those who would make the city more beautiful than it is, but I would have all such schemes begin at the bottom. I would not put money into boulevards and statues, and fine bridges, and elaborate public buildings until the immediate surroundings of the poor are made better and decenter. I would start to build them from the bottom, not from the top. With a good foundation, there need be little worry as to what we rear from it."

A puritan, like so many of the biggest businessmen of Chicago, Crane saw no excuse for forcing the growth of hedonism in the Middle West. "Give the children of the poor a good common school education, from the kindergarten right through the grammar school, with plenty of manual training," he urged. "Give the poor plenty of public playgrounds, plenty of little free libraries. Provide homes for working girls where, if broken down in health or from overwork, they may retire for rest and proper medical attention. And at the other end of the line, let us establish homes for old men and aged women, where the poor and friendless may spend the last days of their lives free from want and misery."

Perplexed by the growing gulf between the classes, Crane was willing to discuss an eventual redistribution of wealth. "This is an age of great disparity between the rich and the poor," he noted. "It is a time of much discontent among the latter, discontent that undoubtedly is justified, as they have not received their rightful share of the prosperity of the country. Consequently, when the time comes for dispersing large fortunes, the bulk of them should go to the poor. Instead of this we are hearing continually of large sums of money being given for purposes that can be of little interest to the poor, or of little benefit to them, and which mainly serve to gratify the vanity of the rich." In his eyes it was a mistake to endow colleges and universities at the expense of our grade schools.

Crane never had a chance at higher education. A native of the industrial city of Paterson, New Jersey, he went to work at nine tending cards in a cotton factory. At fifteen he was busy learning the brass-finishing trade in a foundry. At twenty-three, after losing his job as a machinist in New York, he showed up in Chicago where his uncle, the lumberman Martin Ryerson, lent him the money to start a brass foundry.

Such was the beginning of the Crane Company, famous for the quality of its tubs and toilets, besides being the world largest manufacturer of valves and fittings. If Crane drew $20,000,000 from the company before his death in 1912, $17,000,000 of which went to his family, he took care that $3,000,000 went to deserving causes—$1,000,000 to a children's home, another to United Charities, and still another to the Crane Company pension fund.

In the race to build bigger and bigger business houses, there were not many capitalists who paused, as Crane did, to examine the living conditions of wageworkers and their families. As the Chicago novelist Henry B. Fuller put it, "This town of ours labors under one peculiar disadvantage: it is the only great city in the world to which all its citizens have come for the avowed object of making money. There you have its genesis, its growth, its end, its object; and there are but few of us who are not attending to that object very strictly."

CHAPTER FIVE: *The Builders Quit the Scene*

"A LITTLE LOWER THAN THE ANGELS"

GEORGE MORTIMER PULLMAN was a solemn man. "I wonder if my father is satisfied," he mumbled one morning to a good friend.

"What do you mean?" the friend asked.

"It was my father's chief desire that I should do something for humanity," he replied.

In Pullman's eyes the manufacture of sleeping cars was more than a money-making proposition. Seating every man in plush, he was raising our moral standards. "I have always held that people are greatly influenced by their physical surroundings," he said. "Take the roughest man, a man whose lines have brought him into the coarsest and poorest surroundings, and bring him into a room elegantly carpeted and finished, and the effect upon his bearing is immediate. The more artistic and refined the mere external surroundings, the better and more refined the man."

Railroad presidents were slow to understand this. "Putting carpets on the floor of the cars was considered a very useless piece of extravagance," Pullman recalled, "and putting clean sheets and pillowcases on the beds was even more of an absurdity in the minds of many. They said men would get in between the sheets with their boots on. But they did not. So it was with the most elaborate and costly ornamentation and upholstery . . . criticized as a . . . waste of money on things which passengers would only destroy. It has not proved to be the case."

There was no luxury in Pullman's boyhood. One of the ten children of a carpenter in Brocton, Chautauqua County, New York, he was out working at fourteen for a local merchant. A little later he helped one of his brothers at cabinet-making, then left to become one of the contractors on improvements to the Erie Canal. In 1855, when twenty-four, he was doing business in Chicago as a house-wrecker, looking forward to the time he would have leisure to experiment.

At last, after accumulating a little capital by raising the level of the city streets, Pullman took up inventing in earnest, remodeling two coaches into sleepers for the Chicago and Alton in 1858, and in 1859 a third. These cannot have been too popular with the traveling public, for he spent the next four years managing a general store in the Colorado mine fields. He was not easily downed, however. In the spring of 1864 he patented the folding upper berth, and in the fall of 1865 his other claim to immortality, the adjustable lower.

Though Pullman missed the subtler side of life—he once mailed his poker winnings to a minister with a card signed *J. Pott*—he pushed his way so successfully as to be occasionally envied by sensitive businessmen. In 1865 he built the first of the Pullman cars, "Pioneer A," and installed it on the Chicago and Alton. It cost $20,000 fully equipped, twenty times as much as the remodeled coaches of 1858, but this did not stop him from urging its adoption on all lines. When James F. Joy of the Michigan Central hesitated at running anything as costly as these new cars, the inventor dared him to ask a service charge. The public was more than willing to pay the difference, as Joy found out after comparing the receipts from Pullmans and cheaper sleepers.

Ever eager to advertise his invention, Pullman hooked the "Pioneer" onto the train bearing Lincoln's body from Chicago to Springfield. Soon he was producing chair cars, dining cars, and hotel cars—combined sleeping and restaurant cars—and with business booming abroad, founded the Pullman Corporation of England. At home he had factories in Elmira, Wilmington, and Detroit.

Possibly Pullman was too successful for his own good. Whenever a railroad agreed to lease his cars, there were rhapsodies in all the newspapers. "The interior . . . is perfect home," commented the *Inter-Ocean* on the new hotel car in use on the North Western. "A queen's boudoir could hardly excel it, and our republican adjectives are all inadequate to give any just notion of its magnificence. It is the outcome of years of study by Mr. Pullman, and appropriately bears his monogram on the superb exterior as its only title. In design, it is specially built for the accommodation of Croesuses, bridal parties, etc., who wish to be transported without contact with the common herd."

Reading and rereading this sort of tribute, Pullman grew to believe that his contribution to American civilization was unique—no state of mind in which to face Andrew Carnegie, the sponsor of the rival sleeping car inventor Theodore T. Woodruff. Having earned one eighth of the stock of the Woodruff Company as a reward for forcing Woodruff cars on the Pennsylvania system, Carnegie was thinking of how to get rid of his interest when he bumped into Pullman one night in 1869 on the staircase of the Saint Nicholas Hotel in New York. "Good evening, Mr. Pullman!" he remarked.

"Good evening!" Pullman gruffly returned, suspecting the Scotsman was in town to talk up Woodruff cars at the directors' meeting of the Union Pacific.

"How strange we should meet here!" Carnegie hinted.

To this Pullman made no comment.

"Mr. Pullman," Carnegie continued, "don't you think we are making nice fools of ourselves?"

"What do you mean?" Pullman asked, staring icily at his competitor.

It was absurd to compete with a man of his intelligence, Carnegie explained.

"Well," thought Pullman, now a little warmer in his manner, "what do you suggest doing about it?"

"Unite!" Carnegie cried. "Let's make it a joint proposition to the Union Pacific, your company and mine."

"What would you call it?" Pullman put in, anxious to learn the name of the combine.

"The Pullman Palace Car Company," Carnegie replied.

At this, Pullman melted. "Come into my room and we will talk it over," he murmured. The merger was carried out, and the new company awarded the contract, all to the advantage of Carnegie.

In dealing with the Vanderbilts Pullman did not get off so easily. Furious that the Commodore and his descendants ran only Wagner cars on the New York Central, he leaped at the chance to finance the West Shore Railroad whose roadbed, paralleling that of the Central from New York to Buffalo, promised to hurt its earnings. When the West Shore went bankrupt and then fell into the hands of the Vanderbilts, Pullman realized that the railroad business was not his line. His only consolation for the West Shore fiasco was the friendship of Field, who joined the board of the Pullman Company in the summer of 1877 and ever after held a considerable block of stock.

If Pullman was not the shrewdest of Chicago businessmen, he was one of the most lavish, and he and his wife, the former Harriet Sanger, gave the showiest parties of anyone on Prairie Avenue. "The gardens of Cashmere were not more beautiful than the superb apartments of the Pullman residence, caught, as it seemed, in a shower of roses," the *Tribune* revealed the morning after a fête. Besides his Prairie Avenue mansion, which was decorated and redecorated at a cost of $250,000, he supported two summer homes, one at Elberon, New Jersey, and the other in the Thousand Islands. Even at work he was sumptuous. The Pullman Building on the southwest corner of Michigan and Adams was oppressive; his private office complete with a monumental fireplace. On winter days when richer men than he sat shivering at their desks, he sank into a deep chair by the side of a roaring fire, his only worry the management of the model town of Pullman on the Far South Side. It was there that he centered his manufacturing in 1881.

The architect of both the Pullman Building and Pullman town was Solon Spencer Beman. Trained in the atelier of Richard Michell Upjohn, the creator of the magnificent Venetian Gothic State House at Hartford, he was sympathetic with the millionaire's panting after luxury. When asked to design not only a factory and 1,800 homes for the workers but also a theater, a public library, and a hotel named after the manufacturer's daughter Florence, he tried for a new style, a blend of the Queen Anne and the Ruskinian Gothic. Dominating the scene was the romantic clock tower of the machine shop. A glance at this told Pullman that Beman was a great artist. "I tell you, he's a wonderful young man," he kept reminding reporters.

Having done so much for his employees, Pullman felt he had the right to lay down certain restrictions. "We will not allow any saloons or drinking resorts," he announced, making it clear that no one under any circumstances would be allowed to buy land in the town, and only respectable people entitled to take out leases. "We shall do all we can to develop the better nature of our workmen. . . . I estimate," he added as he inspected the first buildings going up, "that we have spent about $2,000,000 so far. I shall try and benefit humanity where it is in my power to do so."

The theater at Pullman was close to his heart; its formal opening in the winter of 1883 the climax of the social season. According to the *Inter-Ocean* the private train that bore the guests down to the model town "rivaled the drawing rooms of the palace homes when they are thrown open on grand occasions. This train, beautiful without and elegant within, furnished with the loveliness of a great city, rolled out of the dingy depot into the storm, but there was all gaiety on board, and none heeded the howling wind and the driving snow." The locomotive made two stops during the half-hour trip, once at 18th Street to receive Pullman and his family, and again at 22d Street for the convenience of Prairie Avenue neighbors.

At the theater Pullman's intimate friends gathered in the Moorish boxes overlooking the audience for a lecture by Stewart L. Woodford, the New Yorker who nominated Conkling for President in 1876. "A feature about Pullman which commends itself especially to the wives and mothers is the absence of the groggery and the brothel," said Woodford. "This is something for which the women and children will rise up and render thanks to their great benefactor."

For a second Woodford gazed upward at the lavender-and-silver ceiling. "To me," he went on, "Pullman proves in hard, practical dollars and cents that it pays to love your neighbor as yourself. Everywhere is utility, order, cleanliness, and beauty. These are the silent teachers that minister to eye, to heart, to brain. They must make men live more cleanly lives within as well as without. They must help children, women, and men to grow into sweeter, whiter, nobler, and more productive manhood. But," he warned, "place and need and money would have been powerless had not the brain, the vision, the will, and the courage been found. In a word, there were the conditions of just such an effort and just such a result, and the man alone was needed. And *he* was there. He is here. You know him as your neighbor. You love him as your friend. You speak his name and you have christened the town."

Unfortunately not everyone would appreciate his generosity. "I do not dream that the millennium is about to dawn, even at Pullman," Woodford made plain. "It will be strange if the serpent does not hiss, even under the rose leaves of this Eden. Strange if there is not still a fib on the lip of some Eve, and cowardice in the heart of some Adam, even here."

In April—only a few days after the never-to-be-forgotten Vanderbilt Ball in New York—Pullman held another celebration, this time to mark the opening of the library of the model town. For Dr. David Swing, the pastor of Central Church, this was the ideal opportunity to denounce ball-giving on the Eastern seaboard. "There is nothing inexplicable or mysterious in the gold applied by the founder of this library," Swing told the representative citizens who came down by private train. "But should this gentleman give a Vanderbilt Ball we might well be amazed, for there a hundred thousand dollars, less or more, were lavished on the last point between something and nothing. All the scene was transient as the flowers of the evening. Such pageants should come but rarely into our world, and indeed they are fading away. They were frequent in Rome in times of war and plunder, but as reason advances, such applications of money and labor decline. We hope the rich men of the West will always prefer libraries, and parks, and music temples, and even good theaters to the perishable display of the ballroom."

Never stopping to think that the annual fee for the use of the reading room—three dollars—would keep out almost all workingmen, Swing saw Pullman's gift as a kind of civic center. "A library of good books is almost as sacred as a sanctuary," he emphasized. "Here the mind and heart will be allured away from sin and temptation."

Beneath the surface, life in the model town was far from perfect. Rents were 20 to 25 per cent higher than anywhere in the vicinity, and Pullman as exacting on the first of the month as any other landlord. On pay days, when the men lined up at the bank to cash their checks, the company saw to it they settled for their rooms before drawing a penny. "I have seen men with families of eight or nine children to support crying there because they got only 3 or 4 cents after paying their rent," one of the car builders testified. As for living elsewhere, that was out of the question. Any employee who did so was in danger of losing his job.

One of Pullman's foremen stated the company's labor policy in simple terms. "I have no use for American workmen," he said. "They are too damned independent." Unions were not to be tolerated. "If a man belonged to a union, if the company knew it, he was discharged," one of the employees declared.

All the while the model town was expected to show a profit of 6 per cent. The Methodist minister who hoped to lease the Green Stone Church for less than $300 a month, got a cold reception at Pullman's office. "When that church was built," the manufacturer pointed out, "it was not intended so much for the moral and spiritual welfare of the people as it was for the artistic effect of the scene." Dr. Oggel, the leader of the Presbyterians who eventually took over the building, had no objection to this sort of thinking. Using "Thou hast made him a little lower than the angels" for a text, he once preached a sermon on Pullman in the course of which he read a newspaper clipping proposing him for President of the United States.

On the 11th of May, 1894, Dr. Oggel was shocked to learn that the Pullman workers, many of whom had secretly joined the new American Railway Union, had gone on strike. Exasperated by the company's plan of cutting wages but not rents in the depression of 1893 they had been fighting off starvation all winter long, fainting at their jobs for lack of food, and had now taken the only way out. "I don't know how long the strike will last," Pullman observed as he shut down the works. "Financially it is a good thing for the stockholders."

It was not a good thing for the employees. At the end of a week 151 destitute families were begging rations from a hastily organized relief committee. Fortunately for Pullman's subjects, John P. Hopkins, the Democratic Mayor of Chicago, supplied thousands of dollars of dearly needed groceries out of his own pocket.

With each day the tension mounted. Back of Pullman was the General Managers' Association, the strikebreaking combine of the 24 railroads centering in Chicago. Back of the Pullman workers was the American Railway Union, the unified industrial organization of all white railway employees founded by Eugene V. Debs in the summer of 1893.

From the beginning the A. R. U. recognized the danger of incidents. "I understand that the company has already asked for police protection," one of Debs' lieutenants informed the Pullman workers on the first day of the strike. "If you men do your duty as American citizens, there will be no need of police protection. We want no militia here." Under Debs' leadership the discipline of the strikers offered no excuse for armed intervention. "Such dignified, manly, and conservative conduct in the midst of excitement and threatened starvation is worthy of the highest type of American citizenship," the government decided in its report.

But Pullman felt he had nothing to say to his men. When the Civic Federation, newly organized by Lyman Gage to promote good feeling between capital and labor, implored him to submit the dispute to arbitration, he refused not once but twice, horrifying Mrs. Palmer, who set great hopes on the Federation's usefulness in times of crisis. And when the A. R. U. sent word begging him to discuss his differences with the strikers, he did not even open the note.

Outraged, Mark Hanna made a scene in the Union Club of Cleveland. "The damned idiot ought to arbitrate, arbitrate, and arbitrate!" A friend spoke of the fine things Pullman had done for his workmen, of the model town. "Oh, hell!" said Hanna. "Model ——! * Go and live in Pullman and find out how much Pullman gets sellin' city water and gas 10 percent higher to those poor fools!" He added: "A man who won't meet his own men half-way is a God-damn fool!"

Meantime the A. R. U., whose annual convention opened in Chicago on the 9th of June, waited day after day for Pullman to change his mind. On the 22d there was an end to patience. Acting on instructions from their locals, the delegates voted unanimously to boycott all Pullman cars starting the 26th.

"The public should not permit the real question which has been before it to be obscured," Pullman remarked. Dictatorship was menacing "all the industries of the United States and the daily comfort of the millions dependent upon them." The *Tribune* agreed that the tyranny of a labor union was not to be borne. "The question of the merits of this or that side of the strike is not pending. The issue is whether Debs shall prevail or the law." To Medill Debs was "absolute, dictatorial, insolent . . . rushing on with the fury of a maniac."

"We shall absolutely insist upon order," Debs told his followers as Pullman traffic came to a halt. "If there has been an infraction of

* "Primordial American noun, meaning latrine."

the law, let it be proven against this [union] or its officers, but do not charge us with the frailties of the idle thousands over whom we have no control. I hold myself legally responsible for all the things that can be legally established against me, and that is true of every man subject to the direction and control of the American Railway Union."

Richard Olney, the United States Attorney-General, also insisted on order. One of the founders of the General Managers' Association, his first thought was to use the Sherman Anti-Trust Act against the A. R. U. Once the strikers were enjoined from interfering with the mails or interstate commerce, the United States Deputy Marshals could be called out to guard railroad property, and Federal troops summoned on the slightest suspicion of unrest. No use was to be made of the State militia, nor was the Governor of Illinois to be consulted.

No violence was reported at Pullman, but the injunction was issued on July 2d, and Chicago set swarming with United States Deputy Marshals, one of whom was booed and tossed into a ditch the next day. On the 4th Chicago was invaded by a detachment from Fort Sheridan, the training station founded not so long ago by Field and the Commercial Club.

In Springfield Governor Altgeld was indignant. If troops were required, he protested to Cleveland, the militia should have been sent for. The truth was, there was no need of troops. The railroads were not besieged, only tied up for want of men to run the trains. To talk of lawlessness was absurd. "The newspaper accounts have in many cases been pure fabrication, and in others wild exaggeration."

Medill did not think so. "In his insolent letter to the President," he complained, the Governor "conceals, misrepresents and belittles the work of the mob which has held possession of the southwestern part of the city for a week, and which has committed increasing outrages and violence every day of that time. The lying Altgeld substantially declares that all is peaceful and quiet, that there is a condition of concord and fraternal love, that no trains have been molested, that the men have simply quit their work and quietly retired. . . . The real fact in this case might as well be stated without reservation. This lying, hypocritical, demagogical, sniveling Governor of Illinois does not want the law enforced. . . . He should be impeached."

Like all thoughtful citizens, Altgeld was worried by the rioting that broke out after the Federal troops marched in. This was no newspaper story. At night the South Side sky was aglow with flames as gangs of hoodlums—Henry Lloyd suspected they were in the pay of the General Managers' Association—rushed at railroad cars, overturned them, and put them to the torch. Marshall Field was thankful for the presence of the regulars, and said so.

The incidents were suppressed by the 9th, but only with the assistance of the militia, and after twelve men were shot dead and $685,000 worth of property destroyed. On the 10th Debs and the other officials of the A. R. U. were indicted, leaving the strikers leaderless and dismayed. "It was not the soldiers that ended the strike," Debs believed. "It was simply the United States Courts." Though gallantly defended by Clarence Darrow and ex-Senator Lyman Trumbull, the 81-year-old friend of Abraham Lincoln, the labor leader was sentenced to six months for contempt.

When the Pullman plant reopened on August 2d, all A. R. U. men applying for work had to surrender their membership cards. "I think they have had all of the American Railway Union they want," Pullman decided.

The manufacturer was not a man to let bygones be bygones. Late in the summer, when Altgeld appealed to him for a contribution to relieve the suffering of his old hands, 1,600 of whom were jobless and destitute, his only reply was to instruct a vice-president to show him the beauties of the model town. Altgeld then made a personal investigation, with the executive tagging at his heels. Horror-stricken to discover that 6,000 people were starving, four fifths of them women and children, he wrote Pullman once more, this time to recommend that the company cancel all rents since the 1st of October, and stagger the production schedule, cutting the working day in half and doubling the number of employees. Neither proposal made sense to Pullman, who consented to glance at Altgeld's letter only after it was forced upon him by a messenger in the full regalia of the National Guard. The unemployed were miserable, he admitted, but there was nothing he could do about it. In the end Altgeld was driven to ask the people of Illinois for the funds to meet the crisis.

The dogged millionaire had not long to live. Stricken with angina pectoris in his Prairie Avenue mansion, he shuddered half the night and died at dawn on October 19th, 1897. His family, perhaps because they feared reprisals from wayward employees, buried him with care, embedding his coffin in asphalt, and binding it down by steel rails through which no ghoul could hope to claw.

He left an estate of $17,400,000, $1,200,000 of which went to a manual training school.

THE TROUBLES OF C. T. YERKES, JR.

Marshall Field had a clergyman's horror of flippant men. When Charles Tyson Yerkes, Jr., the corpulent plunderer of the Chicago street railways, sat down in his office and bragged of his special talent for corrupting aldermen, he froze with disgust. Later, in the quiet of a good club, he leaned over and told an old banker his opinion of Yerkes' methods. "He shocked me," the great merchant whispered. "He is not safe."

Yerkes was nearly always frank. "The secret of success in my business," he said, "is to buy up old junk, fix it up a little, and unload it upon some other fellows." He broke out laughing on being asked why he didn't run more street cars at rush hours. "Tush!" he cautioned, putting his finger to his lips. "It is the straphangers who pay the dividends."

At meetings of serious-minded businessmen Yerkes was a disturbing influence. "Let us take the land anyway, and apologize afterward," he suggested to a little group of capitalists discussing the acquisition of a piece of property for the World's Fair. At this Field leaped trembling to his feet, protesting that he could not afford to have his name associated with any violation of the law. An anxious half-hour followed as one by one the directors of the Fair labored to convince Field they had no intention of flouting the courts.

Yerkes was forceful, even if undignified. When he learned that a certain Chicago newspaper was about to print certain revelations, he paid a call on the editor-in-chief. "The publication of that article will hurt me," he agreed. "It will hurt me a great deal. It will hurt me personally. I shall be down and out. There will be nothing for me to do. I tell you all this so that you may not underestimate the consequences to me. I also inform you that if you publish it, I, myself, personally, will kill you, sure! Good morning!" The only Chicago capitalist with a prison record, Yerkes couldn't help being touchy at times.

In 1871, when thirty-four, he was sentenced to two years and nine months for misapplying the funds of the city of Philadelphia. The truth might never have come out if his banking house hadn't crashed in the confusion resulting from the Chicago fire, forcing him to disclose that all was not well with the city accounts. He had been highly efficient in marketing Philadelphia bonds, which may explain why he was pardoned in less than a year.

A native Philadelphian, the son of a Quaker bank president, he never absorbed more than a smattering of education. At eight he borrowed $18 from his father, made the family grocer promise to buy all he could supply of a certain brand of soap at 9 cents a pound, bought up the soap in question at 6 cents a pound at auction, and came back home his pockets bulging, a capitalist-to-be. At fifteen he dropped out of high school to go to work as an office boy in a grain commission house. As an apprentice he was supposed to receive no salary for the first year, but was too wide-awake to be denied a bonus of $50. At twenty-two he started his own stock-brokerage office. At twenty-five he went into banking, specializing in high-grade bonds. Probably he annoyed Jay Cooke, who liked to keep the blue chips for himself.

"I don't owe a dollar in Philadelphia," Yerkes used to say. After his release from prison—urged incidentally by a good many of the very best bankers—he made a tiny fortune gambling in the panic of 1873. Two years later he took hold of the Continental Passenger Railway Company, whose stock shot from $15 a share to $100. With the proceeds from this and other clever investments, he paid off his obligations to the city in full, magnificently forgetting that the councilmen had passed a resolution forgiving his indebtedness.

But Yerkes was not at ease in the domesticity of Philadelphia. As soon as his first wife, the mother of his six children, divorced him, he married again and moved to Fargo, South Dakota, where he dabbled unwisely in land and public utilities. In 1881, when he opened a stock and grain brokerage house in Chicago, he had only $40,000 to his name.

He did not do badly in Chicago. As early as 1883 he had Burling and Whitehouse design him a $60,000 Gothic home—now destroyed—on the southeast corner of Michigan Avenue and 32d Street. As early as the winter of 1885 he and his wife showed their faces at a ball for Saint Luke's Hospital. Johnny Hand's orchestra played, and an old chef from Delmonico's superintended the midnight supper. The Potter Palmers were present; so were the Byron L. Smiths, the George M. Pullmans, and the Marshall Fields. "The loftiest minds of the West were there," the *Tribune* reported.

Next spring Yerkes laid out $1,750,000 for the control of the North Chicago Street Railway, a network of street car lines on the North Side. The funds, however, were not his own, but those of William L. Elkins and P. A. B. Widener, two Philadelphians who had helped him seize the Continental Passenger Railway Company. In all likelihood he was their faithful servant for the rest of his life, although Theodore Dreiser, who made Yerkes' life the basis for two painstaking novels *The Financier* and *The Titan,* believed he was on his own.

A distant relation of Senator Stephen B. Elkins of West Virginia, William L. Elkins was once a grocer's clerk, once a paper manufacturer, and once an oil refiner, but most of his $30,000,000 fortune came from street railways. His good friend P. A. B. Widener, who left the largest estate in the history of Philadelphia, showed him the exciting way.

Widener was disarmingly free from awkward scruples. "You can vote first and discuss afterward," he once told a stockholders' meeting, cutting short all questions on the ethics of a lease. A butcher's boy to begin with, he was a knowing one. In his 'teens he cleared $60,000 peddling mutton to the Union armies. In his old age he collected madonnas and wept at the brushwork of Raphael—but this was long after he and Elkins worked their will on the street car lines of Philadelphia, Baltimore, Washington, and Pittsburgh.

In New York Elkins and Widener collaborated with Anthony N. Brady, Thomas F. Ryan, and William C. Whitney, the manipulators of the Metropolitan Street Railway system. Of the three Whitney was by far the most brilliant. If he accumulated a mere $40,000,000, it was because he had other things to think of than traction deals. An inscrutable politician, he was Secretary of the Navy in Cleveland's first administration. A superb sportsman, he had the satisfaction of watching his blue and buff silks win the English Derby in 1901. No dullard in a drawing room, he kept ten houses and also the friendship of Henry Adams. What he might have accomplished if he had given his whole attention to business is too terrifying to consider. His partner Ryan, who piled up $142,000,000, was in many respects his intellectual inferior.

The fact that he was an intimate acquaintance of Elkins, Widener, Brady, Ryan, and Whitney—the great men of the Traction Ring—was always an inspiration to Yerkes. In the fall of 1888, when the citizens of Lake View begged him to provide more trolleys, heat the few that were running, and grant transfers, he made believe he owned the North Chicago Street Railway, or at least talked back as if he did. "Why, gentlemen, you are too modest," he threw off, tossing their protest to the other side of his desk. "There are some things you omitted to demand of me or command me to do. One of them is to turn over the control of the North Side lines to your management. Do you expect me to pay any attention to such a ridiculous document?"

Meanwhile Elkins and Widener had taken over the West Division Railway Company, the West Side counterpart of the North Chicago Company, and installed Yerkes as president. They were also toying with Chicago gas stocks, gambling in the securities eventually merged with People's Gas. Anxious to prove he was his own master, Yerkes gave a $23,000 electrically lit fountain to Lincoln Park, as well as a telescope to the University of Chicago. "Build the largest and finest in the world," he wrote President Harper. "I'll pay the bill."

It was in New York that Yerkes truly expressed his extravagant self. In the spring of 1893 he asked Robert Henderson Robertson, an architect with a number of respectable Romanesque homes to his credit, to create an Italian palace on the southeast corner of Fifth Avenue and 68th Street. Now vanished, this retreat from the anxieties of Chicago supposedly cost $1,500,000 fully furnished. It very well may have. Whenever he went East, Yerkes slept on an $80,000 bed that had once belonged to the King of the Belgians. Rounding out the splendid atmosphere of his new house, he went shopping for paintings at Durand-Ruel's and picked up Turner's *Blue Lights and Rockets* for $67,000. He also invested a delightful sum in oriental carpets.

Cooler capitalists than Yerkes, watching his growing fondness for his Fifth Avenue mansion, wondered if the time had come to bring him low. He began to play the market, and they lent him all he wished. Then, in the middle of the summer of 1896, when money was unusually tight and brokers desperate for collateral, they called his loans, sure that bankruptcy was his only way out.

"Well," said Yerkes as he walked in to face his creditors in P. D. Armour's parlor, "this is the biggest collection of straw hats I ever saw at a funeral!" A few of the younger bankers smiled.

"I'm no good, already busted, a bad egg, a menace to conservative business, and so forth?"

"Yes, you are," someone put in.

"So my loans will be called, and my stock sold tomorrow, what?"

"Correct!"

"Very well," Yerkes declared. "Go ahead! If it's selling of stock you want, you'll see the damnedest exhibition of stock-selling you ever saw in your lives. If the Stock Exchange doesn't close down, your banks will!"

The threat was real. What if he sold not only his own unpledged shares, but also the holdings of Elkins and Widener? The avalanche would bury LaSalle Street. Not daring to take on the Traction Ring, the representative Chicagoans in Armour's parlor agreed to extend the loans. In Field's opinion this was the only wise course. "Mr. Yerkes is not a safe man," he explained to those who asked for his advice. "Such action as is proposed will cause a panic. People will not understand it. Let Mr. Yerkes alone and he will come to his own end."

Just then Yerkes was busy building the elevated system, one arm of which, nicknamed "The Loop," still encircles the choicest downtown real estate. He sometimes considered the public, as when he introduced electric power on the cable-driven lines of the North and West Sides. He was always an expensive executive, however. When carrying out improvements, he handed over the work to certain "construction companies" whose charges were astronomic. And whenever a councilman raised an objection to the granting of a franchise, he opened his wallet. The result of all this was that the capitalization of the North and West Side companies in the first ten years of his management rose from $8,000,000 to $58,700,000—about $29,000,000 more than the cost of the plant and equipment on the books.

But Yerkes grew weary of haggling with aldermen, and in 1895, dismayed by the thought that the franchises of most of his street railways had only eight years to run, looked for a legal method of tightening his hold on the traction system. Using his influence in Springfield, he hurried a set of "Eternal Monopoly" bills through the Legislature. When Governor Altgeld, far from anxious to guarantee his rights for the next ninety-nine years, turned down a $500,000 bribe to veto the measure, Yerkes refused to give up hope. "I admire that man!" he said; then he laid his plans anew.

Two years later, after Altgeld was replaced by the sensible John R. Tanner, Yerkes came near talking the Legislature into approving the Humphrey Bills, the aim of which was to extend the franchises in question for a full fifty years—and with no additional compensation to the city. When this failed, Yerkes arranged for both Houses to pass the Allen Law authorizing the Chicago City Council to execute the provisions of the legislation just rejected in the Capitol. Some said this cost the Traction Ring no less than $500,000. If so, the money was well spent. Tanner signed on the fourth day after the vote.

Surprised by this new move, the Chicago newspaper publishers took it to heart. H. H. Kohlsaat, the politically minded baker in charge of the *Times-Herald,* Victor Lawson, and Joseph Medill, all three thundered against the Allen Law. In self-defense Yerkes bought a newspaper of his own, the old *Inter-Ocean.*

"The truth is," he announced, "that the men now directing the columns of the trust press are far guiltier before the moral law, and if they accomplish their purpose will be far guiltier before the statute law than the half-educated and harebrained agitators of 1886. It is you, Joseph Medill, it is you, Victor Lawson, it is you, Herman Kohlsaat, who are the anarchists of today!" In his exasperation he didn't stop to realize that journalists, who usually think twice before libeling a local millionaire, seldom have any misgivings about abusing capitalists from out of town. As the owner of a home on Fifth Avenue, he was suspect.

"The press of Chicago has no favorable regard or respect," Medill declared, "for a fellow who uses Chicago as a milch cow, and who takes the butter and cream to New York to be consumed there; who grabs franchises in Chicago and uses their excessive profits to

(*Brown Brothers*)

GOVERNOR JOHN P. ALTGELD

(*Brown Brothers*)

CARTER H. HARRISON II, FIVE TIMES MAYOR OF CHICAGO

erect a palace in New York crammed with pictures, statuary, bric-a-brac, and luxuries of the most costly kind."

Carter Harrison, Jr., the calm, good-humored son of the World's Fair Mayor, was not so easily aroused. When sent to the City Hall in 1897 for the first of his five terms, he chuckled to think that Field, Leiter, and Allerton, all of whom owned stock in the Chicago City Railway Company, the South Side street car system, stood to benefit by the franchise-lengthening of the Allen Law quite as much as Yerkes and his Philadelphia friends. The City Railway was to "furnish its share of the expense account," he noted in his autobiography, "letting Yerkes bear the onus of the dirty work." As he read the situation, the traction magnates were likely to be disillusioned. "If Yerkes can pass an ordinance over my veto, I'll eat that brown fedora," he said.

Harrison, who had all of his father's sympathy for the common people, was ideally prepared for the responsibility of leading Chicago in this crisis. A graduate of Saint Ignatius' College, he had a complete understanding of the problems of his Catholic constituents. At home in the German language, having studied three years in the provincial capital of Altenburg, he made friends easily with German-Americans. Well-grounded in the law at Yale, he might have gone on the bench if he hadn't taken an interest in the Chicago *Times*. As its publisher he stood by the Pullman workers in the summer of 1894. Like other kind-hearted Chicagoans, he was distressed by the asocial point of view of Medill and other public figures. "To their way of reasoning, an employer was always right, the employee invariably in the wrong," he complained afterward. "God knows the men involved in the Pullman strike suffered grievously. . . . No way humanly possible of righting the wrongs except the strike."

Though Harrison grew pleasantly huge as he neared middle age, he was only thirty-seven and no more than stout the year he was first elected Mayor. With his magic name and charming personality he had no trouble sidestepping the traction question in the campaign, leaving Yerkes in nervous ignorance of his intentions.

Frantically eager to cultivate the new Mayor, Yerkes hoped against hope that the two could talk things over alone in the City Hall. Unfortunately there was always a third person in the room to overhear any suggestion he might make. At last he called at the Harrison home on Schiller Street, and not knowing that the Mayor's wife and brother were listening on the stairs, brought the conversation near the propositional stage. He was saddened by Harrison's opposition to any franchise over twenty years. "Tell me, Mr. Mayor," he said, "what do you want, anyhow?"

"Mr. Yerkes," Harrison returned, "you may not mean by that query what I think you mean. If I happen to misunderstand, if I misinterpret its significance, please pardon me and consider my words unspoken. If, however, I construe your question correctly, let me say, there is not enough money on God's footstool to induce me to vary my position in the slightest degree."

With that the Mayor went his way preparing Yerkes' downfall. On the 6th of December, 1898, twenty-four hours after Alderman Lyman of the 23d Ward brought the Allen Law to the friendly attention of the City Council, he was addressing mass meetings in each of the 24 wards, drawing perhaps ten times as many people as read the editorials of Kohlsaat, Lawson, and Medill. He was sustained by Ex-Governor Altgeld, and by the Municipal Voters' League, newly organized by the stationer George E. Cole, but no one else had anywhere near his sway over tempted aldermen.

On the evening of the 19th, just a few minutes before the City Council convened to discuss the Allen Law, Harrison's good friend John D. Corey, an insurance broker with a sense of humor, showed up at the City Hall with a hempen noose. All over town he had been joining the Mayor on the platform, brandishing his rope, and waiting for the audience to roar "Hang 'em! Hang 'em!" at any reference to corrupt politicians. Tonight he brought down the house. Forty to 23, the frightened aldermen voted against the Allen Law. Yerkes was through.

In June Yerkes revealed he was leaving Chicago for good. Selling his street car holdings to a syndicate headed by Elkins and Widener, and his elevated stocks and bonds to another group including Field, he moved to London and began planning the Underground for the banking house of Speyer and Company.

The rumor ran through LaSalle Street he was worth $30,000,000 on the day he said good-bye. This must have been an exaggeration, for when he died on the 29th of December, 1905, he had less than $2,100,000 of his own, and his executors had to disregard the provisions of his will setting up an art gallery and a hospital in New York.

If this was not a great fortune, it was a good deal of money for anyone to accumulate who never left off having love affairs. At heart a voluptuary, Yerkes was too fond of sofas to inspect a balance sheet without wincing.

THE LEITERS AT HOME AND ABROAD

One thing was certain, Levi Leiter's son Joseph was not cut out for a society man. Though educated at Saint Paul's and Harvard, he laughed too heartily and wore waistcoats too gorgeous and silk hats too splendid for most people's taste. If he had to use profanity, he did so, no matter who heard him. When fined $250 for using coarse language at a race track, he refused to apologize. "I won't race here any more," he said, "and I'm not going to lose any sleep about racing anywhere, for I'm in the game just for the sport of it." Perhaps he felt his sporting instinct marked him for a grain trader.

In the spring of 1897, when not quite twenty-eight, he woke up one morning in his town house on the North Side and confessed he was weary of the drudgery of managing his father's property. Sauntering over to the Board of Trade, he joined the crowd following grain quotations when he ought to have been reading leases. As summer deepened, and nearly everyone in his set went off to Lake Geneva for the yachting and dancing, he sat up nights guessing the future of wheat prices. He was lucky at the start; late in August he and his friends on LaSalle Street drove September wheat to the dollar mark, 35 cents higher than the low for the year. Though they lost a million of the profits when the commodity dropped 9 cents in three days, this was not enough to spoil the fun.

By the time December came, and thousands of Chicagoans packed the Olympic Theater, tittering at Leonidas and his performing cats and dogs, young Leiter lived for the market. Trembling at every fraction up or down, he dreamed of what he might accomplish if he used his father's millions and his father's credit. In a vision he saw himself dictating the world price of wheat. At last, having won his father over, he rushed in. This was not just another corner; day after day young Leiter's agents kept on buying until they held 18,000,000 bushels of cash wheat and 22,000,000 bushels of futures.

P. D. Armour looked on, half amused. From representatives in Duluth, Minneapolis, and other points in the Northwest he soon heard of 7,000,000 bushels passed over by the Leiter brokers. Unafraid of rising prices, he stepped into the market. The higher wheat soared, the more he bought, positive that the Leiter millions could not stand the strain.

In Christmas week, just when young Leiter was beginning to believe the struggle was over, an avalanche of wheat struck Chicago, all of it Armour's. With contract wheat selling at $1.09, he was more than willing to supply the demand, even if he had to outwit winter weather to do so. As ship after ship jammed the Chicago River, the older men of the Board of Trade took pencil and paper and figured the packer had hired a fleet of tugs to cut the ice on Thunder Bay, another fleet to keep the Soo Canal clear, besides chartering every barge and steamer on Lakes Superior and Michigan.

Young Leiter fooled no one by putting on a bold front for the next few months. Though he offered $1.04 for May wheat in March, and gambled in July futures in May, he had to give up on the 13th of July—the day our troops set foot in Manila. "It is in no sense an assignment for Joseph Leiter," John J. Mitchell of the Illinois Trust and Savings considerately pointed out. "Mr. Leiter senior came home from Washington on Sunday and refused to put up for further wheat deals, and I guess told Mr. Leiter junior to come out of the wet. I suppose his wheat operations have been a little more extensive than his father had looked for."

P. D. Armour was not exactly disappointed by the outcome. "Papa Leiter and I have become great chums," he wrote a relative. "We have had our arms around one another for the last few days, and we are a very loving couple. I feel sorry for the old man to get into such a deal at his time of life. But he is a pretty strong character, and perhaps it is just as well if he don't have so much money to hand down to the next generation." According to the historian of the Board of Trade, the packer made about $2,500,000 out of young Leiter's leap in the dark of finance.

The would-be speculator rather enjoyed talking about his losses. "Nothing could have exceeded Mr. Armour's generosity in his offers of financial help, which were to an extent covering any possible requirement on my part," he told the newspapermen. "It is particularly gratifying to be the recipient of this kind of treatment at this particular time, establishing as it does the fact that the business and personal relations between Mr. Armour and myself are not as strained as they have been reported."

The older Leiter was not half so light-hearted. Sick at the thought of the $2,500,000 due Armour, he realized he would have to dispose of a large part of his downtown real estate. When he called on Field, the only Chicagoan with the millions ready for the emergency, he found the only piece of property he cared for was the site of Schlesinger and Mayer's store on State Street. Purchased in 1885 for $212,000, this was the most desirable of all Leiter's holdings. If he groaned in his sleep the night after he sold it to Field for $2,100,000, no one could blame him. He died six years later worth no more than $14,000,000.

Of the $14,000,000, something like $9,000,000 was invested in Chicago land. The rest was scattered in the street car lines of

Chicago and Washington, the retail jewelry firm of Spaulding and Company, the Pullman Company, the Illinois Trust and Savings Bank, and the Zeigler Coal and Coke Company. This last concern, wholly owned by the Leiter family, controlled mines at Zeigler near Herrin in Southern Illinois. At once Joseph Leiter decided he was fitted for the coal business.

The miners were members of the United Mine Workers of America; for this he saw no excuse. "Labor unions are steadily losing ground in the United States," he announced. There was no room for a union at Zeigler. "Labor unions at Zeigler or elsewhere can't put a collar around my neck and give me orders what kind of labor I shall buy with my money. When I go into the market to purchase labor, I propose to retain just as much freedom as does a purchaser in any other kind of market."

When the union men went on strike over the accuracy of a weighing machine, Leiter felt free to defend himself. A 14-foot oak stockade was thrown up, rapid-firing guns were mounted, and trainloads of strikebreakers were rushed to the mines, armed guards on every car. Many of the blacklegs, however, were far from satisfied with the young millionaire's precautions. Occasionally, terrified by the looks of the union members who met each train on the outskirts of the town, they jumped out of the windows. They were then dragged back to the coaches and kept under lock and key until the train passed inside the stockade. One day the leader of the strikers approached one of Leiter's lawyers with a plea for the freedom of a gang of faint-hearted carpenters who had been caught climbing out of their heavily armed car. "You must let them go," he said. "These men want to get out."

"You must take my word for it that they do not," the lawyer answered.

The president of the United Mine Workers of Illinois was naturally far from enthusiastic. "Leiter can never get intelligent, experienced miners to stay inside that stockade and work under armed guards," he predicted. "Miners are not that kind of men."

Leiter thought differently. As soon as 200 men were at work in the mines and 150 above ground, he faced the future cheerfully. "It has been a hard fight," he conceded, "but so far as we are concerned, there has been no strike." Even if his workers had been peaceable men, he would have insisted on the stockade. "I intended putting it up anyway, and it came in mighty handy." He was used to violence. "I am obliged to carry a brace of revolvers constantly while I am in Zeigler, and in addition I have a bodyguard."

He shortly discovered that mining was a difficult science. In the spring of 1905 an explosion shattered the shaft, taking the lives of 57 men. Mining inspectors laid the responsibility for the disaster on the inexperienced workers he hired to spite the union. In 1910, not long after another explosion rocked the mine, killing 19, he sold the controlling interest in the property to the Bell-Zoller Company, who had no objections to unions as such. Gossip had it he lost $2,000,000 defying the United Mine Workers.

It was hard for Leiter to settle down, even after he married Miss Juliette Williams of Washington, D. C. One day the papers printed a story that he picked a fight in a Pullman car with a mining engineer. "I whipped Joe Leiter because he was rude, boisterous, looking for trouble, and uncivil to his wife and the ladies in the car," the winner of the match told reporters. "I made him take the count."

Leiter's three sisters were cooler than he. Aided by their ever-enterprising mother—a clever woman even if another Mrs. Malaprop—they married superbly. Nancy, the youngest, selected Major Colin Campbell of the Central India Horse. A cousin of the Duke of Argyll, he had the privilege of leading the grand parade at the Durbar. Daisy, the next sister, aimed higher and won Henry Molyneux Paget Howard, the nineteenth Earl of Suffolk and twelfth Earl of Berkshire, whose family seat was at Charlton Park in Wiltshire. But it was raven-haired Mary Victoria, the oldest of the three, who made the most brilliant match. In the spring of 1895, a good three years before her brother surrendered to P. D. Armour, she became the bride of George Nathaniel Curzon. The eldest son of the fourth Baron Scarsdale, he stood to inherit Kedleston Hall in Derbyshire, whose great hall, 66 feet long and 44 feet wide, with alabaster columns 25 feet high, was one of Robert Adam's masterpieces.

If Curzon was distant with most men, it was because most men forgot that Curzons had held Kedleston since King Henry's time. "Let Curzon Holde What Curzon Helde" was the family motto; the family arms were three golden popinjays adorned with collars of scarlet. Thinking on these things, Curzon refined his taste for poetry and architecture. His favorite poem was *The Blessed Damozel;* his favorite building the Taj Mahal, over whose safety he watched lovingly when appointed Viceroy of India in 1899.

In India Mary Victoria could not keep her mind off the coal business. "The estate is being ruined," she wrote her sister Nancy after her brother took charge at Zeigler. "It looks as though it would not be five years before we are poor and needy. Such use of our money as is being made would have killed Papa, and he promised me he would not let the estate be ruined by Zeigler as it was by wheat, alas. . . ." Frightened by the strike, and worn out by the balls she gave as Queen Alexandra's personal representative, she died of a heart attack at thirty-six, leaving three daughters but no sons to carry on the Curzon name.

The Curzon name meant nothing to Joseph Leiter. When Curzon's daughters and the Countess of Suffolk sued him for mismanaging the estate, he called in a reporter and flashed a document in his face. "That will give you an insight upon Lord Curzon!" he fumed, in the white of his anger forgetting that his brother-in-law had been made Baron Ravensdale, Viscount Scarsdale, Earl Curzon of Kedleston, and Marquess Curzon of Kedleston by His Majesty George V. "You know in America it is the order of things for our children to appeal to their parents for money. Lord Curzon has reversed that idea. He appeals to his children for money. He not only appeals to them, but he has—he has admitted it in that letter—made use of their money from the estate to pay the expenses of the household."

As a businessman Joseph Leiter objected to being cross-examined by disrespectful attorneys. "They say I don't know how to manage the estate!" he cried to a newspaperman in the early days of the trial. "Say, young man, I've managed every kind of business in the world, from a hog ranch to a jewelry store, and I believe I know something about handling an estate." The morning he signed a ninety-nine-year lease on the southwest corner of Clark and Madison, he stomped into the courtroom, his dander up. "The arithmetic of the deal," he said, "brings the rental to $480 a square foot, which is just about the top-notch figure in real estate now, not only in America but in the world. I've been working on that proposition for about six months. It is now consummated, and still they say I'm dumb!"

The suit, which lasted eight years and cost the Leiters over a million dollars in legal fees, ended in a compromise, the Countess of Suffolk and Joseph Leiter both resigning as trustees. Less than a year later, in the spring of 1932, he passed away in a rented town house on the North Side. Though he had spent most of his life in Washington, he preferred to die within walking distance of the LaSalle Street of his youth.

His niece Lady Cynthia Curzon, who died the next year, shared his longing for dramatic incidents. Her husband was Sir Oswald Mosley, founder of the British Union of Fascists.

THE PACKERS ON TRIAL

Though Joseph Leiter's plunge into the wheat market provided a pleasant diversion for P. D. Armour, the '90s were not an easy decade for the packers. The '80s closed with a Senate investigation of the industry; highlighting the trade in diseased meat, it shook the people's confidence in the masters of the yards and revealed the need for governmental regulation.

"Do the packers buy any diseased cattle?" a former employee of Nelson Morris and Company was asked.

"They constantly buy them," he replied. "They can slaughter diseased cattle outside the yards. They have other slaughter houses. . . . There is no inspection at those houses. I know of one case where Nelson Morris and Company slaughtered at Flannagan and Hoff's a lot of lumpy-jaw cattle." Cancerous, or lumpy-jawed stock was far from suitable for the table. "There is a lump on the jaw, and frequently there are running sores," testified a commission man from East St. Louis.

If Americans were shocked by this sort of talk, so were Europeans. By New Year's Day, 1895, every port on the Continent was closed to our beef and cattle products, forcing the packers to reconsider the problem of public relations. The struggle to regain the good will of the consumers, so difficult to begin with, was not made any easier by the revelations of General Nelson A. Miles in the winter of 1898.

"You asked about food," Miles told a commission investigating the conduct of the war with Spain. "In my judgment that was one of the serious causes of so much sickness and distress on the part of the troops. . . . There was sent to Porto Rico 337 tons of what is known as, or called, refrigerated beef, which you might call embalmed beef, and there was also sent 198,508 pounds of what is known as canned fresh beef, which was condemned, as far as I know, by nearly every officer whose command used it."

Afterward Miles enlarged on the accusation. "I have overwhelming evidence," he said, "that the embalmed beef was treated with chemicals in order to preserve it. I have affidavits from men who saw the beef undergoing treatment or embalming process. . . . Now as to the canned roast beef, that was different from the embalmed beef. The canned roast beef was the beef after the extract had been boiled out of it. . . . The soldiers report that this canned beef was nauseating. If swallowed, it could not be kept on the stomach."

Colonel Theodore Roosevelt confirmed the popular impression that Miles was telling the truth. "The canned roast beef we had with us was at best unpalatable, and at the worst uneatable and unwholesome," he declared. "The cans, when opened, would usually show on top what looked like a layer of slime." Meanwhile conscientious ministers were busy denouncing the great men of the yards. "Hundreds of graves tell their hideous stories of chemically prepared beef," cried one preacher, "and the silent tears of mothers erect a mournful monument. . . . The old barbarian was a gentleman; the new barbarian is a sneak."

Though the commission found that the refrigerated beef was "pure, sound, and wholesome," and the canned beef "generally of good quality," General Miles never retracted his charges. "I believe that 3,000 United States soldiers lost their lives because of adulterated, impure, poisonous meat," he claimed in an interview seven years after the packers were cleared. In the interval thoughtful citizens had come to realize that the leaders of the industry were not ogres-at-large, but simply businessmen lacking the proper Federal supervision.

P. D. Armour was certainly not a hateful man. One Sunday morning he strode into the Plymouth Congregational Church, curious to hear what Dr. Frank Gunsaulus would say on the topic: "If I had a million dollars." During the sermon he mopped his brow in amazement at the clergyman's educational schemes. "Young man," he asked when the service was over, "do you mean what you just preached?"

"I do, or I would not have preached it," Gunsaulus answered.

Armour then looked him straight in the eye. "I will give you a million dollars," he said, "if you will give me five years of your life." Gunsaulus put his hand in his. Out of their friendship grew the foremost engineering school in Chicago, the Armour Institute of Technology.*

This was not the first time the packer trembled with philan-

* In 1939 Armour Institute was merged with Lewis Institute, founded by the real estate speculator Allan G. Lewis, to form the Illinois Institute of Technology. The chairman of its architectural department is the great German architect Ludwig Miës van der Rohe, whose designs for the new $3,100,000 campus promise to be a dustless answer to the use of historical styles.

thropic fervor. For several years he had been gruffly but tenderly nursing the Armour Mission, a Sunday school founded by his brother Joseph and endowed with $100,000 on his death. Struck by its appeal to children of all races, P. D. Armour added $100,000 of his own to Joseph's legacy besides building a $1,000,000 apartment block whose rents provided the income for an expansion undreamed of by the teaching staff. On Sundays he liked to stroll through the classrooms dropping ice-cold half-dollars down the necks of ticklish colored boys and girls.

Most of all, however, he enjoyed sitting in on the manual training classes. When he and Gunsaulus talked over their educational program, they first thought of a giant manual training school, and only decided on a technical school after learning what Drexel Institute, Pratt Institute, and Cooper Union accomplished. At Cooper Union he was fascinated by the crowded evening classes in drawing. "This school was made out of Peter Cooper's glue, and no wonder it's a good institution," he murmured.

The day Armour Institute opened in the fall of 1893 he was beside himself with happiness. "The religion of Armour Institute," he made plain, "will be sixteen ounces to the pound, but undenominational, and it makes no difference to me whether its converts are baptized in a soup bowl, a pond, or the Chicago River." The fostering of the Mission and the Institute was the richest experience of his career, his only escape from the routine of business. In his lifetime he settled $3,000,000 on these two good works, and after his death his family remembered him by presenting the Institute with another million.

At the Institute he was a different man from the Armour of Armour and Company. He even took a cozy interest in the students' parties. One afternoon he broke in on a group of boys discussing a dance to pay for the cost of a canvas flooring on the fifth-story playhouse. "What's this?" he inquired. "A dance, eh? What's it for? To pay for the canvas, eh? What does it cost? How much do they charge for admission? How much do they expect to take in? Humpf!"

"Oh, Mr. Armour," put in a meek professor, "the boys and girls must have some play, you know."

"Play?" the millionaire snapped, pretending to be angry. "Yes, of course, but—" and here he lowered his voice to a confidential tone—"you tell the boys I'll pay for the canvas, and let them use the gate receipts for supper. Say, what are they going to have for supper? Frappé, eh? What about cake? Whoever heard of boys and girls having a blowout without cake? Send out and get plenty of cake and send the bill to me."

Armour's reward for these good deeds was the constant companionship of Gunsaulus, the only Chicago preacher of Phillips Brooks' stature. Partly Spanish, partly Puritan by inheritance, he argued his convictions with such warm earnestness that he drew the largest and most faithful crowds of any minister in Chicago's history. For twelve years he was pastor of the Plymouth Congregational Church; for twenty years, beginning in 1899, he held forth at the independent Central Church founded by the heretical Presbyterian David Swing. But the pulpit could not absorb all of his energies. He stood six feet tall and weighed 200 pounds, every ounce of which he threw into the struggle for the fine arts in the Middle West. He doted on pottery, and raved over the paintings of Mauve and Israels. He also had an ear for music. Once, in a fit of generosity, he bought and paid for the manuscript of Mendelssohn's *Elijah* and gave it to the University of Chicago. Whenever he had a minute to himself, he browsed in the rare book section at McClurg's—the "Saints and Sinners' Corner" written up in Eugene Field's column in the *News*. He was never at McClurg's for long, since Armour Institute demanded most of his time. He was its first president, and no doubt its greatest. When a rich father complained that his son was in the same class with a Negro, he answered: "He was, but he isn't; the colored boy made 98 in his examinations, the white boy less than 60."

In Gunsaulus' eyes Armour was a genius. "He seemed myriad-minded," the clergyman recollected. "I have been in his office at half-past seven in the morning when a young man sat near him reading him telegrams from the capitals of Europe and the great centers of trade in the Orient. He himself was reading a morning paper, and I was talking to him about some new plans for the Institute. He would look up, touch a button, and tell the gentleman who responded to buy, at the opening of the market, 2,000 shares of this stock or that; and when I asked him if he was not too busy to listen to me, he would proceed to tell me everything I had said to him and give me his answer." The crowning impression was imperial: "Napoleon could not have surpassed Mr. Armour in the number of secretaries to whom he might dictate at one time."

Gunsaulus had such a high opinion of the packer's powers of concentration that he once made the mistake of begging for funds in the midst of a wheat corner. "My dear friend," Armour sputtered when he burst into his office, "you don't seem to know what's going on."

"Mr. Armour, of course I don't," Gunsaulus replied. "But I am here to look after that institution, and we must have this money."

"Have I refused you any money?"

"No, sir; but Mr. Armour, you think me very impractical."

"No, Doctor," Armour smilingly protested, "I don't think you are impractical, but I think there is a lot of daylight between you and the ground."

The packer was never afraid to poke fun at his great and good friend. One night, when traveling with Gunsaulus in the Southwest, he found he could get no sleep at all in the jolting Pullman. "I have tried all of Dr. Billings' nostrums for sleep, and I don't seem to be getting very much of it," he cried out in the dark. "I think I will try you tonight, Doctor. Haven't you one of your long sermons in the carpet-sack?"

On this very trip Armour fixed his shrewd eyes on the surplus of churches in small towns and groaned at the abuse. When an overtalkative brother from a tiny village with four churches on the crossroads stepped up and said he was "proud to grasp the hand of the man who cannot be cornered," the packer was anything but pleased. "I don't think corners in wheat and pork are in it with the way you four fellows are trying to four-corner religion in this town," he objected. "How much is the debt on these churches, all told? You say a thousand dollars would free them? Well, I will give that much, if three of these fellows will resign and the churches will unite."

It was only natural for Armour to hope his children knew the value of a dollar. When Ogden, the older son, returned from a trip to England with no idea of getting ahead in business, he was all disappointment. As he worded it in a conversation with a fellow packer: "Ogden was so impressed with the fact that so many Englishmen had a leisurely life on a small income, with a lot of worthwhile things, that he thought there would be something he would like to do instead of grubbing for money, when we already had more than enough. He thinks he should retire. I told him to be at the yards in his working clothes at seven on Monday morning."

Armour was probably closer to his younger son Philip the Second. Trained like his brother at Yale's Sheffield Scientific School, and endowed like him with $8,000,000 at the beginning of his business life, he took hold easily at Armour and Company. At twenty-five he was a full partner. At thirty-one he died suddenly, forcing Ogden to shape most if not all of the decisions of the firm.

In December, 1900, less than a year after Philip the Second's death, Armour caught cold playing with his grandchildren in the cindery snow of Prairie Avenue. He grew rapidly worse, rallied the day after Christmas, and then, with the Lord's Prayer on his lips, breathed his last before nightfall on the 6th of January. Aside from the $16,000,000 settled on his sons, he had $15,000,000 in his own name.

"Through the wages I disburse and the provisions I supply," Armour once said, "I give more people food than any other man living." Field, who felt Chicago's loss, called him "the most remarkable man I knew." Meantime 2,000 little children, black and white, gathered in the Armour Mission to sing his favorite hymns.

With these and other tributes to cherish, thirty-seven-year-old Jonathan Ogden Armour was left in absolute control of the family business. For advice he could turn to his mother, who lived on until 1927, to his father's old friend Arthur Meeker, or to Patrick A. Valentine, the attorney who married the widow of Philip the Second. There were problems to challenge the greatest of businessmen.

Beginning in the spring of 1905, when the English medical review *The Lancet* ran a series of articles on the unsanitary conditions in the Chicago packing houses, making much of the "innumerable rafters, sharp angles, nooks, and corners where blood, the splashing of offal, and the sputum of tuberculous workers can accumulate for weeks, months, and years," the packers lived in dread of crusading journalists.

Upton Sinclair no sooner dramatized the evil legends of the yards in his best-selling novel *The Jungle* than Senator Beveridge of Indiana pressed for a rigid Federal inspection of meats. Beveridge's bill, with two of its teeth drawn, met only slight opposition in the Senate once President Roosevelt released a government report telling of dead hogs left to rot outside the plants, of slimy killing rooms stinking of men's urine, of meat shoveled up from splintery floors, and of carcasses picked out of privies to hang unwashed in the cooling rooms.

"The packers have done more for this country than any other body of men," protested old Samuel Allerton, frightened by the reforming urge of Beveridge and the other Progressives in the Senate. "I look upon the Progressives," he said, "as the most dangerous political organization that we have ever had. We have anarchists, but they are so positively destructive that they are of no danger, but the crawling Progressives would destroy the foundations of the Republican government."

Though Ogden Armour was calmer than Allerton in dealing with Progressives and muckrakers, he was not a businessman of his father's stamp. "We need not worry about postwar conditions," he observed in the fall of 1917. Tieing up $150,000,000 of the company's funds in inventories, he waited for the boom to follow the armistice. When the price of hides, hogs, and hams tumbled, he and Armour and Company were cruelly embarrassed. "I wish I could go out and get roaring drunk," he told a reporter. "Don't misunderstand me! I have no desire to get drunk. But I would like to be free." "Mellody Farm," his showplace west of Lake Forest, was too splendid to use as a retreat in a crisis.

At the end of 1922 Ogden Armour was $56,000,000 in debt to the family business, and the family business was $38,500,000 in the red. Resigning from the firm, he placed the remains of his fortune in the hands of his creditors.

With the Armours no longer in control of Armour and Company, the leadership in the packing industry passed to the Swifts. Left with $12,000,000 on their father's death in 1903, the seven sons of Gustavus Swift were too prudent to gamble on inventories. As for building a showplace like "Mellody Farm," that was unthinkable. "No man, however rich, has enough money to waste in putting on style," Swift warned his family. He also pointed out that "no young man is rich enough to smoke 25-cent cigars."

THEY THOUGHT AHEAD

Like most intellectuals, Joseph Medill resented big businessmen. Early in 1898, when Marshall Field and Company and six other Chicago firms of the first rank notified McKinley that they would "deprecate war with Spain except as a last resort," the aging editor sprang to the side of warlike William Randolph Hearst. "The people . . . demand war," the *Tribune* declared. "The *merchant princes,* thinking erroneously that war will hurt business, are for peace. It does not take long for Congressmen under such circumstances to make up their minds."

In Medill's opinion Spain was "the yellow dog of nations . . . entitled to the same treatment that all snapping, biting curs receive." Field, who was not so readily upset, was saddened by the outbreak of hostilities. "I entirely agree with the President that diplomacy should have settled the question," he said, "but now that we actually have war, we must all stand by the Government."

Speaking as a merchant, Field was pessimistic. "This is the beginning, and what the ending may be it is probable no man can foresee. War in general always seems to have been easier begun than ended. I don't suppose this war is likely to prove an exception. War unsettles, and while it lasts businessmen are compelled to be more cautious than in times of peace." Irritated by this sort of logic, Medill ordered the *Tribune* staff to play up the pleasant side of our invasion of Cuba. "War Makes Millions for Chicago Businessmen" was the title of one feature article.

The war did not make millions for the *Tribune*. In 1899, in his twenty-fifth year in the editor's chair, Medill had to face the fact that the *Daily News* was Chicago's most popular newspaper, with a circulation of 259,262. The *Morning Record,* lately launched by the *News'* softspoken publisher Victor Lawson, stood second with 222,262. Third was the *Journal,* then edited by John R. Wilson, with 138,816. The *Tribune* was fourth, with only 77,986 readers.

It is hardly likely that Medill gave a thought to the people's dislike of the *Tribune*. If he worried over anything, it was the marriage of his older daughter Katharine to Robert Sanderson McCormick, son of the reaper king's short-lived brother William Sanderson McCormick. The young man was no money-maker. Breaking into the diplomatic service at the age of forty, he went to London in 1889 as First Secretary of our legation. When his expenses amounted to more than he anticipated, he borrowed $90,000 from his father-in-law.

Probably Medill was happier over the marriage of his younger daughter Elinor to Robert Wilson Patterson, Jr. The son of one of the hardiest Presbyterian ministers in the Middle West, he was a serious-minded journalist who got his start on the staff of a religious weekly. Joining the *Tribune* at twenty-three, he married at twenty-eight, and stepped into the managing editorship in 1881 when only thirty-one. In many respects he was an ideal son-in-law. Though not a man of much initiative, he was conscientious about carrying out instructions.

While Patterson looked after the *Tribune,* Medill in his old age watched over his four grandchildren, taking care that they understood the menace of the immigrant to the American way of life. He had one of his grandchildren at his bedside when he passed away on the 16th of March, 1899, twenty-one days before his seventy-sixth birthday.

"My last words shall be," said Medill on his deathbed, "'What is the news?'" The news to his heirs was that he left approximately $4,500,000—a large sum for the proprietor of an unpopular newspaper, and evidence that he was thriftier than his idol Benjamin Franklin.

Looking forward to the time each of his grandchildren would come into more than a million dollars, Medill drew a careful will. Under its terms his controlling interest in the *Tribune,* valued at $2,500,000, was made over to the three trustees of the estate, with the understanding the stock either be sold as a block at once, or put in trust for the benefit of his daughters, the trust to continue for twenty-one years after his death, or until the death of Mrs. McCormick or Mrs. Patterson, whichever was further off.

In case the family decided to hold on to the *Tribune* stock, they were not to change the character of the newspaper. "I want the *Tribune* to continue to be after I am gone, as it has been under my direction," Medill decreed, "an advocate of political and moral progress, and in all things to follow the law of common sense."

To this the family agreed. Promoting Patterson to the editorship, the three trustees, of whom Patterson was one and his brother-in-law McCormick another, set Medill's stock in trust. The other trustee, and by no means the least intelligent, was William Gerrish Beale, the attorney who suggested the terms of the will.

These arrangements were no sooner completed than Mrs. Patterson flashed across the social scene of Washington. It was for her that McKim, Mead, and White created the vast Italian palace still standing at 15 DuPont Circle, a step away from the home of the Leiters. Meantime her sister was mingling with the highest society of the Old World.

Named Minister to Vienna by McKinley in 1901, Robert McCormick was not recalled when our legation was raised to an embassy, and in 1903 was appointed Ambassador to St. Petersburg. Two years later he was transferred to Paris, where an irreverent journalist revealed that his wife was spending more than an ambassador's salary on carriages alone. The McCormicks were just beginning to enjoy themselves when President Roosevelt put an end to his career in 1907.

Though McCormick got the Russian government to honor the passports of American Jews, and made it easier for correspondents of the Associated Press to pass the Russian frontier, he was not the most penetrating of our observers abroad. "The wave of radicalism is subsiding," he announced shortly after receiving the Order of Saint Alexander Nevsky from the Czar of Russia. "It is my opinion that affairs in Russia are shaping themselves in the direction of greater constitutional liberty."

While he was winning social recognition for himself and his family in the courts of Europe, his cousin Cyrus Hall McCormick II was looking for ways to eliminate senseless competition in the farm machinery business. In the summer of 1902, with the blessing of J. P. Morgan and the friendly advice of his cleverest partner George W. Perkins, he signed the final papers incorporating the International Harvester Company, the combine he had been dreaming of for a dozen years.

Cyrus the Second's original plan was to begin by enlarging the McCormick Harvesting Machine Company, which to Perkins' mind was too petty a scheme. "I thought his way of getting at it was not the right way," the Morgan partner later testified in court. "It did not appeal to me as being quite big enough or broad enough to cover what I considered the opportunities at that time." With high, soon-to-be-justified hopes for the expansion of the export trade, and with the organization of an all-year-round sales force his major objective, Perkins assembled an $120,000,000 concern which inside of ten years was doing 85 per cent of the harvester machine and twine-binding business. Besides the McCormick Harvesting Machine Company and three smaller units—the Milwaukee Harvester Company, the Plano Company, and Wardell, Bushnell, Glessner and Company—International embraced the aggressive Deering Harvester Company.

Though the McCormicks had been dominating the industry ever since the eclipse of Obed Hussey, William Deering, a latecomer to Chicago, had recently been undermining their supremacy, challenging their superb agency system by integrating his operations with the sureness of a master financier. As a trader he was terrifying. "Mr. Deering usually has some scheme up his sleeve," Stanley McCormick, the younger brother of Cyrus the Second, warned George Perkins. "He is the kind of man who would make a bluff and then stand by it, no matter what the consequences. Disaster might come to the negotiations from a determination on his part that he would make a gamble of it, that is, he would ask for a certain price, and if he did not get it, he would say: 'Well, we'll just go on as we are now.'" When the time came to distribute the stock of International Harvester, Deering received $21,000,000 for his interest, only $5,000,000 less than the McCormicks.

The son of a prosperous woolen mill owner in South Paris, Maine, Deering didn't enter the farm machinery business until 1870, when he was forty-four, and didn't move his plant to Chicago until 1880. Trained as a physician, he didn't turn businessman until he had to help his father through a financial crisis. Later he speculated in western lands; still later he headed a woolen goods commission house with offices in Portland and New York. A strenuous Methodist, he became a partner in Gammon, Deering, and Steward, manufacturers of reapers, to oblige E. H. Gammon, a fellow Wesleyan from Maine. When Gammon fell ill in the summer of 1873, he agreed to supervise the business for three months, stayed with the struggling firm, and by 1879 was sole owner.

Neither a mechanic nor an inventor himself, Deering had the

brains to hire the best of both. Realizing that an efficient binder would give the McCormicks sleepless nights, he bought up and marketed the finest in existence. When farmers balked at the use of wire, he persuaded a Philadelphia rope maker to spin single strand manila twine for his machines. From that day forward his competitors were on tenterhooks, never knowing what innovation was next. Judging from their dismay, he was a far greater businessman than Cyrus Hall McCormick I, in spite of the fact that he never cut anything like the reaper king's figure in the newspapers.

Deering scorned notoriety as beneath him. "He was never anything else in heart, through all his long life, than a Puritan," claimed a bishop of the Methodist Church. "He loved righteousness and hated iniquity like a Puritan. He loved simplicity and hated ostentation and waste like a Puritan. And he applied these principles to himself even more vigorously than to others." Seeking the proper religious atmosphere for his family, he settled in Evanston, the tranquil Methodist suburb just north of the city. Close at hand, shaded by arching elm trees, was Northwestern University whose Board of Trustees he headed out of a heartfelt sense of duty. He was also the president of Garrett Biblical Institute and the founder of Wesley Hospital.

By the time William Deering died at eighty-seven, his older son Charles Deering was filling the chairmanship of the executive committee of International Harvester, leaving the younger son James Deering free to indulge his love of luxury. On Biscayne Bay at Miami he had F. Burrall Hoffman design him "Villa Vizcaya," perhaps the most extravagant mansion ever ordered by an American millionaire. A tantalizing evocation of the architectural past of Europe, beginning with the Quattrocento and ending with the rococo and Empire styles, "Villa Vizcaya" was five years in the building, with 1,000 artisans, stonecutters, plasterers, cabinet makers, and landscape gardeners toiling under exquisite discipline. In a rare sense it was a museum, for there James Deering treasured the loot of a dozen grand tours, a doorway removed from this palace, a ceiling from that, all deftly inlaid in the intricate plan.

While James Deering was defying his father's Puritan tradition with a hedonistic paradise, Cyrus Hall McCormick II was modeling his life on that of his even-tempered mother. As president of International Harvester, he smoothed the course of labor relations by setting up a company union and a pension system wholly supported by company funds. As a citizen of Chicago's most beautiful suburb, Lake Forest, he headed the Lake Forest Improvement Trust that commissioned Howard Van Doren Shaw to design the delightful grouping of stores across from the railroad station. With this exception, he was no patron of architecture. In town he and his wife lived on Astor Street in a lugubrious Italian palace conceived by McKim, Mead, and White in a diffident half-hour. In Lake Forest they hid themselves at "Walden," a Tudor residence of no particular distinction lost in the midst of an attractive number of acres on the lake front.

If Cyrus the Second was above all an intelligent money-maker, his sister Anita, who married Emmons Blaine, son of the worldly Senator from Maine, personified an idealistic strain in the McCormick family. Left a widow when still a young woman, she burned for the cause of good schools and founded the School of Education at the University of Chicago.

Anita's young brother Harold Fowler McCormick, the most splendid, as he was the most generous of all the children of the reaper king, married Edith, the daughter of John D. Rockefeller. In town they dwelled in gloomy pomp at 1000 Lake Shore Drive, a boulder-hewn mansion defended by a gigantic iron gate. In Lake Forest they enjoyed "Villa Turicum," a desperately expensive dream of Italy from the drafting board of Charles A. Platt.

The descendants of Cyrus Hall McCormick were indeed a powerful family. Backed in business by J. P. Morgan and Company, and allied in marriage with the Rockefellers, they faced the future with a hundred times the confidence of the heirs of Joseph Medill.

THE DEATH OF MARSHALL FIELD

Of course no Chicago businessman had the quiet influence of Marshall Field. In 1904 there was even talk of his running for President on the Democratic ticket. "His spotless character, his long and varied experience in large affairs, his eminent fitness for public position, and his fame as a man of superb business ability would appeal strongly to a class of voters who desire to see a thoroughly safe man at the head of this great and prosperous industrial nation," argued the South Bend *Times*.

Field himself was hesitant. "I have a little reputation now," he said, thinking twice before debating the issues of the day with Roosevelt, "and might not have any left if I became a candidate." Though he longed, like all conservative Democrats, to free the party from Bryan, he had so little ambition to hold office that he passed up the chance to succeed Hay as our Minister at the Court of Saint James.

Still his admirers kept after him. A. Barton Hepburn, the public-spirited president of the Chase Bank in New York, urged him to stand for vice-president. Another Wall Street figure, who preferred to remain anonymous, pointed out that Morgan would "heartily approve," but this was not enough to win Field over. "I am hardly ready to talk about such a proposal," he pleaded. "It has arisen entirely without my knowledge, and this is the first intimation I have had that such a possibility was being considered. I can scarcely believe that there is anything serious in it." As soon as he heard the Democratic National Convention was buzzing with his name, he formally declined the nomination, making it possible for the party to choose Senator Davis of West Virginia as Alton B. Parker's running mate.

On the sidelines Field expressed himself freely on political topics. "Municipal ownership is a fad, like the silver question," he remarked in the fall of 1905, horrified by the suggestion that the City of Chicago operate the street car lines. It was best, he felt, to consult property owners before jumping at conclusions involving property rights. "The time has come when the taxpayers of the city and of the country should have something to say in these matters. At present the taxpayers have nothing to say. People who pay no taxes seem to be running things entirely." As he paid the highest taxes in 1905 of anyone in the United States, he knew whereof he spoke.

He also knew that Americans were too lawless for their own good. "Certainly," he emphasized, "the weakest point in the government of the country today, and one that is destined to bring us the greatest trouble unless we have an immediate change, is the lax enforcement of law. The trouble is that the young people of the land are growing up to have no respect for law and order, and why should they have, when they are not made to respect it?"

In such a state of affairs, no wonder that workers went on strike whenever they pleased. As for the lawmakers, they were no help at all in the crisis. "I venture to say," Field observed, "that one half of the laws are passed with no intention that they shall be obeyed. They are passed purely for blackmailing purposes."

Field appreciated the labor and legal problems of the steel industry as well as the dry goods business. Beginning in 1887, when he joined the Rockefeller syndicate that bought into the Vermillion iron range in Northern Minnesota, he was one of the small group of investors who foresaw the time Chicago would rival Pittsburgh in mills and furnaces. A charter member of the board of the Middle West's first combine, Illinois Steel, he became a director of Federal Steel when it swallowed Illinois, and then of United States Steel when it swallowed Federal. On the board of United States Steel he fought with Schwab on the question of whether the corporation should expand in Pittsburgh or Chicago, and once threatened to resign when the younger man talked of building new plants on the banks of the Monongahela. In the end, as was to be expected, Field had his way. In 1905, two years after Schwab quit to take charge of Bethlehem Steel, United States Steel authorized the construction of the mammoth Carnegie-Illinois works at Gary, 26 miles southeast of the city limits. Chicago was then sure of her share of the business.

Field looked on railroads with more calm. "I will need to see the property," he mused on learning from his good friend Norman B. Ream that Hill and Armour would like his help in reconditioning the Baltimore and Ohio. He thought the matter over, and was never sorry he decided the situation was attractive. Besides lending money to the Baltimore and Ohio, Hill, Armour, Ream, and Field bought a block of common stock at 26 which rose to par before they disposed of most of their holdings to the Pennsylvania.

Meantime Field was coping, his dignity unimpaired, with the emergencies of the store. When H. Gordon Selfridge, the most brilliant member of his staff, deserted him in the spring of 1904, he showed no emotion whatever. According to one of the legends of State Street, Selfridge took the liberty of proposing that the name of the firm be changed to Field, Selfridge and Company, a suggestion which Field did not even acknowledge. "Well," Selfridge threw off, "if it is not done, I shall have to sever my connection with the house."

"Selfridge," Field replied, "the connection is severed right at this instant."

According to another legend Selfridge interrupted his master with "I think I'll go into business for myself."

"When?" Field inquired.

"As soon as you can get someone to take my place."

In twenty minutes Selfridge was a free man.

Selfridge, who was always ambitious, left his home in Wisconsin at fifteen to go to work for Field. "Ten years afterward," he gloried, "almost to the day, I went up to Mr. Field's office and asked to be taken into partnership. To say that Mr. Field was astonished and delighted would be a gross misreading of that famous man's feelings. He was dumbfounded and rather angry. But he allowed me to say what I had to say. I have read somewhere that I 'forced a partnership out of Marshall Field.' Be that as it may, the fact remains that around my twenty-fifth birthday I found myself in the position of junior partner in Field's, with an interest in the business to the extent of 3 per cent of the profits. Two years later my interest was considerably advanced, and in a few years I was taking 10 per cent."

Though Field and Selfridge occasionally clashed, as a careful mind and a meteoric imagination must, the newcomer made a splendid manager of the retail division, guessing the needs of every class of customer, from the thrifty brides for whom he opened the bargain basement to the comfortable housewives for whom he launched the tea room and restaurant serving unreasonably good food at reasonable prices. As tireless as a self-winding clock, Selfridge went to Europe at his own expense to study the great dry goods stores of Paris. If he had any fault, it was that he was fond of experimenting for experiment's sake.

"I can say quite precisely that I never let well enough alone," he bragged, thinking of the day he brought up the idea of branches abroad. "Mr. Field could not see himself playing so far away from home base, and peremptorily ordered me never again to waste his time in discussing such a crackbrained notion."

The end was near. "I had no quarrel with Mr. Field," Selfridge protested. "He was a great man and a great American. He gave me my chance. He carried out the letter and the spirit of the bargain we made together. He was straight as a plummet line. He had confidence in me and I respected him. But while he displayed many evidences of his affection for me, he was austere in his manner and very conservative. He had little finesse in the handling of men, brilliant as he was in running his business. Often I prevailed upon him to do things, take chances, much against his will, and when they came off, he seldom was inclined to unbend and confess that, perhaps, he had been wrong. I fancy he always regarded me as a young man in a great hurry. I was. . . .

"It was ambition that brought about my rupture with Mr. Field. Chaffing under something he had said or done, or left unsaid or undone, I took the train to New York one evening and bought the business of Schlesinger and Mayer. This was a store . . . only a few blocks away from the Marshall Field premises. When I returned and told Mr. Field what I had done, he took the news very quietly—more quietly than I liked. 'Very good, Selfridge,' was all he said. 'I hope you are successful.'"

Ninety days later, his appetite soured and his nerves frayed, Selfridge sold out to Carson, Pirie, Scott and Company. "Under happier circumstances I have no doubt I could have made a success of this store," he said, "but from the moment I entered its doors as proprietor I had the feeling that I was competing with my own people, the people I had been brought up amongst, and with whom I had spent so many happy and gloriously exciting years. I tried to beat down this feeling in my heart. I argued to myself that all was fair in love and business. That I had as much title to a store of my own as Marshall Field. . . . All to no purpose. My unhappiness increased." It was some time before he made up his mind to start life over again in London.

Back at Field's, John Graves Shedd was second in command. Once a farm boy from New Hampshire, he was both aggressive and conservative, closer to the great merchant's ideal of the successful businessman than the ebullient Selfridge. He had only one objection to Field as an employer. "In the years I have been with you," he murmured one afternoon, "you have never told me whether you are pleased with my work."

"Well," Field remarked, "you are here, aren't you?"

James Simpson, the confidential clerk who looked after so many details for Field in these years, seasoned his talk with an impertinence or two beyond Shedd's range. The son of a Scottish mill hand, he was only a drudge in the cashier's office the day he brought himself to Field's notice by pressing for a 50-cent raise. "When I was your age," Field observed, "I got only $5 a week."

"Perhaps you weren't worth any more," Simpson answered.

Leaving greater and greater responsibilities to Shedd and Simpson, Field rounded out his business life as he intended, breathing serenity and leisure. The store, which was incorporated in 1901, was known to be the biggest in the world, and its owner suspected of being the greatest merchant in history. He was certainly the most considerate, thought the ladies who had lunch in the tea room, grateful for the fresh red rose served with the ice cream on the 65-cent special.

At home on Prairie Avenue he entertained graciously, though not splendidly enough for the greatest merchant in history. He was never more at his ease than on Sunday mornings at nine when he opened his dining room to a few of his best friends. As a rule he invited Charles Monroe, a Canadian on the staff of the Bank of Montreal's Chicago branch, Huntington W. Jackson, a congenial attorney, and a deaf but alert insurance broker by the name of James. Sometimes he included Stanley Field, the keen, lean-bodied son of his brother Joseph.

At these intimate breakfasts, with discerning gentlemen at either elbow, Field practiced his quiet sense of humor. When Stanley Field guyed him for buying a lumbering Pierce-Arrow, he broke out with a dry laugh. "I wanted to buy an automobile," he began. "I let it be known I was in the market. All the auto salesmen came around to see me. After each one had told me the fine points of his car, I asked: 'What do you think is the second-best car?' They all said Pierce-Arrow. So I decided that must be the best car."

Mrs. Field rarely presided at these breakfasts or at any other social gathering. Driven abroad by the blustering climate of the Middle West, she took her pleasure in England in the summer and fall, in the South of France in the winter, and in Paris in the spring. There she usually saw her husband for a few weeks. For the rest of the year she tried to forget her wretched health in art galleries, pausing before canvases that spoke to her romantic imagination. She instinctively liked poetic paintings and once bought an ideal head from the studio of Elihu Vedder, a portrait which may have been in her room when she passed away at Nice in February, 1896.

By then neither of her children was living at home. Her daughter

Ethel took up her permanent residence in England shortly after marrying Arthur Tree, son of Judge Lambert Tree, the Chicagoan Cleveland appointed Minister to Brussels and St. Petersburg. The marriage no sooner broke up than Ethel found an Englishman for her second husband. He was Captain David Beatty, a naval officer with a gallant record and a capacity for friendships. One of his admirers was the future George V.

Ethel's brother Marshall the Second would have been no company for his father even if he had stayed on at 1905 Prairie Avenue. A listless young man with a sickly constitution, he showed no aptitude whatever for business, and so little taste for study that he entered Harvard in 1889 with only the vaguest idea of graduating. Next October he married Albertina Huck, the lovely, dark-haired daughter of a local brewer, with whom he drifted to England. Leasing an estate at Leamington in the Midlands, close by Ethel's country home, they spent only part of the year in their house at 1919 Prairie Avenue.

With his wife gone, and with his children in households of their own, Field sometimes called to mind his childhood in the Berkshires. In the summer of 1901 he dedicated a $250,000 library at Conway in memory of his father and mother, surprising the townsfolk with a monster dinner, music, and fireworks. Meantime he was considering the advantages of marrying again.

Since only a remarkable woman would do for the mistress of 1905 Prairie Avenue, it was fortunate that he won the hand of Delia Spencer Caton. The daughter of one of the founders of the famous Chicago hardware house of Hibbard, Spencer, Bartlett and Company, and the widow of the fastidious attorney Arthur Caton, she was one of the great ladies of the South Side, standing near Mrs. Potter Palmer on the social heights.

The wedding, which took place at Saint Margaret's Church in London on the 5th of September, 1905, just eighteen days after Field's seventy-first birthday, was a simple ceremony distinguished by the presence of Whitelaw Reid, our Ambassador at the Court of Saint James. Afterward Claridge's served a breakfast of 21 covers, with cantaloupe rushed from France by telegraph, and *sole diablée* worthy of the Reform Club in the days of Soyer.

But Field's glow of happiness was at best a flicker. On the 22d of November, while he and Mrs. Field were stopping at the Holland House in New York, the news reached him that Marshall the Second had accidentally shot himself in the abdomen loading an automatic revolver in the dressing room of 1919 Prairie Avenue. Half-crazed with anguish, he telephoned for a private train.

At five-nineteen the following afternoon, when he alighted at the 31st Street Station, he found himself at the mercy of a pack of reporters. Bulbs flashed in his ashen face; gossip-mongers pestered him on the steps of Mercy Hospital where Doctors E. W. Andrews, Robert H. Harvey, and Arthur Dean Bevan were doing all in their power to save his son's life. When he left the hospital after his first visit to the sickroom, the snap of a dozen lenses stung him to fury. "Aren't you ashamed?" he asked, striking out with his walking stick in the direction of the nearest photographer.

"Why . . . why . . . why . . . yes, Mr. Field, I am," the offender confessed as he slunk away with his plates.

At four o'clock on the afternoon of the 27th Marshall the Second called for and received the last rites of the Roman Catholic Church, of which he had been a member since his marriage to Albertina. At a quarter to five, with a crucifix clasped in his left hand, he gave up the ghost, leaving his three children, Marshall the Third, age twelve, Henry the Second, age ten, and little Gwendolyn Mary, to the love and kindness of his widow. She then wept wildly and bitterly.

She regained her peace of mind slowly, and only after she came to appreciate the extent of her responsibility. "American wealth is too often a curse," she reflected. "I want it to be the means of the greatest blessing to my sons, the means of fufillment of the highest patriotic ambitions. I should like to see them grow up into politicians, for then they would, it seems to me, employ their wealth to the greatest good for their countrymen."

Though her father-in-law never again smiled in public, he made his usual show of being jolly with the grandchildren. "I know my grandfather had the reputation of being very stern, but with us children he was very indulgent," Marshall the Third recently told the author. "He was delightful. He would laugh and joke with us." The only other relaxation of the grief-stricken merchant was to play a taut game of golf, in any kind of weather.

On New Year's Day, 1906, when the winds were far from mild, he set out for eighteen holes at the Chicago Golf Club with Robert Todd Lincoln. He came down with a sore throat the next morning, and for perhaps the first time in his life neglected to be prudent. He played again within the week, and then, on one of the bitterest days of the year, went the rounds of the links once more with Lincoln. He had a very bad cold when he sent for Stanley Field on the following Sunday afternoon, but not bad enough to stop him from talking until dusk about the future of the dry goods business. At five he suggested a brisk walk. "You shouldn't!" cried Stanley Field, thinking of his uncle's condition. Field waved his objection aside.

"Do you ever go to the Field Museum?" the great merchant dropped as they headed into the lake winds.

"No," Stanley Field returned.

"Have you ever taken any interest in the Field Museum?"

"No."

"I want you to take an interest!" Marshall Field insisted. "That thing is developing beyond anything I expected. I am going to have you elected to the Board of Trustees. I have just agreed to the plans for the new building. Of course, I know the plans cannot be carried out for anything like four millions. So I am having a new will drawn. I am going to leave eight million dollars for the building, eight millions for the endowment."

"When are you going to do all this?" Stanley Field broke in.

"Why," Marshall Field answered, "I have a meeting in New York of Pullman and North Western. Then I shall be home by Friday. I'll sign it Friday."

Doggedly denying that he had a fever, he leaped into his carriage

(*Acme Newspictures, Inc.*)

CHARLES R. CRANE

(Underwood and Underwood)

SENATOR MEDILL MC CORMICK

on Monday afternoon and drove to the Broadway Limited with Mrs. Field and his valet. Before long, however, he realized that he was a sick man. Taking to his berth, he wearily allowed his wife to telegraph Pittsburgh for a physician to meet the train. He swallowed the proper medicines, but tossed all the night long, and the next day tottered helplessly to the reception desk of the Holland House, his valet holding one arm, his wife the other.

In Chicago Stanley Field trembled as he read a wire describing his uncle's state. "Get me something to sleep in on the Century!" he shouted into the telephone. Then he thought of Dr. Frank Billings, the greatest figure in Middle Western medicine. Tracing him to the bedside of President Harper of the University of Chicago, whose death from cancer was expected hourly, he wrung from him the promise that he would race to New York the instant the patient expired.

By Thursday morning Billings was at the Holland House. All day he studied the case with his usual deliberation, checking his conclusions against those of Drs. Walter B. James and E. J. Janeway, who had been before him to the sickroom. But Field was already beyond being saved.

As the shadow of his coming death fell across the nation, a small but distinguished group gathered in the drawing room of his suite, offering his wife and his relatives the vain words of consolation. Marvin Hughitt, the stately president of the Chicago and North Western, paid his respects. So did Norman B. Ream, the expert in the affairs of the Baltimore and Ohio. So did Robert Todd Lincoln. So did William Gerrish Beale, who drafted Field's will as he did Medill's. Though there was no likelihood of the dying man's revising his testament, Beale lingered delicately until the end, which came at four o'clock, Tuesday afternoon, January 16th.

"What a typically American career it is!" remarked next morning's New York *Times*. "The very rich man has died just at the psalmist's limit of life,* leaving a huge estate, which ought not only

* Field was actually 71.

to be unenvied but acclaimed, since the great merchant, whatever his motives, in order to accumulate it must have shared his profits and economies with his customers. And the opportunity to do what he did is still open to every beginner of native or foreign birth in this great and happy land. What is the use of talking about proletariats and classes in the face of such an object lesson that the hopes of American life are still as open as they ever were?"

Newspapers everywhere agreed that the dead man was a model for the young. What other capitalist was at once so rich and so respected? Forgetting its ancient rancor, the Chicago *Tribune* published a cartoon by McCutcheon showing Death closing a book, on the last page of which was written a veritable hymn to the man "about whose fortune [unlike many other great American fortunes] there has never been a suspicion of taint . . . whose faith in Chicago has been steadfast and true, and whose life will be a beacon light to guide future generations to honorable success."

Probably no one had a deeper appreciation of what Field accomplished than Shedd, who wrote that "his employees formed a flawless machine, each part working in splendid harmony and responsive to the controlling touch; they were a regiment advancing in perfect alignment and stepping as one man; they were thousands of individual atoms, brought into absolute business accord by the genius of Mr. Field, and each giving of his best in answer to the scheme of considerate organization instituted by the master heart and mind."

Field was plainly a businessman's businessman, in the sense that Rimbaud was a poet's poet and Cézanne a painter's painter. What did it matter if he lacked the warmth of Armour? Franklin MacVeagh, one of the leading wholesale grocers, testified that all of his "money was fairly made, and he was conspicuous among the immensely rich for the fairness of his competition and the cleanness of his methods. He made no money through oppression or monopoly. He built himself upon no man's ruin. And his business methods from the beginning to the end were so instructive and influential that his fellow citizens were constantly helped by his example."

Harlow N. Higinbotham, with over thirty years' experience in the store, admitted as much, but not without regretting that "Marshall Field's whole life was a serious one" with "no frivolity, fun, or levity." Yet Higinbotham would have been the first to agree that his old master incarnated the principle of order in a frequently disorderly community, a task to furrow the brow of any man. Moreover, he was a director of the National Bank of Commerce of New York, the United States Trust Company of New York, the New York Trust Company, and the Rock Island, as well as of the Merchants' Loan and Trust, the North Western, the Pullman Company, and United States Steel. A man who enjoyed the confidence of those great banks and corporations was not likely to chortle over a trifle.

It was only right for his body to be brought to Chicago on a private train of the New York Central, with a baggage car, dining car, observation car, and two sleepers for the accommodation of his friends, for he was mourned like no other Chicagoan in history. On the day of his funeral the stores of his competitors on State Street shut down from twelve to one, the Board of Trade and the Stock Exchange closed for the afternoon, and 900 business houses were dark from morning to night. As for Marshall Field and Company, it transacted no business from the day he died until the day after he was lowered into his modest grave.

There were three funeral services, the first at eleven o'clock at 1905 Prairie Avenue, the second at twelve in the First Presbyterian Church, and the third at two at Graceland Cemetery. Taking his text from II Samuel 3:38, "Know ye not that there is a prince and a great man fallen this day?" Dr. John Archibald Morrison informed the gathering in the church that the spirit of Marshall Field was eternal. "A great prince has fallen, but in the darkness and gloom of this hour his influence burns with increasing light," he said. "His rare qualities of thought and action have sealed his life with the true patent of nobility, and so long as moral worth is greatness, and integrity of character is kingly, men shall acknowledge that a prince and a great man has fallen today." Moved by these words P. D.

Armour's great friend Dr. Frank Gunsaulus declared that Field "created a definition of Chicago manhood."

On the following afternoon 5,000 employees swarmed into the Auditorium for a memorial service. "What poor man has the right to complain of Mr. Field's millions?" asked Congressman George Adams. "Who has the right to envy his success? All the world knows how it was won—all the world knows that the patient, intelligent industry and square dealing which made Mr. Field one of the richest men in the world are just the qualities by which a right-thinking poor man strives to better his condition and make life easier for his family."

Reverend William Robson Notman was equally impressed with Field's contribution to American life. "He stood for all that is sound and solid and substantial in business, as contrasted with much that is of an unsound and dangerous kind," he disclosed, adding that "so many men, by means of business speculation, flare up like rockets, and like rockets they come down. And as they come down, they bring disaster and suffering to thousands and thousands of innocent people. A business as Marshall Field conducted it leads to no such results."

Dr. Notman might have been less critical of gamblers. Field did not need to speculate, so sharp was his financial vision. When the inventory of his estate was made public, with its holdings in banks, shipyards, railroads, distilleries and breweries, stock farms and stock yards, iron and steel foundries, watch, harvester, and cracker factories, coal, copper, silver, and gold mines, and electric light, gas, telephone, and telegraph companies, all in addition to his stock in the store, it was splendidly real to everyone that he was one of the great investors of the nineteenth century. Wide as was the range of his sympathies, he rarely made a mistake.

Cash on hand for emergencies was, of course, the watchword of his career. On the day he died he had roughly $4,300,000 at his disposal—not counting $8,500,000 due him from the store. As anyone with so much ready money should, he kept in close touch with the best banks. He had over $2,250,000 in bank stocks, $1,000,000 in the Merchants' Loan and Trust, and the rest in the Illinois Trust and Savings, the Corn Exchange of Chicago, the Northern Trust, the First National of Chicago, the First National of New York, the National Bank of Commerce of New York, the United States Trust Company of New York, and the New York Trust Company.

Using his banking connections, he was often the first to hear of bargains in stocks and bonds. But stocks and bonds, however attractive, were never so satisfying as real estate. Counting on the expansion of our great cities, Field tied up half his fortune in land. In New York he owned the $5,000,000 site of the Fifth Avenue store of B. Altman and Company. In Chicago he centered his holdings in the Loop. The northeast corner of Adams and Clark was his. So was the southwest corner of LaSalle and Monroe. So was the home of the Chicago Athletic Association on Michigan Avenue. So was the ground beneath the stores of Mandel Brothers and Carson, Pirie, Scott and Company. And so were dozens of other choice locations, not to mention the ground beneath the wholesale and retail divisions of Marshall Field and Company. It was as if he held the heart of the city in his hand.

Ready cash, stocks, bonds, real estate—it all amounted to $120,000,000. This meant that Marshall Field accumulated approximately four times as much money as P. D. Armour, seven times as much money as George M. Pullman, ten times as much money as Gustavus Swift, twelve times as much money as Cyrus Hall McCormick, fifteen times as much money as Potter Palmer, twenty-four times as much money as "Long John" Wentworth, and twenty-five times as much money as Joseph Medill.

For a man in his position Field had few arguments with tax collectors. When officials of the Illinois Tax Reform Association complained that he never paid more than 10 per cent of his fair share of taxes on real estate, they forgot that he paid the highest taxes of anyone in the country, and that the claim for back taxes against the estate came to only $1,730,000. His executors shortly satisfied the authorities with $1,000,000, and the talk on Prairie

Avenue turned to other subjects, the most fascinating of which was his will.

Its provisions were not mean. To his sister Laura, whose husband was the Chicago real estate operator Henry Dibblee, and whose daughter Frances was the wife of Albert A. Sprague, Jr., son of the founder of the venerable wholesale grocery house of Sprague, Warner and Company, he left $500,000 in trust and $250,000 in cash. To his daughter-in-law Albertina he left $1,000,000, half in trust and half in cash. To his widow, who lived on until 1937, he left $1,000,000 outright in addition to the money made over to her on their wedding day. To his nephew Stanley, whose father headed the Manchester office of Marshall Field and Company until his death in 1914, he left $100,000 in cash, one tenth the sum he settled in cash on his granddaughter Gwendolyn. To employees with twenty-five years of service, he left $100,000 in trust, to tried and true executives, $200,000 outright, and to a host of relatives, over $1,500,000. To his daughter Ethel, the wife of David Beatty, he left $6,000,000 in three different trust funds, $2,000,000 less than he dedicated to the Field Museum.

Finally, as though he wished to make divinely certain that his grandsons would command the awe not only of Chicago but of the civilized world, he placed the rest of his fortune in trust for their benefit, three fifths for Marshall the Third and two fifths for Henry the Second, under terms which made it seem probable that the estate would swell to 300 million dollars in their lifetime. The ablest attorneys in America, men who earned fat livings stretching the dead hands of clients, confessed themselves outdone. "One cannot but be astonished, as one follows the provisions of this will," commented Elihu Root, "at the amazing complications by which the testator sought to tie up his property. He seems to have personified the accumulation of property, and to have regarded accumulation for the sake of accumulation."

Field's first thought was that Marshall the Third should receive $450,000 and Henry the Second $300,000 on their twenty-fifth, thirtieth, thirty-fifth, and fortieth birthdays. Next he provided that one half of the net income of the residuary estate—three fifths of which was Marshall's and two fifths Henry's—be withheld until they reached the age of forty-five, at which time each was to receive his share of income with accumulations. Third, he directed that the other half of the residuary estate be withheld until they were thirty, when each was to receive one third of his share of income. At thirty-five, each was to receive two thirds of his share of income. At forty, each was to receive all of his share of income from that half. At forty-five, each was to receive all of his share of income from both halves. At fifty, each was to receive his entire inheritance.

Too subtle to dictate to the future, Field laid down no rules for the management of Marshall's and Henry's money beyond hinting that it might be expedient to invest, as he had done, one half of the principal in personal property and the other in real estate. There was no danger of this recommendation passing unheeded, for he selected three trustees in whom he had unlimited confidence. The first was his good friend Chauncey Keep. The second was his good friend Arthur B. Jones. The third was the Merchants' Loan and Trust. Its stock soared six points on the day the will was read, and no wonder. In its safekeeping was the greatest fortune ever surrendered to a trust company.

Would Marshall and Henry break into politics with their millions, as their mother intended? Or would they, leaning on the three trustees for advice, grow to be even cooler businessmen than their grandfather? Whatever happened, they had the greatest opportunity for good or evil of anyone in the history of the Middle West.

It all seemed unfair to Joseph Medill's grandson Joseph Medill Patterson.

CHAPTER SIX: *Of Millionaires and Murderers*

A SOCIALIST IN THE HOUSE OF MEDILL

LIFE was full of disappointments for the four grandchildren of Joseph Medill. Brought up to believe that he was one of the creators of American opinion, they made the discovery, once they were away from home, that very few people outside of Chicago had ever heard of the *Tribune,* much less its editor. The grandchildren were high-strung, however, long before they were old enough to read editorials.

Joseph Medill Patterson must have been an unusually sensitive boy. "When we were very little children," his sister Eleanor wrote, "we came into a room—it was my mother's—to find the canary bird dead, lying on the bottom of the cage. I was afraid to touch it. But Joe reached in, took it out, and stood holding it in the palm of his fat little hand; tears poured down his cheeks. I can still see the stiff, tiny claws, and I can still feel my sense of guilt because there was Joe, weeping for our pet, and I wasn't sorry at all. Only scared and a little sick. You know, sometimes an incident like that sticks with you all your life."

Like most little boys who cry easily, Patterson craved more attention than he received. Sent away to Groton at an early age, he felt lonely, so lonely that he afterward criticized his father and mother for giving him an expensive education. He was, he complained, "supported through fashionable day-school, fashionable boarding-school, fashionable summer resorts, fashionable dancing class, etc., by rich (that is, rich for their own community—not for New York) parents, taught to be a perfect gentleman."

Like many millionaires' sons who crave attention, Patterson did not care to be taken for a gentleman. One evening he showed up in the family box at the Auditorium with crinkled tails, mud-caked tan shoes, and a flannel shirt open at the throat. Possibly he found one opera as boring as another. His idea of a pleasant evening, even after his graduation from Yale, was to pick a fight in one of the cheaper saloons of the Near North Side. More than once he was ganged up on and thrown out on his face. Pulling himself together, he grinned through the blood and sweat, positive he was no sissy.

Though he married Alice Higinbotham, the pretty daughter of Marshall Field's partner Harlow N. Higinbotham, and became the father of three little girls, he was too much of an individualist to pass for just another family man. Seven days out of the week he dressed like a roughneck, and rarely looked in the mirror to see if he were well groomed before he set out in the morning. One day he accompanied one of his daughters to school and kissed her good-bye on the steps. A few minutes later the telephone rang at the Patterson home. "I thought I ought to tell you," said the headmistress to Mrs. Patterson, "that I saw your houseman kiss your little girl this morning."

Patterson had other things to think about than his personal appearance. In 1905, after working as a reporter on the family newspaper, and serving a term in the State Assembly, he talked Edward F. Dunne, the good-tempered reformer just elected Mayor of Chicago, into appointing him Commissioner of Public Works. Though Patterson developed plenty of tolerance later on for violent methods of increasing a newspaper's circulation, he held it to be the Commissioner's job to keep peace on the city's sidewalks, and when newsboys took to beating each other up, threatened to yank the newsstands off the corners. He carried out the threat, "They quit their fighting then," he declared.

However, Patterson was harder on businessmen than newspaper owners. He even claimed that certain Chicago capitalists were anarchists. "I say they are, and with emphasis," he told reporters. "I believe men are anarchists, no matter how big their bank accounts, who take the attitude that the law does not exist for them."

This sort of talk brought Patterson's name before the public, but didn't create as much of a stir as a letter he wrote to newspapers in the winter of 1906. Resigning from the Dunne administration, he announced his conversion to socialism. "The whole body of our laws as at present formed are ridiculous and obsolete," he explained. "They are designed always to uphold capital at the expense of the community. . . . I realized soon after I took office that to fight privilege under the present laws would be a jest."

"Joe . . . is impetuous, and a man of strong convictions and emotions," Mayor Dunne commented, puzzled by his resignation. "He has indicated to me that his views tended to socialism, but . . . the holding of such views would not interfere with his continuing in office." Dunne's supporters were not so easy on Patterson. "He worked hard until the novelty wore off," one of them remarked.

Meantime Patterson was warning us that our business leaders were not to be trusted. "It isn't because rich men are bad or a class apart," he admitted. "They are not. But when money possesses them (they practically never possess money), it alters their very soul without their realizing it, and it is simple to see why. It is because money is what a man most wants."

Though only twenty-seven, Patterson had a philosophy of his own. "Money is power and dominion," he said. "It is wine and woman and song. It is art and poetry and music. It is idleness or activity. It is warmth in winter and coolness in summer. It is clothing and food. It is travel and sport. It is horses and automobiles, and silks and diamonds. It is books. It is education. It is self-respect, and the respect of others. No one possesses it, but it possesses everybody. In life, money means everything, and therefore, anybody will do anything to get it. It enslaves those whom it possesses, and it likewise enslaves in a more sordid way those who have none of it. The man who has money masters the destinies of those who have it not.

"I cannot see why money, which is the greatest thing in life, should not be more or less evenly distributed," he pleaded. "By distributing money evenly, I do not mean to say that all the money in the country should be cut up into equal bits and that everybody should get a bit of it. But, on the contrary, I believe that the ownership from which money springs should be vested in the whole community. In other words, as I understand it, I am a socialist. I have hardly read a book on socialism, but that which I have just enunciated I believe in general to be their theory. If it is their theory, I am a socialist."

There were, of course, limits to Patterson's socialism. "Whenever socialism comes in," he said, "I shall abide by its rules, but at present I do not intend to give any money or other property I have to less fortunate individuals." Nor did he have any idea of associating with the foreign-born of New York City. "New York is the last place I'd settle in," he made clear. "It's too cynical and self-satisfied with present conditions. It isn't sufficiently American!"

Patterson was aware of the fact that Karl Marx was not an American author. Marx's *Capital,* he told the readers of the *Saturday Evening Post,* "is so heavy, dry, deep, and closely argued that it is never furnished to beginners. Its first 90 pages, unfortunately, are the most intricate and involved of all."

Patterson may not have been a great reader, but he was none the less a member of the national executive committee of the Socialist Party. At mass meetings in Chicago he was a convincing speaker, as truculent as if he were asking for trouble in a saloon. If he hadn't talked with a strong Grotonian accent, and admitted he was well-born in the first few words, no one would have taken the lean young man with the close-cropped hair and the stubby fingers for a member of one of the leading Chicago families.

"You will never get anything from us capitalists by coming along with your hats in your hand and asking for it," he informed one working-class audience. "The only way you can get it is to fetch us down." As far as he could see, there was no point in playing fair with the boss. "Lie to your employers if they ask you how you voted," he advised. "Lie to them brazenly, courageously, and without an iota of subsequent regret or remorse."

But he was even more dramatic in his autobiographical moments. "I am," he said, "taunted, jeered at, and accused of being a traitor to the social structure in which providence placed me, the social stratum known as the coterie of rich men's sons or grandsons." Suddenly he recalled that Joseph Medill "did not, when fourteen years old, have a valet, as I had, to help dress him, black his shoes, and bring him his coffee while he lay abed mornings."

About this time Patterson published a semi-autobiographical sketch, *The Confessions of a Drone.* "I have an income of between ten and twenty thousand dollars a year," he disclosed. "I produce nothing—am doing no work. I . . . can keep on doing this all my life unless the present social system is changed." To change it was not too difficult. "As long as the working class is satisfied with its present arrangement of poverty, obedience, and laboriousness, the present arrangement will continue. But whenever the working class wants to discontinue the present arrangement, it can do so. It has the great majority."

As things were, a good many rich men's sons failed to take advantage of the opportunities at hand. "I do not think," he went on to say, "that it was entirely natural aptitude that marked me out for a university education, since I remember that frequently I had to pay money to tutors to drill into my head information of a remarkably simple character. I was fond of a good time, and that I had. . . . Having in this pleasant fashion achieved my education, I went to work in my father's business. I 'started at the bottom,' as the saying goes. I became a reporter at $15 a week. If my father had been a broker, I would have started in to sweep out the office at $3 a week. Most of my college friends who went into Wall Street seem to have done just that. But I knew I was play-acting all the time, just as they did."

Patterson was not play-acting, however, when he attacked the

Field will in an article for *Collier's*. Chicagoans of the older generation, who remembered how bitterly Joseph Medill disliked his benefactor, agreed that the young socialist was every inch a grandson of the editor of the *Tribune*.

Though the official estimate of the Field estate was $120,000,000, Patterson argued that it really amounted to $140,000,000, of which $72,000,000 was in trust for Marshall Field III. This sum was "not in the sterile form of gold eagles stored in a vault," he insisted. "His money breeds and multiplies, for it is in the form of real estate, bonds, and stocks, which are like interest-bearing mortgages; which are interest-bearing mortgages—mortgages against the labor of thousands of men. They are perpetual mortgages, too; for, let the thousands of men work their hardest until they close their eyes in final sleep, still the children of these thousands must go on working just as hard in the endless and hopeless task of paying off the mortgages.

"*Endless and hopeless task*—unless socialism comes. Socialism is seeking to arouse the thousands to denounce the perpetual mortgages held by the one, to pay not another dollar of interest on them, to refuse to transfer the hopeless debt to their children and their children's children."

Patterson calculated—how, he did not say—that the two Field boys enjoyed an income of $100,000 a week. "It is particularly galling to these thousands of working people to pay their annual tribute to the two little Field boys," he emphasized. "But from the dollar and cent standpoint, why was it better for the rolling-mill men to be mortgaged to Marshall Field, Sr., whom he never saw, than to Marshall Field III, whom he never saw? Why was it pleasanter for the consumer of gas to pay taxes to Marshall Field, Sr., whom he never saw, than to Marshall Field III, whom he never saw? Does the suburban resident live any worse now that he is paying rent to Marshall Field III than he did six months ago, when he was paying the same rent to Marshall Field, Sr.?

"Socialism says not; says it is no better to pay taxes to the old king in his vigor than to the young king during the regency; says that there should be economic kings no more than political kings; maintains that industrial democracy must succeed the industrial despotism just as the political democracy succeeded the political despotism."

The only American socialist with the right to call a nobleman by his first name—his sister Eleanor married Count Joseph Gizycki, a Pole with a castle in the Ukraine—Patterson protested that he meant what he said when he called for industrial democracy. In the winter of 1909 he denied the rumor that he was losing faith in the socialist cause. "I am a dues-paying member of the socialist party, in good standing, and expect to be one until the end of the chapter," he wrote the editor of the official socialist daily.

But socialism was only one of many careers open to a wealthy Chicagoan. Turning novelist two years after his attack on the Field will, Patterson published *A Little Brother of the Rich,* a study of young America based on his observations at Yale. Paul Potter, the hero of the book, was a Hoosier who went East to college and lived to regret it. Corrupted by the worldliness of his classmates, he jilted his childhood sweetheart and married a woman of low ideals. Soon he sank into the luxury of New York. "Do you call it home to live in a marble palace?" asked a friend who wondered at his extravagance. In the end Paul Potter realized his mistake. "My whole life is a horrible lie!" he confessed.

Next year Patterson expressed his convictions in *The Fourth Estate,* a drama dealing with the struggles of Wheeler Brand, a managing editor who sacrificed the woman he loved for the good of American journalism. In his analysis of the newspaper business Brand undoubtedly spoke for Patterson himself. "Newspapers start," Brand said, "when their owners are poor and take the side of the people, and so they build up a large circulation, and presently, as a result, advertising. That makes them rich, and they begin, most naturally, to associate with other rich men—they play golf with one and drink whisky with another, and their son marries the daughter of a third. They forget all about the people, and then, their circulation dries up, then their advertising—and their paper becomes decadent and feeble."

Having traced the influence of the money power in the modern world, Patterson was now ready to examine the workings of the Roman Catholic Church. In *Rebellion,* a novel brought out in 1911, he showed scant respect for the Roman attitude on divorce. Georgia Talbot Connor, the heroine of the story, was a Catholic wedded to a confirmed drunkard, but forbidden by the family priest to think of a separation. In the end she freed herself from the church, divorced her husband, and married the up-and-coming insurance salesman Mason Stevens.

Rebellion was Patterson's last attempt at fiction. Two years before its publication, he returned to the *Tribune,* prepared to spend the rest of his life in the newspaper business. Forgiven for joining the socialist party, he was elected secretary of the Tribune Company. His cousin Robert Rutherford McCormick was elected treasurer at the same time, suggesting that the day was not far off when the two would rule the family newspaper.

Like Patterson, McCormick was faithful to the principles of Joseph Medill. But while Patterson, paying little or no attention to the foreign-born for the time being, railed at Marshall Field and big businessmen with all of his grandfather's vigor, McCormick concentrated on the menace of the immigrant, feeling that our institutions were in greater danger of being undermined than in Medill's day.

After graduating from Groton and Yale, McCormick came back to Chicago convinced he could best serve the city by improving the tone of its politics. If he hesitated a little before making up his mind, no one could blame him, for he was an aristocrat by temperament. Though no dandy, he dressed with great care, and never appeared in public without being perfectly groomed, all of which must have been irritating to his unfastidious cousin.

In the spring of 1904, having read the law in the offices of Isham, Lincoln, and Beale, and taken a few courses at Northwestern University Law School, McCormick made his political début. Running for alderman of the 21st ward on the Republican ticket, he won. Next year he persuaded the voters that he was the best possible president of the Sanitary District. In this post he was in charge of the sewage system.

McCormick was a competent public servant, but a far from happy one. "As to my life since graduating from college," he wrote the secretary of his class at Yale, "which has been neither so interesting nor so successful as you seem to think, if you were to say that I have felt obliged to spend 90 per cent of my time in saloons, and the remaining 10 per cent in barrooms, you would have it about correct."

At times McCormick wished he were leading a dignified life. "I would advise no one to take to politics as a profession," he told a gathering at the Y.M.C.A. "The tenure of office is uncertain, and there are temptations. I don't mean money temptations, but the temptation that comes when you see your position in jeopardy."

Perhaps the greatest temptation McCormick faced was that of losing his temper. One night at Joliet, at the height of a banquet dealing with drainage canal matters, one of the local dignitaries was so irreverent as to suggest that Joseph Medill had dreamed of steaming down to Joliet in a yacht. McCormick took this to mean that his grandfather was one of the idle rich. Leaping to his feet, he struck the banquet table with all his might. "I came here as an invited guest," he said, "and I do not propose to listen to these insults." He then stomped out of the room. At midnight, when the other guests from Chicago boarded the trolley car that was to take them back home, they found the young man in a corner brooding over his grandfather's reputation.

At the next election the people of Chicago turned McCormick out of office and put a German immigrant in his place. Though this was a disappointment in one way, it was a relief in another. The young millionaire was now free to devote himself to the family newspaper. On March 1st, 1911, he became the president of the Tribune Company, and the editorship, if not already his, was at least within his grasp.

By then new minds were managing the Medill estate. Ambassador McCormick, whose health broke down soon after he retired from the foreign service, no longer had anything to do with the

Tribune. His successor as trustee was his wife, who had him removed to a sanitarium and declared incompetent by the end of 1909. Early next year, when editor Robert Wilson Patterson, Jr., died of apoplexy in a Philadelphia hotel, his widow assumed his duties as trustee, and James Keeley, one of the crack reporters of the Middle West, moved into the editor's office.

In those days the Tribune was an exciting newspaper to work for. Gangs of murderers were prowling the streets, beating, slugging, and killing newsboys. The *Tribune,* which had a gang of its own, proclaimed itself "The World's Greatest Newspaper" on the 29th of August, 1911.

"QUITE A CROQUET GAME"

Though there was violence in the Chicago newspaper business as early as 1905, the circulation wars proper did not break out until 1910, when, according to a spokesman for the *Tribune,* the head of the editorial, business, and circulation departments of the Chicago Hearst papers hired a gang of sluggers to terrify news dealers into boosting sales. The *Tribune* answered this challenge by hiring a rival gang, and the wars were on.

Years later, when the Chicago *Journal of Commerce* sued the Tribune Company for interfering with its newsstand distribution, Robert Rutherford McCormick told how many lives were lost in the battles staged by the private armies. "There was," he confessed, "a great amount of open lawlessness and many flagrant violations of the law, and . . . 27 news dealers and boys were killed and many others injured."

Sometimes McCormick wished the *Tribune* had never called itself "The World's Greatest Newspaper." Asked if the slogan on the masthead was supposed "to convey an idea," he replied that he didn't know. "That was there when I came in," he said, "and it is still there." In his embarrassment he forgot he was elected president of the Tribune Company a good five months before the slogan was adopted.

Shortly before McCormick was elected president, Max Annenberg joined the *Tribune* staff. The son of a Jewish junk dealer from Koenigsberg, East Prussia, he personally selected the sluggers who defended the *Tribune's* side of the argument, and selected them so wisely that the grandchildren of Joseph Medill never held his foreign birth against him.*

Max Annenberg—so he said—might never have left the Hearst papers to work for the *Tribune* if he had not been tired of breathing the air of Pullman cars. "I had a controversy with Mr. Hearst," he testified in the *Journal of Commerce* case. "I was then circulation manager practically of all the newspapers, in addition to the Chicago *American,* and I used to have to travel from New York to San Francisco, and I told Mr. Hearst one day that I would rather work for $8 a week than to travel that circuit. . . . So we had an arrangement that I was to spend six months of every year in Chicago."

When Hearst executives failed to live up to the terms of this agreement, Annenberg decided to ask young McCormick if there was an opening at the *Tribune*. In Annenberg's own words: "I then went over to the Tribune Company, and saw and talked to R. R. McCormick, who was then on the Sanitary Board, and told him I did not want to work on the Hearst papers any longer, and told him why, and I made a contract with them."

"Well, now," Annenberg was questioned by the *Journal of Commerce* attorneys, "everything was peaceful between the publishers and the carriers at that time in 1910, weren't they?"

"I will say they were not."

"What was the trouble?"

"The trouble was between Mr. Lawrence and the *Tribune*."

"What was that trouble?"

* Max Annenberg must not be confused with his brother Moses L. Annenberg, who served twenty-three months in prison for defrauding the Collector of Internal Revenue. At the time of his death in 1942 he was the owner of *The Daily Racing Form* as well as the Philadelphia *Inquirer*.

"Oh, well," Annenberg explained, "the trouble was that when the *Tribune* reduced their price to a cent in October, 1910, the *Examiner* [the morning edition of the *American*] was the only one-cent morning newspaper in Chicago, and when we made known by advertisements and billboards and otherwise that we were coming down to a cent, Mr. Lawrence got busy; he hired a great many labor sluggers working for labor unions under Larry Coffey, who was at one time sporting editor, and then was doing politics in the City Hall; he had such men as Nick O'Donnell, Nick Altman, who was killed in the Briggs House hotel. He had Dutch Gentleman, he had—oh, I can name probably eight or ten more who were instructed to go around in automobiles and slug any boy who cut their order or had their order cut or would permit the *Tribune* to replace an *Examiner*, because it went to a penny—and to give them to understand that they were not only through with the newspaper business, but that they were through on this earth. . . .

"And to meet the opposition, I knew the newsboys of the *Tribune* pretty well, I went around and told them that the Tribune Company would protect them in every way, and that we wanted people to have the *Tribune* if they wanted it. And the controversy got—"

"Wait a minute!" Annenberg was interrupted. "Did you hire any sluggers?"

"Let's see. I had Mossy Enright working for me, Jim Regan, Walter Stephens, and Arthur McBride."

"Quite a few well-known characters?"

"Four well-known sluggers."

"Quite a croquet game?"

"Yes, sir."

"How many other men of that character did you get?"

"At one time, in that battle, there were 60 men employed."

"By you?"

"No, by both of us."

"How many by you?"

"I had about as big an army as Mr. Lawrence had."

"About 30 apiece?"

"Yes, sir."

"How long did this struggle continue in 1910, where you had 30 sluggers and the other fellow had 30 sluggers?"

"Oh, I should say for about two or three years, a couple of years, anyway."

"Was anybody arrested during that time in connection with the struggle?"

"No, not that I know of." *

Meantime the *Tribune* was steadily increasing its circulation. In 1910, before the appointment of Max Annenberg as circulation manager, there were only 188,818 readers of "The World's Greatest Newspaper," and both the *News* and the *American* reached a wider audience. But the figures for 1918 told a different story. With 410,818 readers, the *Tribune* for the first time in its history was the best-selling newspaper in Chicago.

Annenberg had every right to be proud of the results achieved under his leadership. "I maintain," he declared shortly before the *Journal of Commerce* case was settled to his satisfaction, "that the *Tribune* can sell anything from a toothpick to a flat building. That means dominance in the advertising field. Some papers can sell toothpicks and some can sell flat buildings. We can sell anything. You don't need to advertise in any other paper when you advertise in the *Tribune*."

"COLD-BLOODED MURDERERS"

Of course the *Tribune's* peculiar prestige was not without its disadvantages. When editor James Keeley assailed the machine politician William Lorimer, hurting his chances of a career in the United States Senate, Lorimer turned on his attackers and forced

* According to Ferdinand Lundberg, whose *Imperial Hearst* gave the first detailed account of the circulation wars, there was no grand jury investigation worthy of the name.

the Congressional committee judging his fitness for office to examine certain aspects of *Tribune* history. If Lorimer succeeded in nothing else, he proved that the Tribune Building was a favorite resort of criminals, both before and after the outbreak of violence in 1910.

"What is the name of the man who was killed in the *Tribune* office by falling down the elevator shaft?" Keeley was asked by Judge Hanecy of the Congressional committee.

"Killed?"

"Yes; he died shortly afterwards, I think," the Judge put in.

"We killed a man," Keeley began, "a man was killed five or six—"

"When you say *we,* do you mean that you participated?"

"Oh, no, Judge."

"What do you mean by *we?"*

"I was using the word *we* as representing the company," Keeley replied. "I was going to state that we killed a man, or a man was killed, in an elevator shaft, five or six years ago. I think I know what you are driving at now. The man was not killed at all."

"What did happen to him?"

"He was beaten up, thrown down the elevator shaft, and shot at."

"From where to where?"

"He was on the mailing floor."

"Tell us the number of it."

"The first floor below the street level."

"No, but where was he thrown from?"

"I say, he was on the mailing floor, the first floor below the street level, and he was thrown to the pressroom floor, the second floor below the street level."

"How many floors?"

"He was thrown down one."

"One floor?"

"Yes."

"And he was beaten up before that happened, was he not?"

"Yes, sir."

"And made unconscious, was he?"

"No, I think not."

"What happened to him after he was thrown down the elevator shaft to the floor below?"

"I was not in Chicago then. Yes; I was. I left Chicago that day."

"Not because of that?"

"Not because of that, Judge, no."

"What happened to the man?"

"Then he was thrown down the elevator shaft, and I think the fellow that was after him jumped down on him. No; he did not. Some of the pressmen or stereotypers picked up this man and took him over to a big washbasin there, and started to wash the blood off him; and the fellow who was after him came down after him with a gun and shot at him."

"He was prostrate and unconscious, was he not?"

"No; he was standing up at this big wash trough, and was being washed and helped by some of the other men."

"Did he drive the other men who were trying to relieve the injured man away from him?"

"No; they got after the man with the gun."

"Who did?"

"The men who were helping this injured man."

"He shot at the man he had thrown down the elevator shaft first, did he not?"

"I think he did, Judge, as he came down."

"Did the bullet strike the man?"

"I do not think it ever did."

"He was never prosecuted, was he?"

"He was not."

"He was never arrested?"

"He was not."

"And was never indicted?"

"He was not."

"And no prosecution of any kind was made against him by complaint, indictment, or otherwise? By either the *Tribune* or any of its officers or employees?"

"No, sir."

"Was the man who was thrown down the elevator shaft an employee of the *Tribune?*"

"I think he had been until that morning or until the day before. My recollection of the circumstance is that he had been discharged, and that he came in there, and he had a row with this other man over the amount of pay that was due him, and that he first pulled a gun on this man who assaulted him, and shot at him, I believe."

"Do you not know there were no shots fired until the man who threw the other one down the elevator shaft went down and fired?"

"That is right, Judge. They had a fight for the gun, and they beat each other up, I think, with the butts of the guns."

"Was the man who threw the other one down an employee of the *Tribune?*"

"He was."

"In what capacity?"

"In the circulation department."

When asked to define the duties of the "wrecking crew," as the gang of sluggers was sometimes called, Keeley did not hesitate to blame organized labor for the killings. "There have been two wrecking crews," he said, "and the various unions in one trade have been split, one side has been fighting the other, and as a matter of fact, in the last year, they have had gangs of murderers out—"

"Murderers?"

"Yes," Keeley admitted, "cold-blooded murderers, and they have been killing on both sides. That describes the wrecking crew."

"You knew Moss Enright?" Keeley was asked as the Congressional committee fixed its attention on the *Tribune's* friends in the underworld.

"Yes; certainly," Keeley answered. "When I found out who he was I fired him. I got his name. I can give you the names of three other people that Mr. Annenberg had over there that I got rid of."

"Well, who are they?"

"Walter Stephens, Jim Regan, and—well, I can only give you the names of two. There is another one of them. There were four of them."

"Gentleman?"

"No, I do not think they were gentlemen."

"Were they of the Gentleman family? You know I do not mean that as a title, but as a name."

"Yes, I know. I do not think so, Judge. I do not know. I will say that we had Mr. Enright and Walter Stephens and the other man I mentioned, and another man, but what his name was, I do not remember. You probably have it there, and it may recall it to my mind."

"One of the two men whose name is Gentleman was murdered not so long ago in Chicago."

"Yes; a man named Gentleman was killed."

"Somebody went right up to him and put a gun to his stomach and fired it and killed him."

"Yes."

"And that was done in broad daylight, in a saloon there?"

"Yes; on State Street."

"Who was it that did the killing?"

"There seems to be a diversity of opinion as to that."

"Did not somebody confess that he did the killing?"

"Yes; I think he confessed, but I do not know whether his confession was really accepted as the truth."

"Was it not Moss Enright?"

"Moss Enright; yes . . ."

"You knew that Moss Enright made a confession that he killed Gentleman, didn't you?"

"I only knew what I read in the paper or was told in the office, and I have no recollection about the details of that story. If you are driving at the fact that I suppressed it, I will say that I did not. . . ."

"Did not Moss Enright say at the time that he confessed to murdering Gentleman that he worked for the Chicago *Tribune?*"

"I don't know whether he did or not."

"And you don't know that the *Tribune* did not print that part of his confession?"

"I don't know, sir. The paper is the best evidence of that. In the first place, I don't know whether he said it. I said that he did work for the *Tribune* at some period, and I don't know whether he said it or whether we printed it."

Though Keeley held on to his job during the Annenberg terror, he and the circulation manager did not always see eye to eye. In the spring of 1914 he resigned from the *Tribune,* and with $250,000 put up by Samuel Insull took over the management of the short-lived Chicago *Herald,* newly created by the merger of the *Inter-Ocean* and the *Record-Herald.*

As soon as Keeley withdrew, McCormick and Patterson became co-editors and publishers, the former in charge of the business end of the *Tribune,* the latter of the features. Taking a cue from Keeley, who once signed the great German-American painter Lyonel Feininger to draw a comic strip, Patterson followed the funnies eagerly. One day he reached the office with the inspiration for a strip based on the adventures of an orphan. He called for a cartoonist, and the two worked out the continuity for *Little Orphan Annie.*

Meanwhile Annenberg kept close to the news. Far more intelligent than either McCormick or Patterson, he did not intend to see the circulation he created destroyed by a youthful error of judgment.

PREACHERS TO THE PEOPLE

The Chicago in which Max Annenberg was so important was a different city from the one in which Marshall Field went his quiet way to work. It was, indeed, no longer a city at all in the nineteenth-century meaning of the word. By the second decade of the twentieth century Chicago was more of a mart than a metropolis, a city abandoned by the well-to-do.

With the coming of the automobile, thousands of middle-class families decided that life in the suburbs was ideal. Some fathers and mothers crowded west, bringing up their children in Oak Park, Riverside, and River Forest. Others advanced into the North Shore, settling in Evanston, Wilmette, Kenilworth, Winnetka, Hubbard Woods, Glencoe, Ravinia, Highland Park, and Lake Forest.

Though real estate values held firm in the Loop—State Street remained the shopping center of the entire Middle West—this rush to the suburbs undermined property on the South Side. South Michigan Avenue, Indiana Avenue, and Prairie Avenue, once so proud of their palaces and châteaux, sank first into neglect and then into misery, and what well-to-do families were left made their homes near the Midway of the University of Chicago.

If the North Side—that is, the Near North Side centered in Streeterville and the Gold Coast—held its own, it was because a determined group of millionaires, most of them with villas in Lake Forest, insisted on town houses and apartments for winter use on Lake Shore Drive and Astor Street. Even so, ruin attacked the once comfortable streets south of Division and west of Wabash and State.

In this new Chicago—a city of wage earners, many of whom enjoyed large salaries, but few of whom possessed the leisure to criticize the policies of the *Tribune*—Max Annenberg felt free to advise the people on international affairs. "France is a corrupt and immoral nation," he declared in 1914. "Belgium is not much better. But Germany is in the full bloom of health and power."

Annenberg no sooner expressed his admiration of Imperial Germany than Robert Rutherford McCormick made up his mind to experience modern war at first hand. Getting in touch with his mother, and his mother's friends in St. Petersburg, he arranged to visit the Russian front. This decision called for a stout heart. "I wondered whether I retained the physical courage to go upon the battlefield," McCormick revealed in the book he published on his return. "I knew that physical courage was as much dependent upon training and practice as any other form of physical activity. For years I had had none of this training, but, on the other hand, had been steeped as fully as any other in the cult of cowardice which has been such a distinct feature of modern American intellectual thought."

Fortunately life in the Russian trenches was not all blood and thunder. "Around one of the curves," McCormick reported, "we find a cave opening to the rear. In the cave is a table and on the table all kinds of good things to eat. Caviar, sardines, cheese, canned lobster, cake, more caviar, radishes, cold meat, and to drink, tea. . . ."

This is not to suggest that McCormick was a frivolous observer. His book, *With the Russian Army,* was dedicated to Grand Duke Nicolas Nicolaievitch, Commander-in-Chief of all the armies, "who, as a sign of friendship for America, invited me to visit the troops under his command, and who, as a further sign of friendship, permitted me to see the inside of the Russian military organization and frontier fortresses, so that our country might have the benefit of Russia's unequaled experience in military affairs and might be able to adopt such of her methods applicable to our particular conditions."

Under grand ducal auspices McCormick drew near the battlefield. "What," he asked, "is the strange psychology that causes the mind depressed by the sight of wounded men to be cheered by the sound of the cannon that wounded them, the popping corks of the wine of death? What is it causes the drunkard to gladden at the sight of liquor, the drug victim to smile at the poisonous needle? Is it that, born to die, we have an affinity for what destroys and draw back only when too late?" At last McCormick reached the front lines. "Now," he wrote, "we are to visit the place where the wine of death is spilled."

Back in Chicago McCormick rebelled against the limitations of the profit system. "Here I am at home again at my desk," he said, "where the first thing I see each morning is yesterday's balance sheet, same as it used to be before, and I have written a book, not phrasing it as a wise man should with a single eye to sales, but with no higher aim than to serve my country, and as I look over the daily balance sheets, I know that this is stupid and will not pay. But," he added, "I have tasted the wine of death and its flavor will be forever in my throat."

Already a member of the National Guard, he grew a military

mustache and saved his evenings for the study of military history. The more he meditated, the more positive he became that the defenses of our eastern seacoast were inadequate. "With what enthusiasm does anyone think that the American people would rush to arms to drive back an invader of the seaboard?" he asked in 1916 in an article for *Century* magazine. "Eighty per cent of the people of the United States look upon the great fortunes as ill-gotten. The owners of these fortunes, for reasons satisfactory to themselves, have nearly all settled on one or the other seacoast.

"The people back home," he explained, "are hostile to the émigrés. New York and the northeastern seacoast are to them nothing but the homes of the dodging, obligation-shifting idle rich in whose behalf they would certainly feel no call to die. This rich element is itself non-military, and could furnish nothing for protection, nor would the not inconsiderable element depending upon it for ungenerous existence."

Like Joseph Medill, young McCormick was unwilling to count on the foreign-born in an emergency. "In addition to being the chosen home of those richest Americans who have not sought European domiciles, the eastern seaboard," he pointed out, "is the landing-point of foreign immigrants. Immigrants of long standing may have absorbed as much patriotism as the native-born, but the newly arrived immigrants are still foreigners in thought and in law. In the event of invasion thousands upon thousands of them would be legally bound to join the invaders, and none of them would be bound to help defend the country."

In the midst of all these worries McCormick found a congenial spirit in Amie Irwin Adams, the wife of his distant cousin Edward S. Adams. The daughter of General B. J. D. Irwin, the "fighting doctor" of the Civil War and the Indian wars, she sympathized with the young millionaire's impatience at civilian life. In 1915, having secured a divorce from Adams, she made McCormick her second husband.

Meantime Joseph Medill Patterson was doing a great deal of thinking about American foreign policy. In *The Note Book of a*

Neutral, published in 1916, he inferred that the Christian doctrine of the brotherhood of man was obsolete. "Our duty as Americans," he said, "is not to the extent of 1 per cent of 1 per cent to France, Belgium, Germany, or foreign humanity. It is to America, it is only to America, all to America, and to America always."

He was hard on Christian statesmen. "No American," he declared, "has a right to consider any interest save the interest of America. Any American in a position of power or influence who allows any consideration but the selfish interests of America to guide him is a traitor—unconsciously, perhaps, and without a sense of guilt, but still a traitor so far as the results go."

Having proved the quality of his patriotism, Patterson was ready to admit that we were uncivilized. "Our country is inferior to other countries in many, if not most of the higher arts of civilization," he said. America was also a land of loafers. "We are," he went on, "rich, fat, soft, and easy picking for any gunmen among the other nations."

The solution, Patterson hinted, was to model the America of the future on German lines. "The amiable General Bernhardi said that war was a biological necessity, and made for progress. I think he was right, by and large, and that is why I do not think the German idea can be beaten in this war. . . . England is Germanizing its social structure as fast as possible, because so, and only so, can she gain sufficient strength to whip Germany."

With our entrance into the World War on the side of the Allies, Patterson left off preaching about "the German idea." A veteran of the National Guard, he became a Captain in the 149th Field Artillery, joined the Rainbow Division, and saw service for three months in the Lorraine sector. Besides taking part in the defense of Champagne under Gouraud, he fought in the Second Battle of the Marne, the Battle of Saint Mihiel, and the Battle of the Argonne.

Patterson's cousin Robert Rutherford McCormick had an even more distinguished war record. Attached to General Pershing's staff with the American Expeditionary Forces, he ended his military career as a Colonel, the possessor of the Distinguished Service Medal. According to a citation from the War Department, he displayed "rare leadership and organizing ability, unusual executive ability, and sound judgment."

Since he made such a favorable impression on the authorities in the War Department, it was unfortunate that he got on the nerves of the men around him. "I can't imagine McCormick ever doing a kind thing for anybody," one of his fellow officers told the author not so long ago.

Perhaps McCormick dropped one reference too many to Grand Duke Nicolas. "He was always lecturing on social problems," his fellow officer remembered. "He knew that democracy had got out of hand in Russia, and he was afraid that democracy would get out of hand here. He'd talk to us about his Russian experiences and about the bolsheviki and use a lot of big names we'd never heard of. Most of us were wondering what the hell has bolshevism got to do with squads right and squads left."

The men didn't like McCormick any better after he issued orders forbidding them to make friends with Rajah, his German wolfhound. "That's *my* dog!" he cried out whenever he heard footsteps near Rajah's kennel.

HOMER WOULD HAVE LIKED IT

As soon as the war was over, McCormick, Patterson, and Annenberg had to discuss the problem of what to do with the profits of the Tribune Company. The sudden rise in the circulation of the family newspaper provided the millions for almost any adventure, whether the starting of a tabloid in New York, the launching of a national magazine, or the building of a skyscraper in Chicago.

The idea of a tabloid in New York came from Lord Northcliffe, the energetic publisher of the London *Daily Mirror*. "New York's got to have a tabloid," he told Patterson early in 1919. "If the rest of you don't see the light soon, I'll start one myself." Patterson and McCormick did not hesitate for long. On the 20th of June, 1919, the Tribune Company brought out the first issue of the New York *Daily News,* with Patterson in charge and Annenberg to advise him.

According to Simon Michael Bessie, the authority on tabloids, the *News* was an "outright imitation" of Northcliffe's *Daily Mirror,* and a good many editors questioned the wisdom of copying an English model so closely. However, Carr Van Anda of the New York *Times* had no doubts about the *News'* ultimate success. "This paper," he prophesied, "should reach a circulation of 2,000,000." As a practical newspaperman, he realized that no newspaper with Annenberg for circulation manager was likely to fail.

On the first day the *News* sold 200,000 copies. Though the number of readers dropped to 32,000 by the end of the summer, it rose to 220,000 by the 1st of October, 1920, and by 1925 was over 1,000,000. For this Annenberg was mainly to blame. Instead of hiring sluggers to get immediate results, he moved slowly, coaxing the news dealers by offering 2 cents' profit on every Sunday paper —twice as much as they ever received before.

Patterson was willing to experiment with this new technique of winning readers. Leaving McCormick the absolute master of the *Tribune,* he settled permanently in New York in 1925, a puzzle to the publishers of the older dailies. Though no longer a socialist, he liked to feel that he was close to the masses. Once or twice he spent the evening in the Bowery. Often he rode the subway.

It was just as well that he and McCormick made money out of the *News,* for they lost $14,000,000 backing *Liberty Magazine.* A wiser investment was Tribune Tower, the 36-story Gothic skyscraper completed in 1925. Designed by Raymond Hood and John Mead Howells, it shot up on Michigan Avenue just north of the bridge over the Chicago River. To businessmen motoring to and from the North Shore suburbs it served as a reminder that there was no point in advertising in any newspaper but the world's greatest.

Louis Sullivan, who lived in a different world from most businessmen, saw no connection between Tribune Tower and the Chicago tradition in architecture. "It is an imaginary structure—not imaginative," he said. "Starting with false premises it was doomed to false conclusion, and it is clear enough, moreover, that the conclusion was the real premise, the mental process the reverse of appearance. The predetermination of a huge mass of imaginary masonry at the top very naturally required the appearance of huge imaginary masonry piers . . . to give imaginary support. Such weird process of reasoning is curious. It savors of the nursery where children bet imaginary millions."

No such thought occurred to the owners of the *Tribune*. To quote the official souvenir booklet of Tribune Tower: "Words cannot describe the beauty of the Taj Mahal. Man fails to voice the true impression of the magnitude of the Great Pyramid. To say that Tribune Tower is a stone skyscraper which is square in plan and isolated on all sides is to describe a Brahms symphony as a musical composition written for a number of instruments. To appreciate the music of this great master you must hear it. To appreciate the symphony in stone which is Tribune Tower you must see it, experience it, live in the same community with it."

No one could live in the same community with Tribune Tower and not recognize that it was an unusual building. Imbedded in the structure were 30 pieces of stone removed from many of the world's most famous monuments. One of the stones was taken from the Great Wall of China, another from the Parthenon, another from Notre Dame de Paris, and still another from the Alamo.

If these stones were curious, so were the inscriptions carved in the lobby, better known as the hall of inscriptions. One was signed Euripides, another Daniel Webster, and still another Joseph Medill. One was unsigned. It read: "The newspaper is an institution developed by modern civilization to . . . furnish that check upon government which no constitution has ever been able to provide."

The official historian of "The World's Greatest Newspaper" was naturally influenced by such surroundings. "Homer," he wrote, "would have liked to work on the *Tribune*. So would Horace, with his whimsicalities; Herodotus, with his wealth of incident. So would Balzac, Addison, Samuel Johnson, Dickens, Hardy, Kipling, and Mark Twain."

"EVEN AS DID THE GREAT WEBSTER"

If one did not mind listening to the shop talk of Annenberg's henchmen, the *Tribune* was probably an attractive place to work. Yet Medill McCormick, Robert Rutherford McCormick's older brother gave up his job on the family newspaper to seek his fortune in politics. As a vote-getter he was none too successful, reaching the United States Senate only to be retired from office at the end of his first term.

The young millionaire might never have thought of politics as a career if he hadn't married Ruth Hanna, the second daughter of the wise Senator from Ohio. With her to inspire him, he grew to believe that his education at Groton and Yale fitted him for something else than the newspaper business, which wasn't the most dignified of professions in 1907, the year he became publisher of the *Tribune*. Frightened by the rowdyism of the Chicago newspaper world, he almost immediately had five of his business rivals arrested for conspiracy. Three years later he resigned from the *Tribune,* a politician-to-be.

Like many a practical politician, he watched the Progressives battle for the regulation of the trusts. He even became a Progressive himself, but not without expressing his dislike of the professional reformers in the movement. "Think of me on the same platform with Jane Addams!" he protested. He also quarreled with Progressives who imagined that Roosevelt was an idealist. "Fellows," he said, "we must remember that T. R. is great because he understands the psychology of the mutt."

Judging from his first meeting with Harold Ickes, McCormick

did not understand any too well the psychology of the other members of the Progressive party. "I got at once a distinct impression of hostility," Ickes recalled. "He was supercilious and snooty and left me in no doubt he wasn't glad to meet me. I didn't fancy him, either. It was like biting deeply into a green persimmon."

In Ickes' opinion McCormick was a man "to be watched. He had a good deal of ability, and so did his wife. And they both rolled in arrogance as they rolled in wealth. Generally, however, they could be countered, because, in their disregarding selfishness, they tried to move too fast."

No doubt McCormick aimed to dominate the Progressive party in Illinois. In 1912 he ran for the State House of Representatives on the Progressive ticket, won, ran again in 1914, and won again. Flushed with these victories, he called a meeting of the State Central Committee on his own initiative. This was too much for Ickes' followers. "We all went down and tied him up good and tight," Ickes recollected. "No longer could he assume that he was the sole Progressive leader in Illinois. We had the organization by a large margin.

"After we had operated upon Medill (and Mrs. Medill, too, be it said) he asked if he might go back to Chicago with me on the train. It was a mournful procession. Shut up in a compartment, he licked his wounds and deplored the humiliation to which we had subjected him. . . . I was frank with him. I told him that if he would go along with the crowd we would be very happy to have him. But he had to get over the notion that he was a Mark Hanna or even a Hanna son-in-law. The organization was in our hands and we intended to use it for the good of the party."

Perhaps because he fancied that only simple-minded men were loyal under all circumstances, McCormick was not the most dependable of Progressives. On the eve of the Presidential campaign of 1912, he posed as the devoted friend of Senator Robert M. LaFollette, then seeking the Progressive nomination. Once LaFollette took him into his confidence, McCormick did his best to improve the chances of LaFollette's rival, Theodore Roosevelt, and when the Senator found out he was padding the campaign literature with praise of the hero of San Juan Hill, McCormick embarrassed him by tipping off reporters that he was withdrawing from the race. LaFollette denied the canard only to discover that his supporters were deserting him one by one.

One backer, however, stood by LaFollette to the end. This was Charles R. Crane, son of the Richard T. Crane who presumed to criticize D. H. Burnham's Chicago Plan. One of the truly generous millionaires of modern times, Crane was as unpretentious as he was unselfish, and far from eager to hold office. When a mysterious banking syndicate blocked his appointment as Minister to China in 1909, he held his peace until Wilson named him head of our legation in Peking.

As fond of traveling as he was averse to wrangling, Crane made it his princely business to wander over the world seeking out disinterested men. Like Sidonia, the omnipotent banker in Disraeli's novels, he had agents abroad who sent him confidential reports on political trends. When not poring over the dossiers of this personal State Department, he was likely to be calling on rising statesmen or leaders yet to be recognized. In Arabia he fell in with Ibn Saud; in China, with Chiang Kai-shek. In Central Europe he made a firm friend of Masaryk, whose son married his daughter Frances.

At home in America Crane was close to Justice Brandeis, President Harper of the University of Chicago, and President Eliot of Harvard. As soon as he observed that Eliot's health was failing, he presented him with a superb motor car, suspecting that long drives were his heart's delight.

All this while Crane was a thoughtful citizen of Chicago. The day after the Iroquois Theater went up in flames, taking the lives of two of his nieces, he sent for the country's leading specialist on fire prevention and financed a study of theater safety which became the classic on the subject. The next minute he was thinking of the Crane employees. Though he left the management of the company to his younger brother Richard T. Crane II, he insisted on setting up a million-dollar trust fund for the widows and children of workers in the factory. Come election time, he was equally altruistic. Wistfully, and fully conscious that the odds were hopeless, he put up the money for one campaign after another for responsible government in the City Hall. In the end his open-handedness became a legend. "You never had to ask Charles Crane how much money he was going to give a good cause," Harold Ickes told the author. "You always knew he would give until it hurt."

Medill McCormick, who was not so easily distracted, concentrated on his own political future. In 1918, two years after he was elected to Congress on the Republican ticket, he broke into the Senate where he made a name for himself as a nationalist of unusual insight. Unlike many of his colleagues, he saw through a bill guaranteeing fair rents for government workers in the District of Columbia. "Does not this legislation suggest something of the legislation which Mr. Lenin has put into effect?" he asked. He also perceived the danger of allowing foreigners on the Senate floor. Appalled, he introduced a resolution barring them for all time.

Probably no foreigners were more irritating to the young Senator from Chicago than the Czechs and Slovaks with their dream of a democratic republic. As he saw it, it was sheer idiocy to suppose that one race could live in peace and good-will with another. "The treaty-makers," he emphasized, "have compacted within the boundaries of Czechoslovakia the very diverse, warring, racial elements which made representative government and national purpose impossible in Austria-Hungary. . . . At one end of the new State the population must instinctively seek union with its kinsfolk of Germany, and at the other, union with its Magyar brethren, while in the center religious strife has already separated the Slovaks from the Czechs."

Fortunately for our relations with Prague, both Masaryk and Beněs realized that McCormick spoke for himself, and not for the American people. Our first Minister to Czechoslovakia, who was none other than Richard T. Crane III, the son of Charles R. Crane, very likely dropped a hint of the Senator's love of tall talk.

McCormick often referred in public to the education he received as the son of an ambassador. "Certainly," he reminded an audience of Chicago women, "I have naught but good will for those peoples of the Old World whose tongue I speak, among whom I traveled, among whom I went to school as a boy, whose cities and whose countrysides I know, and many of whose statesmen I count among my acquaintances or my friends. But I do not conceal from myself the plain truth that the politics of Europe is in the hands of an International Tammany!"

No wonder he opposed our entrance into the League of Nations. Though he drafted a child labor bill, proposed a waterway from the Great Lakes to the Gulf, drew up a plan for a national budget system, and headed a committee investigating our occupation of Haiti, he did not begin to spend on these projects the time and energy he devoted to exposing the shortcomings of Wilson's scheme for world peace. This was no child's task, for many Americans were eager to participate in an international organization.

Perhaps no one sensed the people's yearning for the League as keenly as McCormick's fellow isolationist Watson of Indiana. "I don't see how we are ever going to defeat this proposition," he complained to Henry Cabot Lodge, the leader of the Irreconcilables in the Senate. "It appears to me that 80 per cent of the people are for it. Fully that percentage of the preachers are right now advocating it, churches are very largely favoring it, all the people who have been burdened and oppressed by this awful tragedy of war and who imagine this opens a way to world peace are for it, and I don't see how it is possible to defeat it."

"Ah, my dear James," Lodge broke in, "I do not propose to try to beat it by direct frontal attack but by the indirect method of reservations." This was, of course, only the bare outline of Lodge's strategy. While he stalled for time in the Senate, hysteria was to be aroused in every State in the Union. Andrew Mellon, Henry Clay Frick, and many other nationalistic millionaires were glad to contribute to a campaign of this sort.

Medill McCormick did his part by explaining that once we

entered the League, hordes of Asiatic immigrants would sweep across our boundaries. "You are willing," he answered an admirer of Wilson, "to see efficient and economical Japanese operating our street railways, to find Hindoo janitors in our offices and apartments, to hear the hands of busy Chinese craftsmen driving rivets, joining timbers, laying brick . . . but I am utterly opposed to a plan which may introduce Asiatic labor into America."

He went on to hint that Wall Street was at work behind the scenes. "If a determined drive is made to have the United States join the European countries, then the activity of the international bankers will be brought in. Then will be brought down the books of the international bankers to help us determine whether they disclose a motive or not, whether they disclose exorbitant profits made out of the necessities of the Allies; whether any of the bankers had Russian or other bonds the future value of which would depend upon their endorsement in American blood. I am not charging anything venal against the bankers," he added.

Meantime the *Tribune* left no doubt of where it stood. "Intellectual internationalism and bolshevik internationalism will corrupt the nationalistic essence of a nation," read one editorial, "and we know that Americans are not willing to have their national essence corrupted."

With the election of Harding, hailed by Medill McCormick as a "man of ripe experience, of deep learning, and of great power," there was no danger of our joining any kind of world government. Even so, the Senator from Chicago anxiously studied developments in Europe. Unlike other members of the foreign relations committee, he felt that France was a menace to world peace. One day he rose from the floor with a resolution forcing the State Department to publish the figures on the military expenditures of the Third Republic.

At this affront to the French government, many thoughtful Americans lost patience with McCormick, and the New York *Times* advised "our French friends . . . to look behind forms to realities, to consider not merely words but the man who utters them. Let them catch any ordinarily intelligent American in Paris and ask him how much importance is to be attached to anything that Senator McCormick does. They would swiftly get the answer: 'None whatever.' The fact that Americans know their own lightweight busybodies and simply laugh at them when they posture on the international stage does not, of course, lessen the gross impropriety of a United States Senator behaving in the fashion of Mr. McCormick. But foreigners ought to be informed, so that they may be reassured, of the way in which our little great men are regarded at home."

McCormick had a different impression of his importance. "I have sought humbly to do my duty, even as did the great Webster," he enlightened the women voters of Chicago. About this time he let it be known that he was eager to become the next President of the United States.

This was not to be. Running for renomination to the Senate in the spring of 1924, he was sentenced to political oblivion by the voters of his own party. On the following 25th of February the forty-seven-year-old millionaire was found dead in his Washington apartment. Some said he died of a gastric hemorrhage; others, of a broken heart.

Though he left his widow and three children a farm near Rockford stocked with the finest Holsteins in the State, a peaceful old age in the country had no appeal for Ruth Hanna McCormick. In 1930, at the end of her first and only term in Congress, she spent $245,000 capturing the Republican nomination for the Senate, only to lose the election to James Hamilton Lewis. Another woman would have hesitated at the expense, but not this daughter of Mark Hanna.*

Wiser than Ruth Hanna McCormick, both Robert Rutherford McCormick and Joseph Medill Patterson sensed that the rebuff

* Afterward she married Congressman Simms of New Mexico who was at her bedside when she died in Chicago on the last day of 1944. As her first husband would have wished, she was a member of the America First Committee.

of her husband in the primaries marked the temporary eclipse of the House of Medill, and for the rest of the decade neither millionaire was aggressive. The fact is, businessmen were shaping all of the decisions of the nation, leaving little if any power in the hands of the intellectuals of the left or the right. If there was no time for reforms, neither was there any room for a philosophy of life based on suspicion of foreigners and the foreign-born. Too many Americans were earning too much money and having too good a time.

If Marshall Field III, whom we left at the age of twelve at his grandfather's funeral, had chosen to live in Chicago in this period, he would have enjoyed the homage due the grandson of the greatest of all Chicago businessmen. But he preferred to live elsewhere, thrusting the burden of ruling the city on the shoulders of Samuel Insull.

CHAPTER SEVEN: *The Age of Insull*

ANXIOUS FOR ELEGANCE

To SAY that Samuel Insull was all-powerful in the '20s does not completely dispose of the decade. Though it was worth a million dollars to be seen talking to the bluff Englishman on LaSalle Street, he was frequently edged off the front page, sometimes by William Hale Thompson, with whom he was on the best of terms, sometimes by the great murderers of gangland, and sometimes by Harold and Edith Rockefeller McCormick, both of whom were anxious for elegance in a hurried world.

Yet Harold McCormick was far from the complete hedonist. If not a poet, he was a poetic character, too vague to will himself a life of pleasure. Often he was troubled in luxurious surroundings by the memory of the Bible readings in the home of his father the reaper king. More often—for he was generous—he was caught in the effort of protecting the fine arts in the Middle West. When Frank Lloyd Wright fell into financial difficulties, he joined the little group of philanthropists who came to the rescue. He also poured hundreds of thousands into the Chicago Civic Opera Company, underwriting season after season of Tito Schipa, Edward Johnson, Galli-Curci, and Mary Garden.

Another millionaire might have made much of these gifts, but Harold McCormick was too sensitive for the role of a braggart. He was also too lovable to quarrel with anyone, and after Edith divorced him in 1921, refused to say anything ill of her. Instead he remembered each of her birthdays with a perfect rose.

Since he dreaded the limelight, he did not know what to make of the publicity that followed the marriages of his children, all three of whom chose partners many years their senior. Mathilde, when only eighteen, became the wife of Max Oser, a Swiss cavalry officer of fifty-three. Her sister Muriel, who went to the altar at twenty-nine, sought her happiness with Elisha Dyer Hubbard, a gentleman farmer the same age as Oser on his wedding day. And Fowler, the present president of International Harvester, was but thirty-two at the time of his union with Anne Urquhart Stillman, the fifty-two-year-old divorced wife of James A. Stillman of the National City Bank of New York.

Though each of these matches brought on a storm of press notices, they did not create anything like the cyclone of notoriety that swept down on Harold McCormick in the summer of 1922 when, shortly after his recovery from a pitilessly publicized gland operation, he married the Polish opera star Ganna Walska. As her fourth husband he was written up in every country on earth.

Madame Walska was indeed a remarkable woman. "The moon is my faithful friend, my inspirer," she confided in her autobiography *Always Room at the Top*. When circumstances interfered with her career as a singer, she weaved one of the satisfying legends of postwar Europe, astounding Chicago with the scale of her establishments. She kept two homes in France, a town house in Paris, and a chateau near Versailles, and in neither was the entertaining mean. Champagne at her table was sipped from seventeenth-century glasses, the gardenias in her finger bowls were flown by plane from London, and the gifts to her guests were handed out by Isadora Duncan girls in tunics.

"My heart," she explained in her autobiography, "is so soaked with sensitivity that life's minutest emotion, even inaudible sound, vibrates in me. Like an enormous sponge that swallows every drop of moisture in the atmosphere, I absorb everything. . . ." She was, however, slow to appreciate the Industrial Revolution, and did not realize the importance of International Harvester until Harold McCormick gently reminded her of the family fortune.

In Madame Walska's own words: "When I moved to my château near Versailles, Mr. McCormick, sweet as only he can be, on learning that I owned a farm, had a charming idea for my birthday, to send me all the machines that International Harvester produces. At six in the morning, to my great surprise, when I looked through the window my eyes were greeted by a whole regiment of robot-soldiers. . . .

"For many days after, all my neighbors, the simple field laborers as well as the rich farmers, were coming to look at those machines with the same admiration that the women would look at an exhibition of rare jewelry. . . . In this quasi-religious atmosphere it was easy for me to catch the spark, the feeling of which not only changed my almost disrespectful disdain for the income from commerce, but filled my heart with gratitude toward those silent, obedient servants of humanity. After that day my whole conception was spiritualized."

But she never succeeded in fathoming her husband's love of Chicago, and in 1931 they parted. She went back to Paris, leaving him in the rich gloom of his father's palace on Rush Street, his home since the divorce from Edith.*

A block or two away, behind the iron gates of 1000 Lake Shore Drive, Edith McCormick held the most fashionable families of Chicago under her peculiar spell. A thin, dark woman with haunted eyes, she never questioned her right to do exactly as she pleased. Once, for no known reason she canceled a dinner for 200 at the last minute. "Were you taken ill?" she was asked.

"No."

"Then perhaps some member of the family was indisposed?"

"No," she replied.

She was ever-independent. Unafraid of the envy of her neighbors, she invested $125,000 in the Emperor's Carpet, a Persian rug from the collection of Peter the Great. Unafraid of a word of criticism from her father, she paid $1,500,000 for the emeralds of

* In 1938, three years before his death, Harold McCormick married his nurse, Miss Adah Wilson, whose portrait was painted by Salvador Dali.

Catherine the Great, $1,000,000 for a diamond dog collar and matching tiara, and $2,000,000 for a pearl necklace. Wreathed in these jewels, wrapped in an ermine cape of 275 skins from Ishima, she would step into her plum-colored Rolls Royce on a windy winter's evening, nod to the two men on the box, each of whom wore her plum-colored livery, and glide down Michigan Avenue to the opera at the Auditorium.

In all Chicago there was no opera-goer more conscientious than Edith McCormick. During the season she set her dinners at seven, and to make sure that none of her guests missed the curtain, timed each course with a jeweled clock at her elbow. At a flip of her wrist, her plum-clad servingmen would rush to remove all the plates from the table, trying the patience of the elderly men and women who had learned to linger over their dessert at Mrs. Potter Palmer's.

What made the scurry all the more perplexing was that Edith McCormick insisted on the highest style, in and out of the season. The menu, supervised by her omniscient butler Denham, was printed in French with raised gold letters, and whenever the table was laid for royalty—as on the occasion of Queen Marie of Roumania's visit to Chicago—the gilded silver service of Napoleon's brother-in-law Prince Camillo Borghese was brought out of the vaults. The service, 1,600 pieces in all, weighing more than 725 pounds, was designed by Percier and Fontaine, the favorite architects of the Emperor, and executed by Biennais and Odiot, the former of whom created the altar for Napoleon's marriage to Marie Louise, the latter, the cradle for the King of Rome. Each plate bore the Borghese arms—a dragon and a crowned eagle displayed against a ducal mantle—surmounted by the imperial crown of France.

Sometimes, fatigued by the glitter of the Borghese silver, Edith let her imagination roam at dinner on the glories of ancient Egypt. One evening she paralyzed the conversation of her guests by crying out that she was the reincarnation of Seti I, the child wife of Tutankhamen. "That was it!" she flashed when a gentleman at her right broke into a description of a couch and stool unearthed in the Pharaoh's sepulcher. "That little chair! As soon as I saw it, I knew. I had known for a long time that I had lived on earth before, but when I saw that chair, I remembered. That was my chair, and I was Seti I. . . . It was a lock of my successor's hair that was found in the tomb."

Now and then an unimaginative Chicagoan would snicker at Edith McCormick's flights of fancy, but most of her neighbors understood that her oddest pronouncements were simply the reachings of a lonely woman. Fretting in solitude, she plunged headlong into the quicksands of philanthropy. With Harold's help she subsidized the opera and provided the endowment for the John McCormick Institute for Infectious Diseases, named after their first-born who died in infancy. Alone, she planned a vast zoo on the Far West Side. When none of these gifts gave her the key to companionship, she issued a dark communiqué from 1000 Lake Shore Drive. "I want to give the public my inner motive for founding the Chicago Zoo Park," she said. "It is for the study of the psychology of animals. When we can make scientific deductions of the actions and reactions of animals, we will find ourselves in a position to reach the human being. We must get nearer animals to reach the human soul."

She failed to appreciate what money meant to others, which was strange, for she spent the war years studying psychology at the home of Jung. While abroad she granted James Joyce an allowance of 1,000 Swiss francs a month, easing if not ending his financial worries, then mystified him by returning with no explanation the present he made her of part of the manuscript of *Ulysses*. "Oh," she said, when the author called at her hotel, "you will need the script. You will possibly have to raise money by it sooner or later." The next day Joyce heard from her attorneys that there would be no more monthly payments.

Back in Chicago she drew close to Edwin Krenn, a young Swiss architect who had happily read Jung from cover to cover before setting out for the New World. During the long winter evenings they talked until all hours, sometimes discussing Jung's philosophy, sometimes the money to be made gambling on local land values. To John D. Rockefeller's daughter real estate speculation was fascinating. Egged on by Krenn and his schoolmate Edward Dato, she founded the real estate firm of Krenn and Dato whose operations, the wonder of sober realtors throughout the Middle West, ran from a chain of apartment towers on the plains of the Northwest Side to a never-to-be-completed summer colony in the old English style.

Krenn was truly grateful. Early each morning, ignoring the motor cars roaring down Lake Shore Drive, he rang Edith McCormick's doorbell, a bunch of wild flowers pressed in his fist.

"THROW AWAY YOUR HAMMER"

While Krenn was performing his delicate duty, gangs of murderers were shooting it out in broad daylight for the control of the bootlegging industry. Dion O'Banion, once a slugger in the circulation wars, was one of the more sentimental killers. He was very fond of his mother, and if he happened to pull a gun on an innocent pedestrian in a tense moment, might even send him a box of cigars at the hospital. Al Capone was not so restless. Depressed by the gunmen's accuracy in picking each other off, he did his best to make the underworld understand that peace would mean bigger profits for everyone. "I told them we were making a shooting gallery out of a great business," he assured a reporter after a heart-to-heart talk with his competitors.

Not that Capone convinced anyone he was a pacifist. "I've been accused of every death except the casualty list of the World War," he protested. On Saint Valentine's Day, 1929, he prudently whiled away the hours chatting with the District Attorney in Palm Beach. At eleven o'clock that morning four men, two of them in police uniforms, walked into a garage at 2122 North Clark Street—just a block or two beyond the boundaries of the Gold Coast—and in a few minutes disappeared in what looked like a police car. An hour or so afterward, when a truckman pushed open the garage door, he stumbled upon the machine-gun-riddled bodies of seven men lying in a pool of blood 40 feet wide. "Only the Capone gang kills like that!" one of the dying men whispered.

Since the Saint Valentine's Day massacre, like the other gang murders of the '20s, would have been unthinkable if newspapers hadn't exposed the impotence of the courts by hiring sluggers and paying no penalty, one way to end the crime wave would have been to force a grand jury investigation of the killing of the 27 newsboys. This, however, did not appeal to Mayor William Hale Thompson. A practical politician, he preferred to tease the *Tribune* rather than mortally offend its owners.

Thompson did not pretend to be an enlightened statesman. When he sat down in an armchair broad enough to accommodate his 200 wobbling pounds, he would roll his bloodshot eyes knowingly, and then undo the first two buttons of his pants, giving his anxious paunch the breathing room it required. A minute later he would be admitting he wasn't very bright. "I am a guy with the guts to speak right out," he described himself. "I've been attacked, lied about, and ridiculed. I may not be smart, but I'm smart enough to follow in the steps of the guys that made success."

Born in Boston, the son of a real estate speculator who moved to Chicago after seeing service under Farragut in the Civil War, Thompson narrowly escaped a college education. Instead he went cowpunching out West, dashing the hopes of his parents who had sent him East to a preparatory school for Yale. Later he held a job as a brakeman on the Union Pacific. When he returned to Chicago, it was not to go into business, but to become the captain of the Chicago Athletic Club's football team. It won an American championship, and there was nothing else to live for. In 1900, when the thirty-one-year-old sport-about-town ran for Alderman, he did so only to win a $50 bet from a friend. To his amazement he carried the ward, and from that day forward politics was his meat and drink.

By 1915 Thompson was an expert at horrifying the best people of Chicago, many of whom were already living in the suburbs. Crying "Throw away your hammer and get a horn!" he was elected Mayor by a landslide. In office he was ever aware of the German vote. The closer we came to siding with the Allies, the louder he raised his voice against meddling on the Continent. When we at last declared war on Germany, he hurriedly decided that he had been for "America First" all along. "Old Glory is good enough for me!" he announced.

In 1919, after trying for the Republican nomination to the Senate, and losing to Medill McCormick, "Big Bill the Builder" consoled himself with a second term in the City Hall. If the victorious Senator was the acknowledged leader of all Middle Western nationalists, the Mayor was an apt pupil. Cruder than McCormick, he was more forceful. Though there is no proof that he promised to "biff King George on the snoot," he published a pamphlet entitled *Shall Your Taxes Be Spent to Make Your Child Hate George Washington and Love the King?*

All this was gratifying to Samuel Insull, who was easily the most nationalistic of Chicago businessmen. When he discovered that Thompson, besides being a dauntless foe of the League, the World Court, and all other international organizations, was willing to appoint a Corporation Counsel of the right sort, he understood that here was the ideal Mayor.

As long as Thompson was in the City Hall, reformers had no chance of revoking franchises or revising utilities rates. At the Mayor's right hand, always on the watch for dangerous legislation, was Corporation Counsel Samuel Ettelson, who happened to be a law partner of Insull's retainer Daniel J. Schuyler.

At press conferences the Corporation Counsel saved Thompson the trouble of answering earnest reporters. "To put the Mayor's thought differently," he would break in when Thompson fumbled, "what he means to say is—" Then he would add: "The Mayor, boys, has given much thought to these questions. He feels deeply on them, far deeper than modesty allows him to admit. The Mayor, boys, has a great heart with a profound love of humanity. With his rugged independence, you may class him as a reincarnation of Abraham Lincoln."

"Now, Sam," Thompson would object, "don't put it too strong!"

"Pardon my outspokenness, Mr. Mayor," Ettelson would reply, "but we who are close to you realize daily that you are a veritable reincarnation of Abraham Lincoln, a Father Abraham come to earth again."

With the election of the Democrat William E. Dever in 1923, there was an end to this kind of talk in the City Hall. Many Chicagoans breathed easier, but not Samuel Insull. Fearing his hold over Thompson would soon be exposed, he read the papers with more interest than usual. When the Chicago *Daily News* struck at Thompson on the eve of Dever's campaign for re-election, beginning publication of a series of provocative articles by Donald Richberg, he reached for the phone. Sending for George Brennan, the boss of the Democratic machine behind Dever, he announced that either the series would stop, or he would spend half a million dollars if necessary to buy enough Democratic committeemen to swing a majority to Thompson. Brennan, who felt this was no bluff, begged the *News* to suppress Richberg's exposé. "I can't afford to lose my organization," he pleaded. The *News* surrendered, positive that Insull could and would buy the election outright if the articles continued.

Thompson easily defeated Dever at the polls. Serious-minded Chicagoans, impressed with the reforms in the school system carried out by William McAndrew, Dever's superintendent of schools, hoped against hope that Thompson would leave him unmolested in office. Such hopes were vain. "Big Bill the Builder" had the luckless superintendent suspended by the Board of Education and tried on the charge of being "a stool pigeon of the King of England."

SUCH WAS SAMUEL INSULL

For all his political power, Insull was a nervous capitalist. One noon, at a banquet for one of the local charities, he flew into a rage at the sight of a newspaper photographer snapping his picture without permission. "I'll see you get fired!" he yelled across the speakers' table, his spectacles dancing, his mustache soaking wet with exasperation. "You see if I don't! If you don't lose your job, my name isn't Samuel Insull!"

It was unfortunate that he lost his temper so easily, for he was a genius at utilities management, as even his bitterest enemies recognized. No wonder he reached for absolute control of the turbines of Illinois. "It matters not," he observed early in his career, "what the legislation of the moment may be, what the opinions of the politicians may be; eventually, all the electrical energy for a given area must be produced by one concern."

Sure of his aim, in 1907 he merged Chicago Edison into Commonwealth Edison and saw to it that its prosperity was enduring. Four years later he seized hold of another 80 odd firms and put together the Public Service Company of Northern Illinois. Like Commonwealth Edison, it was an operating company, and expertly managed. But this was not all. In 1918 he put himself at the head of the decrepit People's Gas, Light, and Coke Company, reorganized its auditing department, and modernized its plants. "Don't you think it is a pity, Insull," a friend asked, "that you have to start learning the gas business at your age?"

"No," he replied. "I'm having the time of my life. I am living it all over again." Thrilled with each new responsibility, he despised the luxury of delegating details.

With Commonwealth Edison, the Public Service Company of Northern Illinois, and the People's Gas under his command, Insull was the dictator of the electric light, gas, and power industry of

Chicago and its suburbs, and since his forte was watching the costs of operating companies, was of real service to the community. Unfortunately he tried for higher honors. Infatuated with the intricacies of high finance, he began experimenting with holding companies. His first was Middle West Utilities, created in 1912 to absorb a chain of power plants in southern Indiana. From the very beginning its financial structure was treacherous. Ten million dollars' worth of stock was issued, of which $4,000,000 was preferred, the rest common. All this was sold to Insull for $3,600,000. As he did not have the cash on hand, he supplied it by marketing all of the preferred and a million of the common for the necessary $3,600,000. He then turned over the proceeds to Middle West in exchange for $330,000 worth of utilities, keeping $5,000,000 worth of common for himself. For this common, as anyone can see, he paid not a penny. Possibly he did not understand what he was doing. "Assuming ordinary normal conditions," he once remarked, "there is no excuse for a man being dishonest, just the same as there is no excuse for a man being unhealthy."

At the outset Middle West controlled only 600 miles of lines serving 140 small towns. By 1917, however, it was operating in 11 States, furnishing power to 385 municipalities, only 228 of them in Illinois. Soon it bought out National Electric Power, the New England network of Albert and Victor Emanuel, and swelled to such a size that Insull in 1928 launched yet another holding company, Midland United. The horizon was clear, yet he trembled at the thought of unfriendly legislation. Taking out insurance against reformers' crossing his plans, he sponsored the most splendid educational campaign in the history of public relations.

"Get busy and do something!" he burst out one morning when a group of key executives confessed they did not know how to cope with public opinion. Overnight, the Illinois Committee on Public Utility Information was organized, with Insull's public relations chief Bernard J. Mullaney in charge. Speakers with the proper attitude toward government ownership were rushed to meetings of the League of Women Voters, the Kiwanis, and other influential audiences, a news bulletin was distributed to 900 Illinois newspapers, and pamphlets by the thousands were mailed to the schools. In the first two years alone of the Committee's existence, 5,000,000 pieces of literature were flung at the American public. "The Illinois plan is no accident!" Mullaney commented.

Mullaney was something of a realist, as those who worked with him well knew. "We are trying," he admitted, "to develop the idea rapidly among the newspapers that public utilities offer a very fertile field for developing regular, prompt-paying customers of their advertising columns. When that idea penetrates the United States, unless human nature has changed, we will have less trouble with the newspapers than we have had in the past." Politicians, he was sorry to say, were not half as dependable as newspaper editors. "I am fairly familiar with legislative practice and procedure and have not many illusions in that quarter," he made clear. "Sometimes the political road has to be traveled. When a destructive bill is pending in a legislature, it has to be dealt with in a way to get results."

Mullaney's boss was vexed by the slow pace of American politics. Never a champion of the people's rights, he lost whatever admiration he once had for democratic processes when, as chairman of the Illinois State Committee on Defense during the first World War, he had everything his own way, and made a brilliant success of the job. "You know," he told the other members of the committee, "I can do whatever I want in this State now."

In 1926 the masterful capitalist invested $237,925.19 in the primaries, $172,925.19 of it in Frank L. Smith's campaign for the Republican nomination to the Senate. The fact that Smith, in his capacity as chairman of the Illinois Commerce Commission, was forbidden by law to accept gifts from officers of utility corporations never entered into Insull's calculations, and no one was more surprised than he when the financing of the Illinois primaries was made the subject of a Senate investigation. At first he insisted that his contributions were none of the government's business; when he finally consented to testify, he did so reluctantly.

The Senators were eager to learn whether Insull used his own money, or Commonwealth Edison's, on Smith's behalf. "You said a little while ago," he was quizzed, "that you might have gotten a little, only a few thousand dollars from the till of the company."

"Oh, no!" he replied. "I said that there might be only a few thousand dollars of this total amount—"

"That you got from the company?"

"That one or the other of my companies might not have been reimbursed for."

"Then you did draw . . . $190,000 out of the till of the company?"

"That I do not know," he answered. "I would have to look that up." Shortly afterward he revealed that the $172,925.19 contributed to Smith's campaign was all of it borrowed from Commonwealth Edison "pending reimbursement of the company from my own funds as soon as I could conveniently arrange for it."

Insull protested that if he went to all this trouble, it was not to protect his business interests, but to watch over the foreign policy of our government. "I have a very strong opinion on the subject of the World Court," he let fall, inferring that Frank L. Smith was of the same mind. "I have some knowledge of international politics from not only an American but a European point of view. I have some decided prejudices in connection with the matter; and the strongest prejudice I have is that if this country became involved in membership in the World Court, they would finally be involved in very close relations with the League of Nations." He was privileged to interfere, he emphasized. "As being responsible for $650,000,000 of investment in Illinois, I have some right to take part in these affairs."

"Do I understand you to mean that you have a special right because you control this money?" he was asked.

"No, sir! No, sir!" he cried. "I have a special duty to the 100,000 stockholders and 150,000 bondholders in the State of Illinois. . . . But that is not the basis of my being interested in public affairs. I became a citizen of the United States because I wanted to exercise the right of franchise and take part in the public affairs of the United States, and the fact that I am a utility man should not be any deterrent to my being allowed to take part in them."

But Senator Norris of Nebraska refused to take Insull for a patriot. "Does anyone believe that he made those contributions . . . because of a patriotic interest in the welfare of his country? Does anyone believe that he was doing anything except making an investment from which he expected ample returns in due time? . . . It is quite apparent," Norris decided, "that his interest in the Senate is a financial one. He is interested in what he can get out of it. He is interested in making money, and in nothing else."

For once Insull did not receive full value for cash expended. Though Smith won the election despite the scandal, the Senate denied him a seat. This was welcome news to Julius Rosenwald, who so dreaded Insull's influence in Washington that he made the mistake, late in the campaign, of offering Smith 10,000 shares of Sears, Roebuck, valued at $550,000, if only he would withdraw.

The attempt to bribe Smith was one of Rosenwald's rare errors of judgment. A sounder businessman than Insull, he would in all likelihood have left a gigantic fortune if he hadn't explored the farthest reaches of philanthropy. On his death in 1932 he was worth no more than $17,415,500, having given away $63,000,000. Distributing such a sum was a troublesome task for a conscientious man. "I can testify," said Rosenwald, "that it is nearly always easier to make $1,000,000 honestly than to dispose of it wisely."

Like many another businessman, Rosenwald abhorred the sentimental approach to charity. "Philanthropy is a sickening word," he declared. "It is generally looked upon as helping a man who hasn't a cent in the world. That sort of thing hardly interests me. . . . What I want to do is to try and cure the things that seem to be wrong."

One such evil was discrimination against the Negro. "I am," Rosenwald once told a colored audience, "the inferior of any man whose rights I trample under my feet. Men are not superior by the accident of race or color; they are superior who have the best heart, the best brain. Superiority is born of honesty, of virtue, of charity, and above all, of the love of liberty. Of one thing you colored men can rest assured: the most intelligent, the grandest are on your side. The sympathies of the noblest are with you. Your enemies are also the enemies of liberty, of progress, and of justice."

Setting up the $20,000,000 Julius Rosenwald Fund, he financed public schools, Y.M.C.A.'s, Y.W.C.A.'s, and universities for the Negro race, besides contributing to the education of Marian Anderson and other colored individuals of talent. The Negro, however, was only one of Rosenwald's many interests. Aware of the hardships of the Jews in the postwar world, he handed out $3,600,000 for Jewish colonies in the Soviet Union. Sensitive to the distress of Central Europe in the '20s, he relieved the suffering of the starving children of Germany. At home he founded the Museum of Science and Industry and donated over $4,000,000 to the University of Chicago.

These millions were not inherited. The son of a Jewish peddler from Westphalia who built up a clothing business in Springfield, Illinois, Rosenwald got his business training selling suits on the road. In 1895, when thirty-three, he laid the foundation of his fortune by buying a one-fourth interest in the mail order house of Sears, Roebuck and Company. This was a canny investment, no matter if he denied he had a flair for business. "I never had any exceptional ability," he claimed. "To say that I had vision and foresight in going into Sears is nonsense. I went in simply because I saw a good chance."

Success did not go to Rosenwald's head. "I never could understand the popular belief that because a man makes a lot of money he has a lot of brains," he one day exclaimed. "Some very rich men who made their own fortunes have been among the stupidest men I have ever met."

Not half so shrewd as Rosenwald, Insull was far more excitable. In the morning, when he flipped on the lights in the bedroom of his vast apartment at 1120 Lake Shore Drive, he tingled from tip to toe at the thought that the power of Chicago was his, that

Commonwealth Edison was his, and Public Service, and People's Gas. Later in the day, when he stepped out of his motor at the entrance to his office building at 72 West Adams Street in the heart of the Loop, he had only to listen to the wrenchings of the trains on the "L" trestles to feel that God had put the coming and the going of the people in his hands. True, the street car lines were not his, nor the bus system, but the "L" was his, with its network north, south, and west. So were the three electric railroads of the city—the Chicago, South Shore, and South Bend, tapping the Far South Side and Gary on its way to the Studebaker plants; the Chicago, Aurora, and Elgin, reaching the pleasant communities on the banks of the Fox River; and the Chicago, North Shore, and Milwaukee, running north through the choice suburbs along the Lake, and cutting northwest into the lowlands of the Skokie Valley. It was at Libertyville, on the valley's edge, that Insull made his country home "Hawthorne Farm." Sitting on his lawn on summer afternoons, he had the satisfaction of spotting the never-ending cables of his power plants on the skyline.

He wore his glory openly, and had only to set foot in one of the better hotels—whether it was the brilliant Blackstone on South Michigan Avenue, the smart Drake overlooking the wonders of Lake Shore Drive, or the enterprising new Palmer House risen on the site of the old landmark—for the guests to start chattering of the money he was making. In 1929, the year People's Gas hit 404, Public Service, 435, Commonwealth Edison, 450, and Middle West, 570, he had, it was thought, $170,000,000 of his own. Charmed with this figure, a good many Chicagoans considered that he was a greater businessman than P. D. Armour, William Deering, or even Marshall Field.

Unlike the titans of earlier times, Insull spread his benevolence far and wide. In 1929 he was the president of 15 corporations, the chairman of 56, and a member of the board of 81. This meant that the sun seldom rose over Lake Michigan without his buying, or thinking of buying, a power-producing unit. He was not one to quibble if the price came too high. "What in hell would you do if someone came along and offered you three times as much as your company was worth?" swore one of the independents when asked why he sold out to Insull. Eventually Middle West was supplying electricity, gas, water, ice, and heat to over 4,000 country towns in Maine, New Hampshire, Vermont, New York, New Jersey, Pennsylvania, Delaware, Maryland, Virginia, West Virginia, North Carolina, Georgia, Florida, Alabama, Tennessee, Louisiana, Mississippi, Texas, Oklahoma, Arkansas, Nebraska, North and South Dakota, Indiana, Illinois, Wisconsin, Michigan, Ohio, and Ontario, Canada. As if this were not enough for one man to look after, Insull took an interest in bankrupt textile mills and paper plants and backed a real estate subdivision on the outskirts of Kansas City.

The prouder Insull grew of this burden, the longer stretched the shadow of Cyrus S. Eaton of Cleveland, the one man of whom he stood in mortal fear. Late in the '20s, when Eaton began buying blocks of Commonwealth Edison, Public Service, and People's Gas for the account of his new investment trust Continental Shares, Insull spent many a sleepless night wondering if a campaign was under way to oust him from the control of the operating companies. It was hardly comforting to recollect that Eaton enjoyed the confidence of Cleveland's richest family, the Mathers. What, Insull asked himself, if he were the Mathers' ally?

As collected as Insull was impatient, as suave as Insull was curt, Eaton would not have been human if he hadn't played on the Chicagoan's anxieties. When the two met on board a transatlantic liner, the Clevelander declined to talk over the utilities situation. In Insull's opinion this was an evil omen. "He made me very nervous," he said afterward.

The truth was Eaton had no intention of embarrassing the creator of Commonwealth Edison. "I had the greatest respect for Mr. Insull's imagination and Mr. Insull's ability," he told the author recently. "I would never have thrown him out of any of the companies. Unfortunately, certain individuals . . . certain friends of Mr. Insull went to him and put certain ideas in his head about me."

Poisoned with suspicion, Insull grew desperate if Continental Shares gained no more than a fraction at the close of the market. At last, in the beginning of 1929, he prepared for the worst. Advertising his need of capital to beat off raids on the operating companies, he founded an investment trust of his own, Insull Utility Investments.

For a time, all was well. Though the holdings which Insull and his family turned over to the trust were worth only $10,000,000, the stock they received in exchange shot to $143,000,000. Even so, Insull was restless. In the fall of 1929 he brought out a second investment trust, Corporation Securities. Like its predecessor, its appeal was to the little people. "Certainly," wrote Frank L. Devers, one of Insull's right-hand men, "there must be some clerk or stenographer, small merchant, or janitor, who has pretty much of a fixed income, and who could easily save $10 a month at 6 per cent interest, and who would like to accumulate money in this fashion. The success of our business has lain in our getting the small fellow to buy."

Meantime Insull was playing an important part in the cultural life of Chicago. Though his wife, who was once an actress, had returned to the stage in 1925 as Lady Teazle in *The School for Scandal,* later producing plays on her own at the Studebaker Theater, it was not drama but grand opera which caught the fancy of the promoter of Corporation Securities. Shortly after the war, perhaps because he understood that Chicago looked up to Edith Rockefeller McCormick as the patroness of the Auditorium, he began supplying cash to the Chicago Civic Opera Company. "We'll have no trouble in obtaining first-class talent," he predicted in the spring of 1922. "There is no place for the singers to go. If they want to stay at home and receive stage money, they may do so, but they'll have to come here to get real money." When certain well-meaning Chicagoans winced at the indelicacy of this approach to the fine arts, recalling that the real estate speculator Louis

Eckstein was endowing the finest summer opera in the world at Ravinia Park without any publicity for himself or his business, Insull was ready with an answer. "I am sure," he said, "that one cannot ignore the dollar without getting into trouble."

The more money Insull invested in the Chicago Civic Opera Company, the more he resented the Auditorium, knowing that no matter how much he contributed, Sullivan's masterpiece would always be associated in people's minds with the liberality of Harold and Edith Rockefeller McCormick. Positive that if Insull and opera were ever to be synonyms, the Auditorium must be abandoned, he shocked Chicago in the winter of 1927 by announcing that its usefulness was over. "Our present lease of the house ends next September," he informed the other guarantors. Adding that "we can get a renewal of the lease for a few years," he went on to say that "this block of buildings ultimately will be torn down, and we are faced with the absolute necessity of moving if we want to preserve our organization." Then he spoke of a new home for opera, to be built on the block bounded by Madison, Market, and Washington Streets and the Chicago River. Forgetting that the Auditorium was large enough to satisfy every need, he rejoiced in the fact that the new home would have 50 per cent more seats, as well as an enormous office building above the theater proper. "It cannot be purely monumental," said Insull of the $16,000,000 structure under contemplation. "It must be commercial, not only self-supporting but profitable."

And so, on the evening of the 4th of November, 1929, many of the most elegant motor cars in America rumbled through the gloom of the Loop, under the trestles of the "L," to the opening of the new opera house on the bank of the Chicago River. In the anxious minutes before the curtain rose on *Aïda,* critical Chicagoans gazed in stupefaction at the work of architects Graham, Anderson, Probst, and White. Was this crushing pile seriously intended to replace the Auditorium?

Opera-goers were disappointed in Insull, but so were investors. The afternoon of the opening, Middle West closed at 295, 275 points below the high for the year. But this was only the beginning of Insull's troubles. In the spring Eaton attacked quotations by unloading a part of his holdings on the open market.

When the Chicagoan protested, the Clevelander proposed that a new company be created of Continental Shares' interest in the Insull utilities, with Insull as manager. At that Insull started, sensing that there was now only one way out. Rather than work under his rival's orders, he would strain his credit to the limit and borrow the millions to buy Eaton out. Many millions were needed—no doubt more than Insull's investment trusts could provide. Although People's Gas was selling at only 255, Public Service at 272, and Commonwealth Edison at 285, Eaton felt that $400 a share was a fair price, and only agreed on $350 after hesitating for weeks. At that price the founder of Continental Shares got $56,000,000 for his investment, $48,000,000 in cash and $8,000,000 in Insull Utility Investments and Corporation Securities stock, both of which he disposed of in the following spring. Gossip in Chicago had it Eaton made $19,000,000 on the deal. Whether the rumor was true or false, he had only kind thoughts for Insull. "He paid me every penny without welching!" he commented.

But Insull was not happy, even though Eaton no longer owned a single share of his securities. With each new day of the depression, there were new creaks, new cracks in the financial structure of Middle West, Midland United, Insull Utility Investments, and Corporation Securities. At his wit's end, Insull ran bravely into debt to the New York and Chicago banks.

Chicago itself was cheerless, and Edith Rockefeller McCormick read no hope in the stars. "I am sure," she said shortly before her death in 1932, "that those living at the time of the birth of Christ must have experienced relatively the same problems which we are experiencing today. Since the birth of Christ there has been no astrological change of house until today. We are in the pains of childbirth, and in proportion to the pain is the severity of the suffering. This is not vicarious suffering, for each one of us is being uprooted. Uprooted, so that we face in the opposite direction to that which has been the direction for two thousand years. This change is inevitable, and no one can escape it. Its great purpose is the control of the balance of the universe. For this reason, there is no fear."

On Friday, the 8th of April, five weeks and four days after Mrs. McCormick issued this warning, Insull was in New York, face to face with the bankers from whom Middle West, Insull Utility Investments, and Corporation Securities had borrowed the sum of $87,250,000. Eleven institutions were involved, seven seriously. The Irving Trust had $5,000,000 at stake; the Guaranty Trust, $6,000,000; the Central Hanover, $7,500,000; the Bankers Trust, $11,000,000; the First National of Chicago, $16,000,000; the Continental Illinois National Bank and Trust, $31,000,000. It was only natural for the Continental to be supremely concerned, for it was the biggest bank in Chicago. The successor to Marshall Field's favorite, the Merchants' Loan and Trust, its leading stockholders were Field's heirs.

For an instant Insull was his old victorious self—his hopes fixed on the quality of the collateral in the bankers' hands. What better security could they ask for than 46,000 shares of Public Service, 110,000 shares of People's Gas, and 180,000 shares of Commonwealth Edison? Was there anything sounder than his operating companies? Then he stopped short, caught by the glances of his creditors. "Does this mean a receivership?" he inquired of Owen D. Young, who had drawn up a chair beside him.

"I'm very much afraid it does," Young returned.

"What did Mr. Insull say to that?" one of the financiers present was asked later on.

"There wasn't much he could say," was the reply. "He seemed utterly broken and humble. I thought he was going to collapse. The only thing he said was: 'I wish my day on earth had come.'"

On Sunday, the 10th, when the bankers gathered in the Chicago Club to draw up the receivers' slate for Middle West, there was no chance for Midland United, Insull Utility Investments, or Corporation Securities. Brooding over the disgrace of four bankruptcies, Insull at first declined to co-operate in clearing the débris. "I finally had to tell him how matters stood," Edward Eagle Brown of the First National Bank recalled afterward. "I said to him in a quiet voice: 'Mr. Insull, you've either got to be a receiver with other receivers, or be left out of the picture altogether.'" Insull then agreed to serve as one of the receivers.

Selecting the co-receivers was a trying problem. "We wanted men of integrity and force," said Edward Eagle Brown, "men who would fight back at Mr. Insull if he persisted in his dominating ways. For thirty-five years he had pursued a course of taking advice from no one and had been pretty successful until near the end. We needed someone to sit down on him if possible. We didn't discuss all this in Mr. Insull's presence. He was the most dominating man I ever knew. You wouldn't discuss such things in his presence, not if you knew Mr. Insull, you wouldn't."

On the 15th, when Edward N. Hurley, the wartime head of the Shipping Board, and Charles A. McCulloch, John D. Hertz's partner in the New York and Chicago bus lines, were appointed co-receivers of Middle West, Insull Utility Investments was going begging at 37 cents, Middle West itself at 25 cents, and Corporation Securities at only 13 cents. But Public Service was selling at $50 a share, People's Gas at 60, and Commonwealth Edison at 65, suggesting that Insull might one day battle his way back to the control of his holding company network.

He never did. Early in June one of the attorneys for the receivers unearthed the evidence that Martin Insull, Samuel's brother, used $170,000 in cash to bolster his personal brokerage accounts. What was worse, the transaction had Samuel Insull's approval. Moreover, there were other unaccountable accounts. On another occasion Martin Insull requisitioned $344,000 in cash and securities, apparently to oblige a friend in want of collateral, but actually to save himself, since he was trading in that friend's name on the Chicago Stock Exchange. On still another occasion Martin Insull borrowed $90,000 in stocks from the portfolio of Middle West, and turned them over to Marshall E. Sampsell, an executive anxious about his

(International News Photos, Inc.)

COLONEL ROBERT R. MC CORMICK

(International News Photos, Inc.)

SAMUEL INSULL ON HIS WAY TO THE TRIAL

credit at the banks. Finally, Sampsell himself put his hands on $400,000 in stocks belonging to the treasury of the Central Illinois Public Service Company, an Insull subsidiary of which he was president. However, as will subsequently appear, the Insulls and Sampsell were freed of all these accusations.

Though Samuel might have staged some sort of a comeback if he hadn't stood by his brother, he was helpless for the moment. When the creditors, meeting at the Continental on the 6th of June, voted to demand his resignation as chairman of People's Gas, Public Service, and Commonwealth Edison, Charles A. McCulloch insisted he retire as co-receiver of Middle West as well. "I told the gentlemen present that Insull had to get out of Middle West," McCulloch declared. "They said they didn't want to give him both barrels on the same day. I said I didn't care what they did. Sam Insull's resignation had to be in my hands by five o'clock that evening. I said I'd fire the first barrel, if I had to."

Later in the day, after Marshall Field's nephew Stanley Field had made plain to Insull that he had no choice but to throw up the chairmanships, McCulloch caught up with the troubled magnate in the hall outside the offices of Middle West. "I told Insull to wait a minute; I wanted to see him," McCulloch reported the incident. "He came into my office, and I said he must have had a bad twenty-five minutes. He said he had. I said, in view of his resignation from the operating companies, I wanted him to resign as Middle West receiver also. He asked if I thought he should. I said, 'Yes.'"

The two businessmen then rode home together in a taxi. "Charlie," Insull put in, patting McCulloch's knee as they roared north on Michigan Avenue, "if I had had a man like you around ten years ago who would tell me no, I wouldn't be out now."

"You're wrong there, Sam," said McCulloch, "for if I had been around ten years ago, you would have chased me down the corridor, as you did other good men."

Insull's only answer was to burst into tears. "I've got a melancholy wife," he dropped when the cab came to a stop at 1120 Lake Shore Drive.

On the 8th, when Insull received the reporters for a last conference, James Simpson, chairman of the board of Marshall Field and Company, was already functioning as the chairman of People's Gas, Public Service, and Commonwealth Edison. "I have ceased to be newspaper copy," said Insull, smiling faintly. "And I am out of public life and no longer a public figure. So I ought to be entitled to privacy."

Thirteen days later, a haggard figure closely resembling Insull stepped down from a boat train in the Gare Saint Lazare in Paris. When newspapermen encircled him, he denied he was the famous financier. Just then a husky fellow with the manners of a bodyguard nabbed one of the reporters by the sleeve. "That wasn't Insull you were talking to, buddy," he said. "You've made a mistake. It wasn't Insull at all. His name doesn't appear in the ship's manifest. You'd better forget it."

By then it was apparent to the wiser bankers of New York and Chicago that Insull was the founder of a new school of accounting, according to which all expenses were considered as assets. All of Middle West's expenses were so considered, with the result that one half of the net income reported from 1912 to 1930 was unearned, fictitious, or unrealized. "By the same reasoning," noted an economist, "one would be entitled to consider the expenses of moving from one house to another as an addition to the value of the furniture."

Middle West, however, was not the only corporation with which Insull carried on experiments in accounting. In spite of the fact that neither Insull Utility Investments nor Corporation Securities had any cash income on hand after interest charges and expenses, both companies paid out cash dividends, entering non-cash and unrealizable items in the income accounts. Furthermore, both companies were gambling on the Stock Exchange, surrendering their best assets for bank loans with which to buy their own stocks, which were worthless, at preposterous prices.

Insull was ever-sensitive to the market value of his stocks. So were his favorite brokers, who unloaded a block of Middle West in

October, 1929, at from $14 to $20 a share above the price for the day, the purchaser being none other than Corporation Securities. Puzzled by this and other transactions brought to light by the receivers, State's Attorney Swanson worried over Insull's absence from Chicago. On the 1st of October he cabled him in Paris, asking him to return and submit to questioning.

Swanson got no answer. Slipping out of Paris, Insull fled to Florence, then to Turin, then to Athens, where he was arrested at the request of the American minister. "I should not be wanted by the police," he grumbled when told that he and his brother had been indicted by the grand jury on the charge of embezzlement. "I have not committed any crimes. The failure of my companies was not fraudulent. I have just been unfortunate and lost lots of money—over a hundred million dollars of my own."

Forty-eight hours later Insull was set free by the local authorities, who declined to surrender him on the ground that the instruments of ratification of the new Greek-American extradition treaty had not yet been exchanged. Heartened by this courtesy of the Athenian government, he refused to give up his passport to the American consul and pointed out that the history of his life was the history of his country. Later on, however, he wondered why his fellow countrymen snubbed him on the streets. "Why is it," he asked a chance acquaintance, "that none of the Americans here want to know me?"

"Well, frankly," the chance acquaintance replied, "they can't understand why you don't go back and face the music."

Driven from Greece in the spring of 1934, Insull was apprehended by the Turkish government and brought back to Chicago. In Cook County Jail, where he was locked up next door to a thirteen-year-old boy charged with the kidnapping and murder of a two-year-old girl, he held his head high. "I still think I did right by leaving Chicago when I did, and I would do the same thing again under similar circumstances," he informed the reporters who filed in to admire his Chinese dragon dressing gown.

When he and sixteen others went on trial for using the mails to defraud, he recollected with not a little pride that his income from salaries alone amounted to $481,000 in 1929, $434,000 in 1930, and $486,000 in 1931. "I will say to the jury that I received those salaries," he testified. "And I think ordinarily, gentlemen, the laborer is worthy of his hire."

This speech made the front pages of the newspapers, but didn't create as much excitement as the testimony of Cyrus S. Eaton, who unexpectedly took the stand in Insull's defense. "I wouldn't have been able to look myself in the face if I hadn't," Eaton admitted to the author. "All LaSalle Street was there," he described the courtroom. "The bankers were 25 deep. They were all waiting for me to assassinate Insull. Instead I told the court the high opinion I had of him."

Throughout the depression the prosperity of People's Gas, Public Service, and Commonwealth Edison was proof that Insull understood, if he did not always practice, the art of business management. Thinking of the good he might have done, the jury freed him and the sixteen other defendants of the charge of using the mails to defraud. Other juries acquitted Marshall E. Sampsell and the Insull brothers of embezzling the funds of Middle West, and with that, the age of Insull was at an end.

In the years to come Insull found it hard to believe that he was one of the little people. On weekday mornings, when he crossed Michigan Avenue to catch a bus, no one turned to stare at his immaculate spats, and he felt forlorn on the scene of his triumphs. He felt forlorn in Paris, too, where he dropped dead of a heart attack in the summer of 1938, leaving $1,000 in cash and $14,000,000 in debts to remind the world of what he once had been.

CHAPTER EIGHT: *In Our Time*

THEIRS THE FREEDOM OF THE PRESS

LONG before the fall of Insull—indeed, as soon as the great depression settled over the Middle West—Robert Rutherford McCormick took it upon himself to free the United States from the domination of the Eastern seaboard where, as he understood it, alien-minded millionaires and unassimilated immigrants were plotting to undermine the American way of life. Alarmed by Franklin D. Roosevelt's evident lack of sympathy for a crusade of this kind, he criticized the New Deal with a vehemence that amazed many a Republican. He also made no secret of his interest in the German experiment in racial purity.

Not that Colonel McCormick—to use the title he bears in civilian life—did all of his thinking on racial lines. In the spring of 1932 he delved into economics and discovered that "the cause of the world-wide depression has been definitely and finally traced to the extravagance of governmental expenditures since the war." Andrew Mellon was partly to blame, he inferred. "It has taken fifteen years of excessive taxation to bring us down to the verge of ruin."

If Colonel McCormick was unorthodox in his economic views, he was even more original in his ideas on education. Coming before the Advertising Club of New York, he proved to his own satisfaction that the great universities of the Eastern seaboard were communist strongholds. "The fact is," he said, "that the pink doctrines which I find taught in the high schools and colleges throughout the country originate in the old established institutions of learning along the coast." No wonder New York City was "the seat of radicalism, socialism, and communism." Hinting that it might be wise to limit the endowments of our universities, he explained that "the excessive extravagance in habits and buildings at tax-supported institutions is merely imitated after the baronial and palatial halls of Harvard and Yale."

Unlike most of our colleges, the Tribune Company was in no wise inconvenienced by the depression. In 1933, the year in which McCormick addressed the Advertising Club, the assets of the company totaled $38,400,000, $4,000,000 of which was invested in cash and securities, $11,000,000 in real estate, and $13,000,000, the biggest sum of all, in pulp-producing mills and timberlands in Ontario.

Perhaps James W. Gerard was right in thinking that McCormick and Patterson were two of "the 59 men who rule America." In 1933 the New York *Daily News* reached 1,428,908 readers, the largest audience of any newspaper in the country. Second only to the *News* was the *Tribune,* with 771,190 readers. According to *Fortune,* the two properties netted $6,700,000 in spite of a drop in advertising.

Since a newspaper's true value is generally considered to be eight times its earnings, the Tribune Company was worth $53,600,000 in 1933, and each of its 2,000 shares of stock, $26,800. Controlling 1,070 shares, the grandchildren of Joseph Medill had easily $28,676,000 in the family business. But this was no more than a fraction of their wealth. Assuming that $26,800 was only half the value of Tribune stock in good times, and that only half the family fortune was tied up in newspapers, the Pattersons and McCormicks had about $100,000,000 when business was booming, and Colonel McCormick himself about $25,000,000.

Of course he had his worries, not the least of which was the possibility of a thorough grand jury investigation of the Annenberg terror. In the summer of 1930, when Jake Lingle, an underworld tipster in the hire of the *Tribune,* was shot dead in the underpass of the Randolph Street Station of the Illinois Central, he realized that the case must be closed quickly, and without probing the past of "The World's Greatest Newspaper." The day after the Lingle funeral, he called a meeting of the Chicago Newspaper Publishers' Association and offered to meet all the expenses in running down the assassin above the usual allowance of the county government. The proposal was accepted, and Charles F. Rathbun, for many years a partner of the firm of Kirkland, Fleming, Green, and Martin the *Tribune's* lawyers, was appointed Assistant State's Attorney with the power of prosecutor. Working with Rathbun on the case was Assistant State's Attorney C. Wayland Brooks, who saw to it that a certain Leo V. Brothers was sentenced to fourteen years in prison for his connection with the crime. In 1940 the *Tribune* was gratified by Brooks' election to the United States Senate, and if he is ever retired from office, the *Tribune* will be disappointed.

As soon as the Lingle case quieted down, McCormick made one of the most interesting speeches of his career. Asked to talk on the Chicago crime wave before the Milwaukee Bar Association, he blamed the gang wars on the presence of immigrants in the Middle West, and denied that the *Tribune* took part in the circulation wars. "Some people," he said, "trace the origin of our crime disturbances to the anarchists of the late '80s. Others refer to the series of violent strikes which raged in Chicago about the end of the last century. Liberal reference has been made to newspaper wars and the *Tribune's* name has been mentioned as participating in these clashes. The fact as to this last is that the circulation competitions which have been dubbed wars were exclusively among afternoon newspapers. They were two in number—one in the late '90s and the other in the early 1900s. The Chicago *Tribune* was not engaged in either as principal or ally."

Later on, when Senator Minton of Indiana quoted from Lundberg's *Imperial Hearst* on the subject of the circulation wars, McCormick declared there was no court record of the killings. "Of course," he said, Minton failed to quote from "the records because there are no records to go to. He picked up and rebroadcast the vaporings of some ex-newspapermen who, having been driven from the profession because of unreliability and other defects of character, have sought existence from the profession by abusing it."

Then, forgetting that he was elected president of the Tribune Company on March 1st, 1911, he implied he had nothing to do with the family newspaper at the time of the Annenberg terror. "It is well known," McCormick said, "to all newspapermen in Chicago—for that matter, in the country—that in 1911 I was not editor, publisher, or business manager of the *Tribune*. . . . I had not been brought up in the newspaper. It was not contemplated by anyone that I would enter the newspaper. The events which led to my entering it three years later were not in sight."

When not giving his personal version of the history of the *Tribune,* McCormick was likely to be defending the freedom of the press. "The freedom of the press is the freedom of the American people," he told the New York State Chamber of Commerce. "Circumstances have imposed upon the publishers of America the holy duty to preserve that freedom and hand it down to posterity. I believe they will not flinch from their responsibility."

Often accused of perverting the news columns of the *Tribune,* McCormick made strange use of the freedom of the press in the spring of 1935. On two successive Sundays Dr. Wilhelm Tannenberg, the Nazi vice-consul in Chicago, was assigned space on the editorial page where he pointed out the advantages of the fascist form of government. Ignoring the pogroms, the concentration camps, and the other undelightful features of the Third Reich, Dr. Tannenberg saluted National Socialism as "that great movement which promised and fought for national unity, courageous leadership, energetic action in the interests of the people, and Germany's equality among the nations of the world." Dr. Tannenberg was disturbed by neither the dissolution of the German labor unions nor the murders of the German labor leaders. "Labor," he said, "has been dignified."

Perhaps because he suspected that very few Chicagoans shared his tolerance for Dr. Tannenberg's political philosophy, McCormick lived largely to himself in the '30s, inviting few friends to his solemn town house at 1519 Astor Street, and almost no one save close relatives to "Cantigny Farm," his estate at Wheaton, due west of the city.* In the gigantic upstairs living room of Cantigny Farm—a room which one of his visitors reported was larger than the waiting room of the 30th Street Station of the Pennsylvania Railroad in Philadelphia—he paced the floor for hours in absolute solitude, glancing occasionally at the ceiling for inspiration. There, written in gold, were the sayings of the French and American generals at Château Thierry, side by side with his own observations at the battlefront.

To the lonely publisher, the great world outside Cantigny Farm was terrifying. Like the sixth Duke of Somerset, who so dreaded the gaze of the vulgar that he had outriders clear the roads whenever he had a mind to set out in his coach, he did not know what to expect from the average man. Fearful of meeting an irreverent reader of the *Tribune,* he stationed policemen with revolvers on his floor at the Tower, and rarely went anywhere without a German wolfhound at his heels. As an afterthought he installed secret panels in his private office.

Yet he often spoke before large crowds, disregarding his personal safety for the sake of his ideals. On the Fourth of July, 1939, he informed the citizens of the western suburb of Downers Grove that the recent Republican victories at the polls were more important than they realized. "It is," he said, "one of the greatest phenomena of history that the American people, unorganized against a thoroughly organized and determined foe, betrayed by their own governors and their government, remained steadfast, resisted the revolution, and successfully defeated their betrayers in the election of 1938. It is because of this defeat that the communists are now conspiring to put us into a European war, so that war powers can accomplish what the police powers are not strong enough to do."

* Close at hand lives Chauncey McCormick, the present president of the Art Institute. A descendant, like the Colonel, of William Sanderson McCormick, he shot into prominence after marrying Marion Deering, granddaughter of the co-founder of International Harvester.

Drawing himself up to his full six feet two inches, the impeccably groomed, superbly dressed publisher of "The World's Greatest Newspaper" went on to sketch his impressions of life in the suburbs. "As I look out among you," he asked, "do I not see many refugees? Have not many of you come to live in these suburban towns to avoid political conditions you have not been able to overcome? . . . that you might go to work without fear that criminals will prey upon your women and children while you are away, that they will be beyond the fury of mobs infuriated by rabid speech and led by trained revolutionists? You know you have.

"Does it occur to you," he continued, "that you are living in a fool's paradise? That the communists are craftily leaving you in your peaceful semi-pastoral lives, while they forge a political and criminal machine strong enough to destroy you?"

When his wife died of pneumonia a few weeks after this speech, he had her buried with full military honors in the garden of Cantigny Farm.* Saddled, and carrying her boots turned backward in the stirrups, her favorite mount looked on as McCormick's servants lowered her flag-draped coffin into the grave. Then a squad from Fort Sheridan fired three volleys, a bugler sounded taps, and the little throng of mourners paused to watch the raising of the flag, which had been lowered to half-mast in the hour of her death.

With his wife gone, the childless millionaire had no one to help him interpret the outbreak of the Second World War to the people of Chicago. But he was not without the comfort of unshakable convictions. "Mr. Roosevelt," he told the readers of the *Tribune,* "is putting himself at the head of a war party in the United States, but it is composed only of communists who seek a catastrophe which would be the end, they think, of capitalism and make Russia the mistress of the world, and of hyphenates who would make vicarious sacrifices to help Great Britain and France."

As a lifelong student of military history, McCormick recognized there was no need for selective service in the summer of 1940.

* In December, 1944, he was married to another divorcee, Mrs. Maryland Mathison Hooper.

"Insanity, nothing less!" was his first reaction. Later on he saw no reason to change his mind. "The draft," he explained after the bill was made law, "was not recommended or required by military considerations. It was, however, a logical element in the warmaking campaign to which the third term entrusts its chances of success." John T. McCutcheon, the most famous of the *Tribune* cartoonists, did not disagree. "Americans will willingly fight for their own country, but they have to be drafted to fight for European countries," read the legend under a McCutcheon cartoon.

As a patriot, McCormick felt it was his duty to reason with the excitable members of the Senate foreign relations committee. "The Germans are not so tough," he testified in Washington. "I have been up against them and there is no use being scared of them."

"What would be your attitude," inquired Senator Pepper, "as to the policy of this country if Hitler should conquer England and proceed to take over and occupy the British bases in what is regarded as this hemisphere?"

"I would not let him do it," McCormick answered.

"I think if things are as serene as Colonel McCormick imagines, the Congress ought to pass the normal appropriations and go home," interrupted Senator Glass.

"I am willing," McCormick returned, "to furnish material to Britain for her own defense, but not to carry a great and terrible war to the continent of Europe. She—" meaning Britain—"should have what she needs for her defense—and I do not think she needs anything."

In McCormick's considered opinion the Lend-Lease or "dictatorship" bill was rushed through Congress on Wall Street's orders. "All the big banks in the East, all of the millionaire society is for putting us into the war," he emphasized.

Speaking as a citizen of the Middle West, he prophesied that the alien-minded millionaires of the Eastern seaboard would sooner or later have an unhappy time of it. "They may force the unwilling majority of their fellow countrymen into the horrors of war," he admitted. "If they do, they face extinction. The normal envy of the rich has been organized by Mr. Roosevelt and his camorra for eight years. The 60 families and their 60,000 cousins have been used to rouse the rabble for three elections. What shift may they expect from the millions upon whom they bring war? Given a terrible injury, the American people, we may fear, will yield to that instinct of intolerance for minorities that has bred a series of disasters throughout history. The stage for a violent revolution is being set by its inevitable victims."

Naturally enough, McCormick was impatient with Middle Western editors who took the Eastern point of view. When Frank Knox, the publisher of the Chicago *Daily News* since the death of Lawson's successor Walter Strong, and S. E. Thomason, the publisher of the popular afternoon tabloid, the Chicago *Times,* ventured to find fault with *Tribune* editorials, he insinuated that his rivals were the tools of Eastern bankers. What if Knox had been the Republican candidate for Vice-President in 1936? What if Thomason had been the business manager of the *Tribune* in days gone by? "These jackals grow too bold!" McCormick roared.

"It is," he cried, "a truism of journalism that little newspapers benefit by getting into controversies with great newspapers. Appreciating this, the *Tribune* has treated the nagging by two little evening contemporaries with silence born of contempt. But when they . . . impugn the patriotism of this newspaper it seems time to take notice.

"The fact is that those newspapers are so deeply in debt that whoever may be held up as editor or publisher is little more than an office boy for the creditors. The financial control is hid in such a labyrinth of financial juggery that the men who do the dirty work may not even know who their masters are. Nevertheless, these jackals think they can hurt the reputation of the *Tribune,* with its ninety-four years of service to Chicago. . . ." Passing quietly over Dr. Tannenberg's contributions to the editorial page, McCormick declared that "the *Tribune* has never uttered a syllable in favor of Hitler's system of government."

At this time the publisher of "The World's Greatest Newspaper" had no daily competitor in the morning field, Hearst having decided to bring out only one paper in Chicago, and that in the evening. Taking advantage of this opportunity to educate a wider audience, McCormick made plain that we had nothing to fear from the Imperial Japanese Government. "What vital interests of the United States can Japan threaten?" he asked on the 27th of October, 1941. "She cannot attack us. That is a military impossibility. Even our base at Hawaii is beyond the striking power of her fleet."

Like his cousin in Tribune Tower, Joseph Medill Patterson had no doubts about Japan. "Of all Oriental peoples, the Japanese are most nearly like us," he advised the readers of the New York *Daily News* on the 17th of November, 1941. "They are physically clean. They even, alone among Oriental peoples, think baseball is a fine game, and like both to play it and to watch it."

The Japanese could be trusted, but not our own government. "The only answer that we can figure out to this 'inevitable war' with Japan is that our administration feels obligated to shore up the British Empire in the Far East. We are already helping the British keep their island home off the European mainland; and the nation we are helping them fend off is the world's most formidable land power at this time. Isn't that enough? Or must we become out-and-out vassals of the British Empire, to do its bidding all around the world for all time so far as we can see?"

Patterson had definite ideas about the Old World, too. "The real menace to modern Europe," as he saw it, was not Nazi Germany, but "Stalin and the Asiatic horde civilization that he represents." When President Roosevelt failed to cheer on the German armies invading Russia, Patterson made no effort to conceal his disappointment. "Roosevelt's War, we think, is the correct name for the war in which we are engaging more intimately every day," he urged in the fall of 1941. "Win or lose, this war should be known to history as Roosevelt's War, because Franklin D. Roosevelt is the man who has got us into it as far as we now are, and is taking us deeper into it."

To be sure, Patterson had not always disagreed with Roosevelt.

In 1932, in 1936, and again in 1940, he backed him for President, giving jovial journalists the impression that the master of the *News* had little in common with the lord of the *Tribune*. It was true that he had a shrewder adviser than his cousin. At his side stood circulation manager Max Annenberg who, knowing that he dearly loved to annoy the best people, may have suggested that he outrage the station wagon set by hailing the New Deal as heaven-sent.*

When Annenberg passed away on the 6th of February, 1941, Patterson revealed how much the circulation manager meant to him.† "Good-bye," he wrote on the editorial page the day of the funeral. "I am going to miss you a lot. For many years you have been my best friend, outside members of my family. Hope to be seeing you some day."

As soon as he was free from Annenberg's influence, Patterson found that there was much to admire in the philosophy of his Washington correspondent John O'Donnell. Trained in the art of leaving certain impressions without saying certain things, O'Donnell was not afraid to speak his mind in Annenberg's lifetime, writing on the 17th of June, 1940, that "a Jewish army is in the making. It is frankly designed to meet the underground whispering campaign that the present war is being fought mainly in the interest of the Jews; that the Jews therefore want to drag everybody into the war, but they themselves stay out." O'Donnell not long afterward received a Nazi iron cross from President Roosevelt.

By the 10th of November, 1941, Patterson was sorry he helped elect Roosevelt to a third term. "We think," he said, "our White House dictator will lose his power over the House of Representatives at the Congressional elections of November 3, 1942—IF there are

* Patterson's daughter Alicia who, in her own words, wanted to be "the best damn newspaperwoman in the world," went to Annenberg for advice when she founded the Nassau County, Long Island *Newsday* in September, 1940. Her present husband is the copper millionaire Harry F. Guggenheim.

† Three years before Annenberg's death, Patterson was divorced from Alice Higinbotham and married to Mary King, the women's editor of the *News*. His home was at Ossining on the Hudson, in an ungainly modern house designed by Raymond Hood, the architect of the News Building.

any Congressional elections in 1942. But at this time Mr. Roosevelt is a dictator, as much so as Hitler, Stalin, and Churchill, and there is no use kidding ourselves that he isn't."

Deep in gloom, Patterson made a handsome contribution to the America First movement and prepared for the worst. "If we go into this war, bleed heavily, and don't win, there will probably be communism in the United States," he predicted. As for the Russians, they were idiots to keep on fighting. "Is it," he asked, "Mr. Churchill's idea that when millions of Russians have been sacrificed in vain, millions of Americans can be sacrified to win a peace which he can dictate?"

Though Colonel McCormick was happy to know that his cousin was thinking like a grandson of Joseph Medill, no one appreciated the wisdom of Patterson's words as fully as his sister Eleanor—his beloved "Cissy"—who, in 1939, had turned newspaper publisher herself, dipping into her personal fortune to buy the Washington *Times-Herald* from William Randolph Hearst. Saving herself the trouble of hiring an editorial staff, she reprinted the editorials of the *Daily News* along with O'Donnell's column.

In 1930, when "Cissy" Patterson stepped into the editorship of Hearst's Washington *Herald* at a salary of $10,000 a year, no one could have foretold that she would find the deepest satisfaction of her life in journalism. She had tried newspaper work before, writing up the hunting season in the Sawtooth Mountains of Idaho for the Chicago Hearst papers, but left off such scribbling for the sake of her career as a society novelist.

Divorced from Count Joseph Gizycki before the end of the First World War, she published her first novel *Glass Houses* in 1926, a year after her marriage to the attorney Elmer Schlesinger. In 1928 she brought out her second, *Fall Flight*. Like the first, it was signed Eleanor Gizycka; evidently for literary purposes, she preferred Gizycka to Schlesinger. But the people of her imagination, even though they wore Locke hats and hunted with Mannlicher rifles, never failed to break into finishing school French in a crisis, and no one supposed that Joseph Medill's granddaughter was at home on the Continent.

She was, she thought, at home in Washington. Left a widow in 1929, she was delighted at the chance to edit the *Herald*. "One can't be a good reporter and a lady at the same time," she decided. "I'd rather be a reporter."

Dropping the name of her second husband, and calling herself simply Mrs. Eleanor Medill Patterson, she stopped at nothing in her eagerness to advertise the *Herald*. One day she deliberately insulted Alice Roosevelt Longworth, taunting her for her feeble efforts in the Senatorial campaign of Ruth Hanna McCormick. One day she horrified the servants in the family palace on DuPont Circle by dressing up as a maid out of work and traipsing through the relief shelters of the city in search of human interest stories. One day she cornered Al Capone and badgered him into giving her an interview. Another time she printed an open letter to President Roosevelt on the first page, denouncing him for prolonging the depression. "It's a good letter," the President told a mutual friend, "but you know she didn't write it."

"Cissy," who answered that she did, couldn't see anything funny in Roosevelt's remark.

Though she quarreled with the columnist Drew Pearson, who was once married to her daughter Felicia Gizycka, she was nonetheless a success at hiring newspapermen. In 1937 she leased both the Washington *Times* and the Washington *Herald* from Hearst, combining them in the *Times-Herald*. No one to experiment with new techniques, she didn't mind if the *Times-Herald* under her ownership, for all its smart typography, was very like a Hearst paper in its emphasis on society gossip and the heartbreaks of little people.

By 1941 she created as much confusion in Washington as her cousin in Chicago and her brother in New York. The *Times-Herald,* with 210,105 readers on weekdays and 210,925 on Sundays, was the most popular newspaper in the capital, just as the *Tribune,* with 1,065,207 readers on weekdays and 1,144,734 on Sundays, was the most popular newspaper in Chicago, and the *News,* with 2,007,797 readers on weekdays and 3,610,483 on Sundays, was the most popular newspaper in New York and the nation.

Reaching over 3,000,000 Americans six days of the week, and nearly 5,000,000 on the seventh, the grandchildren of Joseph Medill were in no mood for self-examination. Taking it for granted that the time had come to show the warmonger in the White House for what he was, on Thursday, the 4th of December, 1941, the three publishers released a confidential report of the joint Army and Navy High Command on a possible American Expeditionary Force. "F. D. R.'s WAR PLANS!" read the headline of "The World's Greatest Newspaper." "GOAL IS TEN MILLION ARMED MEN."

In Washington there was amazement. "What do you think," asked Secretary of War Stimson, "of the patriotism of a man or a newspaper that would take these confidential studies and make them public to the enemies of this country? . . . While their publication doubtless will be a source of gratification to our potential enemies, and a possible source of impairment and embarrassment to our national defense, the chief evil of their publication is the revelation that there should be among us any group of persons so lacking in appreciation of the danger that confronts the country, and so wanting in loyalty and patriotism to their government that they would be willing to take and publish such reports."

Speaking for all three grandchildren of Joseph Medill, Colonel McCormick replied to Secretary Stimson on the morning of Sunday, the 7th of December. "We have known for a long time that the war party was betraying the American people," he said. "Now we have proved it. We regard the achievement as among the greatest contributions to the welfare of our country which this or any other newspaper has ever made."

On the morning of Monday, the 8th, McCormick was of another mind. "America faces war through no volition of any American," he admitted. "Recriminations are useless and we doubt they will be indulged in. Certainly not by us." As proof of the patriotism of the

Tribune, there was an American flag in full colors on the first page.

Pearl Harbor was a surprise to McCormick. But an even greater shock was the appearance, just three days before the Japanese attack, of a new morning newspaper on the streets of Chicago. Its name was the *Sun*. Its owner was Marshall Field III, grandson of the first Marshall Field.

THE RETURN OF MARSHALL FIELD

Colonel McCormick was not very glad to see the *Sun*. "Now we are under attack!" he cried out at the annual convention of the *Tribune's* advertising department. "A government-subsidized newspaper, financed through tax-dodging, is fired at us. It is futile. No newspaper rotten at the heart can ever succeed. No newspaper supported by money taken away from national defense in this hour of peril can have any support from the American people." Turning on Marshall Field III, he called him a "playboy millionaire, playing with his tax-dodging money."

McCormick was too nervous to be accurate. As all of his listeners were aware, there was no truth to the charge that the *Sun* was government-subsidized. Nor was there any foundation in fact for the statement that Field was seeking to avoid paying his due share of taxes.

Having repaid the kindness of the first Marshall Field to Joseph Medill, McCormick went on to accuse his rival of being a slacker. "Field is of age to volunteer," the *Tribune* declared. "He cried for war before it came. Now that it has come, he lets men like MacNider and O'Hare do the fighting while he skulks in his clubs, night and otherwise. . . . The term to fit to him and to all the herd of hysterical effeminates is coward."

If McCormick expected that Field would lose his temper, he miscalculated. As calm as his grandfather, the founder of the *Sun* replied in an editorial one sentence long. "You're getting rattled, Colonel McCormick," he observed.

Chicagoans soon found out that the third Marshall Field bore no resemblance to the hysterical effeminate of McCormick's imagination. Not quite so tall as the publisher of the *Tribune,* and not nearly so heavy, Field at forty-eight was an elegantly gray-haired gentleman whose great charm concealed a greater determination. If he dressed with English ease, and spoke with a mild English accent, it was only natural, for he was something of a stranger to Chicago. Educated in England, he had spent most of his life on the North Shore of Long Island.

When still a little boy, he was taken out of the Colter School on the Gold Coast and entered at Eton by his mother, who settled in England with her three children as soon as the Field estate was turned over to the trustees. Leasing a town house on Berkeley Square and a country home in Herts., she entertained with the usual Edwardian lavishness. One of her guests was Captain Maldwin Drummond, whom she married in the fall of 1908. A member of the Duke of Westminster's set, he frequently played polo at Eaton Hall, the Duke's Gothic seat in Cheshire.

Meantime Marshall Field III was discovering that an English public school was not the best place to study chemistry. "At Eton," he wrote afterward, "the only sop thrown to the modern world of technology was about an hour a week, officially called 'Science.' The situs was a rather ill-equipped laboratory, and the subject had acquired the label of 'Stinks.' Any pupil who evidenced undue interest in the subject was a 'Stinker,' of course, and the whole matter was scarcely tolerated and rarely referred to by either masters or boys. I got a vague idea at different times that water was represented by H_2O, that snakes shed their skins but were fun to fool with, and that caterpillars eventually became butterflies. But our chief occupation in 'Stinks' was mixing liquids, without any apparent idea or purpose except a general hope that a loathsome smell, or possibly even an explosion, might occur."

"I didn't really have a good time at Eton," Field confessed to the author. "You see, I couldn't do much in the way of athletics. I had rheumatic fever in those days." Fortunately he was never too ill to cross the Atlantic. Both at Eton and at Trinity College, Cambridge, he looked forward to the trips he made to Chicago on estate matters. Stepping off the Century, strolling up and down State Street and Michigan Avenue, lunching in the magnificent dining room of the Blackstone Hotel, he felt he was home. "I like English customs," he dropped in an interview with Chicago reporters, "but I want to get back to Chicago, where my grandfather lived."

Yet Cambridge was not a bore. "I found Cambridge utterly delightful," Field wrote, "with every possibility of accumulating knowledge, if one were so disposed; but, as might be imagined, my previous experience had not been conducive to enthusiasm about scientific subjects. I have since found it quite impossible to understand or manipulate anything like a radio, an electric device of any sort, or even an automobile or airplane. Perhaps this is just inherent dumbness, but I like to blame my education."

Coming of age in 1914, Field left Cambridge to see what it meant to be a trustee of his grandfather's estate. En route for New York on the *Lusitania,* he fell in love with Evelyn Marshall, granddaughter of the Charles H. Marshall who built a modest fortune out of the Black Ball packets to Liverpool. Early in 1915 he married her.

The groom's younger brother Henry, who also went to Eton, followed his example in taking a wife on this side of the Atlantic. She was Nancy Keene Perkins of Albemarle County, Virginia, niece of the Nancy Langhorne who became Lady Astor. As readers of the Sunday supplements were soon to be told, Nancy Perkins was not the first woman in Henry Field's life. When just out of Eton, he made love to Peggy Marsh, an American actress at the Alhambra in London. She bore him a son out of wedlock, and he gave her $50,000 in addition to settling $100,000 on the child.

Henry Field had no children by Nancy Perkins. When he died of pneumonia in New York in 1917, two years after his mother passed away in England, his two-fifths share of the estate went to Marshall. His widow then took another grandson of Marshall Field for her second husband. He was Ronald Tree, the son of Ethel Field Beatty by her first marriage. A foxhunter with literary tastes, Tree tried life in New York in the '20s as managing editor of the *Forum*. Afterward he returned to England, serving in the Second World War as parliamentary under-secretary to Brendan Bracken, Churchill's Minister of Information.

For a Field to sympathize with England in a dark hour was nothing new. During the First World War Ethel Field Beatty spent her days and nights collecting winter clothing for the men of the British Navy. Her husband, already an admiral when war broke out, was created Earl of the North Sea and of Brooksby for leading the fleet to victory at Jutland.

Earl's nieces have rarely been slighted in modern times, and Gwendolyn, the sister of Marshall Field III, was no exception to the rule. In the spring of 1923, when she went to the altar of Saint Martin's in the Fields with Archibald Edmonstone, the elder son of Sir Archibald Edmonstone, Bart., three princesses of the royal family graced the ceremony, at the end of which she received Duntreath Castle in Stirlingshire from her father-in-law.

Six years before this, Marshall Field III proved his first allegiance was to the United States, enlisting as a private in the First Illinois Cavalry as soon as we declared war on Germany. "America's richest young man has taken the direct step dictated by unadulterated patriotism," the *Tribune* admitted at the time. "Many will rise to say that Field has done only what everybody should do. They will be careful to ignore the fact that everybody isn't doing it."

"I don't see what the fuss is all about," Field commented. "I am enlisting because I believe it is my duty to serve the United States in this war. That is my personal conviction regarding myself, and myself solely. I am not moralizing over what other people should do." Reaching France in March, 1918, with the 122d Field Artillery, he was promoted to a captaincy and cited for gallantry after seeing service in the Saint Mihiel and Meuse-Argonne offensives.

"He was no playboy and no miser," one of his buddies recalled. "He'd take a couple of drinks, and then he didn't want any more.

If you needed money, he'd let you have it. Don't get the idea, though, that he was a sucker. He didn't throw his money away. He'd lend money to somebody that needed it, but he would expect it back. One the other hand, if it was somebody who needed it real bad, for his wife or folks or something like that, Field would just give him what he needed and never ask for it afterward."

Back in Chicago when the war was over, Field went to work for Lee, Higginson and Company. By the beginning of 1921 he was in the banking business for himself. The partners of Glore, Ward and Company joined him, and he founded the investment house of Marshall Field, Glore, Ward and Company, with offices in New York and Chicago. "I would," he said, "consider it criminal if I did not take advantage of my opportunities to assist in the developing of American industry. Merely having money is not being creative and not doing one's share toward increasing the prosperity and stability of the nation. It is using money, becoming part of the great exchange of ideas, investments, purchases, and sales, that makes a man feel that he belongs to the life of the country."

Banking, of course, was not the only way to put money to work. In the fall of 1927 Field sank $4,000,000 in the Marshall Field Garden Apartments on the North Side, a low-rent housing project which disappointed him by appealing to a higher income group than intended. "Low-rent housing projects," he finally decided, "are the function of the government."

Though the Garden Apartments were his heart's desire, Field was enthusiastic about banking. Field, Glore and Company, as the firm was known following the withdrawal of one of the partners, participated in a $30,000,000 loan to the city of Milan and floated $20,000,000 worth of securities for Italian Superpower, besides bringing out $60,000,000 worth of preferred stock for Republic Iron and Steel and underwriting a $17,500,000 bond issue for Marshall Field and Company.

Under no illusion that Chicago was destined to be the nation's banking center, Field moved to New York in 1921. At 4 East 70th Street, facing the mansion of Henry Clay Frick, he had David

Adler and Robert Works design him a discreetly Georgian town house.* Buying up the largest estate on Long Island for his country home, he called on John Russell Pope to furnish the plans for "Caumsett," at Lloyd's Neck, near Huntington. Like 4 East 70th Street, Caumsett was in the Georgian style, but so undistinguished as to be in no way worthy of the grandson of the greatest of Chicago businessmen.

Caumsett was an estate in the Long Island manner, which is the same thing as saying that both house and grounds were woefully unpretentious despite their size. Though a staff of 85 servants was required to superintend the 1,700 acres of park and woodland, discriminating visitors, glancing at the façade overlooking the Sound, were reminded not so much of a country seat as a preparatory school.

For several years, however, Field made an honest effort to entertain himself at Caumsett. Stocking the woods with pheasants, he went hunting at least once a week in the late fall. Now and then he rode to the hounds. More often he joined the crowd at the Turf and Field Club at Belmont. Like most Long Island country gentlemen, he kept a racing stable and occasionally bred a winner. He also prided himself on the enormous chrysanthemums grown by his expert gardener.

All this was not very exciting, and no more satisfying than serving on the boards of the usual philanthropic organizations. A founder of the Museum of Modern Art and a trustee of the Metropolitan Museum, Field was president of the Philharmonic Symphony Society and the Metropolitan Opera Company as well.

In 1930, when Evelyn Marshall divorced him to marry Diego de Suarez of Florence, Italy, Long Island life was already beginning to pall on the master of Caumsett. Yet he was still unwilling to break with the pattern of his neighbors. Falling in love with the widow of Dudley Coats of London, he made her his second wife. The god-daughter of Edward VII and the good friend of the

* This was torn down in 1937.

Prince of Wales, she was undeniably elegant, but no companion for a discontented man. In 1935 they separated.

Field was now ready to challenge one of the basic assumptions of the American upper classes. There was, he came to believe, "no such thing as an inherent right in private property. Theories to such an effect, like theories concerning the divine right of nobility, were invented by propagandists to justify otherwise untenable positions." Following this trend of thought, he reached the conclusion that a man of his means was not intended to be a passive spectator of the drama of democracy. "For the future of democracy to be sure, for freedom to be more than a word, those with financial and political power must regard the constant rejuvenation of freedom as their pressing duty."

He was not one of those who felt that freedom of the press had already been achieved. "The most essential aspect of democracy—freedom of access to facts, to news—must be revitalized and extended," he insisted. "All shades of opinion, all significant versions of the facts, should have representation, and be given free access to the channels of communication."

Returning to his original conception of the creative use of a great fortune, he decided his funds "could best be utilized as germinal money. That," he afterward made plain, "does not imply either the casual use of the funds, or their squandering. If any given enterprise is to serve social ends, it must within a reasonable time have proved of sufficient utility to society so that society undertakes to support it. The long continuance of any enterprise must be based upon its ability to achieve economic independence and not upon any individual, group, or governmental bounty."

Planning of this kind, calling for personal interference in situations failing to meet the test of freedom, required as much cash on hand as the investment program of the first Marshall Field. For such purposes the estate was reasonably liquid. If half the money was still in land, the other half was mostly in high grade bonds and governments, convertible at an instant's notice.

There were, to be sure, two corporations and one bank in which the estate was seriously involved—Marshall Field and Company, Commonwealth Edison, and the Continental Illinois National Bank and Trust Company. Since the Continental was Chicago's biggest bank, and the Field family the biggest common stockholders, there was nothing remarkable in the fact that the estate was concerned to the extent of $1,500,000, $200,000 more than the amount invested in Commonwealth Edison. In the store approximately $15,150,000 was at stake. This represented a 62 per cent interest in the 6 per cent preferred stock, but no more than a 9 per cent interest in the common, control having passed to the families of John Shedd and James Simpson.

In no doubt of his financial strength, Field severed his connection with Field, Glore and Company in the summer of 1935. In the fall of the next year he took the first step in his new direction by endorsing President Roosevelt for a second term. Long Islanders, who recalled that he voted for Hoover in 1932, were shocked. If they had been better informed they would have understood that supporting Roosevelt meant renewing an old friendship. In the First World War, when the President was Assistant Secretary of the Navy and Field was visiting in Washington, the two had got on very well.

At home in his apartment at 740 Park Avenue Field had no trouble explaining his political change of heart. In January, 1936, on the eve of rebuilding his career, he married Ruth Pruyn Phipps, a sensitive woman who was once the wife of Ogden Phipps of the Pittsburgh dynasty. When Field, early in the Second World War, took over the chairmanship of the United States Committee for the Care of European Children, she fully appreciated the importance of welcoming these refugees to America. By then they had two little girls of their own, Phyllis and Fiona.

Field's three children by his first wife were already grown up. Marshall IV, a graduate of Saint Paul's School, Harvard University, and the law school of the University of Virginia, was married in the summer of 1938 to Joanne Bass, the very beautiful daughter of Robert Perkins Bass, a former Governor of New Hampshire.

Marshall's sister Barbara was then the wife of the textile heir Anthony A. Bliss, whom she afterward divorced to marry Dr. Robert Boggs of Portland, Oregon. Bettine, the youngest of the three, who went to Bennington for a year after finishing at Miss Hall's School in Pittsfield, took McChesney Goodall, Jr., for her husband. A medical student at the University of Virginia, he came from nearby Staunton.

In January, 1942, about six months before the marriage of Bettine and McChesney Goodall, Jr., Field made himself the sole owner of *PM,* the New York tabloid whose angry editorial policy has upset the digestion of every reactionary in Congress. Launched in the summer of 1940 by Ralph Ingersoll, the general manager of *Time* Incorporated, *PM* was conceived as an experiment in adless journalism, an idea so fascinating in itself that John Hay Whitney and many other millionaires bought stock while the paper was still in the discussion stage.

Field, who was one of the original stockholders, was not in the least dismayed to find that *PM,* exactly as intended, succeeded in reflecting the point of view of a group of journalists under no pressure from owner or advertisers. As soon as the other sponsors, worried by the eagerness of the editors, decided they had had enough, he bought their interest at around 20 cents on the dollar. At the time the paper was in the red; three years later, thanks to the perseverance of Ralph Ingersoll and his assistant John P. Lewis, it was in the black, reaching 160,000 readers weekdays, 200,000, Sundays.

"I don't suppose," Field remarked not long after he made *PM* his own, "that anyone can be expected to agree with everything in *PM.* It's very controversial. But I think it's interesting." Overly serious on occasion, *PM* has lived up to its slogan of supplying the "news you can't get elsewhere" by printing more news about more unpleasant people than any newspaper in the country. These people, who happen to be our native fascists, have more than once made plain that they consider *PM* to be an undesirable influence.

Negroes down South, who know that *PM* is one paper that will present their side of a story, feel differently—so differently that whenever they have a grievance to advertise, they pool their nickels, dimes, and quarters for a phone call to John P. Lewis in New York. But colored people everywhere seem to believe that *PM* is on the right track. Taking note of this, *The Defender,* a Negro weekly in Chicago, put Field on the race relations roll of honor "for his leadership in the struggle for full democracy."

Though Field has made a few suggestions to *PM*—he once wrote a letter to the paper correcting its analysis of the cash position of Westinghouse, a company of which he is a director—he has yet to bear down on the staff, who say precisely what they think of public figures without fear of offending his friends of the Caumsett period. If any business is to be transacted, he likes to have the editors use their own judgment. A year or so ago, when *PM* was about to buy the presses of another newspaper, a deal running into several hundred thousand dollars, one of the men phoned Field, who was in Canada just then, to give him the details. "Well," Field interrupted as soon as he heard what was afoot, "do you think it's a good buy?" Told that it was, he said simply, "Well, go ahead."

The editors usually see Field about once a month in his office at 250 Park Avenue. At the end of one of these meetings, he took them all out to a restaurant in the neighborhood featuring a blue plate lunch. Everyone ordered the blue plate special. When the time came for dessert, the waitress put in a good word for the peach pie. "It isn't on the special," she admitted. "It's extra."

"Then," said Field, "I won't have it."

Saving in small ways, like most very rich men, Field has spared no expense to insure the success of the Chicago *Sun,* a newspaper which bears the full imprint of his personality, and by which he must stand or fall as a publisher. When, shortly before the first issue reached the newsstands, he addressed a conference of social welfare workers, the future of the *Sun* was very much on his mind. "I happen to have been left a great deal of money," he said. "I don't know what is going to happen to it, and I don't give a damn. If I cannot make myself worthy of three square meals a day, I don't deserve them."

Field was sharply reminded of Chicago's need in the summer of 1941, when the Fight For Freedom Committee organized a mass meeting at Orchestra Hall in support of the foreign policy of the Roosevelt administration. The crowd, united in its hatred of McCormick, roared its allegiance to any newspaper that might be launched against "The World's Greatest," and late that night, spreading out on Michigan Avenue, began buying every copy in sight of next day's *Tribune,* burning them in indignation.

The invitation was too handsome to be ignored. Getting in touch with Silliman Evans, the promoter of the Nashville *Tennessean,* Field brushed aside all other plans for the invasion of Chicago. Office space was arranged in the News Building on West Madison Street, and the printing plant of the *News* leased for the emergency. The new newspaper, with Evans as publisher, was not to be so hot-tempered as *PM.* Its news columns were to be unbiased, its editorials slanted to favor Roosevelt on domestic and international issues.

At midnight, on Wednesday, December 3d, just as the *Tribune* was breaking the news of F. D. R.'s war plans, Volume One Number One of the *Sun* rolled off the presses carrying the President's congratulations. Inside of ten hours 896,000 copies were sold, so keen was Chicago's curiosity.

Warmed by this reception, the founder of the *Sun* settled down in an apartment at the elegant Ambassador East Hotel on the Gold Coast, and began walking the three miles to work. Reaching the office at nine, he stayed on the job until five or six, looking into every department of the paper when the daily editorial conference was over.

Joseph Medill Patterson, who didn't like to think that Field was getting off to a good start in Chicago, might have been depressed if one of his reporters hadn't discovered that Field and Ingersoll had both been psychoanalyzed by Dr. Gregory Zilboorg. Making the most of the story, the New York *Daily News* declared that Zilboorg's treatment was "just the right cure for that washed-out, futile, satiated feeling that comes to a very rich man about the end of his third honeymoon." Setting out for Chicago without Zilboorg was a dangerous proposition for Field, the *News* hinted. "The question interesting all Field's friends and associates is this: Can Field, without Zilboorg, retain the bloom and zest of his new self? As the months wear by, and the psychiatric merry-go-round runs down, will he still be the same man . . . ?"

Well aware that a certain brand of personal journalism is a reflection of the state of mind of a certain type of publisher, Field made no reply. At the moment he was studying the by-laws of the Associated Press whose members, on McCormick's urging, shortly afterward turned down the *Sun's* application for a franchise. Rejoicing in the AP's decision, McCormick cried out that "the Gestapo is out of American newspaper offices forever," which was his way of saying that the New Deal was foiled for the time being.

Later on, after the Supreme Court forced the Associated Press to amend its by-laws, making it possible for the *Sun* to subscribe to its news service, McCormick found something more important to talk about than the AP's violation of the Sherman Act. The *Sun,* he said, was set up by President Roosevelt "to help in his secret plan to get into war by the back way."

McCormick was disappointed to hear that the founder of the *Sun* was invited to talk on the freedom of the press before a gathering of circulation managers in Ontario. "Marshall Field," he complained, "is an authority on horse racing, yacht racing, and grouse shooting, but he knows little about newspapers and nothing about the great constitutional subject of freedom of the press. It is an evil thing, therefore, that some weasel-minded lawyer should have written a disingenuous speech for him to declaim in a spot where freedom of the press does not exist."

Judging from next day's editorials in the Canadian papers, McCormick had very few admirers across the border. "The Canadian people," the Montreal *Herald* made clear, "are not likely to take any notice save passing contempt for the burbling of a Hitler-crazed Chicago publisher." Premier Hepburn of Ontario was inclined to agree. "Has this man gone wrong in his head, or something?" he asked.

The *Sun* was satisfied. "We had thought," ran its editorial on the incident, "to assure America's friends in Canada that they must not take the *Tribune's* publisher too seriously. We now perceive that it isn't necessary. With us, all Canada is chuckling over the inability of McCormick to face newspaper competition like a man."

Bewildered, McCormick dreamed of regaining his self-respect by libeling the National Maritime Union, CIO. This was a mistake, as he discovered the day after he announced that our merchant crews were "no credit to our nation." "We can understand well enough why Mr. McCormick flew off the handle of his own poison pump," the *Sun* commented, indirectly advising the millionaire that his return to civilian status was long overdue. "A ship of a *Tribune* subsidiary had been torpedoed at sea and the crew so forgot their loyalty to the lord of the tower as to save their lives by leaving the ship. Lese majesty! That was enough to damn the whole merchant marine in the eyes of McCormick. What's more, the merchant sailors belong to unions! That makes their treason to McCormick double."

The rage of the publisher of "The World's Greatest Newspaper" may be imagined. Desperate, he reached for the glory of exposing a communist plot. Though the Studebaker-managed airplane engine plant on the Southwest Side flew an Army and Navy "E" pennant, he found it convenient to believe that many of the workers were loafing, malingering, and gambling, all because of "the communist leadership" of the CIO union. "The Army and other administration agencies have done nothing to stop this sabotage," the *Tribune* protested. "The Roosevelt administration would rather lose the war than alienate its communist supporters."

McCormick could not have made a greater blunder. Field, who had just passed his fiftieth birthday and come into complete control of his grandfather's estate, was in no mood to tolerate the hounding of any labor union, much less an affiliate of the CIO.

As he saw it, the CIO was "perhaps the most powerful factor . . . in modern times" for "the improvement of race relations and the whole fight for modern, industrial democracy."

Studebaker employees, who knew there was no truth in McCormick's charges, gladly co-operated with representatives of the *Sun* in carrying out an investigation of the communist conspiracy. The outcome was unfortunate for the *Tribune*. Summing up the statements of managers and workers, the *Sun* made plain that the attack on the Studebaker plant was a "rotten and reckless piece of work . . . a giant fake" born of the "fevered delusions and prejudices" of a "hate-filled" publisher.

Field was in charge of the editorial page at the time. A few months later, when Silliman Evans resigned to go back to the Nashville *Tennessean,* Field became the publisher of the *Sun* as well as its editor. But he had only begun to plot his new career. Turning Caumsett over to the OWI to be used as a training center, he went on exploring a world undreamed of on Long Island.

Newspaper publishing was only one way to reach an audience. Alarmed at the *Tribune's* influence on the air through radio station WGN and the Mutual Network, Field bought up two radio stations, WJJD in Chicago and WSAI in Cincinnati. Speculating on the room for improvement in popular reference manuals, he took over the Quarrie Corporation, publishers of *The World Book Encyclopedia*. Thinking of the market still to be developed for inexpensive books, he added Simon and Schuster and its subsidiary Pocket Books to the list of his investments. Experimenting with the need for a politically conscious magazine for farmers, he got control of the staid *Southern Farmer,* changing its character by putting in Aubrey Williams of the National Youth Administration as editor. As the owner of the Sunday supplement *Parade,* he was no stranger to the problem of cross-country circulation.

All this while Field was mulling over philanthropic means of combating racial discrimination. The Field Foundation—best known for its sponsorship of the first non-commercial organization to measure public opinion in the United States, the National Opinion Research Center at the University of Denver—was set up primarily to relieve the financial anxiety of minority groups.

In the spring of 1945, when Dr. Edward J. Sparling and most of the faculty of the Central Y.M.C.A. College of Chicago quit in protest against what they believed to be restrictions on Negro students, Field put up part of the money and the Julius Rosenwald Fund the rest for a new institution open to everyone. Headed by Dr. Sparling, it was named after President Roosevelt.

Besides all this, Field is a trustee of the University of Chicago and the Chicago Natural History Museum, as the Field Museum is now called. Impressed with President Hutchins' innovations, he recently made the University a present of a million dollars in real estate. This was a useful sum, if only one fifth the amount he handed over to Museum in 1944.*

Field has his admirers, 1,000 of whom staged a banquet in his honor at the Palmer House on the *Sun's* third birthday. One of the speakers was that liberal Catholic, Most Reverend Bernard J. Sheil, Auxiliary Bishop of the Archdiocese of Chicago. Another was Vice-President Wallace, who insisted that Field was as important in the world of progressive thought as his grandfather in the business world.

About this time the *Tribune's* circulation averaged 964,778 on weekdays and 1,339,368 on Sundays. The *Sun's* audience was much smaller—only 329,441 on weekdays and 408,123 on Sundays. For all that, the *Sun's* showing was respectable. At the end of its first three years it was reaching roughly twice as many readers as the *Tribune* attracted before trying the Annenberg methods.

Field is more than satisfied with the *Sun's* gains, never having thought that it would be an easy matter to edge ahead of the *Tribune*. He admits that the *Tribune* is a habit, and that its

* Presiding over the Museum, fulfilling one of the last wishes of Marshall Field I, is Stanley Field, Marshall Field III's uncle. One of his advisers on anthropology is Henry Field III, the scholarly grandson of the founder's art-loving brother. The son of Minna Field and Preston Gibson, he took the name of Field after his mother divorced Gibson to marry the fox-hunting Englishman Algernon Burnaby.

(*Irving Haberman*, PM)

JOSEPH MEDILL PATTERSON

(*Brown Brothers*)

MARSHALL FIELD III AT A SERVICEMEN'S PARTY

comic strips, amusement pages, and sports columns appeal to a great many Chicagoans who object to McCormick's distortion of the news.

In one sense the battle for Chicago has only begun, for no one knows what part Marshall Field IV will play in humbling "The World's Greatest Newspaper." A lieutenant in the Naval Reserve he was released a few months ago to inactive duty after serving two years on the aircraft carriers *Enterprise* and *Cabot.* The veteran of twelve major engagements, he is entitled to wear a Presidential Unit Citation Ribbon, the Purple Heart, and the Silver Star Medal for heroism.

"NO RIGHT TO LIE"

Distressed by the prestige of the Field publications, puzzled by the strength of the democratic ideal in the modern world, the grandchildren of Joseph Medill labored under a greater emotional strain than many people realized. If Colonel McCormick was the moodiest of the three, and Joseph Medill Patterson the bitterest, "Cissy" Patterson of the Washington *Times-Herald* was the flightiest.

A year or so ago Mrs. Patterson tried to prove that President Roosevelt was a slacker in the First World War, and that our State Department in this war was a haven for draft-dodgers. More recently she compared Marshall Field to one of the inmates of Saint Elizabeth's Hospital for the Insane.

Not so easily rattled as his sister, Joseph Medill Patterson made up his mind on the afternoon of Pearl Harbor that the War Department was entitled to his services. Calling at the White House to present his claims for a commission, he was amazed at the coolness of his reception. Instead of being offered a comfortable chair, he was kept standing, hat in hand, half an hour, while President Roosevelt told him exactly what he thought of the editorial policy of the New York *Daily News.*

Until his death in May, 1946, Patterson brooded over this affront, evening the score in the summer of 1942 by insinuating that Roosevelt was about to become another Caesar. There was a remedy for Caesarism, Patterson pointed out. "Julius Caesar . . . was assassinated in the Roman Senate in 44 B. C."

The day after this editorial appeared in the New York *Daily News* and the Washington *Times-Herald,* Congressman Elmer J. Holland, a Democrat from Pennsylvania, delivered a short speech in the House on the responsibilities of newspaper owners in wartime. "Our American press has been doing a noble job," he said. "But unfortunately, there are a few publishers who take advantage of the right of free speech . . . to expound and promote fascism in America. . . . I now refer," he explained, "to America's number one and number two exponents of the Nazi propaganda line, Cissy and Joe Patterson, who are using their columns to repeat the propaganda broadcasts direct from the Nazi short-wave radio."

To be called to account by a Congressman was a novel experience for the publisher of the New York *Daily News*. "What Holland said about me and my sister is a lie," he protested. "We are not Hitler's followers. We do not seek to bring about a fascist victory, hoping to be rewarded afterwards."

Patterson pleaded that his blood was pure. "One of our grandfathers," he said, "was born of Scotch-Irish parents in New Brunswick, Canada, whence he was removed to the United States. The families of the other three grandparents had been in the United States for several generations. Members served in the Revolutionary, Civil, and World Wars. There is no German, Italian, or Japanese blood in us. We are of Irish extraction (both North and South), with a trace of Holland Dutch."

Of Irish descent himself, Congressman Holland was unimpressed by Patterson's racial background. "No," he decided, "it is not by blood that we can prove our Americanism. It is by word and deed. I would rather put my trust in the patriotism of the boys of my district who are in the services—sons as they are of Slavic steelworkers, Polish mill men, Hungarian craftsmen, Jewish merchants,

Irish railroaders, and the rest, than I would in the finely distilled Americanism of Joseph Medill Patterson. Their love for this country is real and vibrant—a living thing. Patterson's love for this country has been consumed in his hatred for its President."

A few months after this, Patterson's Washington correspondent John O'Donnell reported that "contraceptives and prophylactic equipment" would be "furnished to members of the WAAC, according to a super-secret agreement." One story led to another, until General Marshall came to the defense of the WAACs. Certain individuals, he said, "seem to be intent on the suicide of our own war effort, not to mention the defamation of as fine an organization of women as I have ever seen assembled."

Inaccurate at times, like all reporters, O'Donnell was guilty of a curious twisting of the facts on the 3d of October, 1945, when he claimed that the battle-fatigued soldier whose ears were boxed by General Patton during the Sicilian campaign was a Jew, and that "the secret and astoundingly effective might of this republic's foreign-born political leaders" was "behind the successful drive to disgrace and remove" General Patton from his command. Naming names, he implicated "Justice of the Supreme Court Felix Frankfurter, of Vienna, White House administrative assistant Dave (Devious Dave) Niles, alias Neyhus, and the Latvian ex-rabbinical student now known as Sidney Hillman."

It so happened that there was not one word of truth in all this. The soldier who got slapped was not a Jew, but a Nazarene, a member of a church akin to the Methodist denomination. Neither Frankfurter nor Niles nor Hillman had anything whatever to do with Patton's transfer. On the 18th of October, fifteen days after the publication of the piece in question, O'Donnell admitted that his conjectures were imaginary. "On the evidence," he wrote, "our statements . . . were untrue. We regret having made them."

In the interval the National Citizens Political Action Committee had gone to work, mailing a copy of O'Donnell's column of October 3d to every advertiser in the New York *Daily News*. "We believe," said Chairman Benson of the NCPAC, "this is one of the most scurrilous pieces ever to come from the pen of this notorious writer. It startles us and alarms us. Such articles are worthy only of the most vile hate sheets of Hitler Germany, and the increasing frequency of their appearance in widely circulated American newspapers is real cause for alarm." Benson's words were not without influence. The *News* suffered a sharp drop in advertising, even though R. H. Macy and Company refused to withdraw its copy.

Like his grandfather Joseph Medill, Patterson couldn't see why so much fuss was made over our foreign-born. "The *News,*" he complained, "is neither anti-Semitic nor pro-Semitic." As for censoring O'Donnell's column, that was out of the question, now, or at any other time. "If . . . columnists had to submit all their copy to the home office for approval before publication, they would not be as free to express themselves as they now are, and the traditional American freedom of the press (which is under pretty constant attack, anyway) would suffer."

Mayor LaGuardia was satisfied with neither O'Donnell's apology nor Patterson's excuses. "The whole story," he said over the radio, "was a mean, deliberate, cowardly lie. . . . It was known not to be true when it was written, and it was published knowing it to be entirely false. I suppose this story gave a great deal of amusement to the blasé millionaire owner of the *News*—you know, millionaire Patterson from Chicago. . . .

"Look here, Patterson," LaGuardia warned the hard-pressed publisher, "that kind of stuff may go in Chicago, in the Chicago *Tribune,* but it won't go for long in New York City. See! We concede the constitutional freedom of speech, we concede the freedom of the press, but we do not concede or recognize or know of any constitutional right to lie, to lie about people, to lie about good Americans."

There was no denying the fact that many New Yorkers were out of sympathy with the *Daily News*. Father William E. Kernan, assistant to the rector of the Episcopal Church of Saint James the Less in Scarsdale, took to the radio on Tuesday nights to remind the people that Patterson's racial policy was a denial of the Christian doctrine of the brotherhood of man. The Friends of Democracy, ever on guard against hatemongers in the United States, issued a broadside deploring the *News'* influence. "Wherever [it] is read," said the Friends of Democracy, "anti-Semitism becomes more and more inflamed."

Many of our returning soldiers sensed that the *Daily News* was not their kind of newspaper. Joining the Veterans' Committee against Discrimination, they started picketing the News Building and those department stores still advertising in the *News*. At one of the rallies of the Veterans' Committee Sergeant Marion Hargrove, author of the best-seller *See Here, Private Hargrove!*, left no doubt of how he felt. "By any means you can," he told the audience, "you should beat the hell out of the *Daily News*."

The idea that any American soldier would take exception to the editorials in the *News* had never occurred to Patterson. Dreaming of our political future early in 1945, he pictured the veterans as "sick of having to fight other people's battles and having their country bled white via Lend-Lease." They would, he thought, be glad to enroll in "a nationalist party" that would "stand for American interests."

Unaware of the genuine affection of many servicemen for their late Commander-in-Chief, O'Donnell charged that one man was to blame for Pearl Harbor. "As it now stands," he wrote, "the evidence builds up to the simple, brutal fact that F. D. R., the Big Brain, through blind stupidity and an obsession that Father knows best, was directly and personally responsible for the blood and disaster of Pearl Harbor, the nation's greatest and most disgraceful defeat." Suggesting that our President took the easy way out in 1917, he referred to "the civilian Roosevelt—who never wore the uniform of his country in any war."

In Chicago Colonel McCormick boldly alluded to "the administration leaders who wanted war even at the price of a national calamity," making it clear to everyone that the discrediting of

President Roosevelt was the primary postwar objective of all three publishers in the Chicago network.

Even while the war was on, McCormick was a somewhat severe critic of the Roosevelt administration. Remarking that an ex-employee of the *Tribune* who died in the Philippines had not gone "roaring up and down the country shouting for blood," he declared it was time "that those who willed the war were driven from their hiding places and sent to the front where they can share some of the agony they have created." Congressman Raymond S. McKeough, a Democrat from Illinois, was upset by this reflection on our war leaders. "I challenge Colonel McCormick's patriotism," he cried out in the House, "and I say that that language, at this time, makes him subject, at least to thinking people, as being guilty of treason."

McCormick insisted that he was not only a patriot, but a martyr as well. "I stand before you," he informed a gathering of Republican publishers, "as a living witness of governmental tyranny. The attacks upon me have been many, persistent, vicious, and futile."

Not all of the attacks originated in Washington. At home in Chicago Elmer Gertz, the president of the local chapter of the National Lawyers' Guild, drew up *The People vs. The Chicago Tribune,* a devastating indictment distributed by the Union for Democratic Action. Delving in one daring chapter of the pamphlet into the *Tribune's* relations with "home-grown fascists," Gertz reprinted McCormick's endorsement of *The Red Network* by Elizabeth Dilling, a volume exposing the "dangerous" activities of President Hutchins of the University of Chicago, Harold H. Swift of Swift and Company, and many other highly respected Americans. "I am glad," said McCormick of *The Red Network,* "to have it for reference, and trust that the book will have a large sale so that Americans will know who are the enemies of society within our gates." Mrs. Dilling was one of the 28 persons charged by the United States Government with conspiracy to injure the morale of the armed forces during the war.

Gertz was not alone in his resentment of the *Tribune*. The Chicago *Daily News,* then owned by Secretary of the Navy Knox, ridiculed the lord of the Tower by running a series of cartoons by Carl Jensen portraying the adventures of a certain "Colonel McCosmic." The Chicago *Times,* not to be outdone, revealed that Hitler's own newspaper, the *Voelkischer Beobachter,* hailed "The World's Greatest" for its "purely American thinking and feeling."

Undisturbed by Hitler's tribute, McCormick was faintly embarrassed when Donald Day, for twenty years the *Tribune's* Russophobic correspondent in Northern Europe, decided to do his bit in the war by railing at Roosevelt and the Jews over the Nazi airwaves. Though Day was the only *Tribune*-trained journalist broadcasting for the Third Reich, other enemy radio commentators made a practice of constantly quoting from the *Tribune.* As the *Sun* put it, the *Tribune* was "the darling of the Tokyo and Berlin radios."

"The World's Greatest Newspaper" was Anglophobic, no doubt of that. Incensed at the internationalism of such prominent Rhodes scholars as Herbert Agar, Elmer Davis, and Congressman J. William Fulbright, author of the Fulbright resolution pledging America to world co-operation, McCormick argued that "no Rhodes scholar can escape the suspicion of being, consciously or unconsciously, an alien agent." Fulbright, McCormick claimed, was sent to Oxford "to learn to betray his country and deprive it of its independence."

As one might expect, McCormick was unwilling to believe that the author of *One World* had any following in Illinois. "Why," he cried, "they think Willkie's nuts out there." When Willkie withdrew from the 1944 race for President after his defeat in the Wisconsin primaries, McCormick reflected that "the Eastern money that financed his elaborate campaign, and perhaps Lend-Lease money as well" would unfortunately be available to any candidate picking up his "tawdry banner."

About this time Medill McCormick's daughter "Trini," a determined young woman married to the career diplomat Courtlandt D. Barnes, Jr., created something of a sensation in New York and

Washington by announcing that she had sold her stock in the *Tribune* and given the proceeds to charity. "I've always hated Uncle Bertie," she confided to reporters. Once a devoted member of the America First movement, she took to complaining in public about "what the *Tribune* was spreading." She also began meeting the deficit of *Common Sense,* an earnestly intellectual magazine founded by the anthologist Selden Rodman.

Shortly after Mrs. Barnes took hold of *Common Sense,* it published an enlightening article on the *Tribune* signed by a certain Milton Mayer. "The one million people in Chicago who buy the *Tribune* do so because they like it," Mayer declared. "It expresses their views, not with absolute accuracy, but with sufficient vigor and fidelity to suit them right down to the ground."

Colonel McCormick could hardly object. No doubt he was more benign than ever on the following Saturday night when he went on WGN for his weekly broadcast to the nation. No doubt he was more considerate than usual to the *Tribune* executives who had lunch with him in the private dining room known as the Overset Club. Perhaps he granted an extra privilege to the *Tribune* employees, who already had the right to free dental cleaning, free medical examinations, and cut-rate medical treatment, besides being allowed to borrow money for life insurance and home-building from the *Tribune's* own savings and loan company. Or perhaps, thinking of the annual reception for the employees—at which he shows up in a cutaway—he called for an estimate on a better brand of ice cream than the year before.

McCormick's sixty-fifth birthday was not far off. On the day it fell due, the 30th of July, 1945, an odd thousand Chicagoans headed by attorney Silas H. Strawn gathered in the grand ballroom of the Palmer House for a banquet in his honor. To the surprise of most businessmen, who have always been able to restrain their admiration for McCormick, Mayor Kelly joined Governor Green and Senator Brooks at the speakers' table.

Senator Brooks was the first of the three politicians to pay tribute to the publisher. "No man," he said, "has championed with greater vigor the liberties and rights of the common man." He added that "millions regard him with genuine appreciation as a truly great patriot."

Governor Green was no less enthusiastic. As the leader of the Republican party in Illinois, he had no hesitation in saying that McCormick was "one of America's outstanding patriots."

Though a Democrat, Mayor Kelly felt even closer to McCormick than the Governor. "I have a picture in my library of the guest of honor when he was 25 years old," he revealed. "That is when I first met Colonel McCormick. We have never been very far apart in these forty years, except on some occasions when the Colonel did not agree with my politics."

Before recalling the good old days on the Sanitary District, when McCormick kept him from losing his job after he punched a bureaucrat on the nose, Kelly turned to the publisher's love of Chicago. "I do know," he said, "in all that he has done, he has just been 100 per cent for Chicago."

Kelly, of course, could not pretend to speak for the readers of the *Sun*. At the end of the summer the *Sun's* weekday circulation was 356,624, a gain of 27,183 over last year's figure.

"DISLOYAL AND UNBELIEVABLE"

To suppose that Chicago is shaken to its foundations by the clash of McCormick and Field is to forget that Chicago is a suburban city, and like all suburban cities, less of a metropolis than a shell. Unlike New York, most of whose well-to-do live in town at least in winter, Chicago suffers the lack of a large body of citizens whose very self-interest forces them to worry over good government and other problems affecting the commonweal. The political scene inevitably reflects this unfortunate state of affairs. While New York reaps the benefit of Fusion in the City Hall now and then, Chicago labors under bosses of the Kelly type, incidentally tolerating the most decrepit transportation system of any city in the world.

All this, however, scarcely concerns the suburbs. The bigger businessmen, heading for Evanston, Winnetka, Highland Park, and Lake Forest on the late afternoon trains, dwell in ideal communities from the standpoint of good schools, graftless town halls, and the like. Not unnaturally they tend to forget that all is not perfect in the city in which they spend their working hours. No wonder they are indifferent to the implications of the rivalry of the *Tribune* and the *Sun*.

As for the leading professional men, most of whom are suburbanites, while not indifferent, and often acutely conscious of the pressure of the *Tribune,* they find it next to impossible to rouse the city from its lethargy. The fact that neither the Presbyterian nor the Episcopal Church possesses anything like the prestige of the Episcopal Church in New York is one indication of the remarkable absence of social responsibility.

Under these circumstances, it is hardly surprising that the average Chicagoan, thirty-six years after the outbreak of the Great Circulation War, goes on buying the *Tribune*. No doubt he will continue to do so until the time comes for the leaders of organized labor to launch a truly extensive educational campaign.

Meantime the situation is serious, if not so critical as before the founding of the *Sun*. The *Tribune* is an influential newspaper, as former Secretary of War Stimson knows only too well. Testifying recently before the committee investigating Pearl Harbor, Stimson revealed the odds against the Roosevelt administration in preparing the nation for war in 1941.

"Our General Staff officers," said Stimson, "were working under a terrific pressure in the face of a global war which they felt was probably imminent. Yet they were surrounded, outside of their offices, and almost throughout the country, by a spirit of isolationisms and disbelief in danger which now seems almost incredible. A single incident gives striking evidence of this.

"During the very last week before the Pearl Harbor attack there was made a most disloyal and almost unbelievable attack on the chief work of the Staff. For months the General Staff had been laboring over the construction of a strategic and tactical plan for the fighting of a global war in case it should eventuate.

"The making of such a plan is the highest and most important duty of a General Staff—the chief purpose for which it exists. It is also naturally the most highly secret paper in the possession of the Government. On December 4, 1941, the Chicago *Tribune* published practically in full a copy of that plan.

"The impact of such a blow was very severe. It involved implications which stretched far and suspicions (happily not fulfilled) of disloyalty in the Army itself. The officers of the Army were then trying to do their duty in the deadening, if not actually hostile atmosphere of a nation that was not awake to its danger."

Chicago at this time was no longer the dynastic city of the nineteenth century. No matter if the Swifts continued to watch over the future of Swift and Company, no matter if a McCormick headed International Harvester, the absolute power of the founders of the great business houses was a thing of the past. And thanks to the hierarchic form of the modern corporation, with its minute division of responsibility, no titans loomed on the horizon.

It is in the newspaper business, in the struggle for circulation of the *Sun* and the *Tribune,* that the personal tradition survives, and the battle for Chicago continues.

Notes

CHAPTER ONE: *Queen of the Lake*

MEET MARSHALL FIELD. For Field on thrift, see Marshall Field, *Elements of Success,* p. 6. For Field's appearance, see E. T. Blair, *A History of the Chicago Club,* p. 54. For Field at home, see H. C. Chatfield-Taylor, *Cities of Many Men,* pp. 255-56. For Field on the panic, see *System,* August, 1906, p. 131. For the opening of the store, see Chicago *Tribune,* Oct. 13, 1868. For Field on pedigrees, see *System,* May, 1906, p. 458. For Field on his parents, see *Success,* Dec. 8, 1898, p. 7. For Field's mother, see *System,* May, 1906, p. 460. For Field on college education and drones, see Field, *op. cit.,* pp. 2-3, 8. For Field and the hounds, see Chicago *Tribune,* Jan. 17, 1906. For Field on wastefulness, see Field, *op. cit.,* pp. 5-7. For Field as a clerk, see *System,* May, 1906, p. 462. For Field on high principles and character, see Field, *op. cit.,* pp. 7-8. For Field and "Deacon" Davis, see S. H. Ditchett, *Marshall Field and Company,* pp. 11-12, 14. A copy of Davis' letter is in the possession of Marshall Field and Company.

THEY GOT THERE FIRST. For Miss Bremer's comments, see Frederika Bremer, *Homes of the New World,* I, pp. 605-06. For Ogden's career, see T. W. Goodspeed, *University of Chicago Biographical Sketches,* I, pp. 44, 47, 40, 41, 55, 36, 45-46. See on building of Galena and Chicago Union, Chicago *Tribune,* Dec. 19, 1872. For Newberry's forty acres, see Chicago *Tribune,* Nov. 20, 1868. For Julia Newberry's remarks, see Julia Newberry, *Julia Newberry's Diary,* pp. 42-43, 20. For Newberry's meeting with Wentworth, see Mabel McIlvaine, *Reminiscences of Early Chicago,* pp. 141-42. For Wentworth's memory of Chicago in 1836, see McIlvaine, *op. cit.,* pp. 104-05. For other Wentworth anecdotes, see the Wentworth Scrapbook, Chicago Historical Society.

FIELD FORGES AHEAD. For the number of trains in 1856, see William Bross, *History of Chicago,* p. 81. For Field's comment on Chicago, see *Success,* Dec. 8, 1898, p. 7. For Cooley's impressions of Field, see copy of his letter of Oct. 10, 1898, to Arthur B. Jones, in archives of Marshall Field and Company. For Field's cash on hand, see the official biographical sketch. For Field and the panic of 1857, see *Success, loc. cit.* For Farwell on damnation, see A. F. DeKoven, *A Musician and His Wife,* p. 30. For Farwell's impression of Field, see T. W. Goodspeed, *University of Chicago Biographical Sketches,* I, p. 7. For Ogden's troubles in 1857, see Goodspeed, *op. cit.,* p. 49. For the Wentworth anecdotes, see the Wentworth Scrapbook, Chicago Historical Society. For Joseph Field's comment on his brother's rise, see *System,* May, 1906, p. 464. For Nannie Scott's upbringing, see Chicago *Tribune,* Feb. 24, 1896. For Field's borrowing from Farwell, see A. F. Ferry, *Reminiscences of J. V. Farwell,* II, p. 122. For capitalization in 1865, see Goodspeed, *op. cit.,* p. 8. For Palmer on storekeeping, see *System,* July, 1906, pp. 23-24. For Palmer's early life, see Chicago *Inter-Ocean,* May 5, 1902. For Henry Field on Michigan Avenue, see Ferry, *op. cit.,* II, pp. 172-73. For Willing and Woodhouse's abilities, see the McClintock typescript. For dry goods statistics in 1867, see J. S. Wright, *Chicago, Past and Present,* p. 141. For Carson and Pirie's start, see Chicago *Tribune,* Apr. 25, 1913. For Andrew MacLeish's remark on Field's wages, the author is indebted to Archibald MacLeish. For Field on overworking, see *Success,* Dec. 8, 1898, p. 7. For the anecdotes of Field and Leiter at work, see the McClintock typescript. For the Eastern house and the credit rating, see *System,* July, 1906, p. 27. For Leiter and hats, for the horse worth $400, see the McClintock typescript. For Field's inexorable words, see Marshall Field, *Elements of Success,* p. 11. For Field on the successful merchant, see Chicago *Tribune,* Jan. 17, 1906. For Field's prosperity in 1868, see Chicago *Tribune,* Oct. 13, 1868. For the new building of the store, see Chicago *Tribune,* Oct. 13, 1868. Also Chicago *Times,* Oct. 13, 1868. For Newberry's remark on a nurse, see Joseph Kirkland, *The Story of Chicago,* p. 407. For Newberry's death, see Chicago *Tribune,* Nov. 20, 1868. For the ultimate value of Newberry's estate, see Chicago *Tribune,* May 14, 1886.

RISE OF THE HOUSE OF McCORMICK. For McCormick at breakfast, see W. T. Hutchinson, *Cyrus Hall McCormick,* II, 763. For McCormick on success, see Hutchinson, *op. cit.,* II, 754. For McCormick on his mother's garden, see H. N. Casson, *Cyrus Hall McCormick,* p. 180. For McCormick's father and mother, see Casson, *op. cit.,* pp. 13-14, 24-25. For McCormick on motherhood in Virginia, see Chicago *Inter-Ocean,* Feb. 24, 1880. For McCormick's education, see Hutchinson, *op. cit.,* I, 22. For Mr. Hart's daughters, see Hutchinson, *op. cit.,* I, 25. For invention of the reaper, see Hutchinson, *op. cit.,* I, 83. For Father McCormick's remark, see R. G. Thwaites, *Cyrus Hall McCormick and the Reaper,* p. 239. For McCormick in the iron business, see Hutchinson, *op. cit.,* I, 128. For McCormick vs. Hussey, see Casson, *op. cit.,* p. 88 and F. L. Greeno, *Obed Hussey,* p. 17. For Cyrus McCormick's advice to his brother Leander, see Hutchinson, *op. cit.,* I, 240. For Cyrus McCormick's advice on the Mexican War, see Hutchinson, *op. cit.,* I, p. 24. For the Leander McCormicks in Chicago, see H. L. McCormick-Goodhart, *Hands Across the Sea,* pp. 7, 13. For William McCormick's opinion of Chicago, see Hutchinson, *op. cit.,* II, p. 122. For his wife's interest in the institution of slavery, see Hutchinson, *op. cit.,* II, p. 102. For Leander and William McCormick's complaint of Cyrus and the details of the new contract, see Hutchinson, *op. cit.,* II, pp. 109-10. For William McCormick's remark on the money made selling machines, see Hutchinson, *op. cit.,* I, p. 298. For the New York Central's opinion of Cyrus McCormick in court, see Casson, *op. cit.,* p. 102. For the details on the lawsuit with the

Pennsylvania, see Hutchinson, *op. cit.,* II, p. 759. For McCormick and R. W. Henry, see Hutchinson, *op. cit.,* II, p. 13. For McCormick on religion, see Casson, *op. cit.,* p. 160. For McCormick's donations to the Presbyterian Church, see Hutchinson, *op. cit.,* II, p. 273. For McCormick's marriage, and Mrs. McCormick's rules for the children, see Hutchinson, *op. cit.,* II, pp. 751-52. For McCormick and the Chicago *Times,* see Hutchinson, *op. cit.,* II, pp. 46-47. For the William McCormicks in the Civil War, see Hutchinson, *op. cit.,* II, pp. 118, 113-14, 122. For Cyrus McCormick's letter to the Chicago *Times,* see Hutchinson, *op. cit.,* II, p. 58. For his advice to Lincoln, see Hutchinson, *op. cit.,* II, p. 62. For the *Tribune's* opinion of McCormick, see Chicago *Tribune,* Sept. 18, 1864. For McCormick's opinion of the *Tribune,* see Hutchinson, *op. cit.,* II, p. 48. For Stanton's eulogy of the reaper, see Thwaites, *op. cit.,* p. 255. For Wentworth on McCormick, see Chicago *Inter-Ocean,* May 14, 1884. The McCormick letters dealing with Field are dated Jan. 31, Nov. 29, Dec. 10, Dec. 14, Dec. 26, and Dec. 31, 1864. For William McCormick's mental breakdown, see Hutchinson, *op. cit.,* II, pp. 128-29. For the quarreling of Leander and Cyrus McCormick, see Hutchinson, *op. cit.,* I, p. 105. For the reorganization of the firm, see Hutchinson, *op. cit.,* II, p. 132. For Cyrus McCormick's investments, see Hutchinson, *op. cit.,* II, pp. 158-59, 165, 142. For McCormick and Boss Tweed, see Hutchinson, *op. cit.,* II, p. 308. For McCormick and Napoleon III, see Hutchinson, *op. cit.,* II, pp. 435-36.

MEDILL AND THE TRIBUNE. For the early history of the *Tribune,* see Chicago *Tribune,* June 10, 1907. For Medill's rise in the world and connection with the Republican party, see Chicago *Tribune,* Mar. 17, 1899. For Calvin Cobb's comment on Medill, see Kathryn Maddock, *Joseph Medill,* p. 14. For Medill's personal appearance, see Chicago *Tribune,* Apr. 6, 1923. For Lincoln's letter to the *Tribune,* see *The W. G. N.,* p. 30. For Ray's letter to Trumbull, see T. E. Strevey, *Joseph Medill,* p. 97. For the incorporation of the *Tribune,* see Chicago *Tribune,* Mar. 17, 1899. For Medill's letters to Colfax, see O. J. Hollister, *Life of Schuyler Colfax,* pp. 200, 203. For Medill's letter to Washburne, see Strevey, *op. cit.,* pp. 173-74. Joseph Medill's letter to William Medill is in the possession of the Chicago Historical Society. For Medill and Lincoln, see I. M. Tarbell, *The Life of Abraham Lincoln,* II, pp. 218-19. For Medill on Lee, see Chicago *Tribune,* June 30, 1865. For White on Medill, see Maddock, *op. cit.,* p. 41.

WHEN THE FLAMES STRUCK. For Chicago's position in packing during the Civil War, see the *Mississippi Valley Historical Review,* December, 1923, p. 262. For Morris on education, see Chicago *Tribune,* Aug. 28, 1907. For Morris' early life, see *National Provisioner,* Aug. 31, 1907. For other Morris anecdotes, see Chicago *Tribune,* Aug. 28, 1907. For Allerton's rise in the world, see Chicago *Tribune,* Feb. 23, 1914. For the founding of the Chicago Club, see E. T. Blair, *A History of the Chicago Club,* pp. 16, 4. For White during the fire, see Mabel McIlvaine, *Reminiscences of Chicago during the Great Fire,* pp. 63, 71. For the breakfast of the Chicago Club members, see Blair, *op. cit.,* pp. 33-34. For Storey's despair, see F. B. Wilkie, *Thirty-five Years of Journalism,* p. 193. For Ogden's stamina, see New York *Times,* Aug. 4, 1877. For Potter Palmer's braving of the calamity, see Chicago

Inter-Ocean, Dec. 12, 1886. For the amount of insurance Field carried, see copy of L. Z. Leiter's letter to Joseph Field of Dec. 28, 1871, in the possession of the store. For various anecdotes about the store and the fire, see the McClintock typescript. For the journalist's observation on the store's recovery, see McIlvaine, *op. cit.,* pp. 131-32. A copy of Leiter's letter to Greenbaum is in the possession of the store.

CHAPTER TWO: *The Cash Reward*

MEDILL AND HIS PEERS. For Medill on office-holding, see Chicago *Tribune,* Nov. 10, 1894. For Medill's message to the people, see Chicago *Times,* Dec. 3, 1872. For Hesing's cry of revolt, see Chicago *Times,* May 15, 1873. For Medill and the Field loan, see New York *Daily News,* Sept. 23, 1941. For Medill's declaration of principles, see Chicago *Tribune,* June 10, 1907. For Medill on communists and vagrants, see Chicago *Tribune,* Nov. 23, 1875, and July 12, 1877. For Medill and the reprinting of the article, see Chicago *Tribune,* Apr. 6, 1923. For working conditions on the *Tribune,* see Chicago *Times-Herald,* Mar. 20, 1899. For Storey and the *Times,* see F. B. Wilkie, *Thirty-five Years of Journalism,* pp. 180-81, 135, 151, 310, 273. Also Chicago *Inter-Ocean,* Oct. 28, 1884. For Wentworth vs. Scammon, see Chicago *Tribune,* Nov. 9, 1872 and Nov. 17, 1881. For the Chicago *Daily News,* see C. H. Dennis, Victor Lawson, pp. 5, 6, 68, 67, 48, 141. See also Chicago *Daily News,* Aug. 20, 1925. For Lawson's fortune, see Chicago *Tribune,* Nov. 1, 1925.

A TIME FOR HOTELS. For Kipling on the Palmer House, see Rudyard Kipling, *From Sea to Sea,* II, pp. 139-40. For McCormick's stinginess at the Palmer House, see W. T. Hutchinson, *Cyrus Hall McCormick,* II, p. 751. For Gage and Palmer, see Chicago *Tribune,* Feb. 2, 1890. For Palmer and the hotel help, see Chicago *Tribune,* May 11, 1902. For the Grand Pacific, see Chicago *Inter-Ocean,* Jan. 1, 1884 and Nov. 24, 1879. Also Chicago *Tribune,* Nov. 13, 1895. For the Richelieu, see C. H. Harrison, *Growing Up with Chicago,* p. 113. For Kinsley, see Chicago *Tribune,* Sept. 23, 1894.

FIELD AT HOME AND AT WORK. For Field's working hours, see the Official Biographical Sketch. For the "Millionaires' Table," see E. T. Blair, *A History of the Chicago Club,* pp. 52-54. For N. K. Fairbank and the Chicago Club, see Chicago *Tribune,* Dec. 30, 1885 and Aug. 1, 1876. For Fairbank and the opera house, see Chicago *Inter-Ocean,* Nov. 13, 1880. For Field and the panic of 1873, see Chicago *Times,* Oct. 18, 1873. For the opening of Stewart's store, see Chicago *Tribune,* Aug. 29, 1876. For Lehmann, see Chicago *Tribune,* Jan. 7, 1900. For Young, see Chicago *Tribune,* Dec. 1, 1906. For the opening of the retail on Madison and Market, see Chicago *Times,* Apr. 26, 1872. For Field and Paris gowns, see Chicago *Inter-Ocean,* Apr. 12, 1877. For the Field fire, see Chicago *Tribune* and Chicago *Times,* Nov. 15, 1877. For insurance, see Chicago *Times,* Nov. 16, 1877. For the buying of corner of State and Washington, see S. H. Ditchett, *Marshall Field and Company,* p. 47. For Field and the Merchants' Loan and Trust, see W. H. Harper and C. H. Ravell, *Fifty Years of Banking,* p. 67.

For Solomon A. Smith, see Chicago *Inter-Ocean* and Chicago *Tribune,* Nov. 26, 1879. Also Chicago *Tribune,* Nov. 27, 1879.

RISE OF THE HOUSE OF ARMOUR. For Armour and polished nails, see E. J. Dies, *Street of Adventure,* p. 93. For Armour's working hours, see Chicago *Tribune,* Jan. 7, 1901. For Armour's taciturnity, see Chicago *Record,* Jan. 7, 1901. For Armour vs. Field, see Harper Leech and J. C. Carroll, *Armour and His Times,* p. 346. For Armour and the money-making spirit, see W. T. Stead, *If Christ Came to Chicago,* pp. 79-80. For Armour and facts, see *World's Work,* March, 1901, p. 547. For Armour on the meaning of life, see Chicago *Record,* Jan. 7, 1901. For Armour on ministers and sausages, see Chicago *Inter-Ocean,* Jan. 7, 1901. For Armour and his early habits, see New York *Herald,* Jan. 7, 1901. For Armour on Oneida, see Elbert Hubbard, *Little Journeys to the Homes of Great Businessmen: P. D. Armour,* p. 137. For Armour and the weekly bath, see *World's Work,* March, 1901, p. 541. For Mrs. Armour and Culture, see Hubbard, *op. cit.,* p. 157. For the teacher-caller, see Leech, *op. cit.,* p. 18. For *David Harum,* see Chicago *Record,* Jan. 7, 1901. For Armour and the Almighty, see Hubbard, *op. cit.,* p. 139. For the Plankinton incident, see Chicago *Tribune,* Jan. 7, 1901. For Armour's marriage, see Chicago *Record,* Jan. 7, 1901. For the pork deal, see Leech, *op. cit.,* p. 32. For Armour and gambling, see *World's Work,* March, 1901, p. 541. For Armour and sentiment, see *American Magazine,* February, 1917, p. 15. For Armour on Saint Louis, see Chicago *Tribune,* Dec. 21, 1882. For Armour vs. Morris, see Dies, *op. cit.,* pp. 95-96. For Armour on theaters, see Chicago *Record,* Jan. 7, 1901. For Armour and the coachman, see *World's Work,* March, 1901, pp. 541-42. For Armour and the making of mistakes, see Hubbard, *op. cit.,* pp. 148, 156. For the Saint Paul deal, see Chicago *Tribune,* Jan. 7, 1901. For Armour and his brothers, see Chicago *Times-Herald,* Jan. 7, 1901. For Armour on hogs, Calvin Favorite, and the suits, see Leech, *op. cit.,* pp. 35, 74, 72-73. For Armour and the needy woman, see Chicago *Tribune,* Jan. 7, 1901. For Armour on Swift, Swift on Armour, and the Seaverns story, see Leech, *op. cit.,* pp. 94-95, 238, 236.

RISE OF THE HOUSE OF SWIFT. For Swift on Chicago, see Chicago *Inter-Ocean,* Mar. 30, 1903. For the draperies and George's arithmetic, see Helen Swift, *My Father and My Mother,* pp. 124, 51-52. For Father Swift's exhortation, see *Harper's Weekly,* Nov. 11, 1905, p. 1646. For Morris on Swift, Annie Maria Higgins, and Noble Swift's letter, see Helen Swift, *op. cit.,* pp. 90, 32-33, 63. For Swift's savings on his arrival, see L. F. Swift, *The Yankee of the Yards,* p. 25. For the introduction of refrigeration, see R. A. Clemen, *The American Live Stock and Meat Industry,* p. 236. For Swift stories on employees, managers, yes men, mechanics, dead hogs, cheesecloth, the urchin, offal, scraping hogs, cutting up the pieces, and attending church, see L. F. Swift, *op. cit.,* pp. 159, 173-74, 169, 176, 21, 98-109, 94, 116, 106, 13, 5, 21, 100, 57, 61, 16, 62. For Swift and the "ventilation committee," see Helen Swift, *op. cit.,* p. 125. For the stories of Swift staving off the bankers, see L. F. Swift, *op. cit.,* pp. 36-37, 41. For the story of the Court House steps, see Helen Swift, *op. cit.,* pp. 99-100. For Swift and Doud, see L. F. Swift, *op. cit.,* p. 42.

THE PANIC AND THE PROFITS. For the suicide of Coolbaugh, see Chicago *Tribune,* Nov. 15, 1877. For Hay's distress, see W. R. Thayer, *The Life of John Hay,* II, pp. 1-2. For Leiter and the strike, see Chicago *Tribune,* July 25, 1877. For Parsons and Mayor Heath, also Parsons and the *Tribune,* see Lucy Parsons, *Life of Albert Parsons,* pp. 13-14. For the "red war," see Chicago *Tribune,* July 25, 1877. For the Jews and Collyer's remarks, see Chicago *Tribune,* July 26, 1877. For the viaduct battle, see the Chicago *Tribune,* July 28, 1877. For Parsons on armed assassins, see Chicago *Tribune,* Apr. 26, 1878. For Mrs. McCormick and the communist menace, see W. T. Hutchinson, *Cyrus Hall McCormick,* II, p. 616. For Oakley's report, see Hutchinson, *op. cit.,* II, p. 617. For Armour and the butchers' strike, see Chicago *Inter-Ocean,* Dec. 17, 1879 and Jan. 14, 1880. For Armour and the pork raids, see *North American Review,* August, 1883, pp. 126, 135, 123.

ON THE NORTH SIDE. For the Leadville deal, see Chicago *Record-Herald,* Jan. 21, 1906, Chicago *Tribune,* Apr. 11, 1906, and letter of John Borden II to the author. For the building of the Potter Palmer Castle, see Chicago *Inter-Ocean,* Apr. 29, 1882, Aug. 19, 1882, Mar. 24, 1889. Also Chicago *Tribune,* Dec. 9, 1883. Also Chicago *Tribune,* Apr. 1, 1883. For Boni's comment, see Boni de Castellane, *Comment j'ai découvert l'Amérique,* p. 20. For Perry Smith's house, see Chicago *Tribune,* July 19, 1877. For McCormick's house on Rush Street, see Chicago *Tribune,* May 25, 1880. For McCormick and the coach driver, McCormick and the Paris doctors, and McCormick and oatmeal, see W. T. Hutchinson, *Cyrus Hall McCormick,* II, pp. 768, 751, 769-70. For McCormick and the harness, McCormick and the attorney, and McCormick on his deathbed, see *In Memoriam Cyrus Hall McCormick,* pp. 16, 19, 21. For Cyrus Hall McCormick II on his mother, see *Harvester World,* July, 1936, p. 49. For Henrietta McCormick and the invention of the reaper, see *Memorial of Robert McCormick,* p. 16. For the sale of Leander McCormick's interest, see Hutchinson, *op. cit.,* II, p. 642. For the Mikado Ball, see Chicago *Tribune* and Chicago *Inter-Ocean,* Jan. 2, 1886. For Field on life itself, see W. A. Salisbury, *The Career of a Journalist,* p. 266.

CHAPTER THREE: *The Cost of Grandeur*

FIELD WITHOUT LEITER. For Morgan and Field, see the McClintock typescript. For "hire another office boy," see Chicago *Tribune,* Sept. 15, 1927. For Field on the dissolution, see Chicago *Tribune,* Jan. 27, 1881. For Field vs. Leiter, see the McClintock typescript. For Leiter on trout fishing, see Chicago *Tribune,* Jan. 27, 1881. For Leiter's cash position, see Chicago *Tribune,* Jan. 19, 1883, and Aug. 10, 1904. For the anecdotes of Field in the store, see the McClintock typescript. For sales in 1881, see the official biographical sketch of Field. For the dinners on New Year's nights, see *Fortune,* October, 1936, p. 82. For the fortunes of the partners, see the McClintock typescript. Also Chicago *Tribune,* Dec. 23, 1890, Jan. 17, 1906, Oct. 31, 1927.

THESE WERE THE ARCHITECTS. For Richardson and the Field wholesale store, see M. G. Van Rensselaer, *Henry Hobson Richardson,* p. 36. For

Sullivan and the Field wholesale store, see L. H. Sullivan, *Kindergarten Chats,* p. 161. For Field's remark to Nevers, see the McClintock typescript. For Sullivan's solitude, see H. S. Morrison, *Louis Sullivan,* p. 82. For Sullivan on architecture and Chicago, see Sullivan, *op. cit.,* pp. 72, 143, 146. For Sullivan on Clopet, see L. H. Sullivan, *Autobiography of an Idea,* p. 221. For the opening of the Auditorium, see Chicago *Inter-Ocean,* Dec. 10 and 11, 1889.

TRAGEDY AT HAYMARKET SQUARE. For Medill's coolness to Field, see New York *Daily News,* Sept. 20, 1941. For Medill before the Senate, see U. S. Senate, *Report on Capital and Labor,* II, pp. 959-60, 987, 990, 962, 992. For the strike at the McCormick works, see Chicago *Tribune,* Apr. 8-11, 1885. For Mrs. McCormick's thoughts on the strike, see W. T. Hutchinson, *Cyrus Hall McCormick,* II, p. 696. For Parsons' speech at the McCormick works, see *The Alarm,* Apr. 18, 1885. For bomb-throwing, and the march on the Board of Trade, see *The Alarm,* Dec. 6, 1884, June 27, and May 2, 1885. For the new strike at the McCormick works, see Chicago *Tribune,* Feb. 17, Mar. 1-2, 1886. For the bloodshed at the McCormick works, see Chicago *Tribune,* May 4, 1886. For the Anarchists' proclamation, see Chicago *Inter-Ocean,* May 4, 1886. For the meeting at Haymarket, see Chicago *Tribune* and Chicago *Inter-Ocean,* May 5, 1886. Also Henry David, *The History of the Haymarket Affair,* pp. 200-01, 204. For Field vs. Harrison, see Chicago *Times,* Nov. 5, 1893. For Field and Armour on the police, see Chicago *Inter-Ocean,* May 6, 1886. For Lloyd and his friends, see *In Memoriam Henry Demarest Lloyd,* p. 5. For Medill on Lloyd's viewpoint, see Caro Lloyd, *Henry Demarest Lloyd,* I, p. 93. For Field vs. Gage, see Lloyd, *op. cit.,* I, p. 90. For Altgeld on his looks, see Harry Barnard, *Eagle Forgotten,* p. 18. For Altgeld as a child, and Altgeld's introspection, see Chicago *Inter-Ocean,* Mar. 16, 1902. For the *Tribune* on Altgeld's foreign birth, see Barnard, *op. cit.,* p. 120. For Altgeld on "the same ideas you have," see Barnard, *op. cit.,* p. 118. For Altgeld on the foreign born, see *The Forum,* February, 1890, p. 686. For the *Tribune's* bitter editorials, see Chicago *Tribune,* Mar. 4, 1890, Apr. 28, 1892. For Altgeld on the *Tribune,* see J. P. *Altgeld, Live Questions,* pp. 917, 939-40. For Altgeld on the *Tribune's* cashier, see Chicago *Tribune,* May 1, 1895. For Altgeld's remark to Darrow, see Clarence Darrow, *The Story of My Life,* p. 101. For Altgeld's decision to pardon the Haymarketers, see Chicago *Inter-Ocean,* Mar. 16, 1902. For the *Tribune* on the pardoning, see Chicago *Tribune,* June 27, 1893. For Whitlock's observation, see Brand Whitlock, *Forty Years of It,* p. 75.

FIELD AND THE FUTURE. For Field and Fort Sheridan, see *Yearbook of the Commercial Club 1939-40,* pp. 125-27. For Byron L. Smith, see Chicago *Tribune,* Mar. 23, 1914. For Field's loan to Insull, see Chicago *Tribune,* Nov. 2, 1934. For Insull's reminiscences, see Chicago *Tribune,* May 10, 1925. For Insull and the unemployed, see *New Republic,* Sept. 21, 1932, p. 144. For Edison and Insull, see F. L. Dyer and T. C. Martin, *Thomas A. Edison,* I, p. 332, 368. For Insull's coming to Chicago, see *Collier's,* Dec. 3, 1932, pp. 32-33. For Field and the errand boy, and Field and Funk, see the McClintock typescript.

CHAPTER FOUR: *The Men and the Monuments*

THE WHITE CITY. For Ward McAllister on Chicago, see Chicago *Tribune,* Apr. 10, 16, 23, 1893. Also Chicago *Tribune,* May 2, 1893. For Mrs. Palmer and the Fair, see Chicago *Tribune,* May 5, 1893. Also Chicago *Tribune,* May 8, 1899. For Hunt and the missionary expedition, see L. H. Sullivan, *Autobiography of an Idea,* p. 320. For Burnham's apologies, see *Architectural Record,* January, 1884, p. 292. For Saint-Gaudens on the Fair, see Charles Moore, *D. H. Burnham,* II, p. 47. For Sturgis on the Fair, see *Architectural Record,* August, 1909, p. 127. For Schuyler on the Fair, see *Architectural Record,* January, 1894, p. 291. For Sullivan on the Fair, see Sullivan, *op. cit.,* p. 325. For Field, Higinbotham, and the Fair, see the McClintock typescript. For the Illinois Trust incident, see Harper Leech and J. C. Carroll, *Armour and His Times,* p. 277. For Medill on Harrison, see Chicago *Tribune,* Aug. 28, 1893.

THE DISCIPLINE OF DOING GOOD. For Jane Addams and the sweating system, Jane Addams and the laboring men, and Jane Addams' hopes, see J. W. Linn, *Jane Addams,* pp. 152, 162, 105. For Thomas and "going to hell," see P. A. Otis, *The Chicago Symphony Orchestra,* p. 28. For Ryerson and the Art Institute, the author is indebted to the public relations department of the Art Institute. For the older Ryerson's estate, see Chicago *Tribune,* Sept. 30, 1887. For the estate of Martin A. Ryerson, see Chicago *Tribune,* June 29, 1933. For Hutchinson information, the author is again indebted to the Art Institute. For the jingle about "Old Hutch," see Harper Leech and J. C. Carroll, *Armour and His Times,* p. 260. For Harper and Sanskrit, see T. W. Goodspeed, *William Rainey Harper,* p. 25. For Goodspeed's conversation with Field, see T. W. Goodspeed, *The Story of the University of Chicago,* pp. 31-32. For Goodspeed on Field's lack of generosity, see T. W. Goodspeed, *University of Chicago Biographical Sketches,* I, p. 18. For donations of Field, see Goodspeed, *op. cit.,* I, p. 21. For Rockefeller, the Almighty, and the money, see T. W. Goodspeed, *The Story of the University of Chicago,* p. 169. For Field and the Field Museum, see the McClintock typescript. For Burnham on the cash value of beauty, see Charles Moore, *D. H. Burnham,* II, pp. 101-02. For Crane's misgivings, see Chicago *Tribune,* Dec. 29, 1907. For Crane's death and estate, see Chicago *Tribune,* Jan. 9, 10, 16, 1912. For Fuller's remark, see H. B. Fuller, *With the Procession,* p. 248.

CHAPTER FIVE: *The Builders Quit the Scene*

"A LITTLE LOWER THAN THE ANGELS." For Pullman and his father's hope, see Chicago *Inter-Ocean,* Oct. 25, 1885. For Pullman and our moral standards, see Mrs. Duane Doty, *The Town of Pullman,* p. 23, appendix. For Pullman's early life, see Chicago *Tribune,* Oct. 20, 1897. For Pullman and poker winnings, see New York *World,* Oct. 20, 1897. For the hotel car, see Chicago *Inter-Ocean,* June 18, 1877. For Pullman and Carnegie, see

B. J. Hendrick, *The Life of Andrew Carnegie,* II, pp. 181-82. For Field and the Pullman Company, the author is indebted to the Pullman Company. For the "gardens of Cashmere," see Chicago *Tribune,* Nov. 28, 1889. For Pullman and Beman, see Chicago *Inter-Ocean,* Aug. 16, 1881. For Pullman and saloons, Pullman and the Pullman theater, see Chicago *Inter-Ocean,* Aug. 16, 1881, and Jan. 10, 1883. For Woodford's speech, see Doty, *op. cit.,* pp. 28-31, appendix. For the Pullman library, see Chicago *Tribune,* Apr. 12, 1883. For the testimony of one of the car-builders, see 53rd Congress, Third Session, Senate Document No. 7, *Report on the Pullman Strike,* p. 426. For American workmen, see W. H. Cardwardine, *The Pullman Strike,* p. 100. For unions not being tolerated, see 53rd Congress, *op. cit.,* p. 417. For the rental of the church and Oggel's sermon, see Cardwardine, *op. cit.,* pp. 20-21. For Pullman and the effect of the strike, see Chicago *Tribune,* May 13, 1894. For Hopkins' good work, see Chicago *Tribune,* May 17, 1894. For Debs' lieutenant's advice, see Chicago *Tribune,* May 12, 1894. For the Government comment on Debs' leadership, see 53rd Congress, *op. cit.,* p. xxvii. For Hanna and Pullman, see Thomas Beer, Hanna, pp. 132-33. For Pullman on the meaning of the strike, see New York *Tribune,* July 14, 1894. For Medill on same, see Chicago *Tribune,* July 3, 1894. For Debs' advice to his followers, see Chicago *Tribune,* July 4, 1894. For the Altgeld-Cleveland correspondence, see Allan Nevins, *The Letters of Grover Cleveland,* pp. 358-59. For Medill on Altgeld, see Chicago *Tribune,* July 7, 1894. For the damage done, Debs on the soldiers, and Pullman on the A. R. U., see 53rd Congress, *op. cit.,* pp. xxviii, 143, 563, 566. For Darrow and Debs' trial, see Clarence Darrow, *The Story of My Life,* p. 100. For Altgeld vs. Pullman, see J. P. Altgeld, *Live Questions,* pp. 420-24. For Pullman's burial, estate, and will, see Chicago *Inter-Ocean,* Oct. 24, 1897. Also Chicago *Tribune,* Dec. 9, 1900, Oct. 28, 1897.

THE TROUBLES OF C. T. YERKES, JR. For Field on Yerkes, see *System,* January, 1907, p. 54. For Yerkes on his technique, see *Everybody's,* September, 1907, pp. 355, 358. For Yerkes on the Fair grounds, see *System,* May, 1907, p. 458. For Yerkes' threat to kill the editor, see *Everybody's,* June, 1911, p. 840. For Yerkes' troubles in 1871, see Philadelphia *Public Ledger,* Oct. 20, 1871, Sept. 28, 1872. For Yerkes' youth, see New York *Times,* Dec. 30, 1905. For Yerkes' comeback, see Chicago *Tribune,* Dec. 30, 1905, New York *Times,* Dec. 30, 1905. For Yerkes' Chicago house and the ball for Saint Luke's Hospital, see Chicago *Tribune,* May 13, 1883, Jan. 14, 1885. For the Widener-Elkins' interest in Yerkes' plans, see Chicago *Tribune,* Mar. 27, 1886. For Elkins' rise in the world, see Philadelphia *Public Ledger,* Nov. 8, 1903. For Widener's triumph, see Philadelphia *Public Ledger,* Nov. 7, 1915. For Widener at the board meeting, see *McClure's,* Dec. 1907, p. 328. For Brady, see New York *Sun,* July 23, 1913, New York *Tribune,* July 24, 1913. For Whitney, see New York *Times* and New York *Tribune,* Feb. 3, 1904. For Ryan's estate, see Chicago *Tribune,* Feb. 16, 1932. For Yerkes to the citizens of Lake View, see Chicago *Tribune,* Oct. 28, 1888. For the West Division deal, see Chicago *Tribune,* Sept. 12 and Nov. 13, 1887. For the fountain and the telescope, see Chicago *Tribune,* Mar. 21, 1890, Oct. 12, 1892. For Yerkes' New York home, see Chicago *Tribune,* Apr. 18, 1893, Dec. 30, 1905. Also *Everybody's,* June, 1911, p. 842. For the "straw hat" anecdote, see *Everybody's,* June, 1911, pp. 839-40. For Field's advice on Yerkes, see *System,* January, 1907, p. 54. For Yerkes' loot, see *Quarterly Journal of Economics,* May, 1907, p. 379. For Yerkes on Altgeld, see Harry Barnard, *Eagle Forgotten,* p. 405. For maneuvers in Springfield, see Chicago *Tribune,* Apr. 16, 1897. For the quote of Yerkes on Medill, etc., the author is indebted to Yerkes' leaflet *The Other Side of the Question.* For Medill on Yerkes, see Chicago *Tribune,* Jan. 14, 1897. For Harrison vs. Yerkes, see C. H. Harrison, *Stormy Years,* pp. 138, 152, 51, 148-49. For Harrison's appeal to the people, see Chicago *Tribune,* Dec. 7, 1898. For Yerkes and the deal involving the Chicago "L" system, see Chicago *Tribune,* Feb. 26, 1901. For Yerkes' estate, see Chicago *Tribune,* Mar. 1, 1912.

THE LEITERS AT HOME AND ABROAD. For Joseph Leiter's education, see Chicago *Tribune,* Apr. 12, 1932. For his behavior at the track, see Chicago *Tribune,* July 2, 1931. For the Leiter reserves in wheat, see New York *Herald-Tribune,* Apr. 12, 1932. For Armour's reply, see Chicago *Tribune,* Dec. 19, 1897. For Leiter's offer for May wheat, see Chicago *Tribune,* Mar. 12, 1898. For John J. Mitchell on the corner, see Chicago *Tribune,* June 14, 1898. For Armour on the corner, see Harper Leech and J. C. Carroll, *Armour and His Times,* p. 316. For Joseph Leiter on Armour, see Chicago *Tribune,* June 14, 1898. For the cost to Leiter of the State Street site, see the McClintock typescript. For other details on the sale to Field, and the size of the Leiter estate, see Chicago *Tribune,* June 10, 1904, Feb. 25, 1927. For the investment of the Leiter millions, see Chicago *Tribune,* June 10, 1904. See also Chicago *Record-Herald,* June 29, 1904. For Joseph Leiter and Zeigler, see Chicago *Tribune,* Dec. 6, 1904, July 30, 1904, Jan. 11, 1909, July 28, 1904, Aug. 6, 1904, Aug. 25, 1904, Dec. 1, 1904. See also Chicago *Record-Herald,* Feb. 26, 1907, Chicago *Tribune,* Jan. 11, 1909. For Joseph Leiter's marriage and the trouble in the Pullman car, see Chicago *Tribune,* June 11, 1908, July 18, 1909. For the marriages of the Leiter girls, see Chicago *Tribune,* Nov. 30 and Dec. 27, 1904, Apr. 23, 1895. For Lady Curzon on the Zeigler troubles, see Chicago *Tribune,* Feb. 24, 1927. For her death, see Chicago *Tribune,* July 19, 1906. For Joseph Leiter on Curzon, and Joseph Leiter on the lease of Clark and Madison, see Chicago *Tribune,* Oct. 24, 1923 and Dec. 11, 1926. For the end of the lawsuit and Joseph Leiter's death, see Chicago *Tribune,* May 14, 1931, New York *Times,* Apr. 12, 1932. For Lady Cynthia Curzon's passing, see New York *Herald-Tribune,* May 17, 1933.

THE PACKERS ON TRIAL. For the "diseased meat" stories, see 51st Congress, 1st Session, *Senate Report No. 829,* pp. 185, 178. For Miles on the beef, see 56th Congress, 1st Session, *Senate Document No. 221,* VII, pp. 325-26. For Alger, see R. A. Alger, *The Spanish-American War,* pp. 383-84. For Theodore Roosevelt's comment, see New York *Tribune,* Mar. 26, 1899. For the preacher's remark, see Chicago *Tribune,* Jan. 2, 1899. For Miles' charges, see Harper Leech and J. C. Carroll, *Armour and His Times,* p. 336. For the Armour Mission and the Armour Institute, see Leech, *op. cit.,* pp. 211-12. For other details on the institute, see *Armour Engineer and Alumnus,* May, 1937, p. 35. For the religion of the institute, see Leech, *op. cit.,* p. 213. For the "blowout" at the institute, see Chicago *Tribune,* Jan. 7, 1901. For

Gunsaulus and the Negro, see E. A. Bancroft, *Dr. Gunsaulus, The Citizen,* p. 14. For Armour at the office, chatting with Gunsaulus, and saying his mind in the little town, see *Review of Reviews,* February, 1901, pp. 173-74. For Armour on Ogden Armour's anglomania, see Leech, *op. cit.,* p. 92. For the death of P. D. Armour II, the death of P. D. Armour I, and the size of his estate, see Chicago *Tribune,* Jan. 28, 1900, Jan. 7 and 29, 1901. For Field on Armour, see Chicago *Times-Herald,* Jan. 7, 1901. For the little children singing hymns, see Chicago *Record,* Jan. 14, 1901. For Beveridge's work in Washington, see C. G. Bowers, *Beveridge and the Progressive Era,* p. 233. For Allerton on the Progressives, see Chicago *Record-Herald,* Sept. 29, 1911, Feb. 5, 1912. For Ogden Armour on the post-war picture, see Chicago *Tribune,* Oct. 1, 1917. For the Ogden Armour fiasco, see *Fortune,* April, 1931, pp. 49-50. For the size of Swift's estate, see Chicago *Inter-Ocean,* Mar. 30, 1903. For Swift's warnings to the family, see *National Provisioner,* Apr. 4, 1903.

THEY THOUGHT AHEAD. For Field vs. Medill at time of Spanish-American War, see Chicago *Tribune,* Mar. 18, Apr. 1, May 2 and 15, 1898. For the figures on the *Tribune's* circulation, the author is indebted to a handout of the *Tribune's* advertising department. For the cash advanced to R. S. McCormick, see *The Will of Joseph Medill.* For Patterson's career, see Chicago *Tribune,* Apr. 2, 1908. For Medill on his deathbed, see Chicago *Tribune,* Mar. 17, 1899. For Medill's estate, see New York *Tribune,* Mar. 26, 1899. For Medill's last wishes, see the frontispiece of *The W. G. N.* For Ambassador McCormick's career, see New York *Times* and Chicago *Tribune,* Apr. 17, 1919. For Ambassador McCormick on the decline of radicalism in Russia, see Chicago *Record-Herald,* May 25, 1907. For the preliminaries involved in the creation of International Harvester, see United States of America vs. International Harvester, *Defendants' Record,* Volume XIII, pp. 216, 252. See also New York *Herald-Tribune* and New York *Times,* June 3, 1936. Also *Fortune,* August, 1933, p. 33. For Deering's career, see *In Memoriam William Deering.* For other information on Deering family, see Chicago *Tribune,* Dec. 11, 1913, Feb. 7, 1927. For Cyrus Hall McCormick II's career, see Chicago *Tribune,* June 3, 1936.

THE DEATH OF MARSHALL FIELD. For the South Bend *Times'* comment, see an undated clipping in the possession of the Field estate. For Field's refusal to face TR in open debate, see the McClintock typescript. For Field and the Court of Saint James, see W. R. Thayer, *The Life of John Hay,* II, p. 195. For Field and the Democratic campaign of 1904, see Chicago *Record-Herald,* Apr. 22, 1904, Chicago *Tribune,* July 5 and 9, 1904. For Field on municipal ownership, the tax question, law and order, and strikes, see Chicago *Record-Herald,* Aug. 17 and Oct. 18, 1905. Also Chicago *Tribune,* June 6, 1903, Oct. 23, 1905. For Field in the steel business, see Chicago *Tribune,* Aug. 18, 1887, May 4, 1889. Also Allan Nevins, *John D. Rockefeller,* II, p. 423. For Field and railroads, see *System,* May, 1906, p. 455. Also Edward Hungerford, *The Story of the Baltimore and Ohio Railroad,* II, p. 216. For the legends of Selfridge's departure, see the McClintock typescript. For a first-hand account, see *Saturday Evening Post,* July 27, 1935, pp. 19, 51; Sept. 7, 1935, p. 90. For Field to Shedd, see the McClintock typescript. For Field and Simpson, see New York *Times,* Nov. 26, 1939. For Field at breakfast, the author is indebted to Stanley Field. For Mrs. Field's death, Ethel's first marriage, young Marshall's marriage, and the opening of the library at Conway, see Chicago *Tribune,* Feb. 4, 1896, Jan. 2, 1891, Dec. 26, 1905, July 14, 1901. Also Chicago *Inter-Ocean,* Oct. 24, 1890. For Field's wedding with Delia Caton and young Marshall's accident, see Chicago *Tribune,* Nov. 19, 1904, Sept. 5, Nov. 23, and Nov. 24, 1905. Also Chicago *Inter-Ocean,* Nov. 24, 1905. For young Marshall's death, see Chicago *Tribune* and Chicago *Record-Herald,* Nov. 28, 1905. For Mrs. Marshall Field II on her children's future, see Chicago *Record-Herald,* Sept. 1, 1907. For Stanley Field's conversation with Marshall Field, the author is indebted to Stanley Field. For Marshall Field's death, see Chicago *Tribune,* Chicago *Record-Herald,* Chicago *Daily News,* New York *Times,* Jan. 17, 1906. For the funeral train, see Chicago *Record-Herald,* Jan. 18, 1906. For ceremonies, see Chicago *Record-Herald,* Jan. 20, 1906. For Morrison's sermon, see Chicago *Record-Herald,* Jan. 20, 1906. For Adams' and Notmans' remarks, see *In Memoriam Marshall Field.* For the inventory of the estate, see Chicago *Tribune,* Jan. 25, 1907. For Field's landholdings, see Chicago *Tribune,* Jan. 17, 1906. For the amount of money left by Field, the author is indebted to R. H. Peel of the Field Estate. For Palmer's fortune, see Chicago *Tribune,* May 14, 1902. For taxes against the estate, and the final settlement, see Chicago *Record-Herald,* Sept. 1, 1907, Chicago *Tribune,* Feb. 10, 1908. For Root on Field, see New York *Times,* May 13, 1920.

CHAPTER SIX: *Of Millionaires and Murderers*

A SOCIALIST IN THE HOUSE OF MEDILL. For Eleanor Patterson on her brother, see *Editor and Publisher,* June 24, 1939, p. 7. For J. M. Patterson on his education, see *Sexennial Report,* Class of 1901, Yale University. For Patterson in the opera box, Patterson in the saloons, and Patterson taking his little girl to school, see *The New Yorker,* Aug. 6, 1938, p. 16. For Patterson's threat to the sluggers, see Journal of Commerce Company vs. The Tribune Company, et al., *Transcript of Record,* p. 331. For Patterson on anarchistic capitalists, see Chicago *Tribune,* Nov. 20, 1905. For Patterson's conversion to socialism and hymn to money, see Chicago *Record-Herald,* Mar. 3, 1906. For Dunne's supporter on Patterson, see Chicago *Record-Herald,* Sept. 15, 1906. For Patterson on charity and New York, see Chicago *Record-Herald,* Mar. 17 and Mar. 4, 1906. For Patterson on Marx, see *Saturday Evening Post,* Sept. 29, 1906, p. 5. For Patterson as a socialist orator, see Chicago *Record-Herald,* Mar. 27, and Apr. 2, 1906. Also Chicago *Record-Herald,* June 22, 1908. For Patterson on drones, see *The Independent,* Aug. 30, 1906, pp. 493-94. For Patterson on the Field estate, see *Collier's,* June 2, 1906, p. 26. For Patterson's protest of socialist ambitions, see Chicago *Record-Herald,* Feb. 21, 1909. For Patterson and McCormick on the *Tribune,* see *The W. G. N.,* p. 68. For McCormick in Politics, see Chicago *Record-Herald,* Mar. 3 and Mar. 6, 1904, June 3, 1905, Apr. 23, 1907. Also see *Triennial Report,* Class of 1903, Yale University. For McCormick as president of the Tribune Company, see *The Trib,* March, 1936, p. 7. For Ambassador Mc-

Cormick's collapse, see Chicago *Record-Herald,* May 3 and Dec. 22, 1909. For R. W. Patterson, Jr.'s death, see Chicago *Tribune,* Apr. 2, 1910.

"QUITE A CROQUET GAME." For Moses Annenberg's prison term, see New York *Herald-Tribune,* July 22, 1942. For statements from *Journal of Commerce* case, see Journal of Commerce Publishing Company vs. The Tribune Company et al., *Transcript of Record,* United States Court of Appeals, Seventh District, October Term, 1921, No. 3116, pp. 75, 557, 682-83, 728-29, 730, 703.

"COLD-BLOODED MURDERERS." For statements from Senate hearings, see Sixty-second Congress, Second Session, Senate Document No. 484, *Hearings on the Election of William Lorimer,* pp. 2054-56, 2072-74. On Keeley's leaving the *Tribune,* see J. W. Linn, *James Keeley: Newspaperman,* pp. 185, 189.

PREACHERS TO THE PEOPLE. For Annenberg on France, see Chicago *Tribune,* Aug. 5, 1914, cited in *The War Record of the Chicago Tribune.* For McCormick on courage, cakes, blood-lust, and the wine of death, see R. R. McCormick, *With the Russian Army,* pp. ix, 91, 84, 252. For McCormick on the possible disloyalty of our immigrants, see *Century Magazine,* April, 1916, p. 839. For McCormick's marriage, see New York *Times,* Mar. 11, 1915. For Patterson on one hundred per cent Americanism, American culture, and German ingenuity, see J. M. Patterson, *The Note Book of a Neutral,* pp. 12, 10-11, 18, 22, 19. For McCormick's citation, see New York *Times,* Apr. 12, 1923.

HOMER WOULD HAVE LIKED IT. For Northcliffe's advice, and Van Anda's opinion, see S. M. Bessie, *Jazz Journalism,* pp. 78, 82. For early circulation figures of the *Daily News,* see *The New Yorker,* Aug. 13, 1938, p. 23. For the losses in *Liberty Magazine,* see *The New Yorker,* Aug. 20, 1938, p. 22. For Sullivan on Tribune Tower, see *Architectural Record,* February, 1923, p. 156. For Homer's admiration of the *Tribune,* see *The W. G. N.*, p. 30.

"EVEN AS DID THE GREAT WEBSTER." For McCormick's marriage, see Chicago *Tribune,* June 11, 1903. For McCormick and his rivals, see Journal of Commerce Publishing Company vs. The Tribune Company, *Transcript of Record,* p. 649. For McCormick on Jane Addams and TR, see D. R. Richberg, *The Tents of the Mighty,* pp. 36, 34. For Ickes on McCormick, see H. L. Ickes, *The Autobiography of a Curmudgeon,* pp. 149-50, 166-67. For McCormick and La Follette, see R. M. La Follette, *La Follette's Autobiography,* pp. 555-57. For Crane, see New York *Times* and New York *Herald-Tribune,* Feb. 15, 1939. See also Henry James, *C. W. Eliot,* II, p. 320. For McCormick on fair rents, see *Congressional Record,* Apr. 14, 1922, p. 5512. For foreigners on the floor, see New York *Times,* May 13, 1922. For McCormick on Czecho-Slovakia, see *Congressional Record,* Feb. 16, 1920, p. 2948. For McCormick on the Tammany of Europe, see Sixty-eighth Congress, First Session, *Senate Document No. 51.* For McCormick's career in retrospect, see Chicago *Tribune,* Feb. 26, 1925. For Watson vs. Lodge, see J. E.

Watson, *As I Knew Them,* pp. 190-91. For Mellon and Frick, see George Harvey, *H. C. Frick,* p. 324. For McCormick on Asiatic immigrants, see New York *Times,* Mar. 6, 1919. For McCormick on the international bankers, see New York *Times,* Nov. 23, 1920. For the *Tribune* on internationalism, see Chicago *Tribune,* Feb. 6, 1919. For McCormick on Harding, see Karl Schriftgiesser, *The Gentleman from Massachusetts,* p. 357. For the New York *Times* on McCormick's impertinence, see New York *Times,* Jan. 18, 1922. For McCormick and Webster, see 68th Congress, *op. cit.* For McCormick's death, see New York *Times* and Chicago *Tribune,* Feb. 26, 1925. For Ruth McCormick's expenditures, see Chicago *Tribune,* May 2, 1930.

CHAPTER SEVEN: *The Age of Insull*

ANXIOUS FOR ELEGANCE. For McCormick and Wright's difficulties, see F. L. Wright, *An Autobiography,* p. 503. For McCormick and the Chicago Civic Opera, see New York *Times,* Mar. 12, 1915. For the "perfect rose" story, see New York *Times,* Aug. 26, 1932. For the children's marriages, see *Fortune,* December, 1931, p. 56, *Time,* Sept. 21, 1931, p. 39. For McCormick's operation and remarriage, see New York *Times,* June 18 and Aug. 12, 1922. For quotes from Madame Walska's book, see Ganna Walska, *Always Room at the Top,* pp. 381, 178, 404-05. For her divorce from Harold McCormick, see New York *Times,* Oct. 11, 1931. For his obituary, see New York *Times,* Oct. 16, 1941. For Edith McCormick, the dinner for 200, and her jewels, see New York *Times,* Aug. 26, 1932. For the clock at table, see *Fortune,* December, 1931, p. 124. For Denham and the menu, see New York *Times,* Jan. 7, 1934. For the silver, see Sales Catalog, *Edith Rockefeller McCormick Collection.* For Seti I, the McCormick Institute, and the Zoo Park, see Chicago *Tribune,* Aug. 26, 1932, New York *Times,* Jan. 27, 1923. For Edith McCormick and Joyce, see Herbert Gorman, *James Joyce,* pp. 237, 264. For Krenn and Dato, see New York *Times,* Aug. 26, 1932, Chicago *Tribune,* Aug. 27, 1932.

"THROW AWAY YOUR HAMMER." For Dion O'Banion and Capone, see E. D. Sullivan, *Rattling the Cup on Chicago Crime,* pp. 9-10, 57, 139, 193. For Thompson's personal appearance and "America First," see *Plain Talk,* January, 1928, pp. 43-45, 50. For Thompson and Washington, see W. H. Stuart, *The Twenty Incredible Years,* pp. 294, 296. For Ettelson, see C. H. Harrison, *Growing up with Chicago,* pp. 208-09. For Insull and the Richberg incident, see *The Nation,* Apr. 5, 1933, pp. 368-69.

SUCH WAS SAMUEL INSULL. For Insull's excitement at lunch, the author is indebted to a confidential source. For Insull and "one concern," see M. L. Ramsay, *Pyramids of Power,* p. 56. For Insull and the gas business, see *Collier's,* Dec. 3, 1932, p. 32. For the financing of Middle West, see *Collier's,* Dec. 17, 1932, p. 21. For honesty, see Samuel Insull, *Public Utilities in Modern Life,* p. 35. For the Insull public relations policy, see C. D. Thompson, *Confessions of the Power Trust,* p. 327, Ernest Gruening, *The Public Pays,* pp. 166-67, Federal Trade Commission, *Reports,* Volume XVIIA, p. 17. For Insull during the war, see *New Republic,* Sept. 28, 1932, p. 170. For Insull before the Senate, see Sixty-ninth Congress, First Session, *Hearings before a Special Committee,* pp. 3387-88, 3395, 1824-25. For Norris, see *Congressional Record,* Dec. 6, 1927, p. 120. For Rosenwald see M. R. Werner, *Julius Rosenwald,* pp. 308, 366, ix, 336, viii, 121, 338, 44-45. For Rosenwald and success, see New York *Tribune,* Jan. 7, 1932. For "what in hell" story, see *Atlantic Monthly,* April, 1933, p. 504. For Eaton vs. Insull, see Chicago *Tribune,* Nov. 2, 1934. For Insull Utility Investments, Corporation Securities, and "the little man," see Chicago *Tribune,* Jan. 17, and Sept. 29, 1929, Oct. 17, 1934. For Mrs. Insull and the stage, "stage money," and "the dollar," see Chicago *Tribune,* May 26, 1925, Dec. 17, 1927, Mar. 5, 1922, Jan. 10, 1926. For Insull and the new Opera House, see Chicago *Tribune,* Jan. 29, 1927, Nov. 5, 1929. For the deal with Eaton, see Chicago *Tribune,* Sept. 16, 1932, Oct. 19, 1934. For Eaton's comment on Insull's cheerfulness in paying up, the author is indebted to Eaton. For Mrs. McCormick and the stars, see New York *Times,* Feb. 28, 1932. For Insull's meeting with the bankers in New York and the appointment of receivers in Chicago, see Chicago *Tribune,* Aug. 19, 1932, Feb. 7-8 and 10, 1934. For the "unaccountable accounts," see Chicago *Tribune,* Oct. 1-2, 1932. For Insull's forced resignation and the taxi ride, see Chicago *Tribune,* Feb. 14, 1934. For Insull's plea for privacy and trip to France, see Chicago *Tribune,* June 9 and 22, 1932. For Insull and the new school of accounting, and the sale of that block of Middle West, see *Atlantic Monthly,* April, 1933, pp. 502, 504. For Insull abroad, see Chicago *Tribune,* Oct. 2 and 11, 1932, Mar. 18, 1934. For Insull and doing right, and the laborer and his hire, see Chicago *Tribune,* May 10 and Nov. 3, 1934. For the outcome of all the trials, see Chicago *Tribune,* Aug. 14, Nov. 25, and Dec. 12, 1934, Mar. 12, 1935. For Insull's obituary, see New York *Times* and Chicago *Tribune,* July 17, 1938.

CHAPTER EIGHT: *In Our Time*

THEIRS THE FREEDOM OF THE PRESS. For McCormick on taxation, see R. R. McCormick, *The National Peril,* pp. 5-17. For McCormick and communism in our universities, see Chicago *Tribune,* Apr. 28, 1933. For McCormick and the Tribune's prosperity in 1933, see *Fortune,* May, 1934, pp. 105, 188. For Gerard's appointment of McCormick to the "Fifty-nine Men," see New York *Times,* Aug. 21, 1930. For McCormick's denial of the *Tribune's* participation in the circulation wars, see Chicago *Tribune,* Jan. 27, 1931. For McCormick on Minton, see *Editor and Publisher,* Oct. 1, 1938, p. 9. For the fact that McCormick was elected president of the Tribune Company in 1911, see *The Trib,* March, 1936, p. 7. For McCormick's implied denial of a tie with the *Tribune* at that time, see Chicago *Tribune,* Oct. 2, 1938. For McCormick on the freedom of the press, see R. R. McCormick, *The Case for the Freedom of the Press,* p. 28. For McCormick's indulgence in Tannenberg, see Chicago *Tribune,* Apr. 14 and 21, 1935. For McCormick in his house at Wheaton, the author is indebted to a confidential source. For McCormick on the Fourth, see Chicago *Tribune,* July 5, 1939. For Mrs. McCormick's burial, see Chicago *Tribune,* Aug. 17, 1939. Also *The Trib,* August, 1939, p. 4. For McCormick's second marriage, see New York *Times,* Dec. 19, 1944. For McCormick on the "war party," see Chicago *Tribune,*

Apr. 13, 1939. For McCormick on the draft, see New York *Times,* June 20, 1940, Chicago *Tribune,* Aug. 23 and Oct. 13, 1940. For McCormick before the Senate, see Chicago *Tribune,* Feb. 7, 1941. For McCormick on the alien-minded millionaires, see Chicago *Tribune,* Feb. 17, 1941. For McCormick on his rivals in Chicago, see Chicago *Tribune,* Mar. 22, 1941. For Patterson on Russia and "Roosevelt's War," see New York *Daily News,* Nov. 17, 1939, Oct. 2, 1941. For Patterson on Annenberg, see New York *Daily News,* Feb. 7, 1941. For O'Donnell's iron cross, see New York *Herald-Tribune,* Dec. 19, 1942. For Patterson's gloom, see New York *Daily News,* Oct. 3 and 22, Nov. 16, 1941. For Eleanor Patterson's ambition to be a reporter, see *American Magazine,* August, 1940, p. 10. For other references to Eleanor Patterson, see *Newsweek,* Feb. 6, 1939, p. 30, *Saturday Evening Post,* May 6, 1939, pp. 22-23, 55-62. For Stimson on McCormick's patriotism, see Chicago *Tribune,* Dec. 6, 1941.

THE RETURN OF MARSHALL FIELD. For McCormick's welcome to Field, see *The Trib,* December, 1941, p. 3. For McCormick's taunt and Field's reply, see Chicago *Tribune,* July 26, 1942, Chicago *Sun,* July 28, 1942. For Marshall Field's mother in England, see Chicago *Tribune,* Sept. 4-5, 1908. For Field at Eton, see Marshall Field, *Freedom is more than a Word,* p. 47. For Field and the Chicago reporters, see Chicago *Tribune,* Dec. 24, 1913. For Field on Cambridge, see Field, *op. cit.,* pp. 48-49. For Field's marriage to Evelyn Marshall, see New York *Times,* Feb. 7, 1915. For Henry Field's marriage, death, and relationship with Peggy Marsh, see New York *Times,* Nov. 15, 1916, Feb. 8, 1917, Chicago *Tribune,* Jan. 31, 1919. For Mrs. Drummond's death, see New York *Times,* Sept. 20, 1915. For Nancy Perkins' marriage to Tree, see Chicago *Tribune,* May 5, 1920. For the Beattys, see New York *Times,* July 18, 1932. For Gwendolyn Field's marriage, see New York *Times,* Apr. 6, 1923. For the *Tribune,* on Field's enlistment, see Chicago *Tribune,* Apr. 15, 1917. For Field's comment, see Chicago *Tribune,* Apr. 20, 1917. See also *Literary Digest,* Mar. 27, 1920, p. 98. For Field in the army, see Bruce Grant, *$howdown at $unup,* Chicago *Times,* Oct. 29-Nov. 9, 1941. For Field's entrance into banking, see New York *Times,* Jan. 23 and Dec. 30, 1920. For Field and the creative use of a fortune, see New York *Times,* Dec. 31, 1920. For the Marshall Field Garden Apartments, see New York *Times,* Nov. 19, 1927, Chicago *Daily News,* Sept. 11, 1943. For Field and Field, Glore, see *Fortune,* May, 1930, pp. 104-40. For Field's removal to New York, and his houses, see New York *Times,* June 2 and 12, 1921, Mar. 23, 1937. For Field at "Caumsett," see *Country Life,* April, 1934, pp. 42-45. For Field's divorce from his second wife, see New York *Times,* Nov. 13, 1935. For Field's convictions, see Field, *op. cit.,* pp. ix, x, viii. For the investment of the Field Estates, the author is indebted to R. H. Peel. For the Field holdings in the store and Commonwealth Edison, see Seventy-sixth Congress, Third Session, Temporary National Economic Committee, *Monograph No. 29,* pp. 805, 1055-59. For Field's resignation from Field, Glore, see New York *Times,* July 2, 1935. For Field's endorsement of Roosevelt, see New York *Times,* Oct. 28, 1936. For Field's friendship with Roosevelt in the First World War, the author is indebted to Field. For Field's marriage to Ruth Pruyn Phipps, see New York *Times,* Jan. 16, 1936. For the marriages of Field's three children by Evelyn Marshall, see New York *Times,* June 21, 1938, Feb.

15, 1942, Chicago *Sun,* June 13, 1942. For Field's buying into *PM,* see *Variety,* Jan. 14, 1942. For Field on *PM,* the author is indebted to Field. For Field and the race relations roll of honor, see *PM,* Dec. 29, 1944. For Field on Westinghouse, see *PM,* July 3, 1942. For Field and "three square meals," see New York *Times,* Sept. 19, 1941. For the burning of the *Tribunes,* see *Time,* Aug. 11, 1941, pp. 53-54. For Field at work in Chicago, see *Time,* Sept. 27, 1943, p. 44. For the Zilboorg story, see New York *Daily News,* Nov. 6, 1941. For McCormick on the Gestapo, see New York *Times,* Apr. 23, 1942. For McCormick on the "secret plan," see New York *Sun,* Oct. 9, 1945. For McCormick's Canadian troubles, see Chicago *Sun,* Oct. 9, 1942. For McCormick and the NMU, see Chicago *Sun,* Dec. 22, 1942. For Field on the CIO, see Field, *op. cit.,* pp. 35-36. For the Studebaker incident, see Chicago *Tribune,* Nov. 19, 1943, *Time,* Dec. 6, 1943, p. 59. For Field's complete control of the *Sun,* see New York *Times,* Feb. 7, 1944. For "Caumsett" and the OWI, see New York *Herald-Tribune,* Oct. 3, 1943. For Field's new holdings, see *PM,* Oct. 5, and Dec. 5, 1945, New York *Times,* Nov. 2, 1944, *Time,* June 2, 1941, p. 51; Dec. 17, 1945, p. 62. For the Field Foundation, see New York *Times,* Sept. 3, 1941. For Roosevelt College, see New York *Times,* Sept. 17, 1945. For the University's million dollars, see Chicago *Tribune,* Apr. 6, 1940. For the *Sun's* anniversary party, see Chicago *Sun,* Dec. 5, 1944.

"NO RIGHT TO LIE." For Mrs. Patterson on FDR'S war record, see *Time,* July 24, 1944, p. 48. For her slur on Field, see Washington *Times-Herald,* Oct. 28, 1945. For FDR's reception of Patterson, see *Reader's Digest,* July, 1942, p. 62. For Patterson on Caesar's assassination, see New York *Daily News,* Aug. 2, 1942. For Patterson on the purity of his blood, see New York *Daily News,* Aug. 5, 1942. For O'Donnell's report on the prophylactic equipment, see New York *Daily News,* June 9, 1943. For Marshall's remarks, see New York *Herald-Tribune,* June 22, 1943. For Patterson on the freedom of the press, see New York *Daily News,* Oct. 13, 1945. For LaGuardia on Patterson, see *PM,* Oct. 22, 1945. For the Veterans' Committee, see *PM,* Oct. 18 and Nov. 8, 1945. For O'Donnell on FDR's war record, see New York *Daily News,* Nov. 22, 1945. For McCormick on FDR's administration, see Chicago *Tribune,* Nov. 17, 1945. For McKeough, see *Time,* Feb. 23, 1942, p. 42. For McCormick as a martyr, see Chicago *Tribune,* Feb. 28, 1943. For McCormick on Mrs. Dilling, see Elmer Gertz, *The People vs. The Chicago Tribune,* p. 35. For the *Times* on Hitler's newspaper, see Chicago *Times,* Aug. 24, 1944. For Donald Day and the *Tribune* in Germany and Japan, see *PM,* Mar. 30, 1945, Chicago *Sun,* Mar. 3, 1945. For McCormick on Rhodes Scholars, see Chicago *Tribune,* Aug. 26 and Sept. 23, 1943, New York *Herald-Tribune,* Oct. 2, 1943. For McCormick on Willkie, see New York *Times,* July 15, 1943, Apr. 6, 1944. For "Trini" Barnes, see *Time,* Mar. 13, 1944, p. 81. For Mayer on the *Tribune,* see *Common Sense,* March, 1944, p. 111. For McCormick's paternalism, see *Time,* Dec. 1, 1941, p. 62. For McCormick's birthday party, see Chicago *Tribune* and Chicago *Sun,* July 31, 1945.

"DISLOYAL AND UNBELIEVABLE." For Stimson's remarks, see New York *Times,* Mar. 22, 1946.

Bibliography

MARSHALL FIELD AND MARSHALL FIELD AND COMPANY

EASILY the best short account of Field's life is to be found in T. W. Goodspeed's *University of Chicago Biographical Sketches.* A longer account, but not trustworthy in all details, is H. I. Cleveland's "Fifty-five Years in Business," a series of articles which ran in *System* from April, 1906, through April, 1907. Also to be consulted is S. H. Ditchett's *Marshall Field and Company.* The Dry Goods Economist, 1922. But the most dependable reference is Samuel McClintock's unpublished history of Marshall Field and Company, which is preserved in the archives of the store along with copies of certain letters referring to Field. Other letters referring to Field are in the possession of the McCormick Historical Association.

The official biographical sketch of Marshall Field, issued by the Field Estate, is helpful, if brief. Other sources include:

Crissey, Forrest, *Since Forty Years Ago,* The Fair, Chicago, 1915

DeKoven, A. F., *A Musician and His Wife,* Harper and Brothers, 1926

Dreiser, Theodore, "Life Stories of Successful Men: Marshall Field," *Success,* December 8, 1898

Farwell, J. V. II, Remarks on Fort Sheridan in *Yearbook for 1939-1940,* Commercial Club, Chicago, 1940

Ferry, A. F., *Reminiscences of J. V. Farwell,* Ralph Fletcher Seymour, Chicago, 1928, 2 vols.

Field, Marshall, *Elements of Success,* Northern Trust Company, Chicago, 1896

Field Museum of Natural History, *Addresses Commemorating the Fiftieth Anniversary,* Chicago, 1943

"Fifty Years of Progress," Fiftieth Anniversary Issue, *Field Museum News,* 1943

Hungerford, Edward, *The Story of the Baltimore and Ohio Railroad,* G. P. Putnam's Sons, 1928, 2 vols.

In Memoriam Marshall Field, Privately Printed, Chicago, 1906

MacLeish, Andrew, *The Life of Andrew MacLeish,* Privately Printed, Chicago, 1929

Pierce, F. C., *Field Genealogy,* W. B. Conkey Company, Chicago, 1901

Selfridge, H. G., "Selling Selfridge," *Saturday Evening Post,* July 27, August 10 and 24, and September 7, 1935

GENERAL REFERENCE

Andreas, A. T., *History of Chicago,* A. T. Andreas, Chicago, 1889, 3 vols.
Bross, William, *History of Chicago,* Jansen, McClurg and Company, Chicago, 1876
Bross, William, *The Railroads, History, and Commerce of Chicago,* Democratic Press, Chicago, 1854
Gale, E. O., *Reminiscences of Early Chicago,* F. H. Revell Company, Chicago, 1902
Hansen, Harry, *The Chicago,* Farrar and Rinehart, 1942
Kirkland, Joseph, *Story of Chicago,* Dibble Publishing Company, Chicago, 1892
Lewis, Lloyd, and Smith, H. J., *Chicago: The History of Its Reputation,* Harcourt, Brace and Company, 1929
McIlvaine, Mabel, ed., *Reminiscences of Chicago during the 'Forties and 'Fifties,* Lakeside Press, Chicago, 1913
McIlvaine, Mabel, ed., *Reminiscences of Early Chicago,* Lakeside Press, Chicago, 1912
Pierce, B. L., *A History of Chicago,* Alfred A. Knopf, 1937, 1940, 2 vols.
Wright, J. S., *Chicago, Past, Present, and Future,* Western News Company, Chicago, 1868

WHAT TRAVELERS SAW

Bremer, Frederika, *The Homes of the New World: Impressions of America,* Harper and Brothers, 1858, 2 vols.
Castellane, Boni de, *Comment j'ai découvert l'Amérique,* G. Crès, Paris, 1924
Kipling, Rudyard, *From Sea to Sea,* Doubleday and McClure Company, 1899, 2 vols.
Pierce, B. L., *As Others See Chicago,* University of Chicago Press, 1933

HOTELS

The Palmer House, Chicago, J. M. Wing and Company, Chicago, 1873
Williamson, Jefferson, *The American Hotel,* Alfred A. Knopf, 1930

BANKS AND BANKING

Gage, Lyman, *Memoirs,* The House of Field, 1937
Harper, W. H., and Ravell, C. H., *Fifty Years of Banking in Chicago,* Merchants' Loan and Trust Company, Chicago, 1907
James, F. C., *The Growth of Chicago Banks,* Harper and Brothers, 1938, 2 vols.

REMINISCENCES

Chatfield-Taylor, H. C., *Cities of Many Men,* Houghton Mifflin Company, 1925

CLUBS

Blair, E. T., *A History of the Chicago Club,* H. S. Stone and Company, Chicago, 1898

Glessner, J. J., *The Commercial Club of Chicago,* Privately Printed, Chicago, 1910

EARLY CHICAGO BUSINESSMEN

Newberry, J. R., *Julia Newberry's Diary,* W. W. Norton and Company, 1933

John Wentworth Scrapbook, Chicago Historical Society

THE GREAT FIRE OF 1871

McIlvaine, Mabel, ed., *Reminiscences of Chicago during the Great Fire,* Lakeside Press, Chicago, 1915

JOURNALISM

Abbot, W. J., "Chicago Newspapers and Their Makers," *Review of Reviews,* June, 1895

Dennis, C. H., *Victor Lawson: His Time and His Work,* University of Chicago Press, 1935

Salisbury, W. A., *The Career of a Journalist,* B. W. Dodge and Company, 1908

Wilkie, F. B., *Thirty-five Years of Journalism,* F. J. Schulte and Company, Chicago, 1891

JOSEPH MEDILL AND THE "TRIBUNE"

Cullom, S. M., *Thirty Years of Public Service,* A. C. McClurg and Company, Chicago, 1891

Hollister, O. J., *Life of Schuyler Colfax,* Funk and Wagnalls, 1886

Kinsley, Philip, *The Chicago Tribune: Its First Hundred Years,* Volume 1, Alfred A. Knopf, 1943

Maddock, Kathryn, *Joseph Medill: An Editor of the Old School,* M. A. Thesis, University of Illinois, 1916

Medill, Joseph, Letter to William Medill, dated May 24, 1863, Chicago Historical Society

Strevey, T. E., *Joseph Medill and the Chicago Tribune during the Civil War Period,* Ph.D. Thesis, University of Chicago, 1930
Tarbell, I. M., *The Life of Abraham Lincoln,* Lincoln History Society, New York, 1903, 2 vols.
United States Senate, *Report of the Committee upon Relations between Labor and Capital,* 1885
The W. G. N., The Chicago *Tribune,* Chicago, 1922

THE MC CORMICKS' INTERNATIONAL HARVESTER

Casson, H. N., *Cyrus Hall McCormick,* A. C. McClurg and Company, Chicago, 1909
Gorman, Herbert, *James Joyce,* Farrar and Rinehart, 1939
Greeno, F. L., *Obed Hussey,* F. L. Greeno, Rochester, New York, 1912
Holt, Joseph, *Opinion in the matter of the application of C. H. McCormick for an extension of his patent of 1845,* Washington, 1859
Hutchinson, W. T., *Cyrus Hall McCormick: Seed-Time,* Century Company, 1930
Hutchinson, W. T., *Cyrus Hall McCormick: Harvest,* D. Appleton-Century Company, 1935
In Memoriam William Deering, Privately Printed, Chicago, 1914
In Memoriam C. H. McCormick, Riverside Press, 1884
"In Memoriam Cyrus Hall McCormick II," *Harvester World,* July, 1936
McCormick, C. H. III, *The Century of the Reaper,* Houghton Mifflin Company, 1931
Edith Rockefeller McCormick Collection, Sales Catalog, American Art Association-Anderson Galleries, 1934
Memorial of Robert McCormick, Barnard and Gunthorp, Chicago, 1885
McCormick-Goodhart, H. L., *Hands Across the Sea,* R. R. Donnelley and Sons, Chicago, 1931
Rogin, Leo, *The Introduction of Farm Machinery,* University of California Publications in Economics, Volume 9, 1931
Seward, W. H., *The Reaper, Argument in the Circuit Court of the United States,* Auburn, New York, 1854
Stanton, Edwin, *Argument for the Defendants in McCormick vs. Talcott,* Washington, 1857
Swift, R. B., *Who Invented the Reaper?,* Privately Printed, Chicago, 1897
Thwaites, R. G., *Cyrus Hall McCormick and the Reaper,* State Historical Society of Wisconsin, 1909
United States of America, Petitioner, vs. International Harvester Company et al., *Defendants' Record*
Walska, Ganna, *Always Room at the Top,* Richard R. Smith, 1939

THE PACKERS

Alger, R. A., *The Spanish-American War,* Harper and Brothers, 1901
Armour, J. O., *The Packers, the Private Car Lines, and the People,* H. Altemus Company, Philadelphia, 1906

Bancroft, E. A., *Dr. Gunsaulus, the Citizen,* Privately Printed, Chicago, 1921
Bowers, C. G., *Beveridge and the Progressive Era,* Houghton Mifflin Company, 1932
"Chicago: The Stockyards and Packingtown," *The Lancet,* January 7, 14, 21, and 28, 1905
Clemen, R. A., *The American Livestock and Meat Industry,* Ronald Press Company, 1923
Dies, E. J., *Street of Adventure,* Stratford Company, 1935
Federal Trade Commission, *Report on the Meat Packing Industry,* 1919
Fifty-first Congress, First Session, Senate Document No. 829, *Report of the Vest Committee on the Transportation and Sale of Meat Products*
Fifty-sixth Congress, First Session, Senate Document No. 221, *Report on the War with Spain*
Fifty-eighth Congress, Third Session, House Document No. 382, *Report of Commissioner of Corporations J. R. Garfield on the Beef Industry*
Fifty-ninth Congress, First Session, House Document No. 873, *Neill-Reynolds Report*
Filler, Louis, *Crusaders for American Liberalism,* Harcourt, Brace and Company, 1939
Hendricks, Walter, "Historical Sketch of the Armour Institute of Technology," *Armour Engineer and Alumnus,* May, 1937
Hill, H. C., "The Development of Chicago as a Center of the Meat Packing Industry," *Mississippi Valley Historical Review,* December, 1923
Hubbard, Elbert, *Little Journeys to the Homes of Great Businessmen: P. D. Armour,* Elbert Hubbard, East Aurora, New York, 1909
Leech, Harper, and Carroll, J. C., *Armour and His Times,* D. Appleton-Century Company, 1938
Lloyd, H. D., "Making Bread Dear," *North American Review,* August, 1883
Lorimer, G. H., *Letters from a Self-Made Merchant to His Son,* Curtis Publishing Company, 1901
Norris, Frank, *The Pit: A Story of Chicago,* Doubleday, Page and Company, 1903
Russell, C. E., *The Greatest Trust in the World,* Ridgway-Thayer Company, 1905
Sinclair, Upton, *The Jungle,* Doubleday, Page and Company, 1906
Sixty-fifth Congress, Third Session, *Government Control of the Meat Packing Industry,* Hearings before the Committee on Interstate and Foreign Commerce
Stead, W. T., *If Christ Came to Chicago,* Laird and Lee, Chicago, 1894
Swift, Helen, *My Father and My Mother,* Lakeside Press, Chicago, 1937
Swift, L. F., *The Yankee of the Yards,* A. W. Shaw and Company, Chicago, 1927
Taylor, C. H., *History of the Board of Trade of the City of Chicago,* Robert O. Law, Chicago, 1917

PULLMAN

Carwardine, W. H., *The Pullman Strike,* C. H. Kerr and Company, Chicago, 1894

Doty, Mrs. Duane, *The Town of Pullman,* T. H. Struhsacker, Pullman, Illinois, 1893
Fifty-third Congress, Third Session, Senate Document No. 7, *Report on the Pullman Strike*
Hendrick, B. J., *The Life of Andrew Carnegie,* Doubleday, Doran and Company, 1932, 2 vols.
Husband, Joseph, *The Story of the Pullman Car,* A. C. McClurg and Company, Chicago, 1917
Lindsey, Almont, *The Pullman Strike,* University of Chicago Press, 1942
Pond, I. K., "Pullman: America's First Planned Industrial Town," *Bulletin of the Illinois Society of Architects,* June-July, 1934
Pullman Scrapbook, Crerar Library, Chicago
The Strike at Pullman: Statements, Chicago, 1894 (?)

YERKES

Dreiser, Theodore, *The Financier,* Boni and Liveright, 1927
Dreiser, Theodore, *The Titan,* Boni and Liveright, 1925
Fairlee, J. A., "The Street Railway Question in Chicago," *Quarterly Journal of Economics,* May, 1907
Frost, P. P., "The Chicago Street Railway War," *World's Work,* June, 1905
Hendrick, B. J., "Great American Fortunes and Their Making: Street Railway Financiers," *McClure's,* November and December, 1907, and January, 1908
Leach, J. G., *Chronicle of the Yerkes Family,* J. B. Lippincott Company, 1904
Lefèvre, Edwin, "What Availeth It?", *Everybody's,* June, 1911
Lloyd, H. D., *The Traction Question,* Privately Printed, Chicago, 1903
"The Other Side of the Question," Pamphlet in the Possession of the Crerar Library, Chicago
Russell, C. E., "Where did you get it, Gentlemen?", *Everybody's,* August, September, October, November, and December, 1907, and January and March, 1908
Steffens, Lincoln, "Chicago: Half Free and Fighting On," *McClure's,* October, 1903
Yerkes, C. T., Jr., "Private Control of Street Railways," *Municipal Affairs,* Winter, 1902-03

ARCHITECTURE

Drury, John, *Old Chicago Houses,* University of Chicago Press, 1941
Early Modern Architecture: Chicago 1870-1910, Museum of Modern Art, 1940
Hitchcock, H. R., Jr., *The Architecture of H. H. Richardson and His Times,* Museum of Modern Art, 1935
Hitchcock, H. R., Jr., *In the Nature of Materials: The Buildings of Frank Lloyd Wright, 1887-1941,* Duell, Sloan and Pearce, 1942
Industrial Chicago, Goodspeed Publishing Company, Chicago, 1891, 2 vols.
The Merchants, and Manufacturers of Chicago, J. M. Wing and Company, Chicago, 1873

Moore, Charles, *Daniel H. Burnham: Architect, Planner of Cities,* Houghton Mifflin Company, 1921, 2 vols.
Moore, Charles, *The Life and Times of Charles Follen McKim,* Houghton Mifflin Company, 1929
Moore, Charles, ed., *The Promise of American Architecture,* American Institute of Architects, 1905
Monroe, Harriet, *John Wellborn Root: A Study of His Life and Work,* Houghton Mifflin Company, 1898
Morrison, H. S., *Louis Sullivan,* W. W. Norton and Company, 1935
Saint-Gaudens, Augustus, *Reminiscences,* Century Company, 1913, 2 vols.
Schuyler, Montgomery, "A Critique of the Works of Adler and Sullivan, D. H. Burnham and Company, and Henry Ives Cobb," *Architectural Record,* December, 1895
Schuyler, Montgomery, "Last Words about the World's Fair," *Architectural Record,* January-March, 1894
Sullivan, L. H., *The Autobiography of an Idea,* American Institute of Architects, 1926
Sullivan, L. H., "The Chicago *Tribune* Competition," *Architectural Record,* February, 1923
Sullivan, L. H., *Kindergarten Chats,* Scarab Fraternity Press, Lawrence, Kansas, 1934
Tallmadge, T. E., *Architecture in Old Chicago,* University of Chicago Press, 1941
Van Rensselaer, M. G., *Henry Hobson Richardson,* Houghton Mifflin Company, 1888
Wight, P. B., "Reminiscences of Russell Sturgis," *Architectural Record,* August, 1909
Wright, F. L., *An Autobiography,* Longmans, Green and Company, 1932

THE CRANES

Crane, R. T., *Autobiography of Richard Teller Crane,* Privately Printed, Chicago, 1927
"R. T. Crane Memorial Number," *The Valve World,* April, 1912
"Fifty-Seven Millions for Valves," *Fortune,* June, 1936
James, Henry, *C. W. Eliot,* Houghton Mifflin Company, 1930, 2 vols.

THE UNIVERSITY OF CHICAGO

Goodspeed, T. W., *William Rainey Harper,* University of Chicago Press, 1928
Goodspeed, T. W., *The Story of the University of Chicago,* University of Chicago Press, 1925
Goodspeed, T. W., *University of Chicago Biographical Sketches,* University of Chicago Press, 1922-25, 2 vols.
Nevins, Allan, *John D. Rockefeller: The Heroic Age of American Enterprise,* Charles Scribner's Sons, 1940, 2 vols.

SOCIAL SERVICE

Addams, Jane, *Forty Years at Hull-House,* Macmillan Company, 1935
Bowen, L. DeK., *Growing Up with a City,* Macmillan Company, 1925
Linn, J. W., *Jane Addams,* D. Appleton-Century Company, 1935

MUSIC

Moore, Edward, *Forty Years of Opera in Chicago,* Horace Liveright, 1930
Otis, P. A., *The Chicago Symphony Orchestra,* C. F. Summy, Chicago, 1924
Russell, C. E., *The American Orchestra and Theodore Thomas,* Doubleday, Page and Company, 1927

POLITICAL HISTORY

Abbot, W. J., *Carter Henry Harrison: A Memoir,* Dodd, Mead and Company, 1895
Ahern, M. L., *The Great Revolution,* Lakeside Publishing and Printing Company, Chicago, 1894
Altgeld, J. P., "The Immigrant's Answer," *The Forum,* February, 1890
Altgeld, J. P., *Live Questions,* George S. Bowen and Son, Chicago, 1899
Barnard, Harry, *Eagle Forgotten: The Life of John Peter Altgeld,* Bobbs-Merrill Company, 1937
Beer, Thomas, *Hanna,* Alfred A. Knopf, 1929
Bright, John, *Hizzoner Big Bill Thompson,* Jonathan Cape and Harrison Smith, 1930
Browne, W. R., *Altgeld of Illinois,* B. W. Huebsch, 1924
Cleveland, Grover, *Presidential Problems,* Century Company, 1904
Coleman, McAlister, *Eugene V. Debs: A Man Unafraid,* Greenberg, 1930
Counts, G. S., *School and Society in Chicago,* Harcourt, Brace and Company, 1928
Darrow, Clarence, *The Story of My Life,* Charles Scribner's Sons, 1932
David, Henry, *The History of the Haymarket Affair,* Farrar and Rinehart, 1936
Debs: His Life, Writings, and Speeches, C. H. Kerr and Company, Chicago, 1908
Harrison, C. H., *Growing up with Chicago,* Ralph Fletcher Seymour, Chicago, 1944
Harrison, C. H., *Stormy Years: The Autobiography of Carter H. Harrison,* Bobbs-Merrill Company, 1935
Ickes, H. L., *The Autobiography of a Curmudgeon,* Reynal and Hitchcock, 1943
In Memoriam Henry Demarest Lloyd, Privately Printed, Winnetka, Illinois, 1903
Johnson, C. O., *Carter Henry Harrison I: Political Leader,* University of Chicago Press, 1928

Lloyd, Caro, *Henry Demarest Lloyd,* G. P. Putnam's Sons, 1912, 2 vols.
Nevins, Allan, *Grover Cleveland: A Study in Courage,* Dodd, Mead and Company, 1936
Nevins, Allan, ed., *The Letters of Grover Cleveland,* Houghton Mifflin Company, 1938
Parsons, Lucy, *Life of Albert R. Parsons,* Lucy Parsons, Chicago, 1889
Richberg, Donald, *The Tents of the Mighty,* Willett, Clark, and Dolby, Chicago, 1930
Stuart, W. H., *The Twenty Incredible Years,* M. A. Donohue and Company, Chicago, 1935
Thayer, W. R., *The Life of John Hay,* Houghton Mifflin Company, 1915, 2 vols.
Wendt, Lloyd, and Kogan, Herman, *Lords of the Levee,* Bobbs-Merrill Company, 1934
Whitlock, Brand, *Forty Years of It,* D. Appleton and Company, 1916
Wooddy, C. H., *The Case of Frank L. Smith,* University of Chicago Press, 1931
Wooddy, C. H., *The Chicago Primary of 1926,* University of Chicago Press, 1926

THE "TRIBUNE" AND THE CIRCULATION WARS

Journal of Commerce Publishing Company vs. The Tribune Company, R. R. McCormick, J. M. Patterson, Max Annenberg, and Charles Levy, *Transcript of Record,* United States Circuit Court of Appeals for the Seventh Circuit, October Term, 1921, No. 3116
Lundberg, Ferdinand, *Imperial Hearst,* Equinox Co-operative Press, 1936
Sixty-second Congress, Second Session, Senate Document No. 484, *Hearings on the Election of William Lorimer*

MEDILL AND RUTH HANNA MC CORMICK

La Follette, R. M., *La Follette's Autobiography,* R. M. La Follette Company, Madison, Wisconsin, 1913
McCormick, Medill, *American Prosperity and Peace,* Sixty-eighth Congress, First Session, Senate Document No. 51
Schriftgiesser, Karl, *The Gentleman from Massachusetts: Henry Cabot Lodge,* Little, Brown and Company, 1944
Watson, J. E., *As I Knew Them,* Bobbs-Merrill Company, 1936

CRIME

Asbury, Herbert, *Gem of the Prairie,* Alfred A. Knopf, 1940
Sullivan, E. D., *Chicago Surrenders,* Vanguard Press, 1930
Sullivan, E. D., *Rattling the Cup on Chicago Crime,* Vanguard Press, 1929

THE AGE OF INSULL

Childs, Marquis, "Samuel Insull," *The New Republic,* September 21, September 28, and October 5, 1932
Danielian, N. R., "From Insull to Injury," *Atlantic Monthly,* April, 1933
Dyer, F. L., and Martin, T. C., *Edison: His Life and Inventions,* Harper and Brothers, 1910, 2 vols.
Federal Trade Commission, *Reports on Utility Corporations*
Flynn, J. T., "Up and Down with Sam Insull," *Collier's,* December 3, 10, 17, and 24, 1932
Gruening, Ernest, *The Public Pays,* Vanguard Press, 1931
Insull, Samuel, *Public Utilities in Modern Life* (Selected Speeches 1914-1923), Privately Printed, Chicago, 1924
Ramsay, M. L., *Pyramids of Power,* Bobbs-Merrill Company, 1937
Richberg, D. R., "Gold-Plated Anarchy," *The Nation,* April 5, 1933
Sixty-ninth Congress, First Session, *Hearings before a Special Committee investigating Expenditures in the Senatorial, Primary, and General Elections*
Thompson, C. D., *Confessions of the Power Trust,* E. P. Dutton and Company, 1932
Werner, M. R., *Julius Rosenwald,* Harper and Brothers, 1939

R. R. MC CORMICK AND THE "TRIBUNE"

Alexander, Jack, "The Duke of Chicago," *Saturday Evening Post,* July 19 and 26, 1941
Boettiger, John, *Jake Lingle, or Chicago on the Spot,* E. P. Dutton and Company, 1931
Gertz, Elmer, *The People vs. The Chicago Tribune,* Union for Democratic Action, Chicago, 1942
Ickes, H. L., *America's House of Lords,* Harcourt, Brace and Company, 1939
Linn, J. W., *James Keeley: Newspaperman,* Bobbs-Merrill Company, 1937
McCormick, R. R., *Addresses Broadcast Over W. G. N.,* The Chicago *Tribune,* Chicago, 1940-41
McCormick, R. R., *The Case for the Freedom of the Press,* An Address, 1933
Seldes, George, *Freedom of the Press,* Bobbs-Merrill Company, 1937
Seldes, George, *Lords of the Press,* Julian Messner, 1938
Souvenir of Tribune Tower, The Chicago *Tribune,* Chicago, 1944
The Trib, the house organ of the Chicago *Tribune,* Complete File, 1919—
The War Record of the Chicago Tribune, Compiled for Henry Ford, Undated

JOSEPH MEDILL PATTERSON AND THE NEW YORK "DAILY NEWS"

Alexander, Jack, "Vox Populi," *The New Yorker,* August 6, 13, and 20, 1938

Bessie, S. M., *Jazz Journalism,* E. P. Dutton and Company, 1938
Birkhead, L. M., *The Case against the McCormick-Patterson Press,* Haldeman-Julius Publications, Girard, Kansas, 1945
Patterson, J. M., "Confessions of a Drone," *The Independent,* August 30, 1906
Patterson, J. M., and Ford, Harriet, *The Fourth Estate,* Typescript of play in New York Public Library
Patterson, J. M., *A Little Brother of the Rich,* Reilly and Britton, Chicago, 1908
Patterson, J. M., "Marshall Field's Will," *Collier's,* June 2, 1906
Patterson, J. M., *The Notebook of a Neutral,* Duffield and Company, 1916
Patterson, J. M., *Rebellion,* Reilly and Britton, Chicago, 1911
Patterson, J. M., "The Socialist Machine," *Saturday Evening Post,* September 29, 1906
Stewart, Kenneth, "Case History of John O'Donnell," *PM,* September 23 and 30, and October 7, 1945

ELEANOR MEDILL PATTERSON AND THE WASHINGTON "TIMES-HERALD"

Gizycka, Eleanor, *Fall Flight,* Minton, Balch and Company, 1928
Gizycka, Eleanor, *Glass Houses,* Minton, Balch and Company, 1926
Smith, Beverley, "Herald Angel," *American Magazine,* August, 1940
Walker, Stanley, "Cissy Is a Newspaper Lady," *Saturday Evening Post,* May 6, 1939

MARSHALL FIELD III

Alexander, Jack, "Do-Gooder," *Saturday Evening Post,* December 6, 1941
Field, Marshall, *Freedom Is More Than a Word,* University of Chicago Press, 1945
Grant, Bruce, "$howdown at $unup," Chicago *Daily Times,* October 29, 1941 through November 19, 1941
Temporary National Economic Committee, *Monograph No. 29,* 1940
Wickware, F. S., "Marshall Field III," *Life,* October 18, 1943

Acknowledgments

So MANY people were so helpful to the author during the preparation of this book that he hopes to be forgiven for not naming each and every one. But he would like to express his gratitude to the staffs of the Library of Congress, the Chicago Historical Society, the Newberry Library, the Crerar Library, the University of Chicago Library, and the New York Public Library, without whose complete co-operation this book could scarcely have been written.

The author would also like to thank Marshall Field III, who graciously made available all of the material concerning his grandfather in the archives of Marshall Field and Company; Stanley Field, who sketched his uncle so vividly; the late John V. Farwell II, who talked of the Chicago of eighty and ninety years ago; Richard H. Peel of the Field Estate, who very kindly answered all sorts of questions; Earl Kribben of Marshall Field and Company, who made it so convenient to work in the archives; Joseph T. Ryerson, who opened his collection of Chicagoana; John Borden, who told the true story of the Borden family and Leadville, Colorado; Louis S. Weiss, who carefully discussed Marshall Field III and the Field publications; the late Rowland G. Hazard, who brilliantly brought to life one of the characters in this book; Cyrus S. Eaton, who took the time to relate his impressions of Samuel Insull; Carter H. Harrison, who delightfully recalled the days when he was Mayor; Archibald MacLeish, who imparted his father's recollections of Marshall Field; Daniel Catton Rich, who obligingly read the chapter dealing with the Art Institute; Talbot F. Hanlin, who corrected certain misstatements as to the first skyscrapers; Harvey O'Connor, who pointed out certain aspects of the packing industry; Harold L. Ickes, who described the struggles of the Progressive party in Illinois; Donald R. Richberg, who summed up Samuel Insull; Lloyd Lewis, who spoke of the Chicago *Daily News* in Lawson's time; Professor J. G. Randall, who made it possible to examine a thesis on the town of Pullman; Professor Bessie Louise Pierce, who indicated certain avenues of research; Professor W. T. Hutchinson, who was ever considerate; Professor Tracy E. Strevey, who stressed the significance of the Commercial Club; Herbert A. Kellar, Director of the McCormick Historical Association, who helped the author to refer to certain letters concerning Marshall Field; Walter S. Rogers, who highlighted the career of Charles R. Crane; Melville Cane, who read the manuscript with such care and imagination; and Courtenay Barber, Jr., Dr. L. M. Birkhead, Wallace Brooks, and Elmer J. Holland, who talked over the Chicago *Tribune* and the New York *Daily News*.

Above all the author would like to thank Elmer Gertz, who knows more about the *Tribune* than any man living or dead. Besides discussing the *Tribune* for days on end, Gertz most generously called the author's attention to the *Journal of Commerce* case—not to mention hundreds of other favors.

Finally the author would like to thank Professor Thomas C. Cochran of New York University and Professor Allan Nevins of Columbia University, who had the kindness to comment on the manuscript in its early stages.

A special acknowledgment is due the following for permission to publish excerpts from books, magazine articles, and private papers:

D. Appleton-Century Company: *Cyrus Hall McCormick* by W. T. Hutchinson; *Armour and His Times* by Harper Leech and J. C. Carroll; *Forty Years of It* by Brand Whitlock.

The Architectural Record: "The Chicago *Tribune* Competition" by Louis H. Sullivan; "Last Words About the World's Fair" by Montgomery Schuyler; "Reminiscences of Russell Sturgis" by P. B. Wight.

Dr. Ruth Morris Bakwin: *My Father and My Mother* by Helen Swift (Lakeside Press).

Mrs. George Bambridge and Doubleday and Company: *From Sea to Sea* by Rudyard Kipling, copyright 1899, 1907.

Bobbs-Merrill Company: *Eagle Forgotten* by Harry Barnard, copyright 1938; *As I Knew Them* by James E. Watson, copyright 1936; *Stormy Years* by Carter H. Harrison, copyright 1935.

Daniel H. Burnham II: *Daniel H. Burnham* by Charles Moore (Houghton Mifflin Company).

Mrs. Hobart C. Chatfield-Taylor: *Cities of Many Men* by Hobart C. Chatfield-Taylor (Houghton Mifflin Company).

Chicago Historical Society: A letter of Joseph Medill to William Medill, dated May 24, 1863.

Chilton Company: *Marshall Field and Company* by S. H. Ditchett (*The Dry Goods Economist*).

Dartnell Corporation: "Fifty-five Years in Business" by H. I. Cleveland (*System* Magazine).

Henry David: *The History of the Haymarket Affair* by Henry David (Farrar and Rinehart).

Editor and Publisher: A letter of Eleanor Medill Patterson in the issue of June 24, 1939.

George Grant Elmslie: *The Autobiography of an Idea* by Louis H. Sullivan (American Institute of Architects); *Kindergarten Chats* by Louis H. Sullivan (Scarab Fraternity Press).

Marshall Field and Company: *Elements of Success* by Marshall Field; the unpublished history of Marshall Field and Company by Samuel McClintock; various letters in the archives.

Harper and Brothers: *The Spanish-American War* by Russell A. Alger; *With the Procession* by Henry B. Fuller; *A Musician and His Wife* by Anna Farwell DeKoven.

Carter H. Harrison: *Growing up with Chicago* by Carter H. Harrison (Ralph Fletcher Seymour).

Burton J. Hendrick: *The Life of Andrew Carnegie* by Burton J. Hendrick (Doubleday, Doran and Company)

Elbert Hubbard II: *Little Journeys to the Homes of Great Businessmen: P. D. Armour* by Elbert Hubbard (Elbert Hubbard).

Harold L. Ickes: *The Autobiography of a Curmudgeon* by Harold L. Ickes (Reynal and Hitchcock).

International Harvester Company: "Cyrus Hall McCormick II Memorial Number," *Harvester World,* June, 1936.

Charles H. Kerr and Company: *The Pullman Strike* by W. H. Carwardine.

Alfred A. Knopf: *Hanna* by Thomas Beer.

Mrs. James Weber Linn: *Jane Addams* by James Weber Linn (D. Appleton-Century Company).

A. C. McClurg and Company: *Cyrus Hall McCormick* by H. N. Casson.

McCormick Historical Association: Various letters pertaining to Marshall Field.

R. R. McCormick: *Souvenir of Tribune Tower: The W. G. N.* (The Chicago *Tribune*).

McGraw-Hill Book Company: *The Yankee of the Yards* by Louis F. Swift (A. W. Shaw and Company).

Macmillan Company: *The Life of Abraham Lincoln* by Ida M. Tarbell (Lincoln History Society).

G. P. Putnam's Sons: *Henry Demarest Lloyd* by Caro Lloyd.

The Saturday Evening Post: "Selling Selfridge" by H. G. Selfridge.

Maurice J. Speiser: *Always Room at the Top* by Ganna Walska (Richard R. Smith).

The Stratford Company: *Street of Adventure* by E. J. Dies.

University of Chicago Press: *Victor Lawson* by C. H. Dennis; *Freedom Is More Than a Word* by Marshall Field; *Story of the University of Chicago* by T. W. Goodspeed; *University of Chicago Biographical Sketches* by T. W. Goodspeed.

Vanguard Press: *The Public Pays* by Ernest Gruening.

M. R. Werner: *Julius Rosenwald* by M. R. Werner (Harper and Brothers).

Wisconsin State Historical Society: *Cyrus Hall McCormick and the Reaper* by R. G. Thwaites.

Index